D1602302

RETHINKING AMERICA

RETHINKING AMERICA

FROM EMPIRE TO REPUBLIC

JOHN M. MURRIN

with an introduction by
Andrew Shankman

OXFORD
UNIVERSITY PRESS

OXFORD
UNIVERSITY PRESS

Oxford University Press is a department of the University of Oxford. It furthers
the University's objective of excellence in research, scholarship, and education
by publishing worldwide. Oxford is a registered trade mark of Oxford University
Press in the UK and certain other countries.

Published in the United States of America by Oxford University Press
198 Madison Avenue, New York, NY 10016, United States of America.

© John M. Murrin 2018
Introduction © Oxford University Press 2018

CIP data is on file at the Library of Congress
ISBN 978-0-19-503871-2

1 3 5 7 9 8 6 4 2

Printed by Sheridan Books, Inc., United States of America

In fond memory of Edmund S. Morgan

CONTENTS

PREFACE AND ACKNOWLEDGMENTS

Andrew Shankman

———————

I ARRIVED AT Princeton University in the summer of 1992 for my first semester of graduate school, equally eager and overwhelmed to study with John Murrin. One of my undergraduate professors, Stephen Foster, had known Murrin since their days at Yale working with Edmund Morgan. Another, Allan Kulikoff, had been Murrin's colleague at Princeton for several years. A third, Simon Newman, had been Murrin's student. And a fourth, Alfred F. Young, doubted Murrin's political commitments, but confirmed what the other three said: that Murrin seemed to know everything. Murrin was, Young told me, co-writing an essay for the volume Young was currently editing, an essay that Young assured me was stunning.[1] Murrin, it seemed, fit well the description his Ph.D. adviser Morgan had provided for Ezra Stiles, President of Yale College from 1778 to 1795: he was "a monstrous warehouse of knowledge" exhibiting "so much energy in the sheer joy of learning."[2]

That spring I had first sensed another equally important quality of John Murrin's when I read a brief note he had written to Kulikoff and had enclosed with the final volume of the biographical dictionary *Princetonians*. *Princetonians* ran to five volumes, published between 1976 and 1991, and covered the years 1748 to 1794. Murrin's name appears nowhere as an editor. Yet he devoted a great deal of time to the project due to his deep interest in the history of the university where he worked

for over thirty years, and because of his devotion to the memory and legacy of Princeton's previous early Americanist, Wesley Frank Craven. The
note, to the best of my memory, read "Dear Allan, here is the latest volume of *Princetonians*. I expect you to read every word. John. P.S. Andrew
Shankman is on the admit list." And so, my life changed forever. As I tried
to absorb the note in a hallway outside a classroom, I could concentrate
enough to realize that it was a humorous little letter. It was funny, while
also being ingenuously modest, self-deprecating, and a little bit impish.

As I would come to know, Murrin is joyful both in learning and
mischief. Though Morgan's quotation captures Murrin as well as it
does Stiles, equally revealing is a brief passage from one of Murrin's
essays in *Rethinking America*, "No Awakening, No Revolution? More
Counterfactual Speculations." It is one of the two essays in the volume that
are organized around a counterfactual question, a very difficult exercise
to do well, and one at which Murrin excels. In "No Awakening" Murrin
expunges the first Great Awakening from history to assess what difference that would make for the coming of the American Revolution. The
only way to erase the Awakening is to provide plausible explanations for
the disappearances of George Whitfield, Jonathan Edwards, and Gilbert
Tennant before they could cause any serious trouble. By imprisoning
Whitfield in a Spanish dungeon during the War of Jenkin's Ear, reducing
Edwards to a permanent catatonic stupor, and killing off Tennant with
a bolt of lightning (after all, who didn't know that Tennant was struck
by lightning in 1745 but survived?), Murrin dispatched the three with
wholehearted glee, explaining that it was "one of the forbidden delights
that such counterfactual musings can provide to any suitably degenerate mind." Combining these Morgan and Murrin quotations brings one
closer to knowing Murrin for those who have not met him.

Within days of arriving at Princeton, I had heard about the collected
essays project. My fellow Murrin students (there were always many)
explained that he had written far more essays than I realized, over forty,
possibly more than fifty. Nobody seemed to know for sure, because some
of the best were published in obscure hard-to-find volumes, and some
of the very best were still in a drawer somewhere. I remember wanting
access to that drawer. But I was not to give up hope, for Murrin had a
contract with Oxford University Press and would be publishing his collected essays in two volumes, or was it three? There was spirited debate

about that and the details were hazy. But it was coming soon, quite soon, and the erudition of this monstrous warehouse of knowledge would be widely available. I remember that summer telling somebody that I hoped it would all happen in time for my general exams.

Twenty three years after passing those exams, for me it is a momentous occasion and an enormous pleasure to help make widely available eleven of John Murrin's essential essays treating the American Revolution and the early American Republic. *Rethinking America* addresses essential questions and controversies that have long shaped our understanding of the nation's origins and that should continue to inform the discussions of current and future historians. In doing so, these essays deeply probe themes and issues that are central to the surprising, awe-inspiring, and often deeply troubling formation and development of the United States.

I am grateful to Anthony Grafton and William Chester Jordan of Princeton University, Daniel K. Richter of the McNeil Center for Early American Studies and the University of Pennsylvania, and David Waldstreicher of the CUNY Graduate Center, who read my introduction and helped me with their encouragement to improve it. I also thank Susan Ferber of Oxford University Press, who remained devoted to *Rethinking America* and who imagined that I could be of use to its completion. And above all, my enduring thanks to my adviser and friend John Murrin, the author of the feast.

Notes

1. The essay, "The Making and Unmaking of an American Ruling Class," is included in this volume.
2. Edmund S. Morgan, *The Gentle Puritan: A Life of Ezra Stiles, 1727–1795* (New York: W. W. Norton, 1962), 134.

RETHINKING AMERICA

The Revolutionary Republic of a Radical, Imperial, Whig

The Historical and Historiographical Imagination of John M. Murrin

Andrew Shankman

THE ESSAYS COLLECTED in *Rethinking America* introduce many of the preoccupations that have shaped John Murrin's scholarly life. Foremost among them is his central insight, which he called Anglicization. The process of Anglicization demonstrates that during the first six decades of the eighteenth century the thirteen colonies, in virtually every measurable way—politically, socially, culturally, and economically—became more not less British in their attitudes, outlooks, and actions, and became more fully, willingly, and profitably integrated into the British Empire. As many of the essays in *Rethinking America* treating the years before 1776 show, the colonists, particularly those higher in the social order, proudly embraced a British identity. They believed they were British subjects fully deserving of the liberties they associated with the post-1688 limited constitutional monarchy. Due to their Britishness, they could conclude in the 1760s and 1770s that they should not be subjected to the treatment imperial policymakers were forcing them to endure.

Anglicization is Murrin's overarching insight concerning the revolutionary period, but it is connected to several other issues and questions the essays in *Rethinking America* explore. Among them are: the origins and nature of American federalism; the long success and then sudden spectacular failure and collapse of the British Empire; the colonial origins of class conflict, and the continued impact and significance of social and economic inequality in the early republic; and the great gulf between outcome and intention produced by those who sought a republic, created a democracy, and talked in bold ways about expanding liberty and equality.

To explore these themes, and to bring them together in a coherent whole, Murrin begins where Edmund Morgan insisted historians should start, by paying careful attention to how the people of the past explained what they were doing and why they thought it mattered. On numerous occasions Murrin has described his excitement about making the move in the 1950s from the Midwest to Yale to study with Morgan. He was stimulated by Morgan's fresh approach to the revolutionary period to treat the ideas and convictions of that era as respectfully as his own mentor Perry Miller had taught him to treat the ideas of the Puritans.

Yet like Morgan, Murrin knew it was not a simple prospect to listen to what people of the past said. Statements of the past have a tricky way of being false friends, as Murrin explained in "The French and Indian War, The American Revolution, and the Counterfactual Hypothesis," which is included in *Rethinking America*. In this essay Murrin demolishes the claim that defeat of the French in North America in 1763 directly caused the colonists to seek independence. Historians had long argued that no longer needing to fear the French was the key reason for the movement for independence. In "The French and Indian War" Murrin quoted many eighteenth-century statements that insisted that the colonists would seek independence if the French should ever be defeated. As a result, Murrin wrote, "because the empire did collapse not long after the Peace of Paris, historians ever alert for an apt quotation" built arguments on these statements, "endowed them with prophetic power" since they were "neatly lodged in the sources themselves," and so gravely misunderstood the primary causes of the imperial crisis due to the entirely understandable and "unexceptionable device of quoting what they read."

Murrin's scholarship is shaped by letting the sources guide him and by taking seriously the statements of his subjects. Yet he was not misled by these particular statements, because his understanding of the imperial crisis and the world it produced was part of his vast and deep knowledge of the English-speaking world of the seventeenth and eighteenth centuries. That understanding allowed him to see the ways in which the

American Revolutionary era and the Early Republic were shaped by the colonial period and the British imperial system of which the thirteen colonies were such a vital part. To possess the context to explore the main themes of the essays in *Rethinking America* necessitates spending some time in the earlier colonial period. To understand the American Revolution and the Early Republic requires gaining a fuller understanding of the British colonial and British imperial world from which they emerged.

It is becoming less and less common for scholars to achieve mastery of both the colonial period and the eras of the American Revolution and the Early American Republic. But Murrin's scholarship on the history of British North America before 1750 shows how essential it is to resist treating the American Revolution as a dividing line. In over two dozen essays treating the colonial era, Murrin has shown that in their origins the North American English colonies participated in a sustained seventeenth-century conversation about how best to order political and social relations in the Anglophone early modern world. Over the course of the seventeenth century, what England was and should be was hotly contested. The conflicts were driven by heated disagreements about how best to order and structure Crown/Parliament relations and by bitter divisions among the varieties of English Protestantism. These arguments could overwhelm the realm when constitutional conflicts (which were further intensified by chronic fiscal crisis and the challenge of governing multiple kingdoms) overlapped with religions tensions—which happened with increasing frequency after the start of the Thirty Years War in 1618.[1]

Most of the English North American colonies were founded by groups that were actively participating in these English conflicts. The non-separating Congregationalists of Massachusetts hoped to push the early Stuart church into a much greater assault on church hierarchy. In the Restoration period, the Duke of York (the future James II) sought to use New York to provide an example of a purer and more vital form of Absolutism to motivate his brother Charles II to improve on the anemic English version. In Pennsylvania William Penn hoped to show that the surviving remnant of the countercultural values of the Civil War and Interregnum could still be the basis for a more just and edifying society. And in Carolina the Earl of Shaftesbury and his secretary John Locke tried to fuse the talents of a patriotic landed aristocracy with the cutting-edge social theory of the

Civil War–era thinker James Harrington. They did so to provide an alternative to the absolutism advocated by the Duke of York that they feared would influence the king and to the disruptive upheaval associated with the Interregnum.[2] Each of these colonial experiments represented a position on the seventeenth-century English political spectrum. Yet all were marginal or controversial in England when their adherents resorted to trying them in America. Each of the experiments—dissenting Protestantism in Massachusetts, unadulterated Absolutism in New York, the remnant of Civil War–era counterculture in Pennsylvania, and the early expression of Whig political thought and country ideology in Carolina—hoped to show how English institutions ought to function and to reconstitute English society and politics to more closely follow each colony's example.

Murrin has suggested that a practical definition of "American" in the English colonies was the determination to dissent from English practices or values, to depart from, or actively reject, or critique and seek to transform whatever the mainstream practices of England happened to be at the time of a colonist's opposition. By this definition the English colonies were at their most "American" in the seventeenth century. The exception to this version of a distinct "American" identity was Virginia. After its royal takeover in 1624, it alone among the seventeenth-century English colonies sought to re-create the political institutions of the English mainstream. Yet in the final decades of the seventeenth century (or in Carolina's case the early eighteenth) all of these colonies, including Virginia, suffered acute crisis and nearly collapsed. In the first decades of the eighteenth century no English colony was confident that its past experiences could provide useful guidance for how to build a stable society. This period of crisis began with King Philip's War in Massachusetts and Bacon's Rebellion in Virginia in the mid-1670s, which were followed by the upheaval of the Salem witch trials in Massachusetts, Leisler's Rebellion in New York, the Keithian Schism in Pennsylvania, the Plant Cutters' Rebellion in Virginia in the 1680s and 1690s, and finally the Yamasee War in Carolina in 1715, which almost engulfed the colony.

In descending into crisis mostly at the end of the seventeenth century, the colonies contributed to a general crisis in the English-speaking world. The colonial crises coincided with the dismantling of the Restoration settlement in England as a result of the Exclusion Crisis, the Popish Plot, the Rye House Plot, and Monmouth's Rebellion in the 1670s and 1680s, and finally the Glorious Revolution and the creation of the limited-constitutional monarchy, beginning in 1689.[3] For Murrin, the simultaneity of the transatlantic crises was essential for understanding why the eighteenth-century British colonies were so different from their seventeenth-century pasts. Between 1689 and the 1720s the Glorious Revolution and the limited-constitutional monarchy and fiscal-military state it enabled began to fundamentally resolve the conflicts over Crown/Parliament relations and among the varieties of English Protestantism that had plagued the seventeenth century.

As Murrin discusses in "The Great Inversion, Or Court Versus Country: A Comparison of the Revolution Settlements in England (1688–1721) and America (1776–1816)," included in this volume, the British state and society that developed by the 1720s offered a far more attractive and impressive prospect than the seventeenth-century Stuart state or than any of the seventeenth-century "American" colonial experiments. Britain was becoming capable of mobilizing considerable resources and projecting its will outward as never before. Just as it was becoming able to, in Murrin's phrase, "discover its colonies" by enforcing its Navigation Acts and structuring and governing an empire, the colonies it was discovering were looking for alternatives to the ideas and practices that had brought them all to crisis.[4] Liberty, property, prosperity, and Protestantism protected and nurtured by a limited-constitutional monarchy seemed much more attractive than the ordeals of the seventeenth century.

The eighteenth-century colonies all experienced a complex process at once political, social, cultural, and economic that Murrin has dubbed Anglicization.[5] What he meant by Anglicization would more accurately be called "Britishization," but Murrin coined the term while writing his 1966 Yale Ph.D. dissertation "Anglicizing an American Colony: The Transformation of Provincial Massachusetts," well before thinking in terms of a British history was common.[6] Yet his concept of Anglicization resulted from doing British history long before that approach had a constituency. Anglicization revealed that British history had an essential North American dimension.

Murrin's work on the golden age of colonial America (roughly the forty years after 1720) fits well with the scholarship on Britain that explains the formation of a British identity and a rising British nationalism.[7] Indeed, by focusing only on the British Isles, historians of eighteenth-century

Britain often did not emphasize just how imperial and transatlantic the nationalist story they were telling was. In the royal New England colonies, a political culture developed in which the royal governors, following the example of Whig parliamentary leaders such as Robert Walpole, used the patronage at their disposal to build majorities in their colonial legislatures. Beginning particularly during the 1720s and 1730s, these New England colonies began to replicate the economic diversity and complexity of Britain and to reproduce the social relations and legal culture this sort of economy encouraged. More extensive and widespread commercial relations often extended beyond town boundaries, which led to the rising significance of county government. The growing importance of county government produced a vast increase in offices beyond the town level, such as Justice of the Peace, which were in the royal governors' gift, and those offices became a vital source of this patronage. These social and economic relations produced in New England a more stratified society where provincial elites monopolized local and county offices and dominated colonial legislatures. By the end of the 1730s the royal colonies of New England were producing an emerging ruling class that could realistically aspire to the polite commercial gentility of the British gentry and the rising British middle class.

These interlocking social, political, cultural, and economic developments were a prime example of the process of Anglicization. These developments show the crucial imperial and transatlantic dimension of the formation of eighteenth-century British identity and British nationalism grounded in polite gentility and consumer culture. One of the more effective and powerful depictions of this formation, which also provides a sense of its suddenness and timing, can be found in a passage from Paul Langford's *A Polite and Commercial People*: "The architect John Wood, writing in 1749, listed the novelties introduced since the accession of George II. Cheap and dirty floorboards gave way to superior deal covered with carpets. Primitive plaster was concealed with smart wainscoting. Stone hearths and chimney-pieces, customarily cleaned with whitewash which left a chalk debris on the floor, were abandoned for hardwood embellished with brass locks. Mirrors had become both numerous and elegant. Walnut and mahogany, in fashionable designs, superseded primitive oak furniture. Leather, damask, and embroidery gave seating a comfort unobtainable with cane or rush."[8] Wood dated these tremendous changes, the stuff of polite commercial gentility, and the source of intense national pride and a sense of superiority, as taking place between 1727 and 1749. The English, lowland Scots, and Protestant Irish converged on this polite, commercial, and British culture, and became Britons during the decades of the 1730s and 1740s, at the same time as those living in New England. British identity was a transatlantic development. To a great extent, those living in New England embraced it because they were not simply following a long-established set of behaviors, but were participating in their formation from the start.

This coeval development of British identity in Britain and the New England colonies—this process of Anglicization—was a crucial part of the making of a colonial ruling class, as Murrin discusses in the essay co-written with his former student Gary J. Kornblith, "The Making and Unmaking of an American Ruling Class." In the royal New England colonies, this ruling class increasingly embraced the post–Glorious Revolution British identity that celebrated limited-constitutional monarchy, the accomplishments of the fiscal-military state, and the ideals of liberty, property, and a broad-bottomed pan-Protestantism. This ruling class attached no stigma to accepting offices from royal governors. As Murrin has pointed out, in 1763, on the eve of imperial crisis, fully 71% of the Massachusetts General Court also held the office of JP, a royal office in the governor's gift. Here in New England was J. H. Plumb's explanation for the growth of English political stability with a vengeance.[9]

The messy mid-Atlantic colonies reveal a similar story. Royal New York took longer than Massachusetts and New Hampshire to achieve Anglicized, court-Whig-inspired political stability. But the relations between the royal governor and the elite New Yorkers who dominated local politics and the colonial assembly improved dramatically beginning in the early 1750s with the rise of men such as James Delancey.[10] Murrin has shown that a colony riven by ethnic conflict and divisions within the English community as late as 1710 or so could by the 1740s produce home-grown, highly respectable, and impeccably credentialed British gentlemen such as Delancey.[11] These elites constituted a colonial ruling class that had every confidence the solutions to any pressing issues or problems lay within the British Empire, as evidenced by their ability to rise to positions of prominence as local magnates and thoroughgoing empire men.

In the decade before the Stamp Act Crisis New York's place within the empire had never been more stable and secure, and the political relations between the royal executive and the colonial legislature were more harmonious than they had been in forty years. A similar trend occurred in Pennsylvania. There, colonial American–born British gentlemen and consummate empire men, such as Benjamin Franklin and Joseph Galloway, longed for the King to replace Pennsylvania's proprietary government with royal government. For men such as Franklin, royal government connoted modern, professional administration and the security of British liberty.[12]

Anglicization meant for Murrin the process by which the eighteenth-century colonies converged upon a British identity of polite commercial gentility, the new mainstream institutions and values of limited-constitutional monarchy, a broad Protestant unity, and the dynamic, fiscal-state-driven economic diversity that fueled economic growth in Britain and the empire. Thus, Murrin has shown that the model Bernard Bailyn proposed in *The Origins of American Politics* did not explain the political culture of the northern colonies. Bailyn had argued that royal governors in the colonies had extensive authority on paper, but very little practical power, such as sources of patronage with which to build majorities in colonial legislatures. Colonists believed they had reason to fear over-mighty executives, who were in fact far weaker than was executive authority in Britain. For Bailyn, this unnecessary fear of executive power encouraged devotion to country ideology, a belief system designed to denounce and discredit executive authority. A language of opposition that was marginal in Britain by the 1730s became central to the political culture of the colonies. Thus, colonial politics was brittle and combustible, combining weak executives with a dominant political idiom that encouraged extreme suspicion of central authority. This political structure strongly suggested the inevitability of the American Revolution.[13]

Murrin has shown that Bailyn's model does not explain the royal colonies in New England where governors possessed ample patronage, successfully practiced Walpoleon court Whig methods of political management, and forged harmonious relations with their legislatures prior to the mid-1760s. Nor did the model explain the mid-Atlantic where New York, though never as completely, moved in the direction of New England, and where the most prominent Pennsylvanians in the legislature campaigned to oust the Proprietor and to replace him with royal government. In those colonies, country ideology was present in the same way that it was in eighteenth-century Britain. It was a language of critique expressed by a minority on the outs, was rarely taken seriously by the majority or the influential, and was simply not the dominant political idiom.

But did the southern slave societies Virginia and South Carolina experience Anglicization, and did they, in any way, fit Bailyn's model? When compared directly to the eighteenth-century Anglicizing northern colonies, Virginia and South Carolina would seem to fit Murrin's definition of "American." In various writings Murrin has described a spectrum of settlement ranging from the British Isles to the British West Indies. Britain, almost exclusively white and Anglophone, fully embracing the post–Glorious Revolution world of polite commercial gentility, liberty, property, and Protestantism, and economic diversity was the most heavily Anglicized society in the world. The farther south one traveled along the spectrum of settlement, the less fully Anglicized the eighteenth-century British colonies became. New England most closely replicated Britain's political, social, cultural, and economic practices. The middle colonies were close behind New England, but with more ethnic diversity, more slaves, and less political stability. And the southern colonies were more "American," with more slaves and less economic diversity, while the West Indies were the most "American" colonies, producing societies and economies that looked the least like those of eighteenth-century Britain.[14]

Murrin has also pointed out that eighteenth-century Virginia and South Carolina looked far more "American" when compared to the eighteenth-century northern colonies than they did when compared to their own seventeenth-century pasts. In the eighteenth century these southern colonies also produced highly stratified societies and ruling elites who took their social and cultural cues of polite gentility from the English landed gentry, and who embraced the mainstream British institutions of limited-constitutional monarchy and the Anglican church. Here, if anywhere, Bailyn's model might at first glance seem to explain things. Virginian and South Carolina (and later but much less significantly Georgia) were the only Anglophone societies where country ideology became the dominant political idiom. That was unsurprising, since country ideology glorified the very sorts of people the great tobacco and rice planters insisted they were.[15] One could expect to find intense political instability and a deep suspicion of and hostility toward royal government in societies where powerful local ruling classes took country ideology so seriously.

Yet as Murrin has shown, Virginia, South Carolina, and Georgia became the most harmonious political societies in the English-speaking world.[16] They became so once the royal governors (in Virginia as early as the years just before 1720) learned to take planter elites at their word. Royal governors began to treat their local ruling classes as the respectable, genteel, and patriotic patriarchs they believed they were and to forge a political culture of mutual admiration, respect, and country harmony. The process of Anglicization in the south also showed that widespread access to country ideology, even where it became the dominant political idiom, did not make political conflict or anti-crown sentiment inevitable. Thus, by the mid-eighteenth century the British North American colonies were benefiting greatly from their presence in the empire and had produced confident ruling elites who, in their various ways, took their cues from British society and culture, ruled their provinces, shared mutual respect and harmony with their royal governors, and were far more British in thought and deed than ever before.[17]

It is essential to have some understanding of this process of eighteenth-century Anglicization to fully appreciate Murrin's essays exploring the American Revolution and the early American republic. Understanding the complex, overlapping developments that produced Anglicization allows us to follow Murrin's discussion of how vital cooperation could produce spectacular triumph in North America by 1763. That same understanding is essential to comprehending how this vital cooperation could end with revolutionary violence thirteen years later, and eventually produce a society by the 1820s that none could have imagined in 1776 and that few would have wanted.

The essays in *Rethinking America* treating the Seven Years War (called by the British North Americans the French and Indian War) and the imperial crisis, "The French and Indian War, The American Revolution, and the Counterfactual Hypothesis," "1776: The Countercyclical Revolution," and significant parts of "The Great Inversion, Or Court Versus Country," and "Feudalism, Communalism, and the Yeoman Freeholder: The American Revolution Considered as a Social Accident," show that prior to the late 1760s the default mainstream colonial position was one that by 1776 would be viewed as loyalist. Murrin explains that the gloomy years of defeat in the Seven Years War prior to 1759 resulted primarily because British military officials such as Lord Loudon did not know how to work with confident, prideful, and increasing self-confident, Anglicized colonial Americans. These colonists did not doubt that they were British subjects fully entitled to all the rights and liberties that came with that status.

Britain's imperial enterprise had succeeded by 1750 in producing a sprawling population of aggressive colonial landowners capable of replicating British institutions, society, and culture. On a far greater scale than the other European early modern Atlantic world empires, British imperial policymakers had to consider how to incorporate into their triumphal empire a substantial population of subjects who were locally producing many of their own institutions and methods of governance. The Anglicizing thirteen colonies were, in Murrin's phrase, voluntary-cooperative societies. Inside the colonies the actual coercive power of the British state—best represented by the navy—could not intrude as it could on the oceans. In the colonial interior, to administer imperial policies—to govern the empire—required figuring out how to convince the colonists to voluntarily cooperate with the policies.

This need for voluntary cooperation meant that the British Empire was in reality a federal system, and the critical line dividing power in it was the North American coastline. Britain had coercive power on the oceans that it did not possess in the interior. Murrin shows that in the first phase of the Seven Years War the British betrayed no knowledge of the critical role the coastline played in the practical reality of running the empire. Yet the Seven Years War, Murrin explains, in fact provided two models for the empire—the first showing how it could be lost, the second revealing how it could triumph and expect to enjoy continued harmony and success. The imperial crisis of 1764–1775 began due to three sources of conflict: first, Britain's demand that the colonists pay some of the military costs of defending North America; second, Britain's insistence that the colonists quarter troops; and third, the frustrations, which grew into hatreds, that colonists felt toward the British soldiers in their midst. Murrin explains how from 1759 to end of the Seven Years War William Pitt structured imperial policies that led the colonists to eagerly and voluntarily tax themselves to pay military costs and quarter troops.

The policies also encouraged genuine support and even affection for British soldiers. Murrin's argument fits well with the conclusions of Fred Anderson and John Shy. Victory in 1763 was very much a joint British and colonial affair, and in 1763 the majority of colonists had never been prouder of their British identity and had never felt more secure in their British liberties. The result of six decades of Anglicization was that in 1763 the British Empire reached its apex.[18]

In "The French and Indian War, The American Revolution, and the Counterfactual Hypothesis" and "1776: The Countercyclical Revolution" Murrin explains how, with some exceptions, particularly the brief but effective ministry from 1765 to 1766 of Charles Watson Wentworth, the Marquis of Rockingham, British imperial policymakers drew all the wrong lessons from the war and failed "to think triumphantly." The three great imperial crises of 1764–1766, 1767–1770, and 1773–1775 cumulatively destroyed the colonial willingness to provide voluntary cooperation. British policy, from the perspective of the colonists, seemed to contemptuously deny that they were British subjects and part of the Glorious Revolution legacy that protected liberty and property, primarily by connecting taxation to representation.[19]

Though the empire was a federal system where the critical axis that divided power was the coastline, the twelve years after 1764 also showed that it was a federal system without a justifying federal ideology. As imperial policymakers and their colonial critics were forced into clearer and clearer, and angrier and angrier, conversation (a conversation that Pitt's voluntary-cooperative methods avoided and that Rockingham's strategies in 1765–1766 temporarily ended), they found that they disagreed about the empire's structure. Yet neither the British nor the colonial position could explain how the empire worked. His Majesty's government maintained that it was sovereign. It could tax and legislate throughout Britain and the empire. The colonial critics insisted that, because they were British, they enjoyed liberty and property and so taxation connected to representation. The power to tax, if unchecked, could leach away all property and so too liberty. Therefore, it was a uniquely dangerous power, a power that threatened liberty in a way that the power to legislate (govern behavior but not take a subject's property) did not. Special constraints had to be placed on the power to tax that did not have to be placed on the power to legislate. Thus colonial critics of imperial policy accepted that

Parliament could legislate for the colonies. It could govern their behavior with the Navigation Acts, the Iron Act, and the Hat Act. But only their own colonial legislatures could tax them. Only the colonial legislatures met the two requirements necessary for taxation to be connected to representation: that the taxers were elected by the taxpayers, and that the taxers were required to pay the same taxes they levied on the taxpayers.

Yet in reality, Parliament could for the most part impose its will on the oceans with both legislation, such as the Navigation Acts, and taxation, such as the Sugar Act, especially in its amended 1766 form. Indeed, even the external Townshend duties proved hard to resist. A boycott movement took two years to develop, and only truly got going after Lord Hillsborough ordered the colonial governors to dissolve the colonial legislatures should they dare to discuss a letter from the Massachusetts legislature urging them to denounce the Townshend Acts. It seems unlikely that most legislatures would ever have endorsed the Massachusetts Circular Letter (hardly any had even begun to discuss it several months after receiving it) until they were ordered not to do so, which made it a vital principle regarding the legislatures' freedom and autonomy.[20]

While Parliament could tax and legislate on the oceans, it could only conduct policy in the interior with the colonists' voluntary cooperation. Pitt had shown that the colonists would voluntarily do pretty much all of what the post-1763 coercive measures were demanding that they do. But the Stamp Act Crisis showed that the colonists would withhold their voluntary cooperation from a measure that they believed threatened to destroy their British liberties. And if they did withhold their cooperation, they could quickly nullify and render moot any internal measure. The colonists' sense of an imperial constitution acknowledged Parliament's authority to legislate. Yet internal legislation also required voluntary cooperation in a way that external legislation did not, even though such legislation did not provoke the clear and consistent ideological rejection that taxation did. Neither imperial policymakers nor their colonial critics could imagine a federal ideology that identified the coastline for what it was: the true axis of a separation of powers. Because they could not, the acrimonious conversation continued.[21]

As it did, Murrin argues in "The Great Inversion" and "1776: The Countercyclical Revolution," country ideology began to have the impact Bailyn had mistakenly granted to it for an earlier period. By the late 1760s, for a growing number of people in the colonies country ideology did seem to explain British policy and why a nation created by the Glorious Revolution had slowly but inexorably become a corrupted instrument of tyranny. For the first time country ideology became the dominant political idiom in the northern colonies. And in the southern colonies, where it had long been dominant but had fostered a political culture of harmony and mutual admiration between elites and crown officials, it now provoked bitter suspicion and hostility. The empire was in crisis.

An irony was that British policymakers from a distance could see the colonies as a single unit: America. The policymakers proceeded simultaneously to impose policies on the colonies that provoked them to resist by defending their collective British identity and British liberty. By provoking them all at once, imperial policymakers drove the colonies together and stimulated their common sense of purpose and a distinct unifying identity that little in their disparate colonial experiences had provided before. Yet resisting the British, as Murrin discusses in the co-authored "Feudalism, Communalism, and the Yeoman Freeholder," raised dangerous issues for the Anglicized colonial elites who had, until very recently, been highly satisfied with their place within the British Empire.

Between 1725 and 1765 one key aspect of Anglicization was growing social and economic stratification and the rise of an elite governing class in every colony, developments explored in "Feudalism, Communalism, and the Yeoman Freeholder" and "The Making and Unmaking of an American Ruling Class." As in Britain, the eighteenth-century colonies began to produce conflicts due to disparities in wealth and power, what Murrin called part of a feudal revival. Prior to the great disruption of 1765–1775, colonial British North America was producing in every colony Anglicizing colonial elites, highly loyal empire-minded gentlemen. They were confident they had far more in common with a transatlantic community of polite, commercial, imperial British middle class and gentry than they did with their fellow colonials lower in the social order. The imperial crisis was countercyclical in part because it shattered that confidence. Yet as colonial elites began to resist British policies and provoke conflicts with the empire, they had no choice but to reach out to and invite in their fellow colonials, who had their own additional and considerable grievances about the structure of colonial society. The British were frightened by Stamp Act riots, but so were elite colonial leaders, who grew less and less confident by the final months of 1765 that they were in fact leading anything.[22]

As the need to confront Britain grew more acute after 1770, colonial elites had to balance their fear of power above them with their fear of challenge to their own power from below. "Feudalism, Communalism, and the Yeoman Freeholder" and "The Making and Unmaking of an American Ruling Class" fully endorse Carl Becker's powerful insight that a battle for home rule quickly provoked a sustained, internal conflict over who would rule at home. By 1776 what had begun as a constitutional conflict had become an overwhelming crisis. Constitutional disagreements intensified beyond containment due to the heavy reliance on country ideology to explain Britain's actions. That ideological dimension galvanized elite colonists to continue to encourage resistance. The more they did so, the more they opened up space for those below them in the social order to force their own grievances and concerns into the midst of the imperial crisis. By 1775–1776 the situation was revolutionary as the Coercive Acts, for the first time, provoked the vast majority of colonists to reject Parliament's authority to legislate as well as tax. Yet by 1775–1776 the movement to declare independence could not help but become a widespread argument about existing social, cultural, political, and economic arrangements and relations within the colonies. Country ideology had now produced a virulent hatred and disgust for British government and British institutions. Yet the social upheaval of the previous decade also meant that whatever replaced the world produced by Anglicization, colonial elites would be sharply challenged as they sought to conceive, create, and control it.

Murrin's discussion of the decade of imperial crisis reveals much about the nature of the British Empire and suggests a valuable model for how to draw together and learn from the disparate historiographies that have attempted to explain the coming of the American Revolution. By bringing together all of these issues, themes, and developments, Murrin draws omnivorously on the three historiographical traditions that in the twentieth century vied to explain the Revolution's origins. By taking seriously each of these historiographies, Murrin made himself into what he has often described as a radical, imperial, Whig. As he discusses in "Self-Immolation: Schools of Historiography and the Coming of the American Revolution," and as is implicit in so many of his essays, Murrin has seen great benefit in the classic work of the imperial school best represented by Herbert Levi Osgood, Charles McLean Andrews, George Louis Beer, and later Lawrence Henry Gipson. From them Murrin learned to think carefully about the British Empire as an empire, to pay close attention to its structures and policies and to the men who administered it, and to consider all the challenges and complexities they faced. At the same time, as he studied with Edmund Morgan, read and admired Bailyn and Gordon Wood, and worked alongside John Pocock for many years at Washington University in St. Louis, Murrin was a virtuoso contributor to the neo-Whig historiography that took principles and ideas so seriously. This historiographical school produced Morgan's careful constitutional discussion of imperial relations and Bailyn's, Wood's, and Pocock's recovery of the rich ideological world that explained the significance of country ideology and, eventually, the republican synthesis.[23]

Yet it was clear to Murrin as he earned his Ph.D. and began his career in the late 1960s, as the New Left or neo-Progressive historians began to publish their vital work, that the internal cleavages and class conflicts they were recovering had a central place in the American revolutionary story. The only way to explain how a constitutional conflict in 1764–1765, one that virtually all colonial participants were confident could be resolved within the empire, became a violent, bloody revolutionary upheaval by 1776–1778, was to tell a complete and synthetic story that the imperial, neo-Whig, and neo-Progressive historians could not fully or adequately explain without the others. To more completely explain the emergence and impact of the American Revolution, one had to become a radical, imperial, Whig, which was a sophisticated, complex, and flexible scholarly project that required synthesizing institutional, intellectual, constitutional, social, cultural, political, and economic history—in other words, the project laid out by the concept of Anglicization.

During his career, Murrin's pleas for synthesis, his urging of his fellow scholars to join him in becoming radical, imperial, Whigs, went unheeded. By the late 1980s and early 1990s, Murrin would begin his graduate seminar on the American Revolution and the Early Republic with a lecture setting out the dire consequences for a field in which three highly valuable historiographical literatures refused to engage with one another. By 2005 he was alarmed enough about the impact that refusal had on the study of the origins of the American Revolution that he agreed to give this lecture in public at the McNeil Center for Early American Studies. Then in 2007 John Murrin wrote his final essay, unpublished until now. In "Self-Immolation: Schools of Historiography and the Coming of the American Revolution" he assesses in print the consequences of the three dominant historiographical traditions that sought to explain the American Revolution failing to engage with each other. The result was the self-immolation of each school and, for the previous two decades, almost no work on the causes of the Revolution. "Self-Immolation" was a final plea that scholars become radical, imperial, Whigs. When he delivered the paper at the Columbia Seminar, Murrin noted that this lack of scholarly interest might be changing. In the decade since Murrin wrote, it has. Several books and essays have revived interest in the causes of the Revolution, and recently others have called for synthesis and integration.[24]

Yet we have been here before. Murrin's "The Great Inversion" was an earlier plea that the neo-Whig and neo-Progressive schools talk to one another. And, as Murrin pointed out in a *William and Mary Quarterly* forum assessing Gordon Wood's *Creation of the American Republic*, Wood's book is mischaracterized as solely a history of ideas and ideology.[25] Wood drew heavily on the themes of the neo-progressive school and sought to integrate the material with the ideological. That *Creation of the American Republic* is often assigned to the neo-Whig school, with little awareness of its real debt to the progressive historiographical tradition, makes evident that earlier pleas for integration and synthesis went unheeded.

Despite recent developments, there are reasons to be less than hopeful. Much of the recent scholarship still seems to be re-creating earlier choices and for now, emphasizing economic causes and downplaying ideological and constitutional issues.[26] Indeed, at the conference in Philadelphia that produced *The American Revolution Reborn*, the editors of the 2012 *The Oxford Handbook of the American Revolution* noted that none of the thirty-three essays dealt with the ideological world recovered by Bailyn, Wood, and Pocock and that had played such a vital part in Murrin's radical, imperial, Whig synthesis. The editors certainly did not celebrate the absence; they noted it and thought we should ponder it.[27]

Murrin developed his insight of Anglicization only by crossing methodological boundaries. These crossings led him to creatively synthesize the American Revolutionary era's disparate historiographies. Explaining

the imperial crisis and the American Revolution requires the scholarship of the radicals, the imperials, and the Whigs, and the concept of
Anglicization allows that scholarship to be woven together. Murrin
believes that it is impossible to understand the colonial reaction to
the shift in British imperial policy after 1763 without taking seriously the
insights of the constitutional and ideological perspective provided by the
neo-Whig scholars. Yet doing so should convince us to stop seeking to
distinguish between what was constitutional/ideological and what was
material/economic in the colonial reaction. The leading colonial critics of the Sugar and Stamp Acts, such as James Otis and Daniel Dulany
(Dulany became a loyalist in 1776), were thoroughly Anglicized subjects.
Their critique, insisting on the connection of taxation to representation,
was possible only because their identity and consciousness was fundamentally shaped by post-1688 ideas, ideals, and categories. At the heart of
this Glorious Revolution–inspired mentality was the absolute confidence
that Britons enjoyed the natural right to private property and its protection in ways that were denied to everybody else. The constant refrain "liberty and property" is a reminder that these eighteenth-century subjects
did not distinguish between the constitutional/ideological and the mate-
rial/economic in the ways that we so often still insist they must.

Such distinctions never existed in the early modern era. Public politics,
a public sphere, really began in England with arguments over how far the
Protestant Reformation should go.[28] From the 1570s, and certainly by the
reign of James I, the English could associate the ability to continue this
conversation, and push their monarchs in a more purely Protestant direction, with their monarchs' need to frequently summon Parliaments. And
it was easy for them to understand that monarchs summoned Parliaments
when they needed to tax. Those who controlled taxation had a tremendous impact on whether critical religious conversations could happen.
It was in reaction to charged Parliaments and those sorts of questions
that the early Stuarts began to more vigorously champion Divine Right
and prefer prelates who preached in support of it.[29] Strident defense of
Divine Right led in response to clearer and more frequent articulation of
Parliament's customary role and the possibilities for limits to monarchical authority. As the early Stuarts faced chronic fiscal crisis, more frequent
Parliaments led to more charged encounters and greater entrenchment in
the arguments for Divine Right and limited monarchy.

Nowhere in this story is it helpful to distinguish between the consti-
tutional/ideological and the financial/economic/material. Subjects had
to control their property and the state's access to it to be able to have the
public culture and politics that preserved their liberties and saved their
souls. They needed an economy in which they could further their material
interests, because only subjects secure in their property could ensure the
survival of the institutions that protected and preserved their core ideo-
logical/constitutional and religious values. After the Glorious Revolution
Britons viewed liberty, property, prosperity, and Protestantism as of a
piece—and preserved only by limited-constitutional monarchy. A government that threated any of those things threatened all of them. Subjects
who opposed policies that could threaten their material circumstances
were also opposing policies that could reduce them to a point where
they could no longer protect their liberties and constitutional traditions.
A government imposing policies that degraded liberties and constitutional traditions would escape the limitations that protected subjects'
property and prosperity. Those connections were automatic and axio-
matic for the Anglicized subjects who denounced the Sugar and Stamp
Acts with constitutional arguments, and who over the course of the next
decade tried to comprehend their place in a British Empire that faced a
swiftly escalating imperial crisis.

The breakup of the British Empire produced during that decade was
profoundly disruptive; it violently ruptured all of the significant and
integrative trends that had been shaping the colonies for most of the
eighteenth century. American citizens had to fight a terribly difficult war
and then re-create their polity, economy, and society after having rejected
and destroyed most of the institutions and practices they had grown up
with. Portions of "The Great Inversion," "Feudalism, Communalism,
and the Yeoman Freeholder," and "The Making and Unmaking of An
American Ruling Class," as well as "Fundamental Values, the Founding
Fathers and the Constitution," "Escaping Perfidious Albion," "A Roof
Without Walls," and "War, Revolution, and Nation-Making," explore
the efforts to cope with what Murrin called "The Great Inversion."
With that phrase Murrin meant that fundamentally the core of the
revolution settlement in England was the court-Walpolean fiscal-military state, while the core of the American revolutionary settlement
put the values of country ideology at the heart of the new Republic's

political culture. In the essays in *Rethinking America* treating the post–
Revolutionary War years, Murrin discusses how desperately former
colonial elites, the unmade American ruling class, and their advocates
in the Federalist Party of the 1790s struggled to re-create through policy
the world that the golden age of the colonial era had produced: a world
where a recognizable ruling class possessed political, social, cultural, and
economic power.

That world had been shattered by the American Revolution. Despite
the brilliance of Alexander Hamilton's financial system and the efforts
of the Federalist Party, it could not be put back together again.[30] The
Federalist Party of the 1790s took its name from and hoped to build on
the nationalizing efforts of the supporters of the Constitution of 1787.
The Federalists of 1787–1788 conceived a much more powerful nation-
state than the Articles of Confederation had allowed. And Hamilton
made a mighty attempt to squeeze out of that Constitution a genuine
fiscal-military state. Yet post-revolutionary realities guaranteed that for
a very long time the Constitution would remain "a roof without walls."
With that phrase Murrin meant that the capacity to imagine a national
polity and economy (to envisage a roof) came long before all the various
practices, institutions, and broader national economic and cultural connections (the walls) existed to support the roof. The walls were not there
in part because the nature of the American revolutionary settlement rendered highly suspect those who sought to build them. But the walls were
also not there because the early American Republic faced many of the
same conditions that had made the British Empire a federal system, one
that required imperial policymakers to secure voluntary cooperation in
order to act in the interior. Under the Jeffersonians and Jacksonians, the
early American Republic moved relentlessly across space, but the nation-
state usually found that it could act forcibly in the interior only when
those living there were willing to allow it.[31]

Murrin, I suspect, would caution those scholars who are at present
arguing for a highly effective and powerful early national nation-state.
He would urge them to do the analogous work for the early American
Republic of being a radical, imperial, Whig to explain the American
Revolution. He would welcome their reappraisals of his statements about
a tiny state in a giant land, but would ask them to write finely grained
histories, paying close attention to when, why, how, and under what

circumstances and conditions the nation-state could be active and power-ful, and where, when, and why it could be prevented from being so.[32]

The post-revolutionary nation-state could clearly and forcibly act with real coercive power when it was doing things that were popular in the vast interior. Primarily it could seize land from Indians and European empires and sell it to citizens at ever cheaper prices. The nation-state had a great deal more difficulty (and not much more success than the British Empire) at forcing citizens living on that land to do things they truly did not want to do. The result of the violent disruption of Anglicization, of the great inversion, was to create a nation of many regions and localities. These regions were intensely patriotic and even nationalistic because they were autonomous enough to be able to define the nation in their very different, even mutually exclusive, images. Murrin discusses this develop-ment in "War, Revolution, and Nation-Making," one of the two essays in *Rethinking America* not previously published.[33] The regional and local autonomy resulted from a revolution settlement that was far more country than court, from the sheer immensity of the Republic's size by the 1820s, and due to the apotheosis of the yeoman freeholder, which, "Feudalism, Communalism, and the Yeoman Freeholder" reminds us, no politician could safely question in the early American Republic.

This combination of vast size, deep suspicion of a central state, and glo-rification of the white, male, property-owning head of household made for a violent, racist, and profoundly gendered American democracy. As Murrin discusses in "The Great Inversion," "Feudalism, Communalism, and the Yeoman Freeholder," "Escaping Perfidious Albion," and "The Making and Unmaking of an American Ruling Class," the unmaking of the Anglicizing ruling class, and the defeat of the effort to re-create something like it in the 1790s, unleashed the millions of white adult male heads of household to seize as much of the North American con-tinent as they could. They were supported in their efforts by a nation-state that only reliably and consistently wielded power over them when it assisted their efforts. Rapidly after 1820 the nation's citizens, and those they could coerce in racial and gender hierarchies, collectively produced a vast amount of wealth. But this wealth came much more from the bottom up than it did from the direct involvement of something akin to a fiscal-military state. This process of wealth creation did not reproduce Patrick O'Brien's astute observation about eighteenth-century Britain, where "the economy was driven forward by the state rather than the state being driven by the economy."[34]

The early Republic's far less nation-state managed and frenzied scramble for wealth produced much more wealth and a far greater concentration of wealth than had ever been present in the colonial period. This society and economy produced a great deal of social stratification among white male heads of household. Fluid social mobility went both upward and downward; in effect greater emphasis on freedom, autonomy, and egalitarianism for white men produced among them a great deal of uncertainty, fluctuation, status anxiety, and the broad democratization of marginalization and inequality. Boom and bust and wealth and poverty characterized a republic in which citizens were deeply suspicious of a powerful nation-state, though perhaps it might have been able to alleviate some of the most savage of the hard times. Instead, the solutions offered were usually greater glorification of the yeoman freeholder, the violent seizure of more western land, more intense identification with region, and a growing demand to push each region's core institutions and practices across space. By the 1830s and 1840s these cores had been organized around free labor in the north and slave labor in the south.

The early American Republic had managed to unleash the energies of white men by creating a profoundly democratized political culture built on the autonomy of each citizen from his neighbors, the autonomy of the locality, state, and region from the nation, and the near-total authority of the head of household over the social relations within his household walls. The assumption was that egalitarianism among heads of household would be maintained as hierarchy was banished from the public realm and retreated behind those walls. Yet the result was a society in which equality among white men proved increasingly elusive, which caused ever more frenzied efforts to secure that autonomy and equality through relentless economic growth and geographical expansion. The feverish effort to maintain equality, and the glorification of the yeoman freeholder that drove that effort, grew only more desperate as equality moved further out of reach. The more expansion occurred, the more this bottom-up process of growth and development produced material resources that were inequitably distributed. In the early American Republic, the methods used to lessen inequality among white men were often the most potent sources of inequality among them.

This democratic culture ever more shrilly insisted that white men must be equal when they manifestly were not. White male citizens increasingly found some solace in their whiteness and maleness as many of them could no longer rely on the traditional markers of citizenship: land ownership and material independence. A society of intensely regional localities, which hated dependence and bred suspicion that inequality resulted from the use of corrupt and concentrated power held by somebody somewhere, marched relentlessly across the continent. By the mid-1840s it began to produce an uncontainable crisis. Murrin has said that in the early American Republic the nation-state could primarily seize land from Indians and give it away to citizens but that by the 1850s it could no longer even peacefully manage that. The American Revolution, as he explains it, was a profoundly countercyclical rupture of almost everything that had come before it. The Civil War was an even more violent but logical culmination of a republican experiment whose ideals produced a society where outcomes moved ever further from the best version of intentions.

The U.S. Civil War exposed with overwhelming and bloody violence the dilemmas and challenges of the republican experiment and American identity, the pain of promises and dreams deferred, and the momentous expectations that American citizens of every variety had of their public institutions and civic culture. John Murrin's towering scholarly achievement available in *Rethinking America* help us to better comprehend the origins and development of the tragedies and possibilities produced by the republican revolution that made the United States. This obligation of rethinking is ongoing, indeed perpetual, and never has it been more urgent.

Notes

1. J. P. Sommerville, *Royalists and Patriots: Politics and Ideology in England, 1603–1640* (London: Longman, 1999); Richard Cust and Ann Hughes, eds., *Conflict in Early Stuart England: Studies in Religion and Politics* (London: Longman, 1989); Robert Ashton, *The Crown and the Money Market* (Oxford: Clarendon Press, 1960); P. G. Lake, "Calvinism and the English Church, 1570–1635," *Past and Present* 114 (1987): 32–76; Kenneth Fincham and Peter Lake, "The Ecclesiastical Policy of King James I," *Journal of British Studies* 24 (1985): 169–207; Conrad Russell, *The Fall of the British Monarchies* (Oxford: Clarendon Press, 1991).
2. John M. Murrin, "Colonial Government," in Jack P. Greene, ed., *Encyclopedia of American Political History*, 3 vols. (New York: Scribner's, 1984), 1:293–315;

John M. Murrin, "Political Development," in Jack P. Greene and J. R. Pole, eds., *Colonial British America: Essays in the New History of the Early Modern Era* (Baltimore: Johns Hopkins University Press, 1984), 408–56; John M. Murrin, "Beneficiaries of Catastrophe: The English Colonies in America," in Eric Foner ed., *The New American History* (Philadelphia: Temple University Press, 1990) 3–23; John M. Murrin, "Magistrates, Sinners, and a Precarious Liberty: Trial by Jury in Seventeenth-Century New England," in David Hall, John M. Murrin, and Thad W. Tate, eds., *Saints and Revolutionaries: Essays on Early American History* (New York: W. W. Norton, 1984), 152–206; John M. Murrin, "English Rights as Ethnic Aggression: The English Conquest, the Charter of Liberties of 1683, and Leisler's Rebellion in New York," in William Pencak and Conrad Edick Wright, eds., *Authority and Resistance in Early New York* (New York: New-York Historical Society, 1988), 56–94; John Murrin, "The Menacing Shadow of Louis XIV and the Rage of Jacob Leisler: The Constitutional Ordeal of Seventeenth-Century New York," in Stephen L. Schechter and Richard B. Bernstein, eds., *New York and the Union: Contributions to the American Constitutional Experience* (Albany: New York State Commission on the Bicentennial of the United States Constitution, 1990), 29–71; John Murrin, "The New York Charter of Liberties, 1683 and 1691," in Stephen L. Schechter, Richard B. Bernstein, and Donald S. Lutz, eds., *Roots of the Republic: American Founding Documents Interpreted* (Madison, WI: Madison House Publications, 1990), 47–82; John Murrin, "Pluralism and Predatory Power: Early New York as a Social Failure," *Reviews in American History* 6 (1978): 473–79

3. W. A. Speck, *Reluctant Revolutionaries: Englishmen and the Revolution of 1688* (Oxford: Oxford University Press, 1998); Steve Pincus, *1688: The First Modern Revolution* (New Haven, CT: Yale University Press, 2009); Lionel K. Glassey, ed., *The Reigns of Charles II and James VII and II* (London: Macmillan, 1997); Richard Ashcraft, "Revolutionary Politics and Locke's Two Treatises of Government: Radicalism and Lockean Political Theory," *Political Theory* 8 (1980): 429–86; Tim Harris, *Restoration: Charles II and His Kingdoms* (London: Penguin, 2005); Tim Harris, *Revolution: The Great Crisis of the British Monarchy, 1685–1720* (London: Penguin, 2006).

4. For the phrase, see John M. Murrin, Paul E. Johnson, James M. McPherson, Gary Gerstle, Emily S. Rosenberg, and Norman L. Rosenberg, *Liberty, Equality, Power: A History of the American People*, 1st ed. (New York: Thompson Gale, 1996), chapter three.

5. I have provided an extensive discussion of Anglicization as the central theme of Murrin's work in Andrew Shankman, "A Synthesis Useful and Compelling: Anglicization and the Achievement of John M. Murrin," Ignacio Gallup-Diaz, Andrew Shankman, and David Silverman eds., *Anglicizing America: Empire, Revolution, Republic* (Philadelphia, PA: University of Pennsylvania Press, 2015), 20–56.

6. J.G.A. Pocock, "The Limits and Divisions of British History: In Search of the Unknown Subject," *AHR* 87 (1982), 311–336.

7. J. H. Plumb, *The Growth of Political Stability in England, 1675–1725* (London: Macmillan, 1967); Linda Colley, *Britons: Forging the Nation, 1707–1837* (New Haven, CT: Yale University Press, 1992); John Brewer, *The Sinews of Power: War, Money, and the English State, 1688–1783* (New York: Alfred A. Knopf, 1989); A. L. Beir, David Cannadine, and James M. Rosenheim, eds., *The First Modern Society: Essays in English History in Honour of Lawrence Stone* (New York: Cambridge University Press, 1989); Lawrence Stone, ed., *An Imperial State at War: Britain from 1689 to 1815* (London: Routledge, 1994); Patrick O'Brien, "Inseparable Connections: Trade, Economy, Fiscal State, and the Expansion of Empire, 1688–1815," in P. J. Marshall, ed., *The Oxford History of the British Empire: The Eighteenth Century* (New York: Oxford University Press, 1998), 53–77; Patrick O'Brien, "The Political Economy of British Taxation, 1660–1815," *Economic History Review* 41 (1988), 1–32; Paul Langford, *A Polite and Commercial People: England 1727–1783* (New York: Oxford University Press, 1989); Paul Langford, *Public Life and the Propertied Englishman, 1689–1798* (New York: Oxford University Press, 1991); H. T. Dickinson, *Liberty and Property: Political Ideology in Eighteenth-Century Britain* (London: Methuen, 1977); Neil McKendrick, John Brewer, and J. H. Plumb, eds., *The Birth of a Consumer Society: The Commercialization of Eighteenth Century England* (Bloomington: Indiana University Press, 1982).

8. Paul Langford, *A Polite and Commercial People: England 1727–1783* (New York: Oxford University Press, 1989), 70.

9. John Murrin, "Review Essay," *History and Theory* 11 (1972) 226–275, 268. For a similar process in New Hampshire, see Jere Daniell, "Politics in New Hampshire under Governor Benning Wentworth, 1741–1767," *William and Mary Quarterly* 23 (1966), 76–105.

10. Stanley N. Katz, "Between Scylla and Charybdis: James DeLancey and Anglo-American Politics in Early Eighteenth-Century New York," in Stanley Katz and John Murrin, eds., *Colonial America: Essays in Politics and Social Development* (New York: Alfred A. Knopf, 1983), 394–409.

11. John Murrin, "English Rights as Ethnic Aggression" and "The Menacing Shadow of Louis XIV and the Rage of Jacob Leisler."

12. Gordon S. Wood, *The Americanization of Benjamin Franklin* (New York: Penguin Press, 2004).

13. Bernard Bailyn, *The Origins of American Politics* (New York: Vintage, 1967); Bailyn, *The Ideological Origins of the American Revolution* (Cambridge, MA: Harvard University Press, 1967).

14. John Murrin, "Beneficiaries of Catastrophe" and John Murrin, *Liberty, Equality, Power*, 121–133.

15. T.H. Breen, *Tobacco Culture: The Mentality of the Great Tidewater Planters on the Eve of Revolution* (Princeton, NJ: Princeton University Press, 1985).

16. Murrin, "Political Development."
17. Richard Johnson, "Growth and Mastery: British North America, 1690–
    1748," in Marshall, ed., *The Oxford History of the British Empire* 276–299;
    John Shy, "The American Colonies in War and Revolution, 1748–1783," in
    Marshall, ed., *The Oxford History of the British Empire*, 300–324.
18. Fred Anderson, *A People's Army: Massachusetts Soldiers and Society in the
    Seven Years War* (Chapel Hill, NC: University of North Carolina Press), 23;
    Shy, "The American Colonies in War and Revolution," 308.
19. Jack P. Greene, "Empire and Identity from the Glorious Revolution to
    the American Revolution," in Marshall, ed., *Oxford History of the British
    Empire*, 208–230.
20. The best discussion of the Townshend Acts and the Circular Letter is Merrill
    Jensen, *The Founding of A Nation: A History of the American Revolution,
    1763–1776* (New York: Oxford University Press, 1968), 215–376.
21. For a discussion of the challenges of internal legislation, though the
    colonists did not object to it on ideological grounds prior to the Coercive
    Acts, see Andrew Shankman and Ignacio Gallup-Diaz, "How to Lose an
    Empire: British Misperceptions of the Sinews of the Trans-Atlantic System,"
    in Ignacio Gallup-Diaz, ed., *The World of Colonial America: An Atlantic
    Handbook* (New York: Routledge, 2017), 375–391.
22. Pauline Maier, *From Resistance to Revolution: Colonial Radicals and the
    Development of American Opposition to Britain, 1765–1776* (New York: W.W.
    Norton, 1972), 71–78; Gary Nash, "Social Change and the Growth of
    Prerevolutionary Urban Radicalism," in Alfred F. Young, ed., *The American
    Revolution: Explorations in the History of American Radicalism* (De Kalb,
    IL: Northern Illinois University Press, 1976), 5–36.
23. Edmund S. and Hellen M. Morgan, *The Stamp Act Crisis: Prologue to
    Revolution* (Chapel Hill, NC: University of North Carolina Press,
    1953); Bailyn, *The Ideolgoical Origins of the American Revolution*; Gordon
    S. Wood, *The Creation of the American Republic, 1776–1787* (Chapel
    Hill, NC: University of North Carolina Press, 1969); J.G.A. Pocock, *The
    Machiavellian Moment: Florentine Political Thought and the Atlantic
    Republican Tradition* (Princeton, NJ: Princeton University Press, 1975); Robert
    E. Shalhope, "Republicanism, Liberalism, and Democracy: Political Culture
    in the Early Republic," in Milton M. Klein, Richard D. Brown, and John
    B. Hench, eds., *The Republican Synthesis Revisited: Essays in Honor of George
    Athan Billias* (Worcester, MA: American Antiquarian Society, 1992), 37–90.
24. Woody Holton, *Forced Founders: Indians, Debtors, Slaves and the Making
    of the American Revolution in Virginia* (Chapel Hill, NC: University
    of North Carolina Press, 1999); Michael McDonnell, *The Politics of
    War: Race, Class, and Conflict in Revolutionary Virginia* (Chapel Hill,
    NC: University of North Carolina Press, 2010); Terry Bouton, *Taming
    Democracy: "The People," The Founders, and the Troubled Ending of
    the American Revolution* (New York: Oxford University Press, 2009);

Benjamin Carp, *Rebels Rising: Cities and the American Revolution* (New York: Oxford University Press, 2009); Patrick Spero and Michael Zuckerman eds., *The American Revolution Reborn* (Philadelphia, PA: Penn Press, 2016); Staughton Lynd and David Waldstreicher, "Free Trade, Sovereignty, and Slavery: Toward an Economic Interpretation of American Independence" *William and Mary Quarterly* 68 (2011), 597–630; Gordon S. Wood, "Reassessing Bernard Bailyn's *Ideological Origins of the American Revolution* on the Occasion of Its Jubilee" (unpublished paper cited with the author's permission).

25. John Murrin, "Gordon S. Wood and the Search for Liberal America," *William and Mary Quarterly* 44 (1987), 597–601.

26. A brief but insightful discussion of this concern is Barbara Clark Smith, "Beyond the 'Economic,'" *William and Mary Quarterly* 68 (2011), 639–643. Smith's was a brief response to Lynd and Waldstreicher, "Free Trade, Sovereignty and Slavery."

27. Jane Kamensky and Edward Gray, eds., *The Oxford Handbook of the American Revolution* (New York: Oxford University Press, 2012).

28. Peter Lake and Steven Pincus eds. *The Politics of the Public Sphere in Early Modern England* (Manchester, UK: Manchester University Press, 2007); Patrick Collinson, "The Monarchical Republic of Elizabeth I" and "Puritans, Men of Business, and Elizabethan Parliaments," in Patrick Collinson, *Elizabethan Essays* (London: The Hamledon Press, 1994), 31–57, 58–86.

29. Sommerville, *Royalists and Patriots*; Peter Lake, "Anti-Popery, The Structure of a Prejudice," in Cust and Hughes, *Conflict in Early Stuart England*, 72–106.

30. Andrew Shankman, *Original Intents: Hamilton, Jefferson, Madison and the American Founding* (New York: Oxford University Press, 2017).

31. John Murrin, "The Jeffersonian Triumph and American Exceptionalism," *Journal of the Early Republic* 20 (2000), 1–25. For additional discussion of these issues, see Andrew Shankman, "Toward a Social History of Federalism: Capitalism and the State to and From the American Revolution," *Journal of the Early Republic* 2017 (forthcoming); Andrew Shankman, "Conflict for a Continent: Land, Labor, and the State in the First American Republic," in Andrew Shankman, ed., *The World of the Revolutionary American Republic: Land, Labor, and the Conflict for a Continent* (New York: Routledge, 2014), 1–24.

32. William J. Novak, "The Myth of the 'Weak' American State," *American Historical Review* 113 (2008), 752–772; Brian Balogh, *A Government Out of Sight: The Mystery of National Authority in Nineteenth-Century America* (New York: Cambridge University Press, 2009); Richard R. John, *Spreading the News: The American Postal System from Franklin to Morse* (Cambridge, MA: Harvard University Press, 1995); Max M. Edling, *A Hercules in the Cradle: War, Money, and the American State, 1783–1867* (Chicago: University of Chicago Press, 2014).

33. The other is "Self-Immolation, Schools of Historiography, and the Coming of the American Revolution." For more on the theme of regional autonomy and particularity allowing for mutually exclusive nationalisms, see David Waldstreicher, *In the Midst of Perpetual Fetes: The Making of American Nationalism, 1776–1820* (Chapel Hill, NC: University of North Carolina Press, 1997); Trish Loughran, *The Republic in Print: Print Culture in the Age of U.S. Nation Building, 1770–1870* (New York: Columbia University Press, 2007).

34. Patrick O'Brien, "Inseparable Connections," 64; John L. Larson, *Internal Improvement: National Public Works and the Promise of Popular Government in the Early United States* (Chapel Hill, NC: University of North Carolina Press, 2001).

PART I
An Overview

I

The Great Inversion, or Court versus Country

A Comparison of the Revolution Settlements in England (1688–1721) and America (1776–1816)

AMERICANS HAVE ALWAYS shared one conviction about their Revolution: it was a good thing for the United States and the entire world.[1] The revolutionary generation believed that its principles would benevolently affect social conditions, agriculture, political economy, the fine arts, and even basic demographic trends. Only now are many of these themes being recovered. In the nineteenth century, constitutional questions became increasingly separable from broad social issues in a way that the eighteenth century had never imagined. Thus early chroniclers of the Revolution began to lose some of the movement's context even while quoting directly from its fundamental documents. They explained and defended the Revolution in terms essentially constitutional and political, as the triumph of liberty, equality, and limited government against the menace of irresponsible power and aristocratic privilege—rather feeble dangers, they somewhat paradoxically implied, if only by giving these challenges little real chance of success in America's unique, libertarian environment, which they found at work in the very first settlements. Whatever the Revolution thereby lost in dramatic appeal—and the triumph of the inevitable creates great drama only when the result is tragic—it gained in mythic power even among trained historians. Against its immortal principles, all previous and subsequent events had to be measured.

The Revolution has seemed a living tradition, as against a finite past event, to the extent that Americans have expanded its values to include

Originally published in *Three British Revolutions: 1641, 1688, 1776*, ed. J.G.A. Pocock (Princeton: Princeton University Press, 1980), 368–453.

more people over time. By well-known stages, the republic's definition of citizenship has grown from propertied, white, Protestant, adult, male householders in 1775 to embrace all adults over eighteen today. This theme, and the extension of egalitarianism into economic relationships, have between them organized most serious history yet written about the United States. Complex statistical examinations of social mobility, for example, are really asking whether the Revolution's heirs have fulfilled its promise. Some scholars even see in this country "the first new nation" and in the Revolution the world's first successful revolt against colonialism. To them the revolutionary tradition is not only alive in America, but highly relevant for all mankind.[2] It is exportable. In less discreet hands, this argument almost suggests at times that, if only developing nations can learn to imitate the Federal Constitution and adopt a variant of the American party system, something like the millennium will overtake the globe.

Except perhaps for numerous immigrants to this country, the rest of the world has never quite agreed and, today more than ever, scorns the message. Outsiders who have commented on the American scene over the past two centuries have responded with varying degrees of sympathy. Well into the nineteenth century, European revolutionaries generally admired the American republic, but apart from advocating such specific techniques as written constitutions and the process of ratification, their approval fell short of direct emulation. Since Marx, they have tended increasingly to identify America as the enemy of revolution, not its exemplar.[3] Yet Tocqueville and Lord Bryce toiled thoughtfully and appreciatively to grasp the interaction of American politics and society. One twentieth-century French observer, who dismissed the United States as the only country in world history to go from barbarism to decadence without passing through civilization, evidently abandoned the attempt. In general, foreign critics have found American politics amusing, idiosyncratic, peculiar, trivial, evasive of real issues, bombastic, eccentric, incomprehensible, boring—but inimitable in any case. From this perspective the United States appears less as the mother of democracy than as a precocious child of Britain by a difficult first marriage to mercantilism. The immensely powerful offspring has remained without heirs, but Britain, through a second marriage to nineteenth-century liberalism, has passed on her parliamentary system to much of the world; Western Europe, Canada, Australia, New Zealand, parts of Latin America and the Caribbean, remote Japan, India, and, less happily, South Africa and Rhodesia.

Yet at least since Tocqueville, outsiders—even those who impatiently dismiss the American polity—often succumb to sheer fascination with its social system and, above all, its standard of living. IBM and Pepsi-Cola seem more likely than Thomas Jefferson to sweep the world. American affluence remains highly exportable, although the takers have ironically been Western Europe, Japan, and Taiwan instead of Third World nations, which, while engrossing the attention of modernization theorists, confront the United States through revolution or the threat of revolution rather than through grateful imitation. This trend should not shock anyone, but the misleading image of a "new nation" does appear to have created different expectations. The term applies far more aptly to the United States than to the Third World, in which virtually every society is far older than Jamestown or Plymouth. Only Canada, Australia, and New Zealand truly compare with the United States in this respect, but by the logic of metaphoric tyranny, they are usually considered part of the mature or developed world. Significantly, their traditions range from a loyalist or anti-Revolutionary asylum in Ontario to variants of radicalism in Australia and New Zealand, but none claims a transforming revolutionary heritage. Thus in one sense the American Revolution has severed the United States from its most conspicuous social analogues around the globe without linking it very usefully with the rest of the world.

I

American historians have never convincingly united the idealistic and social themes that have emerged from the Revolution. Justifications of the principles of 1776 have continued without break since the event itself, but a coherent social interpretation of the era finally appeared only with the Progressive generation of Carl Becker, Charles Beard, Arthur Schlesinger, Sr., and John Franklin Jameson. Partly because most Progressives refused to take seriously the lofty pronouncements of revolutionary spokesmen, we remain more divided than ever about the merits of this approach and what, if anything, it has achieved of lasting value. "The popular view of the Revolution as a great forensic controversy over abstract governmental rights will not bear close scrutiny," affirmed Schlesinger. "At best, an exposition of the political theories of the anti-parliamentary party is an account of their retreat from one strategic position to another.... Without discounting in any way the propagandist value attaching to popular shibboleths as such," he concluded, "it may as well be admitted that the colonists would have lost their case if the decision had turned upon an impartial consideration of the legal principles involved."[4] Ideology nearly always masked economic interests, Progressives believed, whether those of merchants, speculators, planters, or small farmers.

Then, twenty-five years ago, Edmund S. and Helen M. Morgan published *The Stamp Act Crisis, Prologue to Revolution.* Emphasizing that revolutionary spokesmen did announce clear and consistent principles, the Morgans left no doubt what they thought was at stake in 1765: "if England chose to force the issue [of taxation without consent]," they explained, "the colonists would have to decide...whether they would be men and not English or whether they would be English and not men." This conviction did not blind the Morgans to a swirl of conflicting interests that varied widely from one colony to another, but on the whole they found ideology and interest mutually compatible rather than antagonistic. More strikingly, perhaps, their account displayed a keener sympathy for the plight of early loyalists than anything yet written in the tradition of Whig history. Their series of vivid personal sketches described them as honest and intelligent men trapped on the wrong side of a revolutionary situation that would never have occurred had London listened to their advice before 1765.[5]

These themes soon acquired different overtones. "Consensus" historians, led by Robert E. Brown, found no room whatever for economic and social conflict in late colonial America, The settlers fought the Revolution to preserve existing liberties against British tyranny and aristocratic arrogance.[6] With a much subtler approach, Bernard Bailyn and his students at Harvard emerged as an "ideological school" that dominated the 1960s, despite persistent radical dissent from Jesse Lemisch and Staughton Lynd. Moving beyond what he saw as a rather narrow constitutionalism in Morgan, Bailyn exuberantly explored the broader ideological world of the late eighteenth century. His patriots, conscious heirs of British opposition writers, explained all history as the desperate struggle of rapacious power against delicate liberty, which, once lost, could never again be recovered. He stressed what had been only a minor motif for the

Morgans—the readiness of each side in the struggle to detect the foulest conspiratorial motives in its opponents. Colonists easily discovered proof that London was plotting to destroy liberty in America, and Englishmen quickly perceived a colonial conspiracy aimed at independence. Critics of Bailyn's recent biography of Thomas Hutchinson apparently fear that this emphasis is now verging on neo-loyalism. The Morgans' decent men caught on the wrong side of a revolutionary dilemma have become possibly the sanest individuals in a paranoid world, even though Bailyn has explicitly stopped short of such a formulation.[7]

But while neo-Whigs, consensus historians, and the ideological school battled to define their versions of the Revolution, Merrill Jensen and a remarkable group of talented students at Wisconsin revived the concern of the Progressives with social conflict and clashing interests. In the last decade they have thoroughly documented acute social tensions in one colony after another, and since 1970 have pretty well dominated the study of the Revolution. Not surprisingly, most of them see Bailyn's ideological interpretation as their chief obstacle or even enemy, and they remain highly critical of his failure to give adequate consideration to economic issues.[8]

In general the ideological school invokes a unique Revolution to explain one of its major concerns: the uniqueness of America. Social conditions are indeed a part of this singularity, but the critical shift to an open or fluid society had occurred long before 1760 and, in any case, did not cause the upheaval after 1765. Ideology did. Surprisingly, the Harvard school has emptied even the colonists' ideology of the economic content it manifestly did possess, as other intellectual historians are now showing. With Morgan somewhere between the two poles on this question, most members of the Wisconsin school seem much less fascinated with the uniqueness of America, They hope to make the Revolution more relevant to our time by linking it, if only by implication, with other great modern upheavals, beginning with that of France in 1789. Only a truly revolutionary Revolution can do the job. And if one compares Alfred Cobban's emphasis on the revolt of minor officeholders in France with James Kirby Martin's similar discovery for all of the colonies, the French and American Revolutions had similarities of origin that most historians have missed, just as on the ideological plane the two movements articulated similar commitments to liberty and equality against the corrupting force of power and privilege.[9]

Thus to a distressing degree the historiography of the Revolution now resembles the children's hand-symbol game of scissors, paper, and rock. Scissors cut paper, paper covers rock, and rock blunts scissors. In this case Morgan's consistent constitutionalism (or neo-Whiggery) slashed through a confusing tangle of Progressive interests, Bailyn's enlarged ideology dulled the Morgans' constitutionalism, and neo-Progressive interests have blanketed Bailyn's ideology.

Increasingly, most colonial specialists seem compelled to pledge firm allegiance to one standard or the other. Despite the mediating efforts of Gordon Wood, J. R. Pole, Kenneth Lockridge, and Eric Foner, a widening gap has opened between the ideological and neo-progressive schools. Each either attacks or, perhaps more devastatingly, simply ignores the contributions of the other.[10] Without pretending to reconcile all differences, this chapter hopes to suggest that the alternatives are not all that stark. An expansion of ideological content to incorporate the economic issues that it really did address will surely help. And a closer attention to economic interests than Beard or Schlesinger attempted will heighten, not lessen, their importance. For example, we should not expect all merchants to have thought or acted alike on political questions. They differed considerably on access to capital, ownership of vessels, the kind of markets they traded with, length of time in their occupation, and the possession of office. Two merchants could behave quite differently, and yet still be pursuing their own particular economic interests.

Any absolute dichotomy between the two schools is unrealistic. The Revolution cannot make sense without both of them. Two trends are now so carefully documented about the period 1760 to 1815 that they appear almost beyond challenge, at least to this historian. Ideological commitment became measurably more intense and precise, foreclosing one option after another in the decades after 1760. By turns oceanic empire, imperial federation, monarchy itself, and Hamiltonian Federalism disappeared as viable solutions to North America's problems. And more rapidly than at any time since 1700, and more universally than at any point since the founding of Jamestown, social conflict escalated into the crisis stage as religious controversy, urban rioting, anti-rent upheavals, the regulator movements, immensely destructive partisan warfare, mutiny in the Continental Line, Shays' Rebellion coupled with a myriad of lesser disturbances in the mid-1780s, the whiskey insurrection, Fries' Revolt,

Gabriel's slave uprising, the Baltimore riots of 1812, and the Hartford Convention paraded past bewildered contemporaries in frightening succession. To this list one could add the Newburgh Conspiracy, various separatist movements in Vermont and Tennessee, and Aaron Burr's strange activities in the West—all with unrealized potential for acute social disturbance.

The historian's task should not be the defense of one of these themes to the exclusion of the other. If at all possible, he should try to explain both. Ideological intensification and social upheaval really did happen—simultaneously. But did they mutually reinforce or impede one another? Or did they interact in different ways at different times? This chapter does assume that the two trends will combine more explosively when they support each other. Working at cross-purposes, they will generate a more mixed and confusing situation. On the whole they did become ever more organically related throughout the era, with the Stamp Act crisis as a major early exception. Social turmoil, which arose over a wide variety of religious, economic, and political issues in the 1750s and 1760s, became inextricably connected to the classic ideological tension between Court and Country in the 1780s and 1790s. Indeed, economic change, the danger of popular upheaval, the emergence of systematic opposition within a republican government, and the imperatives of ideology all united to shape the issues and alternatives of the first American party system after 1790.

One massive uncertainty underlay much of the turmoil. Could thirteen extremely heterogeneous societies with no tradition of continental unity battle their way from colonialism to independence as something resembling a coherent nation? In 1815 the new republic just barely emerged intact from the Age of Revolution, but its unity remained precarious, threatened thereafter by internal forces rather than by European powers feeding upon internal tensions. Its ideological configuration had been set for perhaps the next century, and social violence would henceforth erupt mostly over ethnic conflict (including slavery) rather than over Court-Country issues.

To appreciate how all of these questions interacted until 1815, one must broaden the context considerably. Let me begin, not by employing a French Revolutionary model that became relevant to the men of 1776 only later in their lives, but by comparing the American Revolution with the one major predecessor almost universally admired by contemporaries, however differently they interpreted it: England's Revolution of 1688.[11] Drawing more on J.G.A. Pocock, J. H. Plumb, Isaac Kramnick, Lance Banning, and Drew R. McCoy than upon extensive original research, this chapter suggests an elementary framework for restoring some of the dialogue among colonial historians. What follows is surely not the only way in which the period can be discussed, but I hope it is broad and flexible enough to remain open-ended and inclusive. It does not read out of the Revolution whole areas of experience vastly important to participants.

Much can be learned by contrasting America's "Revolution Settlement" through the War of 1812 with that of England through the Hanoverian Succession and the rise of Sir Robert Walpole. In comparing revolutions, most historians have obtained different results depending upon what they emphasized—the origins, the most extreme stage reached in particular upheavals, or the overall process, structure, and permanence of revolutionary change. To R. R. Palmer, the American and French Revolutions seem broadly similar because the origins of both reflect acute resentment against arbitrary power and legal privilege, even if Americans found less amiss in their social order than Frenchmen did. To both American consensus historians and the European Left since Marx, the two movements remain irrevocably different because the United States never experienced anything as radical as Robespierre's Jacobin republic. Those, such as Crane Brinton, who stress the "anatomy," the "natural history," or the structure of revolutions, have usually tried to reduce all of them to a set of similar stages through which each must pass, culminating in a conservative reaction or counter-revolution.[12]

Any attempt to compare revolution settlements probably resembles Brinton's approach more than the others, for it must ask what everything was like once the process had run its course. But we shall be pondering differences as much as similarities. To take only one conspicuous example, the English Civil Wars generated a Restoration which, modified in 1688 and more often since 1832, has nonetheless survived ever since. Enemies of the French Revolution used their armies to impose upon France a Restoration that quickly fell apart. In our own century the Russian and Chinese Revolutions certainly have created authoritarian governments, but neither is in any meaningful sense a restoration of the Old Regime, as any czarist or mandarin yet living will testify. Although the United

States experienced no true restoration, widespread fears that Federalists intended something close to one fueled political life for a generation after 1789.

The term "Revolution Settlement" is used in this chapter to describe the pattern, whatever it happens to be, assumed by a revolutionary regime after the turmoil itself is over. Once the process has been completed, for an indefinite period of future time internal forces alone will not alter the regime or constitutional system in more than secondary details. This expansion of the time boundary permits important contrasts to emerge, mostly between Britain and America, but also between both of them and France, although the French example shall not be emphasized here. England's Glorious Revolution resolved itself into a stable system of Walpolean politics, operating within the world's most dynamic economy. The American Revolution reached stability with the triumph of Jeffersonian government between 1801 and 1815. The French Revolution gave birth to a Napoleonic Empire that became so deeply entrenched in the society that it could be overthrown only by the combined armies and fleets of the rest of Europe.

A sustained effort at Anglo-American comparison may even suggest why Americans seem unable to resist a dichotomy that pits a political against a social revolution. The perplexity of foreign viewers can be enlightening in this respect, for the United States is not just a political system, nor a dynamic industrial order that mysteriously generates "the American way of life," but a complex interaction between the two. Because the Jeffersonians rescued the polity and the Revolution mostly by divorcing them from larger patterns of economic and social change, this antinomy remains perhaps the single most troublesome legacy of 1776, a continuing barrier to the nation's understanding of what it has become and how it got that way.

II

By 1688 England had long been divided into Court and Country alignments which in the previous decade had coalesced into the Tory and Whig parties. As used here, "Court" and "Country" have strong ideological connotations that suggest the normal though not the possible boundaries of political division. Radical dissent had moved well beyond these limits during the Civil War and Interregnum and, by the very act of doing so, had largely defined acceptable boundaries for subsequent generations. Court apologists were intensely statist and, in their most extreme form, might seek to emulate a continental European monarchy. They tried to endow the government with the resources and vigor necessary to command great respect abroad and maintain order at home. Country spokesmen expressed strong suspicion of government, might even at times seem isolationist in foreign policy, and preferred to rely upon local resources and institutions for the preservation of domestic order. By contrast, the labels Whig or Tory, and later Federalist or Republican, describe political coalitions or "parties" usually constrained to operate within the framework of Court-Country tensions. Within each party, members could assume different positions along the Court-Country spectrum and, especially in Britain, the parties themselves could shift massively from one persuasion to the other.

After the Glorious Revolution the English Court finally abandoned the persecution of dissenters for limited toleration, and it accepted a permanent role for Parliament in the governance of the realm. But in other respects its goals after 1688 merely continued, intensified, and extended the policies of Charles II and James II. William III and his successors still sought the means to restrain opposition at home and to conduct a vigorous foreign policy against French expansion—a standing army, a huge navy, ample revenues to wage war despite the inevitable disruption of trade and customs duties, a reasonably effective bureaucracy, and increased patronage. The Country opposition, staunchly Whig in the 1680s, preferred a militia to a standing army, limited revenues, small government dependent on the voluntary cooperation of the gentry, and place bills and frequent elections to prevent Court patronage from corrupting the House of Commons.[13]

Almost continuous warfare with France imposed terrible strains on these alignments over the next generation. None aroused more acute anxiety than the financial revolution of the 1690s, through which England acquired for the first time a modern fiscal system. A funded national debt which would mushroom spectacularly from £2 million under James II to £130 million by 1763, the Bank of England, the London Stock Exchange, the great recoinage, a permanent land tax and other internal revenues to offset the wartime uncertainties of port duties, heightened reliance upon

an enlarged East India Company and later the South Sea Company—
all these date from the 1690s.[14] Although the point remains much more
debatable, the same era may also have rediscovered the poor as a major
social problem.[15] It certainly did indulge in a quite undisciplined fascination for what Daniel Defoe called "projects"—novelties or improvements ranging from unsuccessful Country experiments such as land
banks to the steam engines of Thomas Savery and Thomas Newcomen.[16]
The number of new patents rose sharply in the 1690s, with sixty-four
issued in the three-year period from 1691 to 1693.[17] In a bizarre way, the
whole trend culminated in the year of the Bubble on the eve of Walpole's
triumph. Thus 1720 witnessed the creation of a company to bleach hair,
another for the transmutation of quicksilver, a firm that proposed to
insure marriages against divorce, and still another that tried to market an
air pump for the brain. Best of all, perhaps, if possibly mythical, was the
stock issue of £3,000 snapped up in a single day for "a company to carry
on an undertaking of great advantage but nobody to know what it is."[18]

In the era of savage party conflict between 1689 and 1714 that brought
voter participation to an amazing peak, these tensions worked an incredible reversal in political alignments. Continuous warfare and the exceptionally high land tax ruined numerous members of the gentry and
yeomanry but offered unprecedented opportunities for assured income
to investors in the public funds and for instant fortunes to other men able
to profit from the government's expanding activities by making shrewd or
lucky investments at the right moment. Many of the gentry sourly concluded that the state was destroying traditional families only to raise a
swarm of greedy parvenus upon their ruin. To an undetermined extent, in
other words, the government's fiscal policy did redistribute wealth.[19] And
in a pattern whose roots lay far back in the seventeenth century, the traditional monopolies, such as the East India and Royal African Companies,
had tended to be Tory, while merchants who had developed newer markets with little Court protection rallied strongly to the Whigs. Especially
in the East India trade, the intruders first broke the monopoly to force
their way in and later took it over for themselves.

Accordingly, the Whigs, by pursuing their anti-French policies,
emerged as the Court party by the Hanoverian Succession, a transformation conspicuous in greater London as early as 1691.[20] Whigs embraced
the new dynasty, the debt, the Bank of England, the great corporations,

a permanent standing army, the world's mightiest navy, and enough patronage to guarantee the docility of Parliament in all but the most extraordinary of circumstances. At the first opportunity they reduced the frequency of elections from three years to seven, quietly restricted the number of eligible voters in many boroughs, eliminated actual contests for seats through prior gentlemanly understandings wherever possible, and almost succeeded in converting the House of Lords into a self-perpetuating corporate body. Whig apologists, to nobody's surprise, often defended moderns against ancients in the "battle of the books" that raged among Augustan literati. Some Whigs even justified 1688 as a Revolution in the modern sense, one that permanently changed things for the better. Lacking from the modern formula was, of course, the legitimation of violence. Court and Country, Whig and Tory, confined their idealization of liberty within boundaries that safely defined public order as a primary value.[21]

Tories, who under Anne seemed to be emerging as the majority party on all issues but the Succession, over which they were badly divided, had originated as the Court supporters of Charles II during the Exclusion Crisis. But as the financial revolution took its toll, they began to question whether France was any more a natural enemy than the Dutch Republic. Beginning in the 1690s, and especially with their exclusion from power after 1714, they tended overwhelmingly to assume the attitudes of a Country opposition. They defended 1688, not as a new departure, but as the restoration of the ancient and virtuous constitutional balance of King, Lords, and Commons, once threatened by James II and now menaced from a new and more sinister direction by the fiscal revolution and the patronage politics of Walpole's "Robinarchy." In sum, they now embarked upon what Pocock has called a "quarrel with modernity," siding with the ancients in the battle of the books. It was now the turn of the Tories to enlist, far more successfully than Court Whigs, the greatest literary talents of the age to denounce a standing army, bloated patronage, and above all the corrupt alliance between government and the money power that threatened to destroy the virtue and independence of the gentry and the House of Commons.[22]

Thus England's Revolution Settlement created a centralized system of Court politics and one-party rule, closely tied to the disturbing new world of high finance and the beginnings of intensive economic growth that may have accompanied it.[23] It was resisted, usually on "Revolution principles," by a Country opposition that was mostly Tory, although it included a remnant of "Real Whigs" who remained faithful to the ideals of the 1680s. This opposition, even in its loosely united "patriot" phase of the 1730s, occasionally extracted concessions from the government. But it never acquired enough strength to regain control of Parliament despite extensive gentry support, considerable voting strength in such remaining open constituencies as the counties and larger boroughs, and highly articulate expression in the press.

III

Now let us shift to North America. This chapter cannot discuss broad colonial developments beyond observing a few trends. First, the generation that experienced the stabilization of Britain's constitutional order also witnessed the institutional elaboration of imperial control. The Board of Trade, the most comprehensive Navigation Act, and the system of vice-admiralty courts all appeared in the 1690s. Army officers, beginning with men who rose through the household of James II while he was still Duke of York, and followed by abler men trained under the Duke of Marlborough, took over and largely defined the office of royal governor in America and the West Indies. By the 1720s a clear pattern had also emerged to determine which colonies would be royal and which would remain proprietary or corporate.[24] Second, colonial military and fiscal practices also took shape in a way that would characterize most of the coming century. The settlers fought their wars with "marching forces" that were institutionally distinct from traditional militia without ever quite becoming a standing army. Apparently with little appreciation for the ideological implications of their decisions, one colony after another also embraced the "Country" fiscal expedients that England had rejected in the 1690s, especially bills of credit receivable in taxes, and land banks. Inflated exchange rates raised havoc and political temperatures in the Carolinas and New England, but these devices worked nicely from Maryland to New York and generally held their value.[25]

As a whole, the colonies did not surrender indiscriminately to Country ideology. Instead political developments in the half-century after the Peace of Utrecht created a spectrum of regimes from north to south. The northern wing produced successful "Court" constitutions in the New Hampshire of Benning Wentworth (1741–1767) and the Massachusetts of William Shirley and Thomas Pownall (1741–1760). New Jersey displayed fainter trends in the same direction after 1750. In New York, an effective system of court politics emerged around 1715 only to decay under inept and greedy governors (1732–1753). In each of these colonies successful governors relied heavily upon various forms of patronage to discipline competing factions and secure the support of the assembly. When used cautiously, such tactics appeared both necessary and salutary in diversifying societies whose factions could jeopardize public order. One measure of the achievement of someone like Shirley was the occasional appearance of Country ideology in newspapers or pamphlets—the effort, as in Britain, of a minority faction unable to gain control of the assembly and use it as a platform against the governor. But when governors did fail and had to duel with the assembly itself, the language of these debates became formal and legalistic, pitting older seventeenth-century definitions of prerogative and privilege against each other.[26]

The southern wing of provinces evolved stable "Country" constitutions in Virginia, South Carolina, and Georgia. In these places strong, independent governors and strong, independent assemblies learned to cooperate voluntarily in the best traditions of Country ideology, usually after an initial period of bitter recrimination. Each had ample power to thwart but not dominate the other and hence took elaborate precautions to avoid real offense. This system worked because a homogeneous planter class, untroubled by serious factional rifts, was producing the tobacco and rice that the empire desired, while the empire provided valuable naval, military, and economic services in return. By mid-century able governors usually got what they sought from the assembly, but they did it through highly ritualized forms of persuasion, not by creating a corps of placemen in the assembly. In these provinces the appearances of Country ideology reflected social harmony, political stability, and effective royal leadership.[27]

North Carolina, divided into competing rice and tobacco regions and troubled by a rapidly growing and exceptionally turbulent back country, never acquired a homogeneous planter class upon which a Country constitution could be built. Similarly Rhode Island and Connecticut, which lacked royal government altogether, deviated from the emerging

"Court" norm of New England. In between the two wings of colonies lay two provinces that really were the kind of exception that proves the rule. Maryland's proprietors continually tried to play Court politics in a Country environment. Pennsylvania found itself imprisoned by a Country constitution—the heritage of early Quakers—in a Court environment of diversifying trade, ethnic and religious rivalries, and persistently clashing interests. Neither colony achieved political stability in the eighteenth century.[28]

Here, too, fiscal systems suggested the possible extremes. In the 1750s, when most of New England voluntarily abandoned paper money for orthodox Court finance, Virginia ardently embraced paper for the first time, eventually provoking Parliament's Currency Act of 1764.[29]

Real limits to parliamentary control of imperial affairs also appeared in this period, most of them by 1713. Parliament amply demonstrated its power over oceanic affairs, which may in fact have been more effective over colonial commerce than it was over Britain's own.[30] But Parliament never successfully extended its authority over internal colonial issues. With only trivial exceptions, British ships monopolized colonial trade, colonial staples were exported to Britain for consumption or reexport, and European and Asian goods reached America via British home ports. Until the reorganization of the 1760s, Parliament got much poorer results regulating commerce between North America and the West Indies, whether through the Molasses Act of 1733 or various measures that tried to interdict wartime trade with the enemy.[31] But Parliament's attempts at internal regulation of the colonies, from the Coin Act of 1708 through the various White Pines, Hat, Iron, and New England Currency Acts, either misfired or were openly ignored and thwarted. Without active local cooperation, imperial officials simply lacked the leverage to secure compliance. To its later discomfort, the empire had drifted into a federal arrangement, with the division of power following an internal-external (or continental-oceanic) axis that hardly anyone but Benjamin Franklin understood or could justify.[32]

These considerations barely indicate how difficult a task the achievement of colonial unity would be. Even more than Italy or Germany in the early nineteenth century, "America" was only a geographical expression before the revolutionary era. Not even a unique language distinguished it from the rest of the British world. Its cultural heritage and its symbols of unity—the Crown, the mixed and balanced constitution, military glory (especially during the Seven Years War)—were predominantly British and in no way exclusively American. Of course New England took great pride in its puritan tradition, but this heritage set off the region from the rest of North America as much as from Britain. In an elementary matter such as the use of common symbols for the continent and its people, Englishmen—who had difficulty distinguishing one colony from another—were measurably more inclined to speak of "America" and "Americans" than were the settlers themselves.[33] Predictions of eventual colonial union and independence came almost exclusively from British placemen and travelers in the New World, not from the actual colonists, who at most mused now and then on the continent's fantastic rate of population growth and the power this trend would bring in a century or two.[34]

Nor had North America evolved anything remotely resembling an integrated continental economy by the 1760s. Instead its separate parts found themselves tied ever more tightly to an imperial economy that was becoming more efficient and more interdependent, often with uncomfortable results for major participants. Per capita colonial imports of British products rose markedly after mid-century. The coastal trade probably was increasing more rapidly than its transatlantic counterparts but not yet fast enough to offset the primacy of the empire as an economic entity. As insurance rates fell and the turnaround time for vessels lessened, profit margins also dropped in the face of increasing competition. Crises in the London money market in 1762 and 1772 rapidly created distress on the other side of the ocean.[35]

Indeed, something like an imperial rather than an American land and labor market had reached a high level of development by the 1760s. Extremely high rents in Ireland and Scotland provoked massive emigration to North America, where land remained plentiful. If not checked in time, this trend, according to some observers, threatened to depopulate Britain's Celtic fringe. It deeply worried powerful landlords in the affected areas, some of whom—such as Lord Hillsborough, the American Secretary after 1768—blamed America for their difficulties and, in consequence, easily became hard-liners on imperial policy.[36]

At one level, then, the American Revolution was a crisis in imperial *integration* which London simply could not handle. Economic, social, and intellectual trends were pulling together the separate societies of the empire in ways that Whitehall neither understood nor appreciated, for events were rapidly outpacing Britain's century-old conception of imperial relationships. Thus in the decade after 1765 the home government performed what should rank with the most stupendous achievements of the age. It united all thirteen colonies in armed resistance to imperial rule, despite their widely varying constitutional systems, the huge social differences between colonies, and the violent cleavages emerging in most of them.

How did Britain do it? Within the scope of this chapter I can address only a few critical themes, and those quite briefly—the underlying thrust of imperial policy, the interaction between ideology and selected interests within the colonies, and the continuing dilemma of colonial unity within this political environment.

IV

To an overwhelming degree Whitehall's policies grew out of the mid-century cycle of Anglo-French wars. The colonial reforms associated with Lord Halifax and the Board of Trade between 1748 and 1754 began with the Treaty of Aix-la-Chapelle that ended the War of the Austrian Succession. Halifax tried to improve imperial control at a time when unity against France seemed especially necessary. Because nearly all of his policies involved administrative rather than parliamentary decisions and thus had to be implemented through the normal channels of royal government, some colonies welcomed the changes while others ignored or resisted them, but nothing resembling *inter*colonial opposition appeared at all.[37] Still more dramatically, every leading item in the Grenville program of 1763 to 1765—the Proclamation of 1763, the crackdown on smugglers, the Currency Act, the Sugar Act, the Stamp Act, and the Quartering Act—can be traced to the panicky demands of provincial governors and imperial administrators during Britain's "years of defeat" from 1754 to 1757. Because most of the problems that prompted these demands had worked themselves out by 1763, and because Britain had adopted quite different measures to win the war, Grenville's program had to seem inappropriate and insulting to the colonists who experienced it, Whitehall quite overlooked the cooperative attitudes engendered by imperial success during the war and opted instead for parliamentary coercion.[38] The settlers eloquently expressed their dissatisfaction by nullifying the Stamp Act, As in seventeenth-century Europe, so also in eighteenth-century North America, warfare remained the primary catalyst to revolutionary change.

The Stamp Act produced a truly unique set of circumstances. Ideology, economic interest, and the heady discovery of colonial unity at both of these levels all combined to generate massive resistance that no one had believed possible even a few months earlier. In fact such a degree of unity was not to recur even in the crisis of 1774 to 1776, for by then loyalists were better organized and far more outspoken. Apart from Rhode Island's Martin Howard, the Stamp Act had no ardent defenders in North America.

For the first time, Parliament had ventured into an area of unenforceable internal legislation so sensitive that all of the mainland colonies instantly felt threatened by it. Recognizing their own powerlessness to avert this catastrophe of taxation without representation and trial without jury, the assemblies could only protest. However, especially after an intercolonial Stamp Act Congress pointed the way, their objections acquired remarkable uniformity. As the assemblies and nearly every pamphleteer quickly recognized, Parliament had ominously polarized imperial and colonial interests but, through its sheer indifference to colonial liberties, had also given the settlers an immense ideological advantage.

What else was the debate over virtual representation about? By smashing the government's chief ideological defense for the Stamp Act, colonial apologists gained a strong moral advantage. Because MPs would pay none of the taxes they imposed on America, the argument went, they could not represent the colonists on this issue even in the sense that they could normally claim to sit for non-voters in Britain. Acquiescence in the measure, reinforced by British self-interest, would only encourage London to devise others. And because stamp duties adversely affected every articulate interest in the colonies—merchants, seamen, lawyers, clergymen, printers, officeholders, planters, litigious farmers, even gamblers and college students—all could unite to resist the danger on the high constitutional ground of "no taxation without representation."[39] This polarization tormented John Dickinson of Pennsylvania, a man acutely sensitive to both interest and ideology. "What then can we do? Which way shall we turn ourselves? How may we mitigate the miseries of our country?" he asked in 1765. "Great Britain gives us an example to guide us. She teaches us to make a distinction between her interests and our own. Teaches! She requires—commands—insists upon it—threatens—compels—and even distresses us into it."[40]

This fusion of interest and ideology created a sense of colonial unity in 1765 that quite amazed the participants. "Can it come within possibility, that all the individuals in the northern colonies should, without prior conference, minutely concur in sentiment, that the British Parliament cannot, agreeable with the inherent privileges of the colonists, tax them without a representation on their part," asked one newspaper essayist, "unless there was some color for such exception?" Britain might even be able to antagonize the colonies into independence, Dickinson warned William Pitt, and "the Attempt [to leave the Empire] may be executed whenever it is made." "But what, sir, must be the Consequences of that Success?" he added, displaying a skepticism about the viability of America hardly unique to him. "A Multitude of Commonwealths, Crimes, and Calamities, of mutual Jealousies, Hatreds, Wars and Devastations; till at last the exhausted Provinces shall sink into Slavery under the yoke of some fortunate Conqueror. History seems to prove, that this must be the deplorable Fate of these Colonies whenever they become independent."[41]

The sheer euphoria of united and successful resistance concealed, nevertheless, important structural defects in the emerging patriot cause. First, because the stakes remained fairly low in 1765, a lot of rather conservative men rallied to the colonial cause who would have hesitated had the issue been as drastic as war or independence. In fact, most of the colonists' leading spokesmen in 1765–1766—chiefly men who skillfully employed legal-constitutional arguments rather than Country rhetoric—either became overt loyalists or hedged conspicuously on Independence by 1776. James Otis, Jr., William Smith of New York, John Dickinson, Maurice Moore, Jr., of North Carolina, Daniel Dulany, and John Joachim Zubly all fit one or the other of these categories. In addition former governor Thomas Fitch, author of Connecticut's official pamphlet against the Stamp Act, probably would have made a similar choice had he not died in 1774. The sample is too small to prove anything conclusive, but it does suggest that constitutional arguments alone lacked the moral force to turn someone into a true revolutionary and that radical Country ideology may often have supplied the difference, at least among intellectuals.

Yet even William Goddard, who used extreme Country rhetoric against all supporters of the Stamp Act, would be suspected of loyalism by his Baltimore neighbors during the early years of the Revolutionary War.[42]

Secondly, success against the Stamp Act concealed the impotence of the assemblies during the crisis. It also gave patriots undeserved confidence in the efficacy of nonimportation. Lord Rockingham's ministry solicited the support of British merchants against the Stamp Act on December 6, 1765, before word of colonial nonimportation agreements reached London on December 12 and 26. During the slack winter-business season, his government committed itself to repeal in the Commons on January 14, long before Britain could seriously feel the economic impact of nonimportation. Why? The ministry knew that the Stamp Act had been utterly nullified north of Georgia—that the "mob" had succeeded where assemblies, colonial agents, and merchants had all failed, and that attempted enforcement could easily produce civil war. Although his government divided privately on this question, Rockingham had no intention of accepting such a risk. But because Parliament needed a more dignified reason for retreat than its own incapacity and the activities of American mobs, the government strongly emphasized the imminence of economic disaster in order to slip repeal through the Commons while saving face with the Declaratory Act. The colonists, who knew little about the ministry's sharp disagreements over the Stamp Act, were understandably inclined to accept Parliament's public reasons for repeal as the real ones and hence overvalued the impact of nonimportation in later crises.[43]

Finally, the dramatic success of the American colonists' resistance to the Stamp Act quite simply obscured their failure in challenging the Sugar Act, which also imposed a tax for revenue. Indeed the Rockingham government amended that statute in 1766 to make it even more blatantly a revenue measure, for it now imposed a uniform penny duty on all molasses, British or foreign, imported into America. As the public celebrations finally quieted in 1766, hardly anyone noticed that the first imperial crisis had resolved itself along the traditional power axis of the empire. Parliament emerged victorious over external or oceanic measures, and the settlers over internal affairs. But neither could admit what had happened. Parliament could justify the exercise of any imperial power only by claiming supreme power, or complete sovereignty. The colonists could resist the Stamp Act consistently only by denying the right of Parliament to levy any tax. The empire was already beginning to disintegrate for want of a sustaining theory that could explain convincingly what Parliament actually could or could not do, what it had or had not done effectively over the previous century.

V

In the next imperial crisis (1767–1770) the settlers extended their resistance from such inland measures as the Stamp Act (or for that matter the older White Pines, Hat, and Iron Acts), where Parliament had never successfully exercised its authority, to oceanic measures where British power was limited only by the efficiency and cost of its enforcement apparatus. Just as the Stamp Act differed from earlier internal legislation in attracting systematic intercolonial resistance on ideological grounds, so the Townshend Revenue Act contrasted with the earlier Molasses Act, which had been evaded locally almost everywhere without appeals to ultimate principle. Since 1763 the activities of the Royal Navy in American waters made smuggling more costly and dangerous.[44] Hence colonial resistance to the Townshend Revenue Act had to be more difficult and structurally more radical than nullification of the Stamp Act had been. This effort jeopardized colonial unity, which remained tenuous at best, and opened troublesome rifts among various interests within and among colonial seaports. It was not particularly successful, and it weakened colonial claims to ideological purity. By 1770, ideology, interest, and the bid for unity simply did not coincide as they had five years before.

The penny duty on molasses, enacted in 1766 with widespread approbation from interested colonial merchants who found it preferable to any other British regulation of molasses since 1733, produced more revenue than all other colonial taxes combined in the prerevolutionary decade.[45] Yet colonial radicals never organized any serious resistance to this measure. Instead the Sons of Liberty united with merchants and seamen trading to the West Indies, the wine islands, and Southern Europe against the Townshend Revenue Act, which taxed items the colonists could legally obtain only through Britain. Although they were painfully slow in getting organized, merchants who concentrated on commerce elsewhere helped force nonimportation upon those who made a living from direct trade with Britain. "While the importers of Wines, Molasses etc., were pursuing their trade to considerable advantage and paying large sums into the [imperial] Treasury for revenues raised out of those articles," complained a Philadelphia merchant in 1770, "the Importers of British Goods were standing still and sacrificing all for the public good."[46] In many ports this cleavage may often have pitted rising merchants exploiting the expanding new markets that had opened since the 1740s against older, better-established mercantile bouses.[47] Apparently the molasses and grain-exporting trades, with their prominent links to distilling, milling, cooperage, shipbuilding, and other occupations, still seemed much too vital to the economic life of colonial cities to sacrifice to the principle of "no taxation without representation." By contrast British importers often used English or Scottish ships, competed directly with colonial artisans, and contributed much less in the form of ancillary employment. Even so, colonial resistance probably created greater hardship in America than it did in Britain, and it disintegrated rapidly when Lord North offered a shadow concession. He repealed the unproductive taxes on lead, glass, and painter's colors and retained the only true revenue producer, the duty on tea.[48]

North's policy shattered organized resistance in 1770 and stimulated savage recriminations among the colonies, but unlike 1766 it produced no real sense of imperial conciliation. Nobody celebrated. Indeed it made a British plot against colonial liberty seem altogether more plausible. If only for this reason the Townshend crisis, more than the Stamp Act controversy, marked a genuine turning point: a hardening of positions, expectations, and political alignments on both sides that would feed directly into the Revolution. Royal government, though stunned and shaken in 1765, had showed strong signs of recuperation by 1767. But in the three years after 1770, incidents that might once have seemed trivial, or at least manageable, paralyzed authority in one colony after another—disagreement over location of the Massachusetts General Court, an unsolved robbery of the East Jersey Treasury, the official fee scale and clergymen's salaries in Maryland and Virginia, paper money in North Carolina, and (a direct offshoot of the Townshend controversy) the Wilkes Fund dispute in South Carolina.[49]

In the midst of this shambles, North's genius soared again. With the Tea Act of 1773 he became the first imperial statesman ever to devise an oceanic measure that could actually be nullified. By restricting the profits to a select few importers, he rallied other merchants against the menace of monopoly. By confining the tea to the East India Company's vessels, he told the Sons of Liberty exactly where to look. They did not have to police the entire waterfront as in 1768–1770. North, by juggling the tea duties in Britain, also managed to reduce the price below that of smuggled tea while retaining the Townshend duty in America, and with it the principle of parliamentary taxation. He got what he deserved, an oceanic version of 1765 culminating in the Boston Tea Party. More ominously, perhaps, ideology now seemed to engulf economic interest at the popular level, for not even the promise of cheap tea could still the angry response.

British indignation at the Boston Tea Party drove the government past enforceable external measures, such as the Boston Port Act, which was implemented with ruthless efficiency, and rushed the ministry into rash internal legislation it could never carry out. The Port Act by itself provoked the First Continental Congress and guaranteed another difficult round of self-imposed commercial sanctions.[50] But the Massachusetts Government Act led directly to war, for not even British bayonets could impose it on the province. And the war may have saved the colonies from an extraordinary excess of virtue. Congress, for the first time, interdicted the vital British West Indian trade as part of its strategy of resistance and also announced a delayed policy of nonexportation that would before long adversely affect a majority of settlers in every colony. Britain responded by proscribing all New England trade except that forbidden by Congress, and soon extended the ban to the other colonies. The earlier Townshend Crisis and Jefferson's later embargo both attest to the enormous social dislocations and resentments a policy of this kind would have produced if pursued for very long, especially with Britain applying commercial pressures from the other side. That the colonists "have not Virtue enough to bear it I take for granted," conceded John Adams in October 1775. "How long then will their Virtue last? till next Spring?"[51]

Merchants as a group had probably never been all that vulnerable to ideology, as the willingness of future patriots to pay the molasses duty of 1766 suggests. "Reduce us all to poverty and cut off or wisely restrict that bane of patriotism, Commerce, and we shall soon become Patriots," mused Henry Laurens, who had been driven into opposition mostly by the rapacity of customs officials, "but how hard is it for a rich or covetous Man to enter heartily into the Kingdom of Patriotism."[52] Before the Sugar Act, corruption in the customs service had normally benefited colonial merchants, especially those in the French West Indian trade. But that statute and subsequent regulations deliberately made it more profitable for a customs officer to fleece the merchants than to cheat his own government. Doubtless this traumatic shift did sensitize some merchants to an ideology obsessed with the dangers of corruption. But on the whole, merchants seem to have divided along lines of interest. Existing studies leave many gaps, but a trend is emerging. Older houses, especially those concentrating in direct trade with Britain, mostly went loyalist. Traders to the islands and southern Europe, often new men, many of whom were building such new cities as Baltimore and Norfolk, sided with the patriots.[53]

Indeed, as war begot Independence in 1775–1776, British importers faced no option beyond what bridge to jump off. If they sided with Britain, the Sons of Liberty would plunder them ashore. If they joined the Revolution, the Royal Navy would destroy them at sea or cut them off from the source of their trade, a fate that did befall James Beekman in New York. Possibly many of them sided with the Crown because their outstanding British contacts gave them unmatched opportunity for royal office—the Hutchinson-Oliver bloc in Massachusetts and the DeLancey family in New York being the most prominent examples. But grain exporters and West Indian traders had greater flexibility. They were far more likely than British importers to own their own ships and, if necessary, they could turn to privateering, an engrossing activity in every port as far south as Baltimore after 1776. Many of these merchants had been dueling with the customs service and the navy for nearly two decades by 1775, for practically every seizure of a colonial vessel I have read about involved one of these trades. For such men and their sailors, the Revolution may have marked only an intensification of an animus already well established. And Independence, including its preliminaries, did extricate them from the awkward constraints of nonexportation provided they could elude the Royal Navy, a task rendered infinitely simpler when London committed the overwhelming bulk of its warships to transporting, supplying, and protecting the army rather than to sustained blockade duty.[54]

VI

Although Bailyn exaggerates the predominance of Country ideology through the 1760s, it had achieved a hugely disproportionate impact by

1775—enough to erode every legitimate royal and proprietary government on the continent, whether it had been a Court or Country structure, stable or unstable. In times of crisis men turn to the most compelling
explanation for their predicament that they can find. As both contestants
in the imperial struggle stumbled blindly into self-fulfilling prophecies,
the most alarming predictions by colonial radicals became not only plausible but true. In Britain, where every packet ship provided appalling
confirmation of the grimmest warnings about colonial Independence,
the government did nothing to avert the avalanche. Whitehall never provided colonial moderates with a viable alternative to continued resistance.
Hence even genuine conservatives at the First Continental Congress
made little effort to block its radical program, and the Second Congress
had no choice but to start organizing for a war that had already begun.[55]

While imperial relations had been deteriorating since the previous
war, immense social cleavages appeared in one province after another.
Because they occurred over a bewildering variety of issues, they had no
uniform effect upon the emerging revolutionary cause. Pennsylvania's
Paxton Riots, prompted by an Indian war, helped drive the assembly into
a demand for royal government that seriously weakened resistance to
imperial measures in that colony through the 1760s.[56] When Anglican
gentry found amusement by horsewhipping humble Baptist worshippers,
they bolstered neither the internal harmony of Virginia nor the cause
of united resistance to Britain. Both the Baptist challenge and growing
dissatisfaction with county courts indicated that Virginia's traditional
pattern of deference had begun to erode.[57] The Regulator movements,
at a bare minimum, made later unity against Britain much more difficult, by pitting backcountry planters against lawyers and merchants with
powerful tidewater connections in North Carolina, and by turning the
backcountry against itself in South Carolina.[58] Similarly New York's land
riots of 1776 left the Hudson Valley divided so many ways, socially and
politically, that no one has yet sorted out all the trends.[59] In each of these
cases, popular upheaval probably impeded more than it furthered the
revolutionary cause.

But the Stamp Act riots unquestionably strengthened radical resistance, as did later assaults on customs officials and the Boston Massacre.
New Jersey's earlier land riots may also have set the farmers of largely
patriot communities against a proprietary clique that would later turn

mostly loyalist.[60] No system of social analysis available to the eighteenth century could adequately explain all of these tumults, much less rally all of the dissidents behind a single standard. The classic Court-Country paradigm simply could not account for everything that was happening.

Yet as the empire collapsed, popular resistance to authority did become contagious and soon found new targets. It even threatened patriot notables such as James Bowdoin in Massachusetts, the Livingston clan in New York, James Wilson and Robert Morris in Pennsylvania, and Charles Carroll and the governing élite of Maryland. The overall pattern of upheaval was hardly uniform. At first it merely worried the planter gentry of Virginia and South Carolina, but once the British army appeared in force in these states, it stimulated vertical tensions of a most difficult and dramatic kind.[61]

The challenge to authority engulfed the assemblies as well. In the entire belt of colonies from New York to Maryland, not a single legitimate assembly ever repudiated the empire, and the provincial congresses that rivaled or replaced them in New York, Pennsylvania, and Maryland were nearly as cautious. Even after Independence, Delaware's convention that drafted its state constitution contained more loyalists than patriots![62] In Massachusetts, where both assembly and provincial congress had set the pace for all other colonies in resistance to Britain, the General Court encountered fierce resistance. The populous eastern towns did not embrace Independence until certain that they could dominate the new state government against recently aroused western farmers. The interior towns, for their part, refused to accept magistrates elected by eastern majorities or a state constitution drafted by such a legislature. Not even the Constitution of 1780 could resolve this tangle.[63]

Thus, as in the English Civil Wars, the Revolution's most radical phase drove many people well beyond the Country wing of the old Court-Country spectrum. Tom Paine's *Common Sense* savagely ridiculed the entire notion of mixed government. Unicameral legislatures in Pennsylvania, Georgia, and Vermont made little pretense at balancing authority. Even the more orthodox constitutions elsewhere drastically reduced executive powers below the Country norm. The most visible features of this radicalism included the continuing proliferation of extralegal committees and conventions at the local level, the overwhelming repudiation of high colonial officeholders, a dramatic expansion in the size of state legislatures, and a democratization of their membership.[64] The frontal assault on deference that all this turmoil revealed often did little to stabilize public authority. People who found new meaning in repudiating their "betters" had not yet discovered compelling reasons for obeying their equals, even when they happened to be organized as a legislature.

Yet by the time the fighting ended, the war had vastly simplified the prerevolutionary pattern of social tensions. Established churches and religious persecution became increasingly unpatriotic. Great landlords lost much of their power, and easterners made basic concessions to the interior, especially on representation, outside New England. These issues gave way to new ones as inflation, high taxation, and military confiscations worked their effects. By 1780 almost every state was divided geographically, and often vertically, between "cosmopolitans" who were more likely to possess education, wealth, and broad experience with the outside world, and "localists" who lacked these attributes and remained tightly identified with their home villages or counties. State legislatures split along these lines in one roll call after another.[65]With commerce badly disrupted and specie scarce, fiscal questions inevitably became the most explosive issues in this situation. Shays' Rebellion was only the most extensive among many riots of the mid-1780s that protested the imposition of orthodox fiscal systems.[66]

Unlike earlier cleavages, these disputes fit neatly within the old Court-Country paradigm. Whichever end of the spectrum one accepted, the issues seemed obvious. On the Country wing, virtuous farmers struggled desperately to protect their land and hence their independence against a darkly corrupt, grasping, anonymous, pervasive, and mysterious money power, which did indeed threaten their autonomy. On the Court wing, the disciples of public order were merely rallying to defend property and protect the "worthy" against the "licentious."[67]

For by the 1780s beleaguered conservatives, alarmed at the swirl of disorder around them, had finally begun to regroup. To many of them only the techniques of Court politics, overwhelmingly rejected everywhere after 1774, could now meet America's needs. The Continental Army officer corps, in particular, viewed the Revolutionary War primarily as an effort to defeat the British through an efficiently organized American military effort. They and their supporters in Congress (usually a minority) evolved plans for the republic between 1779 and 1783 that would require its transformation into an energetic government with sound finances and a respectable, permanent army. Their demands and their unscrupulous tactics alarmed much of the public who believed, often with considerable grounds, that the British had been defeated by the militia (or "the people") as much as by the Continental Line. Thwarted in 1783 by the Peace of Paris and Washington's unshakable integrity as they toyed dangerously with a military *coup d'état*, the nationalists had to wait another four years for a better opportunity.[68]

Events outside the army did indicate broad popular support for the more limited of these goals. The impost plans of 1781 and 1783, which would have given Congress an assured revenue for at least a generation, fell just short of the required ratification by all thirteen states. Interestingly, these measures looked toward a division of power between Congress and the states, similar to the old external-internal axis of the empire. Had either proposal succeeded, no constitutional convention would have met in 1787. But both failed, and left a badly demoralized Congress in a mortifying position. Country ideologues such as Jefferson hoped to populate the Northwest Territory with virtuous yeomen who would quickly receive the powers of self-government. After making a start in this direction, Congress reversed itself. Utterly desperate for any income by 1787, the government sold huge chunks of land to speculators at a pittance per acre and restructured territorial government in a manner that closely resembled royal government (appointive governor, council, and judiciary with an elective assembly), even though this status was meant to be temporary. At this point Country principles were rapidly becoming self-destructive, for the government's very weakness drove it to contrary measures.[69]

Something roughly similar was already happening at the state level. In Pennsylvania especially, the Anti-Constitutionalist (or "Republican") Party, many of whose leaders had been part of the old proprietary faction, pieced together an impressive coalition of various minorities alienated by zealous democrats since 1776. Quakers, sectarian Germans, other neutrals, and former loyalists had all been harassed severely during the war and found such an appeal attractive. Because the old élite proved more adept at pluralistic politics than the more radical Constitutionalists, it would soon be strong enough to ratify the Federal Constitution and replace the Pennsylvania Constitution with an orthodox balanced government in 1790, as Georgia had done a year before.[70]

Yet the Federal Constitution was no automatic result of an inexorable trend toward stronger union. No one seemed gloomier about the
Confederation's prospects for survival than committed nationalists, and
New England leaders—few of whom in any case showed nationalist sym-
pathies through the 1780s—were already exploring the possibilities of a
separate northern confederacy when Shays' Rebellion apparently frightened them off.[71] Convinced that the republic would soon splinter anyway without severe counter-measures, the delegates to the Philadelphia
Convention took some drastic gambles. From virtually their first
moment together, they exceeded their powers by scrapping the Articles of
Confederation to consider an entirely new frame of government. In drafting a constitution that would begin to function as soon as nine states had
joined the system, they announced their willingness to destroy the Union
in order to save it. As of 1787, no one could predict which nine states
might ratify or whether a regionally coherent bloc of states might be left
outside. In antinationalist New England an initial majority in every state
except Connecticut opposed ratification.[72]

Without contending for a nationalist conspiracy or *coup d'état* in 1787,
let us nevertheless concede what Beard rather clumsily argued, that the
United States Constitution was very much an élitist solution to the problems left by the Revolution and the popular turbulence of the 1780s. In
particular its restriction of representatives to one for every thirty thousand people (a figure about twice the size of contemporary Boston) was
consciously designed to secure government by "the wise, the rich and the
good." Only socially prominent men could expect to be visible enough
over that large an area to win elections, and they might well get help
from one another. ". . . The great easily form associations," explained a
troubled New Yorker in 1788, "the poor and middling class form them
with difficulty"—a judgment thoughtfully seconded by William Beers of
Connecticut three years later.[73]

In a word, the Federal Constitution shifted the entire spectrum
of national politics several degrees to the right. By resolving at last the
dilemma of taxation and representation, it gave the new government
access to revenues that the empire had shattered itself trying to establish.
It created a splendid opportunity to attempt traditional Court politics on
a continental scale. As this sudden challenge forced opponents to gather
behind proven Country defenses, more radical alternatives tended to

disappear. In such states as New York, Pennsylvania, and—with significant defections from the original Federalist coalition—Virginia as well,
the localist-cosmopolitan split of the 1780s, which had also been reflected
in the struggle to ratify the Federal Constitution, carried over into the
1790s with strong consistency.[74]

Elsewhere new patterns emerged. New England, which bad been the
most revolutionary and least nationalist region on the continent through
the 1780s and which came close to rejecting the Federal Constitution *en
bloc*, shifted stunningly to become the bastion of nationalist Court politics. The Southern states, generally regarded as fairly conservative during the Revolution, became the regional home of Country principles and
Jeffersonian Republicanism, once coastal South Carolina got far enough
away from its traumatic wartime experiences to join its neighbors. The
Middle States remained, as before, the primary battleground between
the other two regions. For the various state élites had always split into
sectional alignments in the Continental Congress, and they would once
again as soon as the new Constitution went into force.[75]

In other words, although the context was now quite different, the
1790s did mark something of a reversion to pre-1763 patterns of provincial politics. Court techniques again appealed to New England (even to
Connecticut and Rhode Island), the South strongly embraced Country
principles, and the Middle States could go either way.

VII

Implicit divisions among the Founding Fathers became overt in the 1790s.
Above all, they divided over the significance of American Independence.
To Alexander Hamilton and his Federalist followers, Independence
freed America to become another Great Britain. A successful American
Revolution would mean, they believed, that the United States ought to
duplicate England's Revolution Settlement within minimal republican
constraints. The implications of this position went far beyond politics,
for presumably the United States would develop through time much as
Britain had, generating a modern, integrated manufacturing economy.
Fittingly perhaps, the Federalists' Anglophilia (or "Anglomania," according to their enemies) alienated every major ethnic minority in the republic within a decade, except the Hudson Valley Dutch and probably the

sect Germans of Pennsylvania. By 1800 Federalists received their most assured support from old-stock English voters, chiefly in traditional communities with a slow rate of growth. Because the fastest-growing areas of the country produced and marketed primarily agricultural surpluses, this pattern is not at all as contradictory as it may at first appear.[76]

In rapid succession the Hamiltonians adopted measures that fulfilled the worst prophecies of the antifederalists of 1788, most of whom outside New England now rallied behind Madison and Jefferson in opposition. Their deepest concerns also transcended politics. Their vision of the republic saw it expanding through space across the continent while remaining economically and socially at roughly its current stage. With the stakes so momentous, the most consistent position for such a coalition to assume would have been that of an *anti*-Constitution party such as had emerged in Pennsylvania after 1776 and which was pretty much the role Federalists hoped to condemn them to. Instead, led by men who had supported ratification, they assumed the stance of a traditional English Country opposition. They denounced the Federalists for corrupting and perverting an ideally balanced government. This almost instant espousal of strict construction probably contributed more than any other single factor to the rapid legitimation of the new document. Federalists claimed to be implementing it, and Republicans insisted that they were defending it against Federalist excesses. Nobody opposed it. As just about everybody realized right away, the contending regions and interests had all surrendered as much as they dared in the compromises of 1787. The only alternative to the Constitution had already become disunion, a disintegration of the federal republic into its components, rather than experimentation with different systems such as the French could afford to try in the same decade. The continuing unity and viability of the United States depended, ironically, upon its ability to replicate both sides of the central tensions that had afflicted Augustan England.[77]

To Madison, Jefferson, and most committed Republicans, this stance came easily and naturally, for whether they had supported or opposed the Constitution, they instantly recognized Hamilton's policy for what it was. To them Independence meant an almost miraculous opportunity to remain different from and more "virtuous" than Britain. Anything else had to be what they called "corruption," and what the French were about to define as "counterrevolutionary." Like an English Country opposition, at least on political and economic questions, they idealized the past more than the future and feared significant change, especially major economic change, as corruption and degeneration. Huge cities and large-scale manufacturing, especially of luxury items for export, would transform virtuous yeomen into demoralized laborers and thus undermine the very foundations of republicanism. On the other hand, Jeffersonians strongly favored small household manufactures which had no such evil effects and which could significantly reduce America's dependence upon foreign imports.[78] But beyond the political and economic sphere, the parallel with Augustan England does break down. In America's own "battle of the books" during the Federal era, nobody exceeded High Federalists in shrill denunciation of all deviation from classical standards.[79] Not inappropriately, perhaps, Federalists apparently associated theological, literary, and artistic change with political assaults upon the existing social order.

We are now prepared to evaluate America's Revolution Settlement. To an almost incredible degree, American events after 1789 mimicked or even repeated English developments of a century before. America's Revolution Settlement resembles the remake of an old movie classic, except that the new producer has altered the ending to suit the changing tastes of his audience.

Note first the striking similarities. Each Revolution bequeathed intense, brutal party conflict to the next generation, a struggle that mobilized unprecedented numbers of voters, only to yield to a period of one-party rule—the Whig Oligarchy in Britain, the Era of Good Feelings in America. In both cases, because nobody really believed in parties, the contenders sought to destroy or at least absorb one another, not to perpetuate some kind of "party system." The division between Whig and Tory in Britain closely parallels the split between Federalists and Republicans in the United States, with Hamilton assuming the role of Junto Whigs or Walpole, and Jefferson serving as Tory or "Country" gentry—better still, as the "patriot" opposition to Walpole that had united Tories with Real Whigs in the 1730s; for Jefferson took his nomenclature from the late seventeenth century and would have hated to be called a Tory.

Indeed virtually all of England's central issues reappeared in America once Hamilton and his admirers launched their own financial revolution in the 1790s—an overt response to unresolved problems from the Revolutionary War. Hamilton took a debt that had sunk, depending upon the type of security and the provisions individual states had made for redemption, to anywhere from ten to thirty cents on the dollar and funded it at par, creating some of the grosser windfall profits in American history.[80] Nearly all of this gain went to speculators rather than ex-soldiers or planters, as entrepreneurs from New York City, Philadelphia, and Baltimore raced through the Southern backcountry to buy every available security before the local inhabitants (including local speculators) could learn how valuable they were.[81] Thus many Southerners saw only losses for themselves in these arrangements, and New York's Clintonian faction, which had already been forced to surrender lucrative port duties to the new government, was not won over, despite the state's gains. But Hamilton's assumption of state debts meant an immense flow of capital into New England and Pennsylvania, sharply reducing the need for direct taxes there and instantly lowering political temperatures. Certainly for New England, Court politics on a national scale worked wonders that had been utterly impossible when attempted at the state level in the 1780s.[82]

In 1791 Hamilton chartered the Bank of the United States, America's direct copy of the Bank of England. In place of England's great recoinage of the 1690s, the United States government established its own coinage and persuaded "the American Newton," David Rittenhouse, to take charge of the mint, a task Sir Isaac had accepted a century before.[83] Not surprisingly, the New York Stock Exchange also dates from the 1790s, doubtless contributing to a "projecting spirit" that far exceeded anything Defoe's generation had known. By 1792 the speculations of Hamilton's associate, William Duer, had produced the republic's first financial panic. "The stock buyers count him out," complained Jefferson, "and the credit and fate of the nation seem to hang on the desperate throws and plunges of gambling scoundrels."[84] "No man of reflection, who had ever attended to the South Sea Bubble, in England, or that of [John] Law in France, and who applied the lessons of the past to the present time," he added in another letter, "could fail to foresee the issue tho' he might not calculate the moment at which it would happen." The national debt, he admitted, had to be paid. Indeed, unlike Hamilton, he was determined to pay it off as rapidly as possible and end the government's dependence upon the financial community. "But all that stuff called scrip, of whatever description, was folly or roguery, and yet, under a resemblance to genuine public paper, it buoyed itself up to a par with that. It has been a severe lesson: yet such is the public cullability [*sic*] in the hands of cunning & unprincipled men, that it is doomed by nature to receive these lessons once in an age at least."[85]

No mere panic could restrain the "projecting spirit" set loose in the 1790s. Led by Eli Whitney's cotton gin and Robert Fulton's steamboat, the number of federal patents nearly doubled in every five-year period from 1790 through 1814. By 1802 it had reached a level thrice England's peak of the 1690s, which, incidentally, rested on a population base that was nearly identical: 5.5 million people.[86] Similarly the number of American banks exploded from four in 1791 to 29 by 1800, 89 in 1811 when the Bank of the United States expired, 246 by 1816, and over 300 at the onset of the Panic of 1819.[87] Oceanic commerce, mostly stagnant since 1774, grew at an astounding rate. America's $20 million worth of exports in 1790 had multiplied more than five times by 1807, led by the nation's reexport trade as the world's only major neutral carrier after 1793. An even more solid achievement, because it did not rest on European wartime conditions, was the fourfold increase in shipping engaged in coastal and internal trade—about double the rate of population growth. Indeed shipping profited enormously from the overall boom. In 1790 American vessels controlled only 40 percent of the value of American imports and exports. Just six years later this figure had leapt to 92 percent. The tonnage of American registered bottoms tripled between 1790 and 1810, approaching two-thirds of Britain's on a much smaller population base, while American shipbuilding may have roughly equaled the entire British empire's between 1800 and Jefferson's embargo of late 1807.[88] Frantic expansion of this sort created unprecedented extremes of wealth and soon stimulated great concern among the upper and middle classes about the problem of the poor.[89]

Other similarities abound. In every crisis with Indians or foreign powers in the 1790s, Federalists inched the government closer to the statist model first articulated by Continental officers and investors in the critical war years, 1779–1783.[90] For a time the leverage provided by the debt gave Hamilton a virtual placeman system for controlling Congress under a "prime minister"—creating, in effect, a national faction such as Madison thought he had rendered impossible in the persuasive argument of *Federalist Number 10.* Through the whiskey excise Hamilton hoped to establish beyond question the government's power to tax internally. This

Court measure provoked a rebellion in western Pennsylvania within a few years. As the republic verged on war with France, the Federalists extended their imitation of England with the stamp and land taxes of 1798, the second of which touched off Fries' Rebellion in 1799. Federalist repression of this mild and rather comic outburst, combined with the virulent nativism of the government's policy toward aliens, rapidly drove church Germans over to the opposition and forever alienated Pennsylvania from the party of Washington, Hamilton, and John Adams.[91] Hamilton closely supervised the creation of a true standing army at the end of the decade, and Congress added a navy designed to win respect for American merchant vessels on the high seas.[92] Especially after the Jay Treaty, Federalists pursued a pro-British and anti-French foreign policy, partly because the funding program depended for its solvency upon customs duties derived from British trade. (On the other hand, the Federalists, far more than their opponents, took serious steps to limit this dependence by attempting to develop internal revenues as a partial alternative.) Jeffersonians, most of them sincere admirers of the French Revolution, took the opposite approach on these questions. Yet as the new army, the Sedition Act, hysterical nativism, and the threat of electoral reform to guarantee a federalist presidential succession in 1800 all revealed, Hamiltonian statism possessed a high potential for coercing dissent, which Federalists honestly equated with disloyalty. In their hierarchy of political values, liberty and equality had become subordinate to public order and energetic government.[93]

For that matter, just as Whigs and Tories agreed after 1689 that violent protest was no longer acceptable politics, so Federalists and probably a large majority of Republicans accepted Washington's argument that once a government had been validly established by popular consent, it could be changed only by peaceful means. But in America each party still applauded the violent resistance of the Revolutionary War, unlike England where the Civil Wars seemed indecently excessive to virtually the entire governing class by 1689. In this sense, whiskey rebels and others with similar ideas still had a viable tradition to invoke. Yet on balance the similarities with England appear to outweigh the differences even on this issue.[94]

Nevertheless the two Revolutions came out so differently that the result, to steal a phrase from R. R. Palmer, might well be called America's

"Great Inversion" of England's Revolution Settlement. The Court won in England, and the Country in America. Surely one reason was the contrasting pattern of international involvement. While Britain warred with France in all but six years from 1689 to 1714, the United States remained at peace in all but six years from 1789 to 1815 (if we omit Indian conflicts from the comparison). When the republic did go to war, many of the pressures that had transformed England after 1689 appeared instantly in America: an enlarged army, a small but proficient navy, and internal revenues during the quasi-war with France. All of these devices plus improved coastal defenses and a new Bank of the United States reappeared during or immediately following the War of 1812.[95]

But because America's political antagonisms had a strong sectional base, protracted war with any great power would almost certainly have destroyed the fragile Union long before it could have transformed itself into a modern state, which, in the world of 1800, meant above all a government able to fight other governments effectively for an indefinite period. Even more than Englishmen of 1700, Americans could not agree on who their natural enemy was, or, as Washington stressed with peculiar force in his Farewell Address, whether they had one at all. Southern planters, who resented their continuing colonial dependence on British markets for their staples, often did regard Britain as a natural enemy. So did West Indian export merchants in the 1790s when the British took to plundering American vessels in the Caribbean, while merchants specializing in British imports completed this revival of the pattern of 1769 by opposing commercial sanctions and rallying to neutrality and the Jay mission.[96] Yankees, on the other hand, responded similarly to the prospect of war with France. Resurrecting ancestral memories of the traumatic struggles along New England's borders from 1689 to 1763, they evidently still did regard the French as natural enemies, a popish people doomed either to Jacobin anarchy or, especially after the rise of Napoleon, to slavish government.

Thus any major war mobilized hostile interests quite capable of paralyzing the government. Conflict with France soon generated threats of nullification and even disunion in the Anglophobic South after 1798. War with Britain provoked an overt danger of secession in Francophobic New England by 1814. A timely peace defused the crisis in each case. Yet in a real sense Americans could agree to live together only so long as they did not have to experience or share the pressures inevitably associated with a modern central government, and even that minimal understanding was to collapse by 1861.

Two other differences between Augustan England and federal America help to explain the political contrast. The first point is impressionistic but probably accurate, although its dimensions remain uncertain. Compared with England, the United States simply lacked a national governing class, that is, one that had intermarried across state boundaries. The Revolution, and particularly the resulting comradeship among Continental Line officers, undoubtedly stimulated something of the kind, later perpetuated in the Society of the Cincinnati; and while the national capital remained in Philadelphia in the 1790s, High Federalists did everything they could socially to act like a true governing class. But relatively few New Englanders seem to have married outside their region, and while the phenomenon was more common elsewhere, it required—almost by definition—more than a generation for the effects to be felt.[97]

The final contrast may well outweigh the others. By 1700 England had certainly acquired an integrated economy with London at its center, but the United States would achieve nothing fully comparable until the generation after 1815 or even 1840. The Revolution reversed the prevailing trend toward improved, imperial economic efficiency without creating a national, American economy. Many parts of the republic, awkwardly enough, still traded more with the former empire than with the rest of the Union. American vessels (not American produce) were now excluded from the British West Indies, and where about a third of the empire's ships (but not a third of its tonnage) had been built in the colonies as of 1774, Britain now preferred to construct her own at significantly greater cost. American shipbuilding recovered only in the 1790s, mostly as a by-product of European war. Similarly the Mediterranean trade, a rapidly expanding sector before Lexington, utterly collapsed for a quarter-century because American vessels had no navy to protect them from Barbary pirates. The sheer uncertainties of these years, and not the solidity of economic opportunity in the new republic, probably explain the appearance of economic scramblers like William Duer, riding a spectacular cycle from boom to bust. Because imports from Britain, mostly in British ships, did revive after the Revolution, beginning with the famous glut of 1783–1784, the overall pattern seemed ironic in the extreme until perhaps 1793. The

mercantile heirs of the loyalists, primarily British importers and overwhelmingly Federalist politically, appeared to be doing much better than
merchants who concentrated in areas that patriots had once dominated.
From this perspective, if the Revolution really was fundamentally an economic movement, somebody had miscalculated rather badly.[98]

To be sure, coastal and internal trade expanded more rapidly than
American exports (not counting reexports). The margin was about 3:2
from 1790 to 1807 and much more decisive thereafter until war disrupted everything. By 1820 intra-American trade would finally catch up
with American foreign trade. And in the decades 1790 to 1810, greater
New York City displayed unmistakable signs of its rapid emergence as the
continent's center of communications. But as a central city it still could
not compare with London, even the London of 1700. As of the War of
1812, the United States was still a less efficient and less integrated economic entity than the old empire had been. By the time this situation
began to change in the generation after 1815, the political configuration of
the republic had already been defined in a way that excluded the British
Court option.[99]

Thus the results of the two Revolutions differed markedly. In Britain
the Court Whigs won and kept central control over the new Hanoverian
dynasty, Parliament, the debt, the bank, high finance, the major corporations, the army, the navy, the bureaucracy, and the vast network
of patronage. In the United States the Country opposition of Thomas
Jefferson, which defined its aspirations very much in classic British terms,
captured the central government in 1801 and held it. Compared with
the Tory revival in Britain a century before, which had regained control of Parliament and the ministry in the last years of Anne's reign, the
later Federalist resurgence that fell only one state short of retaking the
presidency in 1812 was a less spectacular threat. And as a national force,
Federalists disintegrated much more rapidly after 1815 than British Tories
had after 1714.[100]

VIII

Yet Federalists and Republicans were not mere shadows of earlier Whigs
and Tories, duelling awkwardly after 1789 in the sunrise of Europe's
new revolutionary age. The American parties showed much fainter

tendencies to shift polarities in the course of their struggles, even after the Republicans gained power and the Federalists found themselves in the uncongenial role of a permanent opposition. Both overwhelmingly rejected hereditary monarchy, although they differed considerably over how broadly they construed this repudiation. The etiquette Hamilton devised for President Washington strongly evoked monarchical traditions, his opponents nervously objected, while John Adams' passionate campaign for titles in 1789 and his insistence that functionally the Constitution really had created a monarchy caused him no end of polemical discomfort.[101] To suspicious Republicans, the Federalists seemed to give their dark secret away whenever John Allen and Uriah Tracy, two avowed monarchists from the unlikely state of Connecticut where not even appointive governors had ever taken root, opened their sarcastic and vituperative mouths. Convinced that "the herd have begun to walk on their hind legs," Tracy raged that "it was a damned farce to suppose that a republican government could exist," and that even America must finally have its own aristocracy and king.[102]

As in England, however, each party had discernible Court and Country wings, the normal results of frantic coalition building in time of stress. Among the Federalists, Allen and Tracy represented the extreme, not the norm. But Hamilton's policies explicitly emulated English Court techniques, and on the whole John Adams, the unyielding Country ideologue of 1775, agreed with him. Although he never abandoned his hostility to standing armies, Adams endorsed funding, assumption, the Bank, the Jay mission and treaty, and at first greatly admired Hamilton. "The Secretary of the Treasury is so able, and has done so well," he wrote in 1791, "that I have scarcely permitted myself to think, very closely whether he could or could not have done better," although he did believe that Hamilton should have pushed harder for internal revenues. Adams found speculation deplorable but inevitable. "The funding system is the hair shirt which our sinful country must wear as a propitiation for her past dishonesty," he explained. "The only way to get rid of speculation is to hasten the rise of our stocks to the standard beyond which they cannot ascend." Fear of disunion and disorder now outweighed the dangers of malignant power that had tormented him in the 1770s. "The rivalries already arisen between the State Sovereignties and the National Sovereignty, and the other rivalries which if not already in action, will soon appear between

Ministers of State and between the legislative, executive and judicial powers give me more serious apprehension, than National Debt, Indian Wars and Algerine depredations"—that is, the three issues out of which a national bureaucracy, army, navy, and their accompanying patronage already seemed likely to emerge.[103] Eventually, of course, Adams and Hamilton did split, mostly over the army issue after 1798. Yet even in the 1790s some Federalists opposed each Hamiltonian measure, sometimes on explicit "Country" grounds. Once out of power, a few of them could develop these themes more fully, as when Senator Isaac Tichenor of Vermont fumed against James Monroe—of all people—for overlavish support of a standing army during the War of 1812. On the whole, however, the rarity of such defections is far more striking. Although younger Federalists copied Republican styles of mass politics, they held strongly to their old policies. In 1811 they voted unanimously to recharter the Bank which, despite the administration's support, died at Republican hands.[104]

More fascinating are tensions among the Republicans. In several respects Republican attitudes, like popular upheaval during the Revolution, strayed past the accepted boundaries of Country ideology. Republicans often extended to any navy the kind of rhetoric aimed at a standing army in England, where Country thinkers saw the navy as a politically safe *alternative* to larger armies. When Republicans extended the suffrage beyond property holders, they clearly outran neo-Harringtonian prescriptions, but this trend—common among northern Republicans by 1800 or so—did not become widespread in the more orthodox South until the Jacksonian era.[105] Similarly when radical Republicans fought to repudiate English common law for simplified codes or digests, they attacked a major prop to Country ideology in England and hence rang alarm bells through their own party. The Sedition Act of 1798 persuaded virtually all Republicans that no such thing as a common-law crime should exist under federal jurisdiction.[106] But at the state level moderate Republicans combined successfully almost everywhere with Federalists to protect common law.[107] Even Jefferson, who at times could sound quite radical on this theme, retreated hastily when confronted with an ominously viable alternative—French civil law in Louisiana.[108]

This issue aside, Jefferson fits the specifications for a Country ideologue almost perfectly. Country terminology happily avoids the muddle Jeffersonian scholars usually get into when they worry about whether, or how and why, an "agrarian" like Jefferson could advocate commercial expansion and internal improvements of so many different kinds, including "manufacturing" after 1807. Evidently he was not really an "agrarian" after all.[109] But as Pocock and McCoy have shown, Country thinkers believed that commerce was a basic civilizing force and that the exchange of agricultural surpluses for other necessities strengthened the economic viability of the virtuous landowner. They were indeed suspicious of immense cities, of luxuries which might "effeminate" virtuous and "manly" qualities, and of the money power by which people who did no work and performed no visible useful function got rich at someone else's expense. Confined to the household level, manufactures were acceptably virtuous. Jefferson matches the model on all these points, even if his deep Anglophobia inclined him to quote Scots more often than Englishmen.[110]

Jefferson agreed that the Revolutionary War debt had to be paid, but he loathed funding systems and the very idea of a permanent debt. To redeem this obligation, his "wise and frugal government" had to spend less than it received. Always fearful of banks, he tried to prevent the chartering of the Bank of the United States in 1791, and after it expired he attempted to prove with logarithms in 1813 that the republic could not afford banks.[111] Speculative booms and busts appalled him and made him tremble for the nation's future, whether in 1792 or 1819.[112] He opposed any standing army beyond a decentralized, frontier, constabulary force, although he did support the West Point Academy as a place through which its officers could be rotated to learn the technical side of their trade.[113] Like English Country spokesmen, he favored a navy if only to regain for America's agricultural surpluses the world markets that the Revolution had closed. Thus he launched the Barbary War to keep open the newly revived Mediterranean trade.[114] Only with assured overseas markets could the United States remain agricultural, prosperous, and free of undue dependence upon British credit and buyers.

Madison and Gallatin shared most of these values. Madison was less given to rhetoric about the tree of liberty and the blood of tyrants, and as an author of *The Federalist,* perhaps more inclined to praise public order. Although he and Gallatin reconciled themselves to the Bank in a way that Jefferson never did, Madison's economics involved the same concern—to protect America's agricultural surpluses by making the rest of the world bid for them competitively. He and Gallatin seemed more skeptical than Jefferson about the navy. Could the United States afford one large enough to make a real difference? Indeed for Gallatin, retirement of the debt overruled almost all other considerations and strongly reinforced his deep antimilitarist beliefs. Only when the government had an assured surplus revenue should it start to think seriously about fleets and internal improvements. Madison did agree with Hamilton that population pressure would eventually force the United States to follow the economic pattern of Europe—sprawling cities, huge manufactures, and the network of social dependencies that these phenomena involved. But while Hamilton's policies tried to hasten this trend in the interests of national strength, Madison—much to Hamilton's surprise—struggled to postpone the evil day in the name of republican virtue.[115]

Nevertheless the Jeffersonians did attract a number of "Court" Republicans, defined here as men whose social and economic values resembled Hamilton's much more closely than Jefferson's, Madison's, or Gallatin's. General Samuel Smith of Baltimore—wealthy merchant, Revolutionary War hero, and strong advocate of the Federal Constitution—entered Congress as a Hamiltonian. "Gentlemen might speak of equality," he scoffed in an early speech, "but in practice the thing was impossible." Yet he soon went over to the opposition when the Washington administration did nothing to protect his ships against British depredations in the Caribbean. Always a bit contemptuous of Jefferson's idealism and Madison's policies, he vainly tried to arrange an accord between Jefferson and Adams in 1800. Although he rarely got his way with the administration on commercial policy after 1801, his brother did become Jefferson's Secretary of the Navy, and Samuel did serve in a frustrating role as the administration's chief link with the merchant community.[116] Jacob Crowninshield, a Salem merchant who made his fortune after 1790 in the Far Eastern and Continental European trades, had acquired a strong dislike for the British during the course of doing so. Quite logically, his experience and attitude brought him into the Republican Party.[117] Elbridge Gerry of Massachusetts followed a more tortuous path from antifederalist with a keen distrust of the people in 1787–1788 (the people of New England, he told the Philadelphia Convention, "have . . . the wildest ideas of Government in the world"), to Hamiltonian with an anti-Southern bias a few years later, to Adams Federalist, to Jeffersonian. Like Smith, he hoped Jefferson would acquiesce in Adams' reelection in 1800, in exchange for the succession in 1804.[118]John Armstrong's strange career led him from authorship of the extremely inflammatory Newburgh broadsides in 1783 to the secretaryship of war in Madison's cabinet.[119] In New York the Clintonian, Livingston, and Burr factions all had conspicuous entrepreneurial elements that would make possible a coalition of moderate Republicans and Federalists against Madison's reelection in 1812.[120]

Whatever Burr's famous conspiracy was really about, one element of it represented the ultimate danger to liberty in Country terms. Burr actively tried to subvert the officer corps of both navy and army, and he did bring the army's commanding general, James Wilkinson, into his scheme. Despite his killing of Hamilton, he apparently had considerable Federalist support. Emphasizing "the weakness and imbecility of the federal government" under Jefferson, Burr boasted to one potential recruit "that with two hundred men, he could drive Congress with the president at its head into the river Potomac" and "that with five hundred men, he could take possession of New York." Wilkinson tried to win over a reluctant major by arguing "that the very existence of an army and democracy was incompatible; that Republics were ungrateful; jealous of armies and military merit; and made no provision for the superannuated and worn out officers . . . who were left to starve." The major stayed out of the conspiracy, but he agreed with the general's opinion. Interestingly, in the cypher used between Burr and Wilkinson, 76 meant "democracy," 89 stood for "aristocracy," and 96 represented the navy.[121]

Pennsylvania produced a small but active group of Court Republicans. Merchants and manufacturers such as Tench Coxe, John Nicholson, John Swanwick, Charles Pettit, and Blair McCleanachan, plus the able lawyer Daniel Cunyngham Clymer, entered the 1790s either as overt Hamiltonians or with principles difficult to distinguish from Hamilton's, but each of these men eventually defected to the Republicans. Their motives varied from dissatisfaction with the funding program (Pettit and McCleanachan demanded even better terms for security holders), to an interest in manufacturing with Anglophobic implications that Hamilton did not share (Coxe and possibly Nicholson), to ethnic and social resentment against Federalist snobbery (McClenachan again, and Swanwick). Quite a rarity among Jeffersonians, Coxe had been a loyalist during the Revolution, while Swanwick was the son of a British placeman and loyalist. Swanwick also entered public life while a younger member in the mercantile firm of Robert Morris, "financier of the Revolution" and arch-Federalist.[122] As Federalism rapidly collapsed in Pennsylvania after 1800, such men often found themselves working with Federalists against radical Republicans, such as Michael Leib. Yet moderate Republicans always remained in command. Their support of Madison made the difference in his reelection in 1812.

The Court-Country paradigm heavily colored nearly all participants' perceptions of the issues and personalities of the era. The political rhetoric of the age implicitly assumed a spectrum of possibilities from an extreme Court position on the right, through Hamiltonianism, then various stages of moderation in the middle, then a pure Country position on the left, and on to radical Jacobinism (most evident, perhaps, in Pennsylvania) as a new option on the extreme left. Wherever one stood on this spectrum, he was likely to suspect anyone to his right of sinister conspiracies against liberty. Hamilton so accused Burr, Adams attacked Hamilton, Jefferson and Madison indicted Adams, John Randolph and the Quids denounced Madison, and Michael Leib raged against Gallatin in these terms. Conversely, everybody to one's left had to be flirting with disorder and anarchy. High Federalists never quite trusted John Adams, for they remembered his radicalism of the 1770s. Jefferson, of course, was to them a hopeless demagogue. For example, even after four years of mild Republican rule, Fisher Ames still expected a dawning age of democratic terror. "Our days are made heavy with the pressure of anxiety, and our nights restless with visions of horror," he groaned in the placid year of 1805. "We listen to the clank of chains, and overhear the whispers of assassins. We mark the barbarous dissonance of mingled rage and triumph in the yell of an infatuated mob; we see the dismal glare of their burnings and scent the loathsome steam of human victims offered in sacrifice." Even a brief glimpse of reality only drove him to deeper despair, for as he confessed in the same essay, "there are not many, perhaps not five hundred even among the federalists, who yet allow themselves to view the progress of licentiousness as so speedy, so sure, and so fatal, as the deplorable experience of our country shows that it is . . ."[123] Somewhat more genially, the moderate Republican governor of Pennsylvania, Thomas McKean, remarked of the radicals: "who is there to control the wanton passions of men, suddenly raised to power and frisking in the pasture of true liberty, yet not sufficiently secured by proper barriers?"[124] Even when they went past conventional Country positions, men still used the rhetoric. Opponents of common law attacked its malignant corruptions. Many Republicans denounced a navy with arguments borrowed from the classic controversy over standing armies.

Yet when they faced one another, Federalists and Republicans accurately recognized what were basically Court and Country coalitions, respectively. Both parties also understood that westward expansion and the continuing immigration of non-English elements strongly favored the Republicans over the Federalists But only when their own position had become quite hopeless did Federalists seriously try to exploit the Republicans' most conspicuous weakness—African slavery.[125]

Although most American historians like to boast that Federalists and Republicans created the world's first example of a modern party system, Ronald Formisano, a close student of the "second American party system," has challenged this view. To him the contest between Hamiltonians and Jeffersonians embodied the antiparty deferential values of the eighteenth century more than it anticipated the mass parties of the 1840s. Federalist decline was so rapid and complete that no "system" ever existed for very long, and in any case, state and national politics were far from integrated along party lines.[126] However we define the threshold that permits use of the term "party system," these strictures, by emphasizing the underlying similarities between Augustan Britain and Federalist-Jeffersonian America, nicely support a central argument of this chapter.

Finally, did Republicans really take on Federalist traits after 1801 until by 1816 they "out-Federalized the Federalists"? Did the responsibilities of power turn the Country into the Court? Did Republicans switch positions much as English Whigs had a century before? Certainly the "Old Republicans" (or "Quids") who prided themselves on faithfulness to "the principles of '98" believed that too much of Hamilton had sneaked inside Jefferson, and historians since Henry Adams have found the theme equally attractive. To be sure, Jefferson was not as radical after 1801 as some of his earlier pronouncements had hinted he might be. Much to Gallatin's relief, he did not interfere with the Bank. Although he and Madison had questioned the value and desirability of the burgeoning reexport trade in the 1790s, they decided to defend it when it came under British attack after 1806. But they resorted to the more drastic embargo, rich as it was in Revolutionary precedents, only when Britain challenged American access to European markets for agricultural products.[127] Yet in 1816 Republicans did enact a second Bank of the United States and the nation's first protective tariff, while Madison vetoed an internal improvements bill solely on constitutional grounds.

Still, the argument is fairly weak. Even after 1816 Republicans differed from their antagonists far more than they resembled them.[128] Before 1812 and again after 1816, they worked consistently and successfully to pay off the national debt, a commitment that would survive in American politics until World War II. All internal taxes were repealed as soon as possible, another legacy that endured into the present century. The army and navy were again reduced to prewar size. Even during the War of 1812 Madison's government attempted none of the repressive measures that Federalists had inflicted upon Republicans in 1798. More than any other single factor, the regional lopsidedness of the two parties tended to keep both safely within their respective traditions.

The very success of Republicans in assimilating ex-Federalists did attract alien souls to the coalition, including for the first time a powerful Northern element committed to heavy manufactures. Yet the Tariff of 1816 was designed merely as a temporary response to British dumping tactics and, in any case, had little Southern support—almost none by 1820.[129] As early as 1813 Jefferson complained "that in proportion as avarice and corruption advance on us from the north and east, the principles of free government are to retire to the agricultural states of the south and west, as their last asylum and bulwark."[130] Momentarily he seemed correct, but the pattern did not take hold. Occasional deviations aside, Jeffersonian and Jacksonian government held amazingly steadfast in protecting its virtue from the corrupting influences of economic modernity. By the 1830s things had been righted once again, and the most commercial elements began to organize separately as National Republicans before they finally emerged as the Whig Party. Jackson dismantled the Bank, and South Carolina the tariff. In one state legislature after another, Democrats displayed their suspicion of corporations, America's over-mighty subjects. In New York City, men of truly great wealth gathered almost unanimously under the Whig banner by 1840.[131] The United States became in the 1830s the only country in the world that I know of to repay its entire national debt and then fret virtuously about how to spend, or not spend, its surplus revenue.

Similarly the federal government remained minuscule, a midget institution in a giant land. It had almost no internal functions except the postal system and the sale of western lands. Its role scarcely went beyond what would have pleased even most Antifederalists in the 1780s, the use of port duties and the revenue from land sales to meet its own limited expenses. Thus when the Adams administration occupied Washington, D.C. for the first time in 1800, congressmen and senators physically outnumbered executive officials and clerks combined! This ratio slipped very little over the next thirty years.[132] The American army of five to ten thousand men held fast at a level roughly comparable to Charles II's weak force, even though by 1830 the population of the United States would be double that of England in the 1680s, and the difference in per capita wealth must have been much greater. To take a guess, the American navy may not have exceeded the strength of the Tudor fleet of three centuries earlier, despite the fantastic growth of commercial shipping after 1790.[133]

Can we explain this contrast by defining the United States as naturally a "Country" society, so committed to the principles of English opposition ideology that alternatives were scarcely conceivable, much less attainable?[134] Court principles, as we have seen, did take root as far south as Maryland in the provincial era, and after a devastating setback in the Revolution, they reappeared in the 1780s and, in the next decade, came amazingly close to defining the new government's character for an indefinite future. Without the French Revolution, which gave Republicans the leverage to organize voters on an unprecedented scale and take possession of Pennsylvania and New York, Federalists might have triumphed even while outnumbered. After all, England's natural majority, the Tories, managed to lose to the Whigs by 1714. At this level the consensus school has a compelling point to make, for a broader electorate than Britain's, organized into nearly equal districts and constantly stimulated by westward expansion and immigration, gave the French example something to work with and thus contributed decisively to Jefferson's "Revolution of 1800."[135]

But at another level the vital difference between Britain and America was not so much the voting population or even ethnic and religious pluralism, but the South. From this perspective, Country principles did become inseparable from American politics after the titanic battles of the 1790s, not because everybody shared them, but because they overwhelmingly characterized a region that established something close to political hegemony within the republic after 1801. Had the Union begun and ended north of the Potomac, Federalists probably could have created a variant of Britain in America, with themselves as a genuine ruling class presiding over a modernizing economy. And American polities would then have acquired a more overt class basis. But slaveholding planters, by dominating the federal government without serious interruption from 1801 to 1861, made regional Country principles into national political practices until the party of Lincoln emerged to threaten everything they cherished. In response they tried to withdraw into a smaller union that could sustain their system, but were smashed into submission by invading armies from the industrial North. Even then, whenever the South remained free to function openly in national politics, it severely limited Northern options. A united South could still tip the balance in a closely divided North. To take only the most conspicuous example, no incumbent Northern president ever won reelection until William McKinley in 1900, except Lincoln while the South was out of the Union, and Grant with the aid of Reconstruction governments and votes. No incumbent Southerner ever failed to gain reelection until John Tyler was repudiated by his own party in 1844 and James K. Polk chose not to run again four years later. The decision of 1800 had enduring effects for a full century of presidential politics, another good reason for considering it an essential element in America's Revolution Settlement.[136]

Yet the political defeat of Federalism did not destroy the old Court forces in American society at large. In league with Republican moderates, they retained control of the judicial system which they used, often despite the known wishes of state and national legislatures, to encourage the redistribution of property in favor of wealthy entrepreneurs—the complex process by which "instrumentalism" evolved into "legal formalism" between the Revolution and the Civil War.[137] They discovered that they did not have to dominate politics or the central government to manipulate America's vast resources. In fact by mid-century judicial barriers against legislative interference probably seemed more valuable than any possible benefits that active political participation could bring. Thus, reluctantly at first but inevitably nonetheless, they largely abandoned

national politics to the "plain republicans" and shifted their activities—
and most of the potential for "corruption"—to the state and local levels
of the Northeast and later the Northwest, where their enterprise, boost-
erism, ability, and greed ran amok across the land. Rapidly transforming
Jefferson's "fee-simple empire" into the world's most commercial and
industrial society, they soon outstripped the regulatory capabilities of
local jurisdictions while Jeffersonian and Jacksonian opponents stood
impotent guard over the inactive virtue of the central government. For
that matter, the very inexpensiveness of democratic government may have
contributed significantly to the frantic pace of industrial growth, for in
the United States—unlike Britain—the government's military and naval
needs, or even its civil expenditures, provided almost no drain upon the
nation's productive resources. Even the Civil War proclaimed only a temporary interruption, and not a permanent change, in this pattern.[138]

In this way the Great Inversion became complete. America's Revolution
Settlement centralized the Country and decentralized and largely depoliticized the Court. Big money, quite capable of buying a state legislature
here or there and hence of acquiring real weight in the Senate by the
1880s, otherwise would not again play a sustained role in national politics
between Jefferson's victory and the Hanna-McKinley triumph of 1896.[139]
Because a decentralized and depoliticized Court is a contradiction in
terms, this result merely stresses the decisiveness and permanence of the
Settlement. Court politics, a real option before 1801, had become impossible by 1815. One is tempted to add the old cliché, that the Republicans
won all the battles but evidently lost the war, except that the same verdict
also applies to the Federalists—if we assume that their deepest aspiration
was general recognition and acceptance of their status as a ruling class.
Both parties would be equally appalled by what the United States has in
fact become.

IX

The rest of the globe is correct about America. Aspects of its Revolution
still inspire admiration abroad, especially its concern with human rights
and dignity. But the Revolution Settlement is truly unique in its totality and quite inimitable in the way it has affected, or failed to affect,
larger patterns of American life. Only in America did anti-Court forces,

so conspicuous in their resistance to the war-making needs of European states between 1550 and 1789, win and retain possession of a central government designed by its framers, ironically enough, to make the United States competitive with other powers.[140] After 1801 they kept statist impulses well in check, almost resurrecting the Articles of Confederation within the Constitution. If the percentage of a government's revenue derived from internal sources or direct taxes can serve as a reasonable though crude indicator of its power and influence, the United States did not reach the level of eighteenth-century Britain until fifty years ago.[141] The Third World, which inevitably links economic development to vigorous government, has little to learn from "plain republicanism" which, even in its own day, remained more nostalgic than modernizing. As armed citizens swarmed across the continent, the heirs of Jefferson continued to praise growth as expansion, not development, even while being trampled from behind by stampeding industrialization.[142]

What this tradition and Settlement should mean to us is another matter. In historiographical terms, the ideological school is right about the uniqueness of America (though a generation too early in the chronology of its triumph), but only because the Wisconsin school is correct about the overall pattern of social tensions. The most committed variety of Revolutionary resistance did evolve through Antifederalism into Jeffersonian democracy, and most "reluctant patriots" and ex-loyalists found their way into the Federalist Party.

Did Country domination of the central government check in hidden ways the rapacity of great wealth and contribute, somehow or other, to the material well-being of lesser people? Can anyone attach a quantitative value to the "politics of recognition" for ethnic minorities that Jefferson's party and its successors learned to practice with consummate skill? Humble immigrants could achieve a sense of dignity through politics and minor office-holding that was probably available to them in no other way. At the moment we lack adequate answers to these questions, partly because they are seldom posed quite so bluntly.[143] But prior to our bureaucratic age, Country rule does seem to have kept the sense of alienation to a minimum, or at least channeled it in an unusual direction. In America, except for the generation of older Federalists after 1800 and Southerners after 1850, alienation has been directed at the society rather than the polity, until our own Vietnam-Watergate era.

Another and less flattering interpretation remains possible, inspired by the mammoth nineteenth-century disjunction between the wildly expanding participation in elections on the one hand, and the drastically shrinking responsibilities of the central government on the other. In the United States has politics instead of religion been the true "opiate of the people"—and of their historians?

Notes

1. The author wishes to thank James M. Banner, Jr., Richard Buel, Jr., Douglas Greenberg, Ronald Hoffman, Robert F. Jones, James M. McPherson, James Kirby Martin, Drew R. McCoy, Stephen E. Patterson, Theodore K. Rabb, and Lawrence Stone for their helpful criticisms of this chapter as it went through various drafts.

2. Perceptive developments of the "new nation" theme include William N. Chambers, *Political Parties in a New Nation: The American Experience, 1776–1809* (New York, 1963); Seymour Martin Lipset, *The First New Nation: The United States in Historical and Comparative Perspective* (New York, 1963); Thomas C. Barrow, "The American Revolution as a Colonial War for Independence," *William and Mary Quarterly,* 3rd Series, 25 (1968), 452–64 (hereafter *WMQ,* 3rd Series unless otherwise stated); and Richard B. Morris, *The Emerging Nations and the American Revolution* (New York, 1970).

3. R. R. Palmer, "The Fading Dream: How European Revolutionaries Have Seen the American Revolution," in *The Walter Prescott Webb Memorial Lectures: Essays on Modern European Revolutionary History,* ed. Bede K. Lackner and Kenneth Roy Philp (Austin, Tex., 1977), pp. 89–104.

4. See, generally, Richard Hofstadter, *The Progressive Historians: Turner, Parrington, Beard* (New York, 1968). The quotation is from Schlesinger, "The American Revolution Reconsidered," *Political Science Quarterly*, 34 (1919), 76–77.

5. Edmund S. and Helen M. Morgan, *The Stamp Act Crisis, Prologue to Revolution* (Chapel Hill, 1953). The quotation is from p. 113.

6. Brown. *Middle-Class Democracy and the Revolution in Massachusetts, 1691–1780* (Ithaca, N.Y., 1955); Robert and B. Katherine Brown, *Virginia, 1705–1786: Aristocracy or Democracy?* (East Lansing, Mich., 1964).

7. Major statements by the ideological school for the period before 1789 include Bernard Bailyn, *The Ideological Origins of the American Revolution* (Cambridge, Mass., 1965); Bailyn, "The Central Themes of the American Revolution: An Interpretation," in *Essays on the American Revolution*, ed. Stephen G. Kurtz and James H. Hutson (Chapel Hill, 1973), pp. 3–31, especially 15 and 23; Bailyn, *The Ordeal of Thomas Hutchinson* (Cambridge, Mass., 1974), especially p. 380; Pauline Maier, *From Resistance to*

Revolution: Colonial Radicals and the Development of American Opposition to Britain, 1765–1776 (New York, 1972); and Gordon S. Wood, *The Creation of the American Republic, 1776–1787* (Chapel Hill, 1968). For extensions into the period after 1789, see John R. Howe, Jr., "Republican Thought and the Political Violence of the 1790s," *American Quarterly*, 19 (1967), 147–65; Richard Buel, Jr., *Securing the Revolution: Ideology in American Politics, 1789–1815* (Ithaca, N.Y., 1972); and Lance G. Banning, *The Jeffersonian Persuasion: Evolution of a Party Ideology* (Ithaca, N.Y., 1978).

8. For a fuller discussion of the Wisconsin school, many of whose works will be cited individually in this essay, see John M. Murrin's review of *The Human Dimensions of Nation Making: Essays on Colonial and Revolutionary America*, ed. James Kirby Martin (Madison, 1976), in New York History, 58 (1977), 97–101. Examples of growing dissatisfaction with the ideological interpretation include Jackson Turner Main's review of Gordon Wood, in *WMQ*, 26 (1969), 604–7; and cf. half a dozen reviews of Pauline Maier's book in the standard journals; Gary B. Nash's review of the Kurtz and Hutson Essays (above, n. 7) in *WMQ*, 31 (1974), 311–14; the exchange between Bailyn and Nash in *WMQ*, 32 (1975), 182–85; Joseph A. Ernst, "Ideology and the Political Economy of Revolution," *Canadian Review of American Studies*, 4 (1973), 137–48; Jesse Lemisch's "Bailyn Besieged in His Bunker," *Radical History Review*, 3 (Winter 1977), 72–83; a broad attack by maybe half the participants at the Journal of Interdisciplinary History's Conference on the American Revolution which met at Harvard in May 1975; and Edmund S. Morgan's review of Bailyn's *Ordeal of Thomas Hutchinson*, in *The New York Review of Books*, 21 March 1974, pp. 7–10. These attitudes are hardly confined to Jensen's students at Wisconsin. For example, see *The American Revolution: Explorations in the History of American Radicalism*, ed. Alfred F. Young (DeKalb, Ill., 1976).

9. Cobban, *The Social Interpretation of the French Revolution* (Cambridge, 1964); Martin, *Men in Rebellion: Higher Government Leaders and the Coming of the American Revolution* (New Brunswick, N.J., 1973); R. R. Palmer, *The Age of the Democratic Revolution: A Political History of Europe and America, 1760–1800* (Princeton, 1959–64). Marc Egnal and Joseph A. Ernst apply a Marxist perspective to the Revolution in their "An Economic Interpretation of the American Revolution," *WMQ*, 29 (1972), 3–32. For the economic content of eighteenth-century ideology, see Isaac Kramnick, *Bolingbroke and His Circle: The Politics of Nostalgia in the Age of Walpole* (Cambridge, Mass., 1968); J.G.A. Pocock, *The Machiavellian Moment: Florentine Political Thought and the Atlantic Republican Tradition* (Princeton, 1975); and Drew R. McCoy, "The Republican Revolution: Political Economy in Jeffersonian America, 1776 to 1817" (Ph.D. dissertation, University of Virginia, 1976; publication expected. Chapel Hill, 1980).

10. Wood, "Rhetoric and Reality in the American Revolution," *WMQ*, 23 (1966), 3–32, tries to link his ideological emphasis with the older social interpretation, and his *Creation* (esp. chs. 12–13) revives Beardian themes

from an unexpected direction, a point most of his reviewers seem to have missed. See also Wood's review of Jackson Turner Main's *Political Parties before the Constitution* (Chapel Hill, 1973), in *Canadian Historical Review*, 55 (1974), 222–23; Lockridge, "Social Change and the Meaning of the American Revolution," *Journal of Social History*, 6 (1972–73), 403–39; Foner, *Tom Paine and Revolutionary America* (New York, 1976). For Pole see below, n. 63.

11. Isaac Kramnick, "Augustan Politics and English Historiography: The Debate on the English Past, 1730–35," *History and Theory*, 6 (1967), 33–56; J. P. Kenyon, "The Revolution of 1688: Resistance and Contract," in *Historical Perspectives: Studies in English Thought and Society in Honour of J. H. Plumb*, ed. Neil McKendrick (London, 1974), 43–69; and H. T. Dickinson, "The Eighteenth-Century Debate on the 'Glorious Revolution,'" *History*, New Series, 61 (1976), 28–45.

12. Palmer, *Age of the Democratic Revolution*; Palmer, "The Fading Dream"; Briton, *The Anatomy of Revolution*, rev. ed. (New York, 1952).

13. J. H. Plumb, *The Growth of Political Stability in England, 1675–1725* (London, 1967); J. R. Jones, *The Revolution of 1688 in England* (New York, 1972); J. R. Western, *Monarchy and Revolution: The English State in the 1680s* (London, 1972).

14. P.G.M. Dickson, *The Financial Revolution in England: A Study in the Development of Public Credit, 1688–1756* (London, 1967); Kramnick, *Bolingbroke and his Circle*, especially 39–48; Peter Laslett, "John Locke, the Great Recoinage, and the Origins of the Board of Trade, 1695–1698," *WMQ*, 14 (1957), 370–402; D. W. Jones, "London Merchants and the Crisis of the 1690s," in *Crisis and Order in English Towns 1500–1700: Essays in Urban History*, ed. Peter Clark and Paul Slack (London, 1972), pp. 311–55.

15. Charles Wilson, "The Other Face of Mercantilism," *Royal Historical Society*, Transactions, 5th Series, 9 (1959), 81–101.

16. Kramnick, *Bolingbroke and His Circle*, 188–200; J. Keith Horsefield, *British Monetary Experiments, 1650–1710* (Cambridge, Mass., 1960), chs. 12–17.

17. K. G. Davies, "Joint-Stock Investment in the Later Seventeenth Century," *Economic History Review*, 2nd series, 4 (1952), 285 (hereafter, *EcHR*).

18. The material on 1720, including the quotation, closely follows Kramnick, *Bolingbroke and His Circle*, pp. 66–67.

19. J. H. Plumb, "The Growth of the Electorate in England from 1600 to 1715," *Past & Present*, 45 (November 1969), 90–116; Plumb, "Political Man," in *Man versus Society in Eighteenth-Century Britain: Six Points of View*, ed. James L. Clifford (Cambridge, 1968), pp. 1–21; Geoffrey Holmes, *The Electorate and the National Will in the First Age of Party* (London, 1976); H. J, Habakkuk, "English Landownership, 1680–1740," *EcHR*, 1st Series, 10 (1939–40), 2–17; J.G.A. Pocock, *Machiavellian Moment*, ch. 13.

20. Gary De Krey establishes this point in "Trade, Religion, and Politics in London in the Reign of William III" (Ph.D. dissertation, Princeton University, 1978).

21. Plumb, *Political Stability*, ch. 6; Kramnick, "Augustan Politics and English Historiography"; Jeffrey Nelson, "The Contradictions of Freedom: Ideology and the Emergence of the Liberal State in Great Britain," paper read at a conference of the American Society for Eighteenth-Century Studies (Philadelphia, November 1976). See also J. P. Kenyon, *Revolution Principles: The Politics of Party, 1689–1720* (Cambridge, 1977).

22. Kramnick, *Bolingbroke and His Circle*, passim; Pocock, *Machiavellian Moment*, especially pp. 422, 477.

23. N.F.R. Crafts, "English Economic Growth in the Eighteenth Century: A Re-Examination of Deane and Cole's Estimates," *EcHR*, 2nd Series, 29 (1976), 226–35.

24. Stephen S. Webb, "The Strange Career of Francis Nicholson," *WMQ* 23 (1966), 513–48; Webb, "Army and Empire: English Garrison Government in Britain and America, 1569 to 1763," *WMQ* 34 (1977), 1–31. Cf. Charles M. Andrews, *The Colonial Period of American History* (New Haven, 1934–38), IV, passim.

25. John M. Murrin, "Anglicizing an American Colony: The Transformation of Provincial Massachusetts" (Ph.D. dissertation, Yale University, 1966), ch. 3; Leslie V. Brock, *The Currency of the American Colonies, 1700–1764: A Study in Colonial Finance and Imperial Relations* (New York, 1975), especially chs. 2–4.

26. Bernard Bailyn, *The Origins of American Politics* (New York, 1968), argues that massive acceptance of Country ideology by the colonies explains why America and Britain parted ways in the Revolutionary era. He has been challenged by Jack P. Greene, "Political Mimesis: A Consideration of the Historical and Cultural Roots of Legislative Behavior in the British Colonies in the Eighteenth Century," which appears with Bailyn's reply and Greene's rejoinder in *American Historical Review*, 75 (1969–70), pp. 337–67 (hereafter, *AHR*). On individual colonies, sec Jere R. Daniell, "Politics in New Hampshire under Governor Benning Wentworth, 1741–1767," *WMQ*, 23 (1966), 76–105; John M. Murrin, "Review Essay," *History and Theory*, 11 (1972), 245–72; Robert M. Zemsky, *Merchants, Farmers and River Gods: An Essay on Eighteenth-Century American Politics* (New York, 1971); John A. Schutz, *William Shirley, King's Governor of Massachusetts* (Chapel Hill, 1961); Beverly W. McAnear, "Politics in Provincial New York" (Ph.D. dissertation, Stanford University, 1935), which still provides the most detailed account available of internal New York politics, especially from Governor Robert Hunter (1710–19) to William Cosby (1732–38); Patricia U. Bonomi, *A Factious People: Politics and Society in Colonial New York* (New York, 1971); Stanley N. Katz, *Newcastle's New York: Anglo-American Politics, 1732–1753* (Cambridge, Mass., 1968); Larry R. Gerlach, *Prologue to Independence: New Jersey in the Coming of the American Revolution* (New Brunswick, N.J., 1976), especially pp. 21–23; Gerlach, *William Franklin: New Jersey's Last Royal Governor, New Jersey's Revolutionary Experience*, Pamphlet No. 13 (Trenton, 1975).

27. David Alan Williams, "Anglo-Virginian Politics, 1690–1735," in *Anglo-American Political Relations, 1675–1775*, ed. Alison G. Olson and Richard

M. Brown (New Brunswick, N.J., 1970), pp. 76–91; Williams, "Political Alignments in Colonial Virginia Politics, 1698–1750" (Ph.D. dissertation, Northwestern University, 1959); Leonidas Dodson, *Alexander Spotswood, Governor of Colonial Virginia, 1710–1722* (Philadelphia, 1939); Robert M. Weir, "'The Harmony We Were Famous For': An Interpretation of Pre-Revolutionary South Carolina Politics," *WMQ* 26 (1969), 473–501; M. Eugene Sirmans, *Colonial South Carolina: A Political History, 1663–1763* (Chapel Hill, 1966); W. W. Abbot, *The Royal Governors of Georgia, 1754–1775* (Chapel Hill, 1959).

28. Lawrence F. London, "The Representation Controversy in Colonial North Carolina," *North Carolina Historical Review*, 11 (1934), 255–70; Sydney V. James, "Colonial Rhode Island and the Beginnings of the Liberal Rationalized State," in *Essays in Theory and History: An Approach to the Social Sciences*, ed. Melvin Richter (Cambridge, Mass., 1970), pp. 165–85; Mack Thompson, "The Ward-Hopkins Controversy and the American Revolution in Rhode Island: An Interpretation," *WMQ*, 16 (1959), 363–75; Richard L. Bushman, *From Puritan to Yankee: Character and the Social Order in Connecticut, 1690–1765* (Cambridge, Mass., 1967); Charles A. Barker, *The Background of the Revolution in Maryland* (New Haven, 1940); Donnell M. Owings, *His Lordship's Patronage: Offices of Profit in Colonial Maryland* (Baltimore, 1953); James H. Hutson, "Benjamin Franklin and Pennsylvania Politics, 1751–1755: A Reappraisal," *Pennsylvania Magazine of History and Biography*, 93 (1969), 303–71 (hereafter, PMHB); Robert S. Hohwald, "The Structure of Pennsylvania Politics, 1739–1776" (Ph.D. dissertation, Princeton University, 1978).

29. Brock, *Currency of the American Colonies*, ch. 6; Joseph A. Ernst, "Genesis of the Currency Act of 1764: Virginia Paper Money and the Protection of British Investments," *WMQ* 22 (1965), 33–74.

30. Oliver M. Dickerson, The Navigation Acts and the American Revolution (Philadelphia, 1951), argues for the effectiveness of the system; Thomas C. Barrow, *Trade and Empire: The British Customs Service in Colonial America, 1660–1775* (Cambridge, Mass., 1967), finds widespread evasion. But careful investigation will probably reveal nothing in North America to match the scale of smuggling in the home islands. Cal Winslow, "Sussex Smugglers," in Douglas Hay et al., *Albion's Fatal Tree: Crime and Society in Eighteenth-Century England* (New York, 1975), pp. 119–66; Hoh-cheung and Lorna H. Mui, "Smuggling and the British Tea Trade before 1784," *AHR*, 74 (1968–69), 44–73; idem., "'Trends in Eighteenth-Century Smuggling' Reconsidered" and W. A. Cole's rejoinder, "The Arithmetic of Eighteenth-Century Smuggling," both in *EcHR*, 2nd Series, 28 (1975), 28–49, provide a good introduction to the literature.

31. Lawrence A. Harper, *The English Navigation Laws: A Seventeenth-Century Experiment in Social Engineering* (New York, 1939), ch. 19; Dickerson, *Navigation Acts*, ch. 3; and James M. Shepherd and Gary M. Walton, *Shipping, Maritime Trade and the Economic Development of Colonial North*

America (Cambridge, 1972), pp. 91–92, 205–6, all agree on these points. Benjamin W. Labaree, partly by arguing that coffee consumption after 1790 must have been to some degree a substitute for tea, contends that three-fourths or more of the colonial tea supply was smuggled. But import data for the 1790s show that tea consumption also continued to increase, thus implying little relationship between the two. Compare Labaree, *The Boston Tea Party* (New York, 1964), ch. 1, especially p. 7, with U.S. Bureau of the Census, *Historical Statistics of the United States, Colonial Times to 1970* (Washington, 1975), II, 902 (hereafter, *U.S. Hist. Stats.*).

32. Joseph J. Malone, *Pine Trees and Politics: The Naval Stores and Forest Policy in Colonial New England, 1691–1775* (Seattle, 1964); Richard B. Morris, *Government and Labor in Early America* (New York, 1946), pp. 154–56 on the Hat Act; Arthur C. Billing, *British Regulation of the Colonial Iron Industry* (Philadelphia, 1933); Brock, *Currency*, pp. 325–33, on Rhode Island's very gradual compliance with the New England Currency Act.

33. Richard L. Merritt, *Symbols of American Community, 1735–1775* (New Haven, 1966), especially ch. 7.

34. Though it is not the author's main point, this distinction will emerge from a careful reading of J. M. Bumsted, " 'Things in the Womb of Time': Ideas of American Independence, 1633 to 1763." *WMQ* 31 (1974), 533–64. See also Bernhard Knollenberg, *Origin of the American Revolution: 1759–1766* (New York, 1960), pp. 7–8, 283 n. 4.

35. James A. Henretta, *The Evolution of American Society, 1700–1815: An Interdisciplinary Analysis* (Lexington, Mass., 1973), p. 42, Table 2.1; James E. Shepherd and Samuel H. Williamson, "The Coastal Trade of the British North American Colonies, 1768–1772," *Journal of Economic History*, 32 (1972), 783–810, especially 800–801, 804 (hereafter, *JEcH*); Gary Walton, "New Evidence on Colonial Commerce," *JEcH*, 28 (1968), 363–89; David C. Klingaman, "The Coastwise Trade of Colonial Massachusetts," Essex Institute, Historical Collections, 108 (1972), 217–34. Egnal and Ernst, "An Economic Interpretation of the American Revolution," use much of the same data for quite different purposes. Carville V. Earle, *The Evolution of a Tidewater Settlement System: All Hallow's Parish, Maryland, 1650–1783* (Chicago, 1975), ch. 5, argues for the increasing self-sufficiency of tobacco plantations in the eighteenth century. But his own data (see esp. pp. 122–23) show a significant decline after the 1740s in nearly all of his 27 selected items. Only spinning wheels surpassed all previous highs in the 1760s.

36. Bernard Bailyn, "1776: A Year of Challenge—A World Transformed," *Journal of Law and Economics*, 19 (1976), 437–66. In this valuable essay, Bailyn has begun to analyze the kind of social change that he believes is relevant to the coming of the Revolution.

37. Jack P. Greene, "An Uneasy Connection: An Analysis of the Preconditions of the American Revolution," in *Essays on the American Revolution*, ed. Kurtz, and Hutson, especially pp. 65–74.

38. John M. Murrin, "The French and Indian War, the American Revolution and the Counter-factual Hypothesis: Reflections on Lawrence Henry Gipson and John Shy," *Reviews in American History*, I (1973–74), 307–18.

39. Daniel Dulany offered the fullest refutation of virtual representation in his Considerations on the Propriety of Imposing Taxes . . . (1765), in *Pamphlets of the American Revolution, 1750–1776*, ed. Bernard Bailyn (Cambridge, Mass., 1965–), I, 598–658. See, generally, Morgan, *Stamp Act Crisis*, and his "Colonial Ideas of Parliamentary Power, 1764–1766," *WMQ* 5 (1948), 311–41.

40. Dickinson, *The Late Regulations respecting the British Colonies . . .* (1765), in *Pamphlets*, ed. Bailyn, I, 683.

41. "A Plain Yeoman," *Providence Gazette*, 11 May 1765; Dickinson to Pitt, 21 December 1765, both reprinted in *Prologue to Revolution: Sources and Documents on the Stamp Act Crisis, 1764–1766*, ed. Edmund S. Morgan (Chapel Hill, 1959), pp. 72, 119.

42. Compiled from *The Dictionary of American Biography* and other standard biographical sources. On Goddard, see Ward L. Miner, *William Goddard, Newspaperman* (Durham, N.C., 1962), pp. 153–62, 169–72; and *Tracts of the American Revolution*, 1763–1767, ed. Merrill Jensen (Indianapolis, 1967), pp. 79–93.

43. P.D.G. Thomas, *British Politics and the Stamp Act Crisis: The First Phase of the American Revolution, 1763–1767* (Oxford, 1975), pp. 145–51, 162, 187–88, 214–15. Cf. Paul Langford, *The First Rockingham Administration, 1765–1766* (Oxford, 1973), pp. 117–25.

44. Neil R. Stout, *The Royal Navy in America, 1760–1775: A Study of Enforcement of British Colonial Policy in the Era of the American Revolution* (Annapolis, 1973).

45. *U.S. Hist. Stats.*, II, 1200.

46. Henry Drinker to Abel Jones, 29 April 1770, PMHB, 14 (1890), 42. Easily the best history of the Townshend Crisis is Merrill Jensen, *The Founding of a Nation: A History of the American Revolution, 1763–1776* (New York, 1968), chs. 8–14.

47. Stephen E. Patterson, "Boston Merchants and the American Revolution" (M.A. thesis, University of Wisconsin, 1961). A similar theme is implicit in Edward C. Papenfuse, *In Pursuit of Profit: The Annapolis Merchants in the Era of the American Revolution, 1763–1805* (Baltimore, 1975).

48. Egnal and Ernst, "An Economic Interpretation of the American Revolution," isolate British importers (that is, colonial merchants importing from Britain) as the mercantile group with the most severe grievances against the empire. But so far every local study suggests that they were loyalist to a heavily disproportionate degree—possibly more so than any other groups except high Crown officeholders and northern Anglican clergymen. By contrast, merchants concentrating in the West Indian or South European trades (including the wine islands) were strongly patriot. John W. Tyler is now pursuing this subject in a doctoral thesis at Princeton University. Meanwhile, see: Arthur M. Schlesinger, Sr., *The Colonial Merchants and*

the American Revolution, 1763–1776 (New York, 1918), pp. 591–92 and passim (for Southern factors); Virginia D. Harrington, *The New York Merchant on the Eve of the Revolution* (New York, 1935), pp. 349–51; Thomas M. Doerflinger, "The Economic Structure of Philadelphia's Merchant Community, 1756–1791" (Senior thesis, Princeton University, 1974), a careful and imaginative study, especially 63–66. Charles Akers in a study (in progress) of Boston's wealthy Brattle Street Church finds that about one-fourth of its merchant members were loyalists, nearly all British importers or factors who owned few ships; David Edward Maas, 'The Return of the Massachusetts Loyalists" (Ph.D. dissertation, University of Wisconsin, 1972), especially p. 142, gives the same percentage of loyalists among Boston merchants generally but analyzes them by levels of wealth, not patterns of trade. On the growth of mercantile specialization after 1750, see Philip L. White, *The Beekmans of New York in Politics and Commerce, 1647–1877* (New York, 1956), pp. 538, 540, 545–48, and passim—a neglected study of exceptional value; Walton, "New Evidence on Colonial Commerce"; Shepherd and Walton, *Shipping*, passim. On the shifting coalitions behind non-importation and widespread artisanal support, see Ronald Hoffman, *A Spirit of Dissension: Economics, Politics, and the Revolution in Maryland* (Baltimore, 1973), chs. 2, 4; Richard Walsh, *Charleston's Sons of Liberty: A Study of the Artisans, 1763–1789* (Columbia, S.C., 1959); and Charles S. Olton, *Artisans for Independence: Philadelphia Mechanics and the American Revolution* (Syracuse, 1975). On smuggling and British seizures after about 1755, see Victor L. Johnson, "Fair Traders and Smugglers in Philadelphia, 1754–1763," *PMHB*, 83 (1959), 125–49; Richard Pares, *War and Trade in the West Indies, 1739–1763* (Oxford, 1936), pp. 326–468; Dickerson, *Navigation Acts*, ch. 9; Stout, *Royal Navy*; Arthur L. Jensen, *The Maritime Commerce of Colonial Philadelphia* (Madison, 1963), ch. 10; Jesse Lemisch, "Jack Tar in the Streets: Merchant Seamen in the Politics of Revolutionary America," *WMQ* 25 (1968), 371–407.

49.   Donald C. Lord and Robert M. Calhoon, "The Removal of the Massachusetts General Court from Boston, 1769–1772," *Journal of American History*, 55 (1968–69), 735–55 (hereafter JAH); Larry R. Gerlach, "Politics and Prerogatives: The Aftermath of the Robbery of the East Jersey Treasury in 1768," *New Jersey History*, 90 (1972), 133–68; Jean H. Vivian, "The Poll Tax Controversy in Maryland, 1770–76; A Case of Taxation with Representation," *Maryland Historical Magazine*, 71 (1976), 151–76 (hereafter *MHM*); *Maryland and the Empire, 1773: The Antillon—First Citizen Letters*, ed. Peter S. Onuf (Baltimore, 1974), especially pp. 1–39; George M. Curtis III, "The Role of the Courts in the Making of the Revolution in Virginia," in *The Human Dimensions of Nation Making*, ed. Martin, pp. 121–46; Robert M. Weir, "North Carolina's Reaction to the Currency Act of 1764," *North Carolina Historical Review*, 40 (1963), 183–99; Jack P. Greene, "Bridge to Revolution: The Wilkes Fund Controversy in South Carolina, 1769–1775," *Journal of Southern History*, 29 (1963), 19–52.

50. David Ammerman, *In the Common Cause: American Response to the Coercive Acts of 1774* (Charlottesville, 1974), especially ch. 2.

51. Adams to James Warren, 19 October 1775, *Letters of Members of the Continental Congress*, ed. Edmund C. Burnett (Washington, 1921–36), I, 236.

52. Laurens to William Livingston, 19 April 1779, ibid., IV, 163.

53. See the authorities cited in notes 47–48, above.

54. David Syrett, *Shipping and the American War, 1775–1783: A Study of British Transport Organization* (London, 1970). A modern study of privateering would be quite useful.

55. Ammerman, *In the Common Cause*, ch. 3. Ammerman is more inclined than I to trace conservative weakness to a broad American consensus. For the willingness of Congressional moderates to grasp at almost any hope of conciliation, see Milton M. Klein, "Failure of a Mission: The Drummond Peace Proposal of 1775," *Huntington Library Quarterly*, 35 (1971–72), 343–80.

56. James H. Hutson, *Pennsylvania Politics, 1746–1770: The Movement for Royal Government and Its Consequences* (Princeton, 1972).

57. Rhys Isaac, "Evangelical Revolt: The Nature of the Baptists' Challenge to the Traditional Order in Virginia, 1765 to 1775," *WMQ* 31 (1974), 345–68; Anthony Gregg Roeber, "Faithful Magistrates and Republican Lawyers: The Transformation of Virginia's Justices of the Peace, 1705–1805" (Ph.D. dissertation, Brown University, 1977).

58. James S. Whittenburg, "Planters, Merchants, and Lawyers: Social Change and the Origins of the North Carolina Regulation," *WMQ* 34 (1977), 215–38; Richard M. Brown, *The South Carolina Regulators* (Cambridge, Mass., 1963).

59. The range of recent interpretations can be derived from Staughton Lynd, "Who Should Rule at Home? Dutchess County, New York, in the American Revolution," *WMQ* 18 (1961), 330–59; Sung Bok Kim, "A New Look at the Great Landlords of Eighteenth-Century New York," *WMQ* 27 (1970), 581–614; Bonomi, *A Factious People*, ch. 6.

60. Gary S. Horowitz, "New Jersey Land Riots, 1745–1755" (Ph.D. dissertation, Ohio State University, 1966); Alison G. Olson, "The Founding of Princeton University: Religion and Politics in Eighteenth-Century New Jersey," *New Jersey History*, 87 (1969), 133–50.

61. Martin, *Men in Rebellion*, passim; Stephen E. Patterson, *Political Parties in Revolutionary Massachusetts* (Madison, 1973), chs. 5, 6, and 8; Robert J. Taylor, *Western Massachusetts in the Revolution* (Providence, 1954), chs. 2–4; Edward M. Countryman, "Consolidating Power in Revolutionary America: The Case of New York, 1775–1783," *Journal of Interdisciplinary History*, 6 (1975–76), 645–77 (hereafter, *J Intdis. H*); Lynd, "Who Should Rule at Home?"; Roger Champagne, "New York's Radicals and the Coming of Independence," *JAH*, 51 (1964–65), 21–40; Bernard Friedman, "The Shaping of the Radical Consciousness in Provincial New York," *JAH*, 56 (1969–70), 781–801; Stephen Brobeck, "Revolutionary Change in Colonial

Philadelphia: The Brief Life of the Proprietary Gentry," *WMQ* 33 (1976), 410–34; John K. Alexander, "The Fort Wilson Incident of 1779: A Case Study of the Revolutionary Crowd," *WMQ*, 31 (1974), 589–612; Hoffman, *A Spirit of Dissension*, chs. 7–10; Hoffman, "The 'Disaffected' in the Revolutionary South," in *The American Revolution*, ed. Young, pp. 273–316; Thad W. Tate, "The Coming of the Revolution in Virginia: Britain's Challenge to Virginia's Ruling Class," *WMQ* 19 (1962), 323–43; Robert M. Weir, "Who Shall Rule at Home: The American Revolution as a Crisis of Legitimacy for the Colonial Elite," *J Intdis. H*, 6 (1975–76), 679–700.

62. Carl Becker, *The History of Political Parties in the Province of New York, 1760–1776*, 2nd ed. (Madison, 1960), pp. 176–78, 239–43; Gerlach, *William Franklin*, pp. 30–32; Herbert E. Klingelhofer, "The Cautious Revolution: Maryland and the Movement toward Independence: 1774–1776," *MHM*, 60 (1965), 261–313; Richard A. Ryerson, *The Revolution Is Now Begun: The Radical Committees of Philadelphia, 1765–1776* (Philadelphia, 1978), describes the overthrow of the Pennsylvania assembly in 1776; Jackson Turner Main, *The Sovereign States, 1775–1783* (New York, 1973), pp. 165–66, discusses Delaware in 1776.

63. Patterson, *Political Parties*, pp. 143–48, 152; J. R. Pole, *Political Representation in England and the Origins of the American Republic* (London, 1966), pp. 226–44; Van Beck Hall, *Politics without Parties: Massachusetts, 1780–1791* (Pittsburgh, 1972).

64. Countryman, "Consolidating Power"; Pole, Political Representation, pp. 226–44; Martin, "Men in Rebellion; Jackson Turner Main, "Government by the People: The American Revolution and the Democratization of the Legislatures," *WMQ* 23 (1966), 391–407.

65. Main, *Political Parties*, especially chs. 12–13.

66. Richard B. Morris, "Insurrection in Massachusetts," in *America in Crisis: Fourteen Crucial Episodes in American History*, ed. Daniel Aaron (New York, 1952), pp. 20–49; for a partial list of other riots and disturbances, most of which have never been studied, see John P. Kaminski, "Democracy Run Rampant: Rhode Island in the Confederation," in *Human Dimensions of Nation Making*, ed. Martin, pp. 247–48 n. 13.

67. Wood, *Creation of the American Republic*, chs. 10, 12–13; J.G.A. Pocock, "Virtue and Commerce in the Eighteenth Century," *J Intdis. H*, 3 (1972–73), 119–34.

68. E. James Ferguson, "The Nationalists of 1781–1783 and the Economic Interpretation of the Constitution," *JAH*, 56 (1969–70), 241–61; Richard H. Kohn, "The Inside History of the Newburgh Conspiracy: America and the Coup d'Etat," *WMQ* 27 (1970), 187–220; John Shy, *A People Numerous and Armed: Reflections on the Military Struggle for American Independence* (New York, 1976), pp. 135–224; Russell F. Weigley, *The Partisan War: The South Carolina Campaign of 1780–1782* (Columbia, S.C., 1970); William A. Benton, "Pennsylvania Revolutionary Officers and the Federal Constitution," *Pennsylvania History*, 31 (1964), 419–35; Edwin G. Burrows, "Military

Experience and the Origins of Federalism and Antifederalism," in *Aspects of Early New York Society and Politics*, ed. Jacob Judd and Irwin H. Polishook (Tarrytown, N.Y., 1974), pp. 83–92; Norman K. Risjord, "Virginians and the Constitution: A Multivariant Analysis," *WMQ* 31 (1974), 613–32.

69. E. James Ferguson, *The Power of the Purse: A History of American Public Finance, 1776–1790* (Chapel Hill, 1961), chs. 8, 11; Jackson Turner Main, *The Antifederalists, Critics of the Constitution, 1781–1788* (Chapel Hill, 1961), ch. 4; Stephen E. Patterson, "After Newburgh: The Struggle for the Impost in Massachusetts," in *Human Dimensions of Nation Making*, ed. Martin, pp. 218–42; Merrill Jensen, *The New Nation: A History of the United States during the Confederation, 1781–1789* (New York, 1950), pp. 350–59.

70. Douglas M. Arnold, "Political Ideology and the Internal Revolution in Pennsylvania. 1776–1790" (Ph.D. dissertation, Princeton University, 1976); Kenneth Coleman, *The American Revolution in Georgia, 1763–1789* (Athens, Ga., 1958), pp. 271–75.

71. New England's antinationalism is stressed by both H. James Henderson, *Party Politics in the Continental Congress* (New York, 1974) and Joseph L. Davis, *Sectionalism in American Politics, 1774–1787* (Madison, 1977). See also, Rufus King to John Adams, 2 November 1785; Theodore Sedgwick to Caleb Strong, 6 August 1786; James Monroe to Patrick Henry, 12 August 1786; Monroe to James Madison, 14 August 1786; Monroe to Thomas Jefferson, 19 August 1786; Monroe to Madison, 3 September 1786, in *Letters of Members of the Continental Congress*, ed. Burnett, VII, 247–48, 415–16, 424–25, 427, 445, 461; James Winthrop's "Agrippa" paper No. 12, in *Essays on the Constitution of the United States Published during Its Discussion by the People, 1787–1788*, ed. Paul Leicester Ford (New York, 1892), p. 92.

72. Forrest McDonald, *We the People: The Economic Origins of the Constitution* (Chicago. 1958), pp. 136–48, 182–202, 235–54, 321–46. Cf. Kaminski, "Democracy Run Rampant: Rhode Island in the Confederation."

73. Wood, *Creation of the American Republic*, pp. 514–16; Alfred F. Young, *The Democratic Republicans of New York: The Origins, 1763–1797* (Chapel Hill, 1967), p. 392, for the New York quotation; Buel, *Securing the Revolution*, pp, 101–2, for Beers.

74. Young, *Democratic Republicans*; Arnold, "Political Ideology and the Internal Revolution in Pennsylvania"; Leonard J. Sneddon, "State Politics in the 1790s" (Ph.D. dissertation, State University of New York at Stony Brook, 1972), ch, 2; Norman K. Risjord and Gordon Den Boer, "The Evolution of Political Parties in Virginia, 1782–1800," *JAH*, 60 (1973–74), 961–84.

75. Henderson, *Party Politics in the Continental Congress*; Mary P. Ryan, "Party Formation in the United States Congress, 1789 to 1796," *WMQ*, 28 (1971), 523–42; Henderson, "Quantitative Approaches to Party Formation in the United States Congress: A Comment," with Ryan's response, *WMQ*, 30 (1973), 307–25.

76. Kenneth W. Keller, "Diversity and Democracy: Ethnic Politics in Southeastern Pennsylvania, 1788–1799" (Ph.D. dissertation, Yale University, 1971); Edward C. Carter II, "A 'Wild Irishman' Under Every Federalist's Bed; Naturaliration in Philadelphia," *PMHB*, 94 (1970), 331–46; David Hackett Fischer, *The Revolution of American Conservatism: The Federalist Party in the Era of Jeffersonian Democracy* (New York, 1965), pp. 201–26.
77. Lance G. Banning, "Republican Ideology and the Triumph of the Constitution, 1789 to 1793," *WMQ*, 31 (1974), 167–88.
78. Banning, *The Jeffersonian Persuasion*, passim; Drew R. McCoy, "Republicanism and American Foreign Policy: James Madison and the Political Economy of Commercial Discrimination, 1789 to 1794," *WMQ*, 31 (1974), 633–46; McCoy, "The Republican Revolution," especially chs. 3–7.
79. Linda K. Kerber, *Federalists in Dissent: Imagery and Ideology in Jeffersonian America* (Ithaca, N.Y., 1970), ch. 4. Cf. Thomas Jefferson to Moses Robinson, 23 March 1801, *The Writings of Thomas Jefferson*, ed. Andrew A. Lipscomb and Albert Ellery Bergh (Washington, 1903), x, 236–37.
80. Ferguson, *Power of the Purse*, pp, 252–53, 256–57, 329.
81. Whitney K. Bates, "Northern Speculators and Southern State Debts: 1790," *WMQ*, 19 (1962), 30–48.
82. Hall, *Politics without Parties*, ch. 11; Snedden, "State Politics in the 1790s," p. 28; Ferguson, *Power of the Purse*, pp. 331–32.
83. Bray Hammond, *Banks and Politics in America from the Revolution to the Civil War* (Princeton, 1957), ch, 5; Brooke Hindle, *David Rittenhouse* (Princeton, 1964), pp. 331–32.
84. Jefferson, quoted in Robert Sobel, *The Big Board: A History of the New York Stock Market* (New York, 1965), p. 19. Cf. Robert F. Jones, "William Duer and the Business of Government in the Era of the American Revolution," *WMQ*, 32 (1975), 393–416.
85. Jefferson to Henry Remsen, 14 April 1792, quoted in Nathan Schachner, *Thomas Jefferson, a Biography* (New York, 1951–57), I, 466.
86. Calculated from *U.S. Hist. Stats.*, II, 959.
87. Hammond, *Banks and Politics*, pp. 144–45, 190.
88. Computed from *U.S. Hist. Stats.*, II, 750–51, 886, and B. R. Mitchell and Phyllis Deane, *Abstract of British Historical Statistics* (Cambridge, 1962), pp. 217, 220. In seven years for which data survive, 1800–1807, American shipbuilding averaged 111,200 "gross tons" per year. For the British Empire in all eight years, the average was 106,600 "net tons." Even if one subtracts 5–9% from gross tons to get net tons, the results are very nearly comparable. See John G. B. Hutchins, *The American Maritime Industries and Public Policy, 1789–1914: An Economic History* (Cambridge, Mass., 1941), p. 303, n. 50 on this point. Elsewhere (p. 226 n. 15) Hutchins, following Albert Gallatin, suggests that as of 1800 tonnage figures for American carriers (not shipbuilding) may have been inflated by as much as 200,000 tons out of the

reported total of 972,000, which is accepted in U.S. Hist. Stats. Presumably sales abroad would account for the difference.

89. David Hackett Fischer, *America, A Social History*. Volume I: The Main Lines of the Subject (forthcoming) discusses the new polarization of wealth in this period, as does Edward Pessen for a slightly later era in his "The Egalitarian Myth and the American Social Reality: Wealth, Mobility, and Equality in the 'Era of the Common Man,'" *AHR,* 76 (1971), 989–1034. Although the numbers of poor began to increase rapidly in colonial cities around 1750, poverty inspired major reform movements only in the 1790s. Gary B. Nash, "Urban Wealth and Poverty in Pre-Revolutionary America," *J Intdis. H,* 6 (1975–76), 545–84; Nash, "Social Change and the Growth of Prerevolutionary Radicalism," in *The American Revolution,* ed. Young, pp. 3–36; Young, *Democratic Republicans,* pp. 252–56, 518–45. Cf. David J. Rothman, *The Discovery of the Asylum: Social Order and Disorder in the New Republic* (Boston, 1971), especially chs. 1, 7.

90. Richard H. Kohn, *Eagle and Sword: The Beginnings of the Military Establishment in America, 1783–1802* (New York, 1975).

91. Poorly discussed in the secondary literature, the internal taxes of the Adams administration can be followed in *American State Papers: Finance* (Washington, 1832–59), I, 579–80, 616–22, 681–88, 718–27; Kohn, *Eagle and Sword,* pp. 157–73; Keller, "Diversity and Democracy," ch. 7.

92. Kohn, *Eagle and Sword,* chs. 10–13; Marshall Smelser, *The Congress Founds the Navy* (Notre Dame, Ind., 1959).

93. Jerald A. Combs, *The Jay Treaty: Political Battleground of the Founding Fathers* (Berkeley, 1970); Buel, *Securing the Revolution,* chs. 7–12—a major revision of Leonard W. Levy's *Freedom of Speech and Press in Early American History: Legacy of Suppression* (Cambridge, Mass., 1960), which, at least on the question of seditious libel, finds little difference between Federalists and Republicans. On the Disputed Elections Bill, designed to guarantee a Federalist succession in 1800, see Buel, pp. 208–10, and Albert J. Beveridge, *The Life of John Marshall* (Boston, 1916–19), II, 452–58.

94. I am not aware of any study of American ideas of public order and revolution in the 1790s.

95. Palmer, "The Great Inversion: America and Europe in the Eighteenth-Century Revolution," in *Ideas in History: Essays presented to Louis Gottschalk by His Former Students* (Durham, N.C., 1965), pp. 3–19.

96. Fischer, *Revolution of American Conservatism,* pp. 207–8; Young, *Democratic Republicans,* pp. 42, 47, 455; Paul Goodman, *The Democratic Republicans of Massachusetts: Politics in a Young Republic* (Cambridge, Mass., 1964), ch. 5.

97. Wallace Evan Davies, "The Society of the Cincinnati in New England, 1783–1800," *WMQ,* 5 (1948), 3–25, and Ethel E. Rasmussen, "Democratic Environment—Aristocratic Aspiration," *PMHB,* 90 (1960), 155–82, are both highly suggestive, especially when contrasted with James Sterling Young, *The Washington Community, 1800–1828* (New York, 1966). The

point about inter-marriage derives mostly from reading hundreds of
biographical sketches of graduates of Harvard, Yale, and Princeton, but
I have never attempted to measure the differences. James McLachlan, author
of *Princetonians, 1748–1768: A Biographical Dictionary* (Princeton, 1977),
shares this opinion.

98. Charles R. Ritchcson, *Aftermath of Revolution: British Policy toward the
United States, 1783–1795* (New York, 1969); Hutchins, *American Maritime
Industries*, chs, 6–8; James A. Field, Jr., *America and the Mediterranean
World, 1776–1882* (Princeton, 1969), pp. 27–49; Jones, "William Duer";
McCoy, "The Republican Revolution," p. 182.

99. *U.S. Hist. Stats.*, II, 750, 886; Allan R. Pred, *Urban Growth and the
Circulation of Information: The United States System of Cities, 1790–1840*
(Cambridge, Mass., 1973), pp. 28–29 and passim.

100. Plumb, *Political Stability*, ch. 5; G. W. Trevelyan, *England under Queen
Anne: The Peace and the Protestant Succession* (London, 1934), remains
the fullest narrative of the Tory resurgence. For the Federalist revival and
its limitations, see Fischer, *Revolution of American Conservatism*; Harry
W. Fritz, "The Collapse of Party: President, Congress, and the Decline
of Party Action, 1807–1817" (Ph.D. dissertation, Washington University,
1970); James M. Banner, Jr., *To the Hartford Convention: The Federalists
and the Origins of Party Politics in Massachusetts, 1789–1815* (New York,
1970); Victor Sapio, "Maryland's Federalist Revival, 1808–1812," *MHM*,
64 (1969), 1–17; James H. Broussard, "Regional Pride and Republican
Politics: The Fatal Weakness of Southern Federalism, 1800–1815," *South
Atlantic Quarterly*, 73 (1974), 23–33; J.C.A. Stagg, "James Madison and the
'Malcontents': The Political Origins of the War of 1812," *WMQ*, 33 (1976),
557–85; Norman K. Risjord, "Election of 1812," in *History of American
Presidential Elections, 1789–1968*, ed. Arthur M. Schlesinger, Jr. (New York,
1971), I, 249–72; Irving Brant, *James Madison: Commander-in-Chief, 1812–
1836* (Indianapolis, 1961), ch, 8; Frank A. Cassell, "The Great Baltimore Riot
of 1812," *MHM*, 70 (1975), 241–59.

101. On presidential etiquette, compare Broadus Mitchell, *Alexander
Hamilton: The National Adventure, 1788–1804* (New York, 1962), p. 13,
with Jefferson's view, in *The Life and Selected Writings of Thomas Jefferson*,
ed. Adrienne Koch and William Peden (New York, 1944), pp. 175–76. On
Adams, see James H. Hutson, "John Adams' Title Campaign," *New England
Quarterly*, 41 (1968), 30–39; Wood, *Creation of the American Republic*, ch.
14; Manning J. Dauer, *The Adams Federalists* (Baltimore, 1953), ch. 3. Cf.
James D. Tagg, "Benjamin Franklin Bache's Attack on George Washington,"
PMHB, 100 (1976), 191–230.

102. Fischer, *Revolution of American Conservatism*, pp. 22–23.

103. Adams to Councillor Trumbull, 31 March 1791; Adams to Henry Marchant,
3 March 1792, John Adams Letter Book, 1789–1793, pp. 158, 16–69,
Massachusetts Historical Society, Microfilms of the Adams Papers owned

by the Adams Manuscript Trust, Part II, Reel 115 (Boston, 1955), quoted with permission. See also John R. Howe, Jr., *The Changing Political Thought of John Adams* (Princeton, 1966), especially chs. 4, 7; Joyce Appleby, "The New Republican Synthesis and the Changing Political Ideas of John Adams," *American Quarterly*, 25 (1973), 578–95.

104. Dauer, Adams Federalists contains much useful information about alignments on specific issues; Richard A. Harrison, sketch of Isaac Tichenor, *Princetonians: A Biographical Dictionary, II* (forthcoming). For the bank issue in 1811, sec Hammond, *Banks and Politics*, p. 224.

105. For English Country support of naval power, see John Trenchard and Thomas Gordon, Cato's Letters: or, Essays on Liberty, Civil and Religious, and Other Important Subjects, 6th ed. (London, 1755), II, No. 64. For the argument against standing armies, see ibid., III, Nos. 94–95, and Trenchard, An Argument Shewing, that a Standing Army Is Inconsistent with a Free Government, and Absolutely Destructive to the Constitution of the English Monarchy (London, 1697); see also Lois G. Schwoerer, "No Standing Armies!" The Anti-Army Ideology in Seventeenth-Century England (Baltimore, 1974). Republican use of these arguments against a navy can be followed throughout Smelser's Congress Founds the Navy. On suffrage, see Chilton Williamson, *American Suffrage from Properly to Democracy, 1760–1860* (Princeton, 1960), especially chs. 8–9.

106. Levy, *Legacy of Suppression*, especially pp. 238–48, and ch. 6, passim.

107. Richard E. Ellis, *The Jeffersonian Crisis: Courts and Politics in the Young Republic* (New York, 1971).

108. George Dargo, *Jefferson's Louisiana: Politics and the Clash of Legal Traditions* (Cambridge, Mass., 1975).

109. Examples include Richard E. Ellis, "The Political Economy of Thomas Jefferson," in Thomas Jefferson: The Man, His World, His Influence, ed. Lally Weymouth (London, 1973), pp. 81–95; and Marshall Smelser, *The Democratic Republic, 1801–1815* (New York, 1968), especially ch. 1. These references are not in any sense meant to be invidious. The present writer was equally or more perplexed by Jefferson's economic views until the appearance of Pocock's "Virtue and Commerce" and McCoy's "Republican Revolution."

110. Ibid. Garry Wills nicely developed Jefferson's preference for Scottish over English writers in the first of three lectures on Jefferson delivered at Princeton University, fall term, 1975. See, however, ch. 8, n. 18, above.

111. Jefferson's Anas (available in numerous editions) contains his strictures on Hamiltonian finance. For his views on banks in 1813, see Hammond, Banks and Politics, p. 195.

112. For Jefferson's reaction to the Panic of 1819, which left him insolvent because he had underwritten a friend's obligation, see his letter to John Adams, 7 November 1819, *The Adams-Jefferson Letters: The Complete Correspondence between Thomas Jefferson and Abigail and John Adams*, ed. Lester J. Cappon (Chapel Hill, 1959), II, 546–47.

113. Kohn, *Eagle and Sword*, pp. 253, 262, 302–3. For the very narrow role of the West Point Military Academy before the War of 1812, see Edward C. Boynton, *History of West Point and Its Military Importance during the American Revolution: And the Origin and Progress of the United States Military Academy* (New York, 1964), chs. 10–11.

114. Julia H. Macleod, "Jefferson and the Navy: A Defense," Huntington Library Quarterly, 8 (1944–45), 153–84.

115. On Madison, see McCoy, "Republican Revolution," pp. 114, 120, 128–29, 166, 179, 212, 254, 256–57, 271–73, 296–97, 305–9, 311; on Gallatin, see Henry Adams, *The Life of Albert Gallatin* (Philadelphia, 1879), especially pp. 218–19, 270–74, 304, 321–22, 362; and Alexander S. Balinky, "Albert Gallatin, Naval Foe," PMHB, 82 (1958), 293–304; Balinky. "Gallatin's Theory of War Finance," WMQ, 16 (1959), 73–82.

116. Frank A. Cassell, *Merchant Congressman in the Young Republic: Samuel Smith of Maryland, 1752–1839* (Madison, 1971). The quotation is from p. 49.

117. William T. Whitney, Jr., "The Crowninshields of Salem, 1800–1808: A Study in the Politics of Commercial Growth," Essex Institute, Historical Collections, 94 (1958), 1–36, 79–118; John H. Reinoehl, "Some Remarks on the American Trade: Jacob Crowninshield to James Madison, 1806," HMQ, 16 (1959), 83–118.

118. George A. Billias, *Elbridge Gerry, Founding Father and Republican Statesman* (New York, 1976), especially ells. 11, 16, 19. For the quotation, see *The Records of the Federal Convention of 1787*, ed. Max Farrand, rev. ed. (New Haven, 1937), I, 123.

119. C. Edward Skeen, "Mr. Madison's Secretary of War," PMHB, 100 (1976), 336–55.

120. Young, Democratic Republicans, pp. 243–50. For political alignments in 1812, see the authorities cited in n. 100, above.

121. *The Case of Aaron Burr*, ed. V. B. Reed and J. D. Williams (Boston, 1960), pp. 119–22. 154, 174, 178.

122. Richard A. Harrison's sketch of Clymer, in Princetonians, II (forthcoming); Jacob E. Cooke, "Tench Coxe, Alexander Hamilton, and the Encouragement of American Manufactures," *WMQ*, 32 (1975), 369–92; Cooke, "Tench Coxe, American Economist: The Limitations of Economic Thought in the Early Nationalist Era," *Pennsylvania History*, 42 (1975), 267–89; Robert D. Arbuckle, "John Nicholson and the Attempt to Promote Pennsylvania Industry in the 1790s," ibid., 42 (1975), 99–114; Roland M. Baumann, "'Heads I Win, Tails Von Lose': The Public Creditors and the Assumption Issue in Pennsylvania, 1790–1802," ibid., 44 (1977), 195–232; Baumann, "John Swanwick: Spokesman for 'Merchant-Republicanism' in Philadelphia, 1790–1798," PMHB, 97 (1973), 131–82.

123. Works of Fisher Ames, ed. Seth Ames (Boston, 1854), II, 354.

124. Adams, Gallatin, p. 313.

125. Donald L. Robinson, *Slavery in the Structure of American Politics, 1765–1820* (New York, 1971).

126. Formisano, "Deferential-Participant Politics: The Early Republic's Political Culture, 1789–1840," *American Political Science Review*, 68 (1974), 473–87. Cf., Paul Goodman, "The First American Party System," in *The American Party Systems: Stages of Political Development*, ed. William N. Chambers and Walter Dean Burnham (New York, 1967), pp. 56–89; Sneddon, "State Politics in the 1790's," passim.

127. McCoy, "The Republican Revolution," pp. 251–57. The range of disagreement and factionalism among republicans can be gleaned from Norman K. Risjord, *The Old Republicans: Southern Conservatism in the Age of Jefferson* (New York, 1965); Kim T. Phillips, "William Duane, Philadelphia's Democratic Republicans, and the Origins of Modern Politics," PMHB, 101 (1977), 365–87; and John S. Pancake, "The 'Invisibles': A Chapter in the Opposition to President Madison," *Journal of Southern History*, 21 (1955), 17–37.

128. Smelser, *The Democratic Republic*, ch. 15. Even New York's General Incorporation Law of 1811 was aimed primarily at stimulating household manufacturing. See Ronald E. Seavoy, "Laws to Encourage Manufacturing: New York Policy and the 1811 General Incorporation Statute," *Business History Review*, 46 (1972), 85–95.

129. Norris W. Preyer, "Southern Support of the Tariff of 1816—A Reappraisal," *Journal of Southern History*, 25 (1959), 306–22.

130. Jefferson to Henry Middleton, 8 January 1813, *Writings*, ed. Lipscomb, XIII, 203.

131. For major revisions of Bray Hammond's entrepreneurial interpretation of the bank war, see Jean Alexander Wilburn, *Biddle's Bank: The Crucial Years* (New York, 1967); James R. Sharp, *The Jacksonians versus the Banks: Politics in the States after the Panic of 1837* (New York, 1970). See also Frank Otto Gattell, "Money and Party in Jacksonian America: A Quantitative Look at New York City's Men of Quality," *Political Science Quarterly*, 82 (1967), 235–52; Herbert Ershkowitz and William G. Shade, "Consensus or Conflict? Political Behavior in the State Legislatures during the Jacksonian Era," *JAH*, 58 (1971–72), 591–621.[132]

132. Young, The Washington Community, 31, Table 2.

133. U.S. Hist. Stats., II, 1142.

134. A major theme of Bailyn's *Origins of American Politics*.

135. Brown, *Middle-Class Democracy*. But by denying the impact of either deference or conflicting interests on colonial and revolutionary politics, Brown deprives the subject of the contingencies it obviously possessed as late as 1800 or even 1812, Young's Democratic Republicans carefully documents Clintonian mobilization of poorer voters as the 1790s progressed. Pole, *Political Representation*, Appendix II, provides statistics on voter turnout in several states. See also J.G.A. Pocock, "The Classical Theory of Deference," AHR, 81 (1976), 516–23: Lance Banning, "Jeffersonian Ideology and the French Revolution: A Question of Liberticide at Home," *Studies in Burke and His Times*, 17 (1976), 5–26.

136. Among many possible items, sec especially Richard H. Brown, "The Missouri Crisis, Slavery, and the Politics of Jacksonianism," *South Atlantic Quarterly*, 65 (1966), 55–72; and Robert Kelley's brilliant synthesis, "Ideology and Political Culture from Jefferson to Nixon," *AHR*, 82 (1977), 531–62.

137. Morton J. Horwitz, "The Emergence of an Instrumental Conception of American Law, 1780–1820," *Perspectives in American History*, 5 (1971), 287–326; Horwitz, "The Rise of Legal Formalism," *American Journal of Legal History*, 19 (1975), 251–64; Gerard W. Gawalt, "Sources of Anti-Lawyer Sentiment in Massachusetts. 1740–1840," ibid., 14 (1970). 283–307; William E. Nelson, Americanization of the Common Law: The Impact of Legal Change on Massachusetts Society, 1760–1830 (Cambridge, Mass., 1975), chs. 8–9, especially pp. 173–74.

138. Richard D. Brown, Modernization: *The Transformation of American Life, 1600–1865* (New York, 1976), and his "The Emergence of Urban Society in Rural Massachusetts, 1760–1820," *JAH*, 01 (1974–75), 29–51, nicely develop a number of these themes, Peter Temin, *The Jacksonian Economy* (New York, 1909), demonstrates the government's trivial role in the economy, while Pred's Urban Growth charts what is really the emergence of a national economy. C. Vann Woodward, "The Age of Reinterpretation," *AHR*, 66 (1960–61), 1–19, stresses America's "free security" after 1815.

139. Richard J. Jensen, *The Winning of the Midwest: Social and Political Conflict, 1888–1896* (Chicago, 1971); Wallace D. Farnham," 'The Weakened Spring of Government': A Study in Nineteenth-Century American History," *AHR*, 68 (1962–63), 662–80; Pocock, "Classical Theory of Deference," p. 523.

140. *Crisis in Europe, 1560–1660*, ed. Trevor Aston (New York, 1965) is excellent on European dimensions of this question. Need one add that the French monarchy collapsed during a fiscal crisis created by wartime expenditures?

141. Throughout the eighteenth century, customs duties provided only about a fourth of British revenues, and usually less than the land tax alone. Mitchell and Deane, *British Historical Statistics*, pp. 386–88. In the United States, internal revenues remained inconsequential until the Civil War, did not consistently exceed customs until about 1911, and finally surpassed eighteenth-century British ratios only with American entry into World War I. *U.S. Hist. Stats.*, II, 1106.

142. Henry Nash Smith, *Virgin Land: The American West as Symbol and Myth* (Cambridge, Mass., 1950); Major L. Wilson, "The Concept of Time and the Political Dialogue in the United States, 1828–48," *American Quarterly*, 19 (1967), 619–44.

143. A refreshing exception is Robert Kelley, *The Transatlantic Persuasion: The Liberal-Democratic Mind in the Age of Gladstone* (New York, 1969). The term "politics of recognition" comes from Robert E. Lane, *Political Life: Why and How People Get Involved in Politics* (Glencoe, Ill., 1959). p. 243.

PART II
Toward Revolution

2

No Awakening, No Revolution?

More Counterfactual Speculations

AT LEAST SINCE Herbert Levi Osgood proclaimed the Great Awakening as the first truly American event, historians have pondered its impact upon independence. Vernon L. Parrington saw it as a last explosion of clerical fanaticism from which the settlers happily escaped into saner preoccupations, such as the Revolution. John C. Miller linked it to class resentments surrounding the Massachussetts Land Bank, presumably another foretaste of 1776. Perry Miller tried to startle everyone by stressing the utter modernity of Jonathan Edwards; but his most distinguished student, Edmund S. Morgan, has emphasized quite a different contrast. He has juxtaposed the religious worldview of colonial spokesmen in 1740 against the astonishingly secular outlook of the Founding Fathers by 1790 and has tried to suggest how the Awakening helped to move America from the first position to the second.[1]

Since the mid-1960s, Alan Heimert has set the terms of debate. He has divided late eighteenth-century Americans into evangelicals and antievangelicals, linking evangelicals to the Revolution and proclaiming Edwards as the intellectual progenitor of Thomas Jefferson and Andrew Jackson. His antievangelicals (or "liberals") either resisted the Revolution or embraced it awkwardly and with reservations. Heimert's claims soon drew heavy and withering fire from Morgan and Sidney Mead, and an ironic appreciation from William McLoughlin. Reaction since then has slowly grown more favorable. Richard Bushman, Harry Stout, Gary Nash, and Rhys Isaac have all seen clear revolutionary potential in the religious upheaval that began in the 1730s. Probably no one would now deny that

Originally published in *Reviews in American History*, 1 (1983), 161–171.

an extraordinarily high correlation exists between New Lights and patriots. Remarkably few evangelicals in the Thirteen Colonies (unlike Britain
and Nova Scotia) rallied to the crown in 1776.[2]

The other half of Heimert's equation has not fared well. Many antievangelicals behaved as he described them, but far too potent a group did
not. Indeed, if evangelicals clustered in a very narrow band of the political spectrum (somewhere to the left of center), antievangelicals can be
found at every point. Among other things, they defined both extremes,
providing the most radical patriots (Thomas Paine, Jefferson, Dr. Thomas
Young, Samuel Adams, Ebenezer McIntosh, Ethan Allen), and virtually
all of the loyalists. To put the matter differently, antievangelicals supplied
nearly all positions of leadership, both radical and moderate, within the
patriot camp—signers of the Declaration of Independence, members of
Congress and the Philadelphia Convention of 1787, army commanders,
and even the sons of liberty and the organizers of anti-British mobs. With
a few exceptions that will shortly be noted, evangelicals followed but
did not lead. Antievangelicals defined the terms of resistance to Britain,
guided the republic to victory, set most of the agenda for the "internal
revolution" after 1776, and wrote (and probably led resistance to) the
Constitution of 1787.

A frank class analysis could resolve this enigma if it could demonstrate
that evangelicals clustered among the "meaner sort" but used their weight
to give power to those antievangelicals among the elite who shared their
social goals. Nash and Stout flirt with such an interpretation but do not
state it explicitly; both are doubtless aware of numerous exceptions to any
such pattern. As a result, the debate continues, but increasingly without
any sharp focus. It no longer seems obvious what aspect of the Revolution
the Awakening is supposed to explain.

Counterfactual arguments have their terrors for historians, especially
when they lack a rigorous statistical base. Yet, as I argued ten years ago
in discussing the impact of the Canada cession upon the Revolution,
they can also clarify issues that have become muddied and suggest useful avenues for future research. The historiography of the Awakening
has reached just such an impasse. One way of realizing where we are is
to obliterate the Awakening and then try to discover what remains in its
absence. This exercise, for all the risk of indiscipline it entails, might at
least tell us what we are trying to say.[3]

Of course in annihilating a major historical event, we should make as few actual changes in the known record as are needed to procure the result. I propose to remove from the scene, before certain critical points in their careers, the three men who did most to make the Awakening a North American and trans-Atlantic event: George Whitefield, Jonathan Edwards, and Gilbert Tennent. More than any other person, Whitefield drew together into a common experience the separate, local revivals that had agitated parts of the British world by 1740. In his absence, these local upheavals can continue to wax and wane much as they had been doing since the 1690s, but they will never reach the threshold of general awareness of "a great and extraordinary outpouring of the Spirit." To sustain our enterprise, he must disappear before 1739. Similarly, Edwards not only provided the Awakening with its most sophisticated theological exposition, but he also created a literary genre of crucial importance to its success—the published revival narrative, which found numerous imitators once he had invented the model. Edwards must go before completing *A Faithful Narrative of the Surprising Work of God* in 1736. Tennent forced the disagreements in the American Presbyterian Church to the point of schism by 1741, and he contributed more than anyone else to the task of joining local Middle Atlantic revivals to those in New England. His existence is intolerable, for our purposes, by 1738 or 1739. Finally, some readers might wish a similar fate upon John Wesley, but his impact upon America was never large before the Revolution, and I hesitate to adopt a counterfactual premise that might remove the entire Methodist movement from Anglo-American history. If he must be neutralized, let us give his hitherto unrequited romance in Georgia a consummation so blissful that it sustains him for several more years at his High Church, ritualistic phase. He does not turn in 1738 to Martin Luther and the Moravian Brethren for spiritual rebirth.

As should already be obvious, one of the forbidden delights that such counterfactual musings can provide to any suitably degenerate mind is the invention of proper circumstances for dispatching the other three men. Whitefield crossed the Atlantic in perilous times. On his return from Georgia in 1738, we can blow him off course and invite his capture by Spanish *Guarda Costa,* who take him to Havana and lose him in a dungeon. Instead of awakening thousands, he can become another minor cause of the War of Jenkins' Ear. We should detain him in these wretched

conditions long enough to outgrow his angelic youth, and perhaps transform him into a solitary mystic without an audience by the Peace of Aix-
la-Chapelle in 1748.

Edwards, sadly, cannot survive even his first Northampton revival
of 1734–35. Staring too fervently at the bellrope during one of his most
quickening sermons, he suddenly became mesmerized and had to be carried, a hopeless catatonic, from his pulpit by his weeping congregation.
He had not even started to write *A Faithful Narrative.*

Tennent, who really was struck by lightning in 1745 while preparing a
blast or two against the Moravians, can perhaps experience this discomfort in a more fatal way seven or eight years earlier. He never delivered his
fiery manifesto on *The Dangers of an Unconverted Ministry,* and his aged
father did not force issues to a schism. Thus Tennent never invited James
Davenport to supply his vacant pulpit while he toured New England, nor
did Davenport follow behind him.[4]

With the Awakening gone, what can we now ask? Basically three questions: 1) Would colonial resistance to British measures after 1763 have
reached the point of armed rebellion by 1775? 2) If it had, would the
Revolution have turned out differently with no Awakening to draw upon?
3) With no Awakening, would the republic of 1800 have been significantly
different from the one we now love and study? The rest of this essay will
suggest that we already know enough to provide clear answers to the first
and third questions. Without the Awakening, colonial resistance would
have taken very much the same forms it did and within the same chronology, but the America of 1800 would have been an unimaginably different
place. Far more difficult is the second question, to which no unequivocal
answer can yet be given.

Resistance to the Stamp Act was so universal and intense that one
hardly needs to invoke the Awakening to explain its success, except in
Connecticut. Apart from Martin Howard of Rhode Island, the stamp tax
had no committed defenders in North America. In fact, a surprising number of people who would later be unable to repudiate the crown provided
the settlers with their most cogent defense against Parliament—James
Otis, Jr., Thomas Fitch, William Smith, Jr., John Dickinson, and Daniel
Dulany. Of course actual nullification of the measure required forcible
intervention by urban mobs, particularly in Boston, Newport, New York,
and Charleston. Boston led all other cities in popular fervor in both

1740 and 1765, with the Boston *Gazette* defending the radical position in each case. But evangelical elation had declined sharply in 1742, and no one has yet connected the youthful converts of Whitefield, Tennent, and Davenport to the rioters of 1765. To be the same men, most would have had to be between 45 and 50 years old by then. To be younger men but still evangelical, we need to discover a later revival for Boston. Much the same generational argument applies to the other cities, with an interesting variation for Philadelphia. That port stood just behind Boston and ahead of New York and Charleston in the intensity of its excitement over Whitefield. In 1765 it did less than any of the others to resist the Stamp Act. No doubt evangelicals found the Stamp Act reprehensible, but there is no reason to believe that they exerted a decisive influence in 1765, or anything of the kind. Nearly all of their neighbors agreed with them.[5]

Much the same analysis applies to the Townshend Crisis. Resistance centered in the ports, where evangelical passion had been declining for a generation while continuing to erupt sporadically in the countryside. Opposition to Britain spread to the colonial legislatures when Lord Hillsborough forbade any assembly to consider the Massachusetts Circular Letter. Everything we know about the lower houses before 1768 argues for the predictability of their response. In any case, resistance achieved only a limited success before it collapsed in 1770, leaving the colonies badly divided. Here too, no good evidence has yet been offered for suggesting that the crisis would not have occurred without the Awakening or that it would have been resolved in any significantly different way.[6]

The final imperial crisis from the Tea Act through Lexington can also be explained quite satisfactorily without invoking the Awakening. The flash point again occurred in the nonevangelical port cities, Boston above all, and when Britain responded with the Coercive Acts, the countryside was rapidly drawn into a movement of massive resistance. Here we should expect to find a decent share of active evangelicals, but again colonial anger was so deep and widespread by the autumn of 1774 that we do not need them to account for what happened. The First Continental Congress developed its program without seeking guidance from the elect, and the war began shortly before the Second Congress met. Significantly, the town of Concord, site of the heaviest fighting on the first morning of the war, had split badly over the Awakening. It now united behind the Revolution.[7]

Even without the Awakening, the Revolution would have happened. But could it have succeeded? Would the colonies have been able to agree upon independence by July 1776? (Without the barrier of independence, the Howes' Peace Commission later that summer would have stood a better, though still not a good, chance of restoring the Empire.) Could Americans have won the war?

On these questions we find, for the first time, that some evangelicals were strategically located where their political decisions really mattered. The New Light Susquehannah Company faction had gained control of Connecticut politics during the Stamp Act Crisis and now guided that province steadily and exultantly toward independence. In New Jersey, where over a third of the population became active loyalists while others stood neutral, patriot leadership fell heavily to Presbyterians from the Princeton area, home of the college that had done more than any other to perpetuate and spread the Awakening. Quite appropriately, President John Witherspoon led a fresh New Jersey delegation to Philadelphia just in time to swing the colony's vote in favor of independence by July 2. Pennsylvania experienced its own internal revolution in June 1776 when a movement dominated by backcountry Presbyterians overthrew the moderate, antiindependence, Quaker-Anglican elite that had controlled provincial politics.[8]

Elsewhere we can record evangelical support for independence, but its decisiveness seems highly dubious. Massachusetts Baptists, the most evangelical group in the province by the 1770s, were caught largely by surprise during the rush of events. So indifferent had many of them been to imperial issues that their neighbors suspected them of loyalism. They had played no conspicuous part in the resistance movement, but now at the culminating stage they climbed aboard. Similarly Virginia Baptists had struggled for a decade against the Anglican gentry who drove the Old Dominion into independence. They too rallied to a cause that others defined, but they seem to have provided no decisive impact upon policy until the fight for Anglican disestablishment in the 1780s.[9]

Even when a correlation exists, how much can we make of it? Connecticut, for example, appears beguilingly simple and obvious until we ponder the alternatives. A New Light party did lead the colony to independence. But had the Old Lights retained power past 1766, would they have behaved much differently? Governor Fitch, had he remained in office past 1766 and lived past 1774, might indeed have gone loyalist. He showed every sign of such behavior. Yet he probably would have been no more difficult a problem for patriots than loyalist governor Joseph Wanton in neighboring Rhode Island, who was jettisoned in the final crisis. When the crunch came, Connecticut Old Lights rallied overwhelmingly to the Revolution, as did Old Light Congregational clergy throughout New England. The only sizable pocket of loyalism in the state was Anglican, a faith that had grown rapidly in reaction *against* the Awakening. The argument would be more perverse than any I care to defend, but a case could be made that the net effect of the Awakening was to increase loyalism more than patriotism. More probably, it increased both the number of Anglican loyalists and the intensity of patriot resistance.[10]

In Pennsylvania, by contrast, the Revolution often seemed to be almost a civil war between Presbyterians and Quakers. This evaluation, however, does not place the province in the Awakening camp. As with Congregationalists, few prominent Presbyterians, New Side or Old, went loyalist, and the proportion was probably no higher among the inconspicuous and inarticulate. We can, of course, trace the revolutionary activities of such New Side Presbyterians as the Reverend George Duffield of Philadelphia. Even so, the decisive event in Pennsylvania was the rising of backcountry Scots-Irish, many of them without resident clergymen, yet strongly rooted in Ulster traditions of Presbyterianism. Radical as they were (and they soon helped to launch the most daring constitutional experiment of the period), they remained in all likelihood an antievangelical, Old-Side band of patriots. That leaves New Jersey as a fairly unequivocal case of New Lights dragging their fellows into independence and a bracing republican vision of the future. Only months later would the Princeton radicals begin to discover what could happen if they gave a revolution in New Jersey—and nobody came but the British.[11]

Without an Awakening, one might argue, continuing opposition to independence in New Jersey might have stiffened the resistance of like-minded men throughout the Middle Atlantic region as a whole and thus postponed or even prevented the Declaration. New York, after all, abstained even in July 1776. But any such argument is tenuous and must rely upon an escalating succession of imponderables. Had the war continued, the logic for independence would almost certainly have prevailed eventually, as it soon did in antievangelical New York. To the war itself we must now turn.

Could the military conflict have been won without an Awakening? Here we approach the most difficult and fascinating problem of all. The war, we now realize, was an extremely brutal and draining experience. It stands just behind the Civil War as the most destructive conflict in our history. Did evangelicals somehow provide the resiliency and stamina to endure a struggle that the less righteous would have abandoned?[12]

Possibly so. The argument deserves serious consideration and can sustain far more research than it has yet received. Some hasty answers to the problem are clearly inadequate. Perry Miller, for example, has insisted that, while secular leaders spoke their lofty eighteenth-century language of natural rights, ordinary soldiers responded far more warmly to appeals based on biblical covenants. Perhaps. Leaving aside the realization that both Old and New Lights could endorse covenant and even millennial rhetoric, this contention lacks specificity. Does it apply chiefly to the Continental Army, which probably did have a disproportionate share of New Light chaplains? Two strong arguments suggest otherwise. First, the Continentals did not *behave* that way. They were no reincarnation of Oliver Cromwell's Ironsides from the previous century. Their outlook and grievances were far more secular. They did not defend themselves as the elect of God nor charge into battle chanting Psalms. Some of their chaplains undoubtedly hoped to make things otherwise, which may explain the intense mortification of the Reverend Samuel Spring, a committed evangelical. He learned that during his brief furlough from the Army, his men had rejoiced heartily to be rid of him. Second, most Continentals were the wrong age and probably from the wrong social class to match the profile that has been emerging of who got converted in eighteenth-century revivals. Most of them were too young, and their family and communal roots were too weak.[13]

On the other hand, as John Shy and others have contended, maybe the Continentals were not the decisive weapon after all. Maybe the militia really did tip the balance, politicizing the neutral at heart, holding loyal to the patriot cause every area not under British military occupation, and providing logistical support to George Washington and Nathanial Greene, or even desperately needed reinforcements at several critical phases of the contest. Here, if anywhere, we should look for a direct impact of evangelicals upon the military struggle. Did they serve disproportionately in the tiring services required of the militia? This question can be researched but so far has not been. From everything we know about both evangelicals and the militia, we ought to expect richer results here than with the Continental Army. Evangelical conversions occurred most often within established families of church members, and the militia was a communal, family-based institution. For whatever reason, evangelical ministers (unlike Old Lights, who far more often had clerical forebears) were disproportionately descended from militia officers. If the militia really accomplished all that Shy claims, perhaps evangelicals contributed more to the militia than to any other patriot institution. Here above all, a counterfactual question can give us a specific and important problem to investigate.[14]

Less concretely, the kind of emphasis stressed recently by Stout and Isaac also seems more appropriate to the war years, or at least to the period from 1774 on, than to earlier crises. Both men emphasize the sharp difference between the evangelicals, with their oral, face-to-face culture and emotional sermons, and the older colonial elite, with its polite, urbane, genteel, literary culture. Patrick Henry derived much of his influence, Isaac thoughtfully suggests, from his special talent for bridging the two worlds. Without in any way underplaying the importance of this insight or even trying to suggest that a counterfactual hypothesis can begin to measure its significance, we might still argue that the evangelical style of exhortation found its truest role in winning the war, not bringing it on. Baptists were by far the most vigorous evangelical group in America by the 1770s, but apart from a few individuals such as Elder John Allen of Boston (whose heterodoxy prevented him from winning a pulpit), they have not yet been detected provoking the imperial crisis. They responded to what others created.[15]

We might also discover that evangelicals contributed significantly to the internal revolution of the 1770s and 1780s. The role of Presbyterians in Virginia and Baptists everywhere in the fight for ecclesiastical disestablishment is too well known to discuss here. But we still do not understand where evangelicals stood on other urgent, nonreligious, social questions. How large a presence were they in the reformed state legislatures of the era? If they appeared in significant numbers, did they cluster with Jackson Turner Main's localists or cosmopolitans? Or did Baptists perhaps behave differently from New Side Presbyterians and

New Light Congregationalists in this respect? In New England, for example, Congregational New Lights eventually emerged as Federalists while Baptists went Jeffersonian. If such a split was general, can we speak meaningfully of an evangelical alignment or party in the very early republic? Only when we have mapped the boundaries of the evangelical social vision through rollcall votes and local records can we properly grasp its meaning and impact.[16]

The internal revolution leads naturally to our final question, which need not detain us long. Everything we have learned recently about American political culture in the nineteenth century underscores the importance of the evangelical upheaval. In the early eighteenth century, the denominations bidding for hegemony in North America were Congregational, Quaker, and Anglican. As the two Great Awakenings did their work, the lead shifted decisively to Baptists, Methodists, and Presbyterians, all major beneficiaries of the revivals. Without their contribution, the American republic after 1800 would have been an utterly different place from what we know. Speculation about its behavior would be quite pointless.

Nevertheless, partly because colonialists and early national specialists often seem to communicate as poorly with each other as New Lights did with Old Lights, some points of confusion remain that deserve short notice. Above all, Jonathan Edwards can in no sense be regarded as the intellectual progenitor of Jefferson and Jackson. The very notion would have startled and dismayed all three gentlemen. Although the Democratic party could and did attract Baptist support, it remained overwhelmingly a pluralistic and antievangelical coalition down to the Civil War and beyond. New Divinity men lopsidedly supported the other side—the Federalist, Antimasonic, Whig, Know-Nothing and Republican parties. So powerful is this correlation that, if we are determined to attribute a major political and military upheaval to revival fervor, we would do far better to choose the Civil War, not the Revolution. The Union Army, not the Continentals, sometimes marched to combat singing *The Battle Hymn of the Republic,* whose millennial tone has no counterpart among either Confederate or Revolutionary War songs.[17]

The Awakening did not create the Revolution. It surely contributed to its success, but how decisively we still do not know. More important, the Revolution liberated the spirit of the Awakening, which had grown tepid and largely ineffective among all but Baptists by the 1770s, when church membership and attendance may have been approaching an all-time low. The success of the Revolution, and the exhilarating prospects that it aroused, inspired a new generation of respectable evangelicals to reshape the social landscape of the United States. Far more dramatically than their predecessors of 1740, they imposed their social vision upon their fellow citizens until their reformist ardor drove an angry South to secession. Without the Great Awakening and its successors, there would have been a revolution in 1775, but in all probability, no Civil War in 1861.[18]

Notes

1. Herbert Levi Osgood, *The American Colonies in the Eighteenth Century,* vol. 3 (1924), pp. 409–10; Vernon L. Parrington, *Main Currents in American Thought,* vol. 1 (1926), pp. 148–63; John C. Miller, "Religion, Finance, and Democracy in Massachusetts," *New England Quarterly* 6 (1933): 29–58; Perry Miller, *Jonathan Edwards* (1949); Edmund S. Morgan, "The American Revolution Considered as an Intellectual Movement," in *Paths of American Thought,* eds. Arthur M. Schlesinger, Jr. and Morton White (1963), pp. 11–33.

2. Alan Heimert, *Religion and the American Mind from the Great Awakening to the Revolution* (1966); Edmund S. Morgan, review of Heimert in *William and Mary Quarterly* 3rd. ser., 24 (1967): 454–59; Sidney Mead, review of Heimert in *Journal of Religion* 48 (1968): 274–88; William McLoughlin, review of Heimert in *New England Quarterly* 40 (1967): 99–110. See also, Richard Bushman, *From Puritan to Yankee: Character and the Social Order in Connecticut, 1690–1765* (1967); Harry Stout, "Religion, Communications, and the Ideological Origins of the American Revolution," *William and Mary Quarterly* 3rd ser., 34 (1977): 519–41; Gary Nash, *The Urban Crucible: Social Change, Political Consciousness, and the Origins of the American Revolution* (1979), ch. 9; Rhys Isaac, "Evangelical Revolt: The Nature of the Baptists' Challenge to the Traditional Order in Virginia, 1765–1775," *William and Mary Quarterly* 3rd ser., 31 (1974): 345–68; J. M. Bumsted, *Henry Alline, 1748–1784* (1971), on Nova Scotia.

3. John M. Murrin, "The French and Indian War, the American Revolution, and the Counterfactual Hypothesis: Reflections on Lawrence Henry Gipson and John Shy," *Reviews in American History* 1 (1973): 307–18.

4. For the importance of Edwards's *Faithful Narrative* in its trans-Atlantic setting, see Michael J. Crawford, "The Invention of the American Revival: The Beginnings of Anglo-American Religious Revivalism, 1690–1750" (Ph.D. diss., Boston University, 1978). For Tennent the best study is Milton J. Coalter, Jr., "The Life of Gilbert Tennent: A Case Study of

Continental Pietism's Influence on the First Great Awakening in the Middle
Colonies" (Ph.D. diss., Princeton University, 1982); for the lightning
incident, see pp. 282–84.

5. Edmund S. and Helen M. Morgan, *The Stamp Act Crisis: Prologue to
Revolution* (1953); Benjamin H. Newcomb, "Effects of the Stamp Act on
Colonial Pennsylvania Politics," *William and Mary Quarterly* 3rd ser., 23
(1966): 257–72. The sharp decline in conversions in Boston can be plotted in
John W. Raimo, "Spiritual Harvest: The Anglo-American Revival in Boston,
Massachusetts, and Bristol, England, 1739–1742" (Ph.D. diss., University of
Wisconsin, 1974), pp. 244–46.

6. The best account of the Townshend Crisis is Merrill Jensen, *The Founding of
a Nation: A History of the American Revolution, 1763–1776* (1968), chs. 7–14.

7. David Ammerman, In the Common Cause: American Response to the
Coercive Acts of 1774 (1974); Robert L. Gross, *The Minutemen and their
World* (1976).

8. Oscar Zeichner, *Connecticut's Years of Controversy, 1750–1776* (1949); Alison
B. Olson, "The Founding of Princeton University: Religion and Politics
in Eighteenth-Century New Jersey," *New Jersey History* 87 (1969): 133–50;
Larry R. Gerlach and Sheldon S. Cohen, "Princeton in the Coming of the
American Revolution," *New Jersey History* 92 (1974): 69–92; Paul H. Smith,
"New Jersey Loyalists and the British 'Provincial' Corps in the War for
Independence," *New Jersey History* 87 (1969): 69–78.

9. William G. McLoughlin, *New England Dissent, 1630–1833: The Baptists
and the Separation of Church and State,* vol. 1 (1971), ch. 31; Rhys Isaac,
The Transformation of Virginia, 1740–1790 (1982), part 2. In the Middle
Colonies, some Baptists, led by Morgan Edwards, did go loyalist, but their
theological position would have to be investigated carefully before deciding
whether they were New Lights. Edwards, for example, was flirting with
Universalism by the 1780s.

10. Glenn Weaver, "Anglican-Congregationalist Tensions in Pre-Revolutionary
Connecticut," *Historical Magazine of the Protestant Episcopal Church* 26
(1957): 269–85, esp. the list of Anglican churches by date of founding on
p. 278; John W. Tyler, *Connecticut Loyalists: An Analysis of Loyalist Land
Confiscations in Greenwich, Stanford [sic] and Norwalk* (1977); David
S. Lovejoy, *Rhode Island Politics and the American Revolution, 1760–1776*
(1958), pp. 182–84. For Fitch, see *Dictionary of American Biography*.

11. Richard A. Ryerson, *The Revolution Is Now Begun: The Radical Committees
of Philadelphia, 1765–1776* (1978); "Republican Theory and Partisan
Reality in Revolutionary Pennsylvania: Toward a New View of the
Constitutionalist Party," in Peter Albert and Ronald Hoffman, eds.,
Sovereign States in an Age of Uncertainty (1982). Leonard J. Trinterud,
*The Forming of an American Tradition: A Re-examination of Colonial
Presbyterianism* (1949), ch. 14; James McLachlan, *Princetonians, 1748–
1768: A Biographical Dictionary* (1976), on Duffield, see pp. 51–53; Elizabeth
I. Nybakken, "New Light on the Old Side: Irish Influences on Colonial

Presbyterianism," *Journal of American History* 68 (1981–82): 813–32; John
M. Murrin, "Princeton and the American Revolution," *Princeton University
Library Chronicle* 38 (1976–77): 1–10; Adrian C. Leiby, *The Revolutionary
War in the Hackensack Valley: The Jersey Dutch and the Neutral Ground*
(1962).

12. Howard H. Peckham, ed., *The Toll of Independence: Engagements & Battle
Casualties of the American Revolution* (1974), pp. 131–34; Richard Buel, Jr.,
Dear Liberty: Connecticut's Mobilization for the Revolutionary War (1980).

13. Perry Miller, "From the Covenant to the Revival" (1961), reprinted in his
Nature's Nation (1967), pp. 90–120; Edward C. Papenfuse and Gregory
A. Stiverson, "General Smallwood's Recruits: The Peacetime Career of
the Revolutionary War Private," *William and Mary Quarterly* 3rd ser., 30
(1973): 117–32; John R. Sellers, "The Common Soldier in the American
Revolution," in *Military History of the American Revolution: Proceedings of
the Sixth Military History Symposium, USAF Academy, 1974,* ed. Stanley
J. Underdal (1976), pp. 151–61; Mark E. Lender, *The New Jersey Soldier,* New
Jersey's Revolutionary Experience, No. 5 (Trenton: New Jersey Historical
Commission, 1975); Charles Royster, *A Revolutionary People at War: The
Continental Army and American Character, 1775–1783* (1979), pp. 373–78,
modifies the above studies but not in a way that changes expectations
about the evangelical composition of the Army. On Spring, see Richard
A. Harrison, *Princetonians, 1769–1775: A Biographical Dictionary* (1980),
pp. 166–71 at p. 168.

14. John Shy, *A People Numerous and Armed: Reflections on the Military Struggle
for American Independence* (1976), esp. chs. 7, 9; Harry S. Stout, "The Great
Awakening in New England Reconsidered: The New England Clergy,"
Journal of Social History 8 (Fall 1974): 21–47; James Walsh, "The Great
Awakening in the First Congregational Church of Woodbury, Connecticut,"
William and Mary Quarterly 3rd ser., 28 (1971): 543–62.

15. In addition to material already cited, see Rhys Isaac, "Preachers and
Patriots: Popular Culture and the Revolution in Virginia," in *The American
Revolution: Explorations in the History of American Radicalism,* ed. Alfred
F. Young (1976), pp. 125–56.

16. Jackson Turner Main, *Political Parties before the Constitution* (1973). For
linkages to Federalists and Jeffersonians after 1790, see John Brooke, "A
Society, Revolution, and the Symbolic Uses of the Dead: An Historical
Ethnography of the Massachusetts Near Frontier, 1730–1820" (Ph.D. diss.,
University of Pennsylvania, 1982).

17. Nathan O. Hatch's *The Sacred Cause of Liberty: Republican Thought and
the Millennium in Revolutionary New England* (1977) shows that both
Old and New Light Congregational clergy overwhelmingly supported the
Revolution and, later, the Federalist party. Among the extensive literature
on nineteenth-century political culture, perhaps the best introductions are
Lee Benson, *The Concept of Jacksonian Democracy: New York as a Test Case*
(1961); Robert Kelley, *The Cultural Pattern in American Politics: The First*

Century (1979); and Paul E. Johnson, *A Shopkeeper's Millennium: Society and Revivals in Rochester, New York, 1815–1837* (1978).

18. Nathan O. Hatch, in "The Christian Movement and the Demand for a Theology of the People," *Journal of American History* 67 (1980–81), 545–67, demonstrates the liberating impact of the Revolution upon religion. See also, Patricia U. Bonomi and Peter R. Eisenstadt, "Church Adherence in the Eighteenth-Century British American Colonies," *William and Mary Quarterly* 3rd ser., 39 (1982): 245–86, esp. p. 274.

3

The French and Indian War, the American Revolution, and the Counterfactual Hypothesis

Reflections on Lawrence Henry Gipson and John Shy

I

HISTORY IS NOT fiction. Historians reject the liberty, essential to historical novelists, of inventing personalities and other details about a past era. Instead we must stick to what we can prove, or reasonably infer, from the data we study. Thus whenever someone begins to speculate heretically about "might-have-beens," historians almost instinctively react by erecting this principle into an impassible barrier. "We cannot have the events other than they are," A. J. P. Taylor has recently pronounced with doctrinal certainty. "Some historians like to play at the game 'if it had happened otherwise.' This only goes to show that they would be better employed writing romantic novels where dreams come true."[1] But, one might ask, is that what historical novelists really do? *War and Peace*, for example, derives its overwhelming impact from Leo Tolstoy's artistic discipline which deliberately subordinates fictional invention to genuine history. Tolstoy created individuals and incidents, but he accepted the reality of the larger events of the age of Napoleon. American historical fiction follows the same pattern. Nathaniel Hawthorne, Margaret Mitchell, and Kenneth Roberts never felt at liberty to undo the founding of Massachusetts, the Revolution, or the Civil War.

Originally published in *Reviews in American History*, 1 (1973), 307–318.

Yet paradoxically most of us attempt in practice what we reject in theory. To make sense out of the past, historians do fantasize about their subject. Every time a historian evaluates a particular decision or policy option in terms of contemporary alternatives, he is thinking counterfactually because he has to, unless he is prepared to assert that real choices did not exist in the past or that, if they did, historians should ignore them. Traditional military histories and good biographies are largely written in these terms. Although this quality resembles the literary imagination in major respects, it serves a different function for historians. Generally speaking, historical novelists remain faithful to great events while they invent or embellish particulars. By contrast, the historian must adhere to the details of the past while speculating about larger patterns. To explain his data, he must ask whether it could have fallen together in some combination other than what actually occurred. Only by posing this question can he decide which of his verifiable "facts" were decisive and which were peripheral in generating the larger "events" he hopes to reconstruct.

This essay argues through a single complex example that we might be better historians if we render explicit what we already do implicitly. Because counterfactual thinking embarrasses us, even terrifies us by its sheer lack of rules, we employ it haphazardly rather than systematically. The predictable result is sloppy scholarship. We can reduce this difficulty only by devising ways to validate counterfactual hypotheses. And in the last analysis, they can be formulated and assessed only in terms of the data from which they arise. Had George III invented the airplane, he might have won the War for Independence. But this particular counterfactual argument is absurd on its face because it violates what we already know about the science of the period. Other might-have-beens are more plausible and merit serious attention. One of them has managed to influence nearly every attempt to understand why the Revolution happened when it did.

II

The late Lawrence Henry Gipson was one of few American historians to erect counterfactual arguments into explicit research tools. Throughout his lengthy career he often repeated one major point: "that the American Revolution," as he put it in 1948, "was an aftermath of the Anglo-French conflict in the New World [between 1754 and 1763]." Had Canada remained French after 1763, he asked, "would not Americans have continued to feel the need as in the past to rely for their safety and welfare upon British sea power and British land power, as well as upon British resources generally?"[2] Britain's honest, rational, but expensive attempt to administer vast new territory acquired largely for the benefit of the older colonies clashed inevitably, Gipson believed, with their lessened sense of dependence. Britain had to ask them to accept in time of peace a series of impositions they had not felt even in time of war. The result was revolution, for despite the Empire's manifest needs, the colonies responded by demanding "greater autonomy than ever."[3]

In Gipson's hands, an avowedly counterfactual assumption became a basis for sorting out the importance of particular events—in this case, for deciding that the Canada cession outweighed the Stamp Act, for example, as a cause of the Revolution. This particular counterfactual argument is essential to his entire history. It enables him to convert the Revolution into an enormous tragedy in which the British Empire destroys itself through an excess of altruism, decency, and concern for order.[4]

But this assumption did not originate with Gipson. Indeed, few organizing principles in American history can boast of lengthier genealogies, for the argument antedated the Revolution itself by at least one generation. "I have been told by Englishmen . . . that the English colonies in North America, in the space of thirty or fifty years, would be able to form a state by themselves entirely independent of Old England," Peter Kalm, the Swedish naturalist, reported after visiting New York in 1748. "But as the whole country which lies along the seashore is unguarded, and on the land side is harassed by the French, these dangerous neighbors in time of war are sufficient to prevent the connection of the colonies with their mother country from being quite broken off."[5] "The possession of *Canada*, far from being necessary to our Safety, may in its Consequence be even dangerous," warned William Burke after the fall of Quebec. "A Neighbour that keeps us in some Awe, is not always the worst of Neighbours."[6] Even high French officials seemed to agree. Britain's conquest of New France will "be one more cause acting to hasten her ruin by favouring the defection of her colonies in North America," one of them observed as early as 1758; "they will soon be richer than Old England and will undoubtedly shake off the yoke of the mother country."[7] Had Canada remained

French, lamented Governor Thomas Hutchinson in 1773, "none of the spirit of opposition to the Mother Country would have yet appeared & I think the effects of [the Canada cession] worse than all we had to fear from the French or Indians."[8]

Because the Empire did collapse not long after the Peace of Paris, historians, ever alert for an apt quotation, have seized passages of this sort and endowed them with prophetic power. And because this particular counterfactual argument is neatly lodged in the sources themselves, scholars have embraced it through the unexceptionable device of quoting what they read. In this way a counterfactual argument has acquired the analytical function of a verifiable "fact." Partly for this reason, the Canada cession has emerged as a major cause of the Revolution across the entire interpretive spectrum. It characterizes not just Gipson's "imperial" approach, but even George Bancroft's fervently nationalistic account.[9] It is a staple item in American textbooks. Yet the argument never has attracted thorough analysis, probably because it is counterfactual, and historians are not quite certain how to handle such material. Since it already plays an important role in our understanding of the Revolution, it demands careful investigation. It can, in fact, be approached in several ways, all derived from other available data of the pre-Revolutionary era.

First, Gipson's argument assumes that the "Gallic Peril"[10] had to discourage colonial resistance to Britain. Its removal would thus stimulate opposition. If so, we ought to learn something from the earlier political behavior of colonies exposed to this danger or isolated from it. The outbreak of Queen Anne's War did not prevent the Massachusetts assembly from embarking upon a bitter quarrel with its governor in 1702–04, nor did it deflect the assembly of vulnerable New York from a path of remarkable radicalism a few years later.[11] King George's War generated a similar response in New York, where the governor found himself pathetically impotent by 1748.[12] The aftermath of that war is also instructive. Although Britain returned Louisbourg to France, thus strengthening the Gallic Peril, and although French expansion assumed alarming dimensions shortly after the peace, this threat did not forestall the eruption or continuation of serious political crises in New Hampshire, New York, New Jersey, and North Carolina.[13] To be sure, these controversies remained local, not intercolonial, but the will to redress perceived grievances was quite apparent in them all. Unlike the situation after 1763, no common target emerged against which all the colonies could direct their energies at the same time. On the other hand, Virginia provides a stunning example of a province all but immune to the French threat until after 1750. Instead of stimulating demands for independence, this security reinforced what must have been the most harmonious political system in the Empire. Between 1720 and 1753, no issue of consequence ever divided the governor from the assembly. Virginia remained loyal to the imperial connection despite the lack of an overriding military need. Ironically, the Pistole Fee controversy spoiled the record of harmony in 1753, just as the colony was being drawn into the Anglo-French contest for control of the Ohio Valley.[14] Of course, contrary examples also existed, especially the Massachusetts of Governor William Shirley, who used war and expansion to solidify his immensely successful system of political management. But the point remains that war with France could strain imperial relations as easily as it could bolster them.[15]

Still another approach to this question involves analysis of a somewhat broader range of quotations about the impact of Anglo-French tensions upon colonial politics, and vice versa. Benjamin Franklin flatly denied that the acquisition of Canada would jeopardize colonial loyalties, while a Boston newspaper essayist suggested that the continuing presence of French Canada along the colonial frontier might actually inspire Versailles to stimulate colonial resistance to Britain.[16] Other spokesmen, both British and colonial, were more explicit. During the parliamentary debate on repeal of the Stamp Act, a proponent of British sovereignty declared, "ask France what Occasion She wou'd wish for y[ou]r Destruction, she will answer, let Divisions be kept up and fomented between you and your Colonies . . . as the surest Means to her of compassing the great Object of her Ambition."[17] "Do you think that all your rival powers in Europe would sit still and see you crush your once flourishing and thriving colonies, unconcerned spectators of such a quarrel?" the Virginia planter, George Mason, warned the London merchants even more bluntly in 1766. "Recollect what happened in the Low Countries a century or two ago. Call to mind the causes of the [Dutch] revolt [against Spain]."[18] European powers, fearing that Britain had "grown too powerful" in the last war, could only applaud "civil discords" within the Empire, echoed John Dickinson during the next crisis, because these dissensions "would afford opportunities of revenging all the injuries supposed to be received from her."[19] Thus while Gipson and his sources contend that elimination of the Gallic Peril had to generate an imperial crisis, these other writers perceived an opposite connection. Imperial strife might revive the Gallic Peril for Britain. And, of course, the Franco-American alliance of 1778 very nicely proved their point.

A third consideration is equally telling. The French government may have left North America by 1763, but the French *Canadiens* remained behind, very much alive and still dangerous. Colonists did not protest Britain's decision to garrison North America with regulars after the war because the need seemed obvious. If the *Canadiens* rebelled, the cycle of war could begin anew. Indeed, the Quebec Act of 1774 alarmed the northern colonies precisely because, in their view, it did revive the Gallic Peril. The Loyalist Daniel Leonard grimly stoked their smoldering fears. If we challenge Britain to war, he observed in December 1774:

> Inconceivably shocking the scene; if we turn our views to the wilderness, our back settlements a prey to our ancient enemy, the Canadians, whose wounds received from us in the late war, will bleed afresh at the prospect of revenge, and to the numerous tribes of savages, whose tender mercies are cruelties. Thus with the British navy in the front, Canadians and savages in the rear, a regular army in the midst, we must be certain that whenever the sword of civil war is unsheathed, devastation will pass through our land like a whirlwind.[20]

As Leonard realized, Britain in 1775 possessed the maritime dominance she had used to crush the French in the previous conflict *plus* all the geographical assets of New France as of 1754. The colonies could avoid conflict with Canada only by preserving peace with Britain. In other words, the Revolution erupted *despite* general recognition that it would almost certainly produce another Canadian war. Only a quick conquest of their troublesome neighbor could avert this fate, Congress assumed, and when that failed by 1776 the Gallic Peril had revived—only to stimulate rather than retard the revolutionary cause. For, as James Hutson has recently argued, the Declaration of Independence came *when* it did because Patriots feared a mythical "Partition Treaty" between Britain and France. In exchange for Canada, France would help Britain subdue her rebellious colonies, a prospect so terrifying to American leaders that nothing short of independence seemed likely to sway France in their favor.[21] In fact, Canada soon became a staging ground for British regulars instead of angry French *habitants*, but this development was hardly predictable in the decisive years 1775–76. And Indian behavior along the frontier, coordinated out of British territories that had once formed New France, actually did resurrect for the colonies many of the specific difficulties of 1754 with no Empire to turn to for aid.[22] Lord North certainly understood the military value of Canada. So long as the Empire holds Canada, he wrote in 1778, the colonies "will be always obliged to pay attention to Great Britain."[23]

III

Removal of the Canada cession as a milestone toward revolution leaves rather different markers behind. To oversimplify the options a little, it returns the Stamp Act and other specific issues to the central place that Patriots always gave them. Instead of pretexts for the manifestation of a selfish American nationalism, as Gipson saw them, these particular crises again emerge as causes of the Revolution. Without them there would have been no revolution and no American nation, at least not in the immediate future.

Yet Gipson was correct in one sense, for important links can indeed be established between his "Great War for the Empire" and the American Revolution. The best research on this question proceeds from John Shy, whose *Toward Lexington: The Role of the British Army in the Coming of the American Revolution* (Princeton, 1965) deserves recognition as one of the most perceptive contributions to Revolutionary history since World War II. He shows that Britain's victories over France generated a great fund of colonial good will towards the mother country. The army itself remained quite popular in the colonies until it was sent to Boston in 1768. Outside New England, these favorable attitudes persisted into the 1770s, including a surprising willingness to enlist in the king's forces. Properly exploited, these loyalties could have been mobilized to tighten imperial bonds. Instead a persistent misapplication of means to ends, with the army usually involved somewhere along the way, finally dissipated the good will. Somehow particular policy decisions, seemingly rational in themselves, consistently missed the point at the level of implementation.[24]

In a separate essay, Shy has also taken an explicitly counterfactual approach to the coming of the Revolution. By comparing the policy

suggestions of Henry Ellis, a hard-liner on imperial issues, with those of
Thomas Pownall, an avowed friend of the colonies, he shows that even
Pownall's proposals would have badly antagonized America. His conclusion exudes pessimism about the Empire's prospects for surviving the crisis, for he can find no likelihood that Britain's ruling class could ever have
agreed on a colonial policy leading anywhere but toward Lexington and
independence.[25]

Yet Shy's book, taken in conjunction with other recent studies, suggests a startling pattern about British policy formation in the 1760s, a
pattern no one has quite pieced together so far. He demonstrates that the
Quartering Act of 1765 was a useless, ill-conceived irritant in imperial relations. The quartering of British soldiers had raised serious tensions early
in the war, but colonists had resolved them by erecting public barracks for
the redcoats in major provincial cities, while the assemblies had regularly
voted essential supplies. Yet after the war General Sir Thomas Gage began
to worry about his lack of power to quarter soldiers in smaller communities while marching them from one post to another. Although the problem had not yet arisen, he asked London to obtain legislation enabling
him when necessary to quarter troops in private homes. Eventually the
ministry, nervous over this challenge to traditional English liberties, gave
the problem to Pownall, who claimed expertise on the subject because he
had been governor of Massachusetts during its quartering dispute of 1758.
Accordingly, Pownall's statute addressed the problems of 1758, which had
already taken care of themselves, rather than the new theoretical issue
of 1765. The Quartering Act met no real needs. It did create real problems by compelling colonial legislatures to do what so far they had all
done voluntarily. Thus it gratuitously antagonized assemblies that were
proud of their record of cooperation with the army while, ironically, it
also denied Gage the one power he had requested-to quarter soldiers in
private homes.[26]

Surprisingly, this bizarre sequence of events is beginning to look
like the norm rather than a silly exception. The Proclamation of 1763,
the Sugar and Currency Acts of 1764, and in a looser way even the
Stamp Act all had similar origins. A decent case can be made for the
Proclamation of 1763, but it also dated back to wartime treaties with
particular Indian tribes, protecting their lands against white encroachment.[27] The Sugar Act with its attack on smuggling is another matter.

Alarmed by colonial trading with the enemy early in the war, the Board of Trade began to collect data from which the customs commissioners compiled a full report in 1759. Significantly, the most recent item in the report dated only from 1757. In fact, the smuggling problem was also taking care of itself, for as British forces overran Canada and the Caribbean, hardly any place remained worth smuggling to by 1760. Yet after the war the Board of Customs and the Treasury both used this report to help draft the Sugar Act. London's response was again anachronistic. The Sugar Act was more germane to the difficulties of 1757 than to the changed realities of 1764.[28]

The Currency Act is comparable. Virginia's emissions of paper money early in the war prompted London merchants to protest loudly lest the value of planter debts depreciate. Nothing happened at the time because Virginia needed paper to carry on the war, and in any case her paper held its value until 1762, when it dropped slightly in the wake of a London fiscal crisis. The merchants immediately complained, the government dug out their protests of several years back, and Parliament finally embalmed them in the Currency Act of 1764—another mischievous irritant soon regretted even by many of its merchant supporters. Yet the ministry continued to enforce what several of its influential members fully recognized as a bad law, rather than appear too soft toward the colonies in the wake of the Stamp Act crisis.[29]

In less specific terms the Stamp Act can also be traced to the gloomy years of French victory, 1754–57, when the traditional requisition system had revealed its inability to provide badly needed revenues. All royal (and some nonroyal) governors pleaded with London to obtain a general parliamentary tax upon the colonies. Instead Britain found a different answer by 1758—William Pitt's subsidy policy in which Parliament used specie grants to reimburse particular colonies in direct ratio to their military efforts. By offering valuable rewards to specie-poor colonies, it actually stimulated competition among them in support of imperial goals. Its achievements far surpassed anything that requisitions had ever accomplished. At an annual expense to Britain of £200,000 (later reduced to £133,000), the colonies raised about twenty thousand provincials per year through 1762, paying about half the cost themselves. Yet by adopting the Stamp Act after the war, Britain in effect honored the panicky demands of 1754–57, not the solid achievements of 1758–62.[30]

Thus Britain possessed, in effect, two sets of imperial precedents after 1763. To govern her colonies she could extend the lessons of victory by continuing to do what had won the war. Or she could revert to earlier, more strident suggestions about how she *ought* to have won the war. Without major exception, London bypassed the lessons of victory to embrace projects stimulated by fear of defeat. With the Gallic Peril finally eliminated from North America, Britain espoused reforms once deemed necessary to meet that threat. In the process she alienated her mainland colonies—and thus revived the Gallic Peril. Parliament's subsidy policy stands out in this respect. With reasonable efficiency it provided provincial troops in large numbers, probably stimulated a dramatic rise in colonial importations of British goods, helped to stabilize paper currencies, and encouraged hearty cooperation with the mother country—all of this while respecting traditional colonial liberties.[31] Yet after the war London regressed, almost without reflection or debate, to the attitudes of 1754–57, which in turn rested upon still earlier assumptions and demands that had never worked properly and which were, in any case, quite inadequate to the needs of the 1760s.[32]

Fiscal considerations alone probably cannot explain this choice. Direct taxation of the colonies promised to raise only about a fourth of the annual £400,000 needed to maintain ten thousand redcoats in America after 1763. Well-placed subsidies might have fielded as many provincials at less cost to Britain by stimulating a larger voluntary response from the colonies. The contempt of redcoats for provincial troops discouraged the search for alternatives, as did the king's wish to save as many regiments as he could from demobilization after the war. Yet it remains quite remarkable that, so far as I know, the subsidy option was never even considered. Apparently English leaders thought of subsidies not as acceptable instruments of policy, but as desperate wartime expedients justified only by a terrible emergency. Despite their conspicuous success, in other words, they could not compete as *legitimate* precedents with earlier failures or risky, untried suggestions.

Thus with amazing consistency Britain's imperial policies of 1764–66 carefully addressed the specific problems of 1754–57, most of which were well on the way toward resolving themselves through various informal mechanisms. But if London was running only a decade behind the times during the Stamp Act controversy, this gap tended to widen, not narrow, as imperial relations worsened. The second colonial crisis (1767–70) found Charles Townshend unearthing the concerns of 1748–54, when the Board of Trade had identified the lack of an independent salary for the governor as the crucial weakness in several royal colonies, especially New York. Even more dramatically than the quartering problem, this issue had been dead for fifteen years, but Townshend's memory of his youthful experience at the Board of Trade after 1748 kept it alive for him. Not surprisingly, his policy did not strengthen a single colonial governor. It did unravel informal accommodations that had worked reasonably well in most northern colonies for years.[33] Then, in the final crisis of 1774, Parliament reached back even farther to the early years of the century. The Massachusetts Government Act resurrected the Board of Trade's ancient nostrum of depriving charter governments of special privileges by act of Parliament.[34] This time the Empire came apart with the charter, possibly a fitting response when a policy of 1701 had emerged as Britain's brightest idea for 1774.

IV

This sketch of counterfactual possibilities suggests, finally, that we should seek the origins of the Revolution less in inexorable trends propelling the colonies into nationhood no matter what Britain did, and more in British public attitudes that relentlessly confronted the colonies with a series of disturbing choices. From 1758 to 1763 Britain came close to resolving her imperial difficulties. But restricted to a set of ideas that had long been institutionalized and bureaucratized among colonial administrators at the Board of Trade, she proved incapable of even recognizing her own achievements, much less perpetuating them.

As Parliament's uncompromising insistence on complete sovereignty indicated, English politicians could not easily distinguish the realm from the Empire and hence were not willing to concede genuine rights to the colonies as against Parliament. In other words, English statesmen had severe difficulty thinking *either* imperially *or* federally. The war provided a catalyst for all kinds of change, but evidently it could not alter the habitual way that politicians looked at old problems, not even when it forced them to make specific decisions which, by 1763, were in fact liquidating those problems. In this sense, rather than Gipson's, the Revolution truly was a paradoxical aftermath of the Great War for the Empire. Britain may actually have lost her colonies because, in the last analysis, the English simply did not know how to think triumphantly.

Notes

1. *The Times Literary Supplement* (London), March 23, 1973, p. 327.
2. Gipson, "The American Revolution as an Aftermath of the Great War for the Empire, 1754–1763," *Political Science Quarterly* 65 (1950): 86, 103–4.
3. Gipson, *The Coming of the Revolution, 1763–1775* (New York: Harper, 1954), p. xii.
4. For what was probably Gipson's last affirmation of the importance of the Canada cession, see his *The British Empire before the American Revolution* (Caldwell, Id.: The Caxton Printers, 1936–72), XIII, pp. 346–47.
5. Adolph B. Benson, ed., *The America of 1750: Peter Kalm's Travels in North America: The English Version of 1770* (New York, 1937), I, pp. 139–40.
6. William Burke (supposed author), *Remarks on the Letter Addressed to Two Great Men*, in *A Letter to the Author of That Piece* (London, 1760), p. 51. For discussions of the debate over the Canada cession, see Clarence W. Alvord, *The Mississippi Valley in British Politics: A Study of the Trade, Land Speculation, and Experiments in Imperialism Culminating in the American Revolution* (Cleveland, 1917), I, pp. 56–53: William L. Grant, "Canada versus Guadaloupe, an Episode of the Seven Years War," *American Historical Review* 17 (1911–12), 735–43; and Jack M. Sosin, *Whitehall and the Wilderness: The Middle West in British Colonial Policy, 1760–1775* (Lincoln: University of Nebraska Press, 1961), pp. 3–26.
7. The Marquis de la Capellis, as quoted in Guy Fregault, *Canada: The War of the Conquest*, Margaret M. Cameron, transl. (Toronto: Oxford University Press, 1969), pp. 231–32. For other French examples, see George Bancroft, *History of the United States from the Discovery of the Continent* (Boston, 1834–74), IV, pp. 460–61.
8. Quoted in Gipson, "The American Revolution as an Aftermath of the Great War," p.104.
9. Bancroft, *History of the United States*, IV, pp. 460–62.
10. The phrase is Edward Channing's. *A History of the United States* (New York, 1905–25), II, Ch. 5.
11. Everett Kimball, *The Public Life of Joseph Dudley: A Study of the Colonial Policy of the Stuarts in New England, 1660–1715* (New York, 1911), Ch. 5; Beverly W. McAnear, "Politics in Provincial New York, 1689–1761" (Ph.D. diss., Stanford University, 1935), Chs. 6–7, esp. pp. 236–44.
12. Stanley N. Katz, *Newcastle's New York: Anglo-American Politics, 1732–1753* (Cambridge: Harvard University Press, 1968), Ch. 7; Patricia U. Bonomi, *A Factious People Politics and Society in Colonial New York* (New York: Columbia University Press, 1971), pp. 149–66.

13. Jack P. Greene, ed., *Great Britain and the American Colonies, 1606–1763* (Columbia: University of South Carolina Press, 1970), pp. xli–xlv; Jere R. Daniell, "Politics in New Hampshire under Governor Benning Wentworth, 1741–1767," *William and Mary Quarterly* 3rd ser., 23 (1966): 94–105; Gary S. Horowitz, "New Jersey Land Riots, 1745–1755" (Ph.D. diss., Ohio State University, 1966); Lawrence F. London, "The Representation Controversy in Colonial North Carolina," *North Carolina Historical Review* 11 (1934): 255–70. For New York, see note 12 above.

14. David Alan Williams, "Political Alignments in Colonial Virginia Politics, 1698–1750" (Ph.D. diss., Northwestern University, 1959); Percy S. Flippin, "William Gooch: Successful Royal Governor of Virginia," *William and Mary Quarterly* 2d ser., 5 (1925): 225–58, and 6 (1926): 1–38; Jack P. Greene, "The Case of the Pistole Fee," *Virginia Magazine of History and Biography* 66 (1958): 399–422.

15. John A. Schutz, *William Shirley, King's Governor of Massachusetts* (Chapel Hill: University of North Carolina Press, 1961). Cf. James Alan Rogers, "Northern Colonial Opposition to British Imperial Authority During die French and Indian War (Ph.D. diss., University of California, Santa Barbara, 1968).

16. Leonard W. Labaree et al., eds., *The Papers of Benjamin Franklin* (New Haven: Yale University Press, 1959–), IX, pp. 90–91; *The Boston News-Letter* No. 2991, December 28, 1758, p. 2.

17. Edmund S. Morgan, ed., *Prologue to Revolution: Sources and Documents on the Stamp Act Crisis, 1764–1766* (Chapel Hill: University of North Carolina Press, 1959), p. 153.

18. Mason to the Committee of Merchants in London, June 6, 1766, in Kate Mason Rowland, *The Life of George Mason, 1725–1792, Including his Speeches, Public Papers, and Correspondence* (New York, 1892), I, p. 387; cf. Stephen Johnson in *The New London Gazette,* October 4, 1765, reprinted in Bernard Bailyn, "Religion and Revolution: Three Biographical Studies," *Perspectives in American History* 4 (1970): 154.

19. John Dickinson, "Letters from a Farmer in Pennsylvania (1767–68)," in Forrest McDonald, ed., *Empire and Nation* (Englewood Cliffs, N.J.: Prentice-Hall, 1962), p. 67.

20. John Adams and Jonathan Sewall (should be Daniel Leonard), *Novanglus and Massachusettensis; or Political Essays, published in the Years 1774 and 1775, on the Principal Points of Controversy, between Great Britain and Her Colonies* (Boston, 1819), p. 145. Cf. David Hartley's speech in the House of Commons, March 27, 1775, in William Cobbett, comp., *The Parliamentary History of England from the Earliest Period to the Year 1803* (London, 1806–20), XVIII, p. 561.

21. James H. Hutson, "The Partition Treaty and the Declaration of American Independence," *Journal of American History* 58 (1971–72): 877–96.

22. Jack M. Sosin, "The Use of Indians in the War of the American Revolution: A Re-Assessment of Responsibility," *Canadian Historical Review* 46 (1965): 101–21.

23. North to William Eden, April 23, 1778, in Benjamin F. Stevens, comp., *Facsimiles of Manuscripts in European Archives relating to the American Revolution* (London, 1889–98), IV, No. 447.

24. Shy, *Toward Lexington*, esp. pp. 140–48, 343–58, 376–98.

25. Shy, "Thomas Pownall, Henry Ellis, and the Spectrum of Possibilities, 1763–1775," in Alison G. Olson and Richard M. Brown, eds., *Anglo-American Political Relations, 1675–1775* (New Brunswick, N.J.: Rutgers University Press, 1970), pp: 155–86; cf. Jack P. Greene, "The Plunge of Lemmings: A Consideration of Recent Writings on British Politics and the American Revolution," *South Atlantic Quarterly* 67 (1968): 141–75.

26. Shy, *Toward Lexington*, pp. 178–90. Cf. Stanley M. Pargellis, *Lord Loudoun in North America* (New Haven, 1933), pp. 187–210; Jack P. Greene, "The South Carolina Quartering Dispute, 1757–1758," *South Carolina Historical Magazine* 60 (1959): 193–204; John J. Zimmerman, "Governor Denny and the Quartering Act of 1756," *Pennsylvania Magazine of History and Biography* 91 (1967): 266–81: Gipson, *British Empire before the American Revolution*, XI, pp. 39–69.

27. Ibid., IX, pp. 41–54; cf. Shy, *Toward Lexington*, pp. 45–83.

28. Thomas C. Barrow, "Background to the Grenville Program, 1757–1763," *William and Mary Quarterly* 3rd ser., 22 (1965): 93–104; Victor L. Johnson, "Fair Traders and Smugglers in Philadelphia, 1754–1763," *Pennsylvania Magazine of History and Biography* 83 (1959): 125–49; Richard Pares, *War and Trade in the West Indies, 1739–1763* (Oxford, 1936), pp. 395–470. The near-heroic achievements of smugglers in home waters lend perspective to the colonial problem. See Hoh-cheung and Lorna H. Mui, "Smuggling and the British Tea Trade before 1784," *American Historical Review* 74 (1968–69): 44–73.

29. Joseph A. Ernst, "Genesis of the Currency Act of 1764: Virginia Paper Money and the Protection of British Investments," *William and Mary Quarterly* 3rd ser., 22 (1965): 33–74; Ernst, "The Currency Act Repeal Movement: A Study of Imperial Politics and the Revolutionary Crisis, 1764–1767," ibid. 25 (1968): 177–211. In all fairness to Ernst and Barrow (note 28 above), I should emphasize that I have used their data for purposes quite different from theirs.

30. Bancroft, *History of the United States*, IV, pp. 159–81; George Louis Beer, *British Colonial Policy, 1754–1765* (New York, 1907), pp. 31–51.

31. Colonial imports from Britain in 1760 were nearly double those of 1756, when in turn they had exceeded the total for every previous year except 1753. U.S. Bureau of the Census, *Historical Statistics of the United States, Colonial Times to 1957* (Washington, D.C.: Government Printing Office, 1960), p. 757. Because exchange rates turned on the balance of payments

within a particular colony, specie subsidies and British expenditures for the army obviously helped to stabilize colonial paper. Cf. Ernst, "Genesis of the Currency Act," pp. 55–56. Despite their importance, parliamentary subsidies have attracted little attention so far. Pargellis mentions them only to contrast the effectiveness and efficiency of regulars against the higher cost and wastefulness of provincials. *Lord Loudoun*, pp. 352–55. Gipson barely notes the existence of this policy during his lengthy discussion of the war years. Instead he withholds the question until he reaches the immediate background of the Sugar and Stamp Acts, and then he couples it with the liquidation of colonial war debts after 1763. The artistic effect of this strategy is to contrast British generosity during the war with colonial parsimony after the war. At no point does he regard subsidies as an available policy option, and indeed he never really evaluates their impact. Ibid., X, pp. 38–110.

32. See, generally, James A. Henretta's excellent study, "*Salutary Neglect*": *Colonial Administration under the Duke of Newcastle* (Princeton, N.J.: Princeton University Press, 1972); and Greene, *Great Britain and the American Colonies,* pp. xi–xlvii.

33. Sir Lewis B. Namier. "Charles Townshend, His Character and Career," in his *Crossroads of Power: Essays on Eighteenth-Century England* (London: Hamish Hamilton, Ltd., 1962), pp. 194–212; P. D. G. Thomas, "Charles Townshend and American Taxation in 1767," *English Historical Review* 83 (1968): 33–51. For an example of an informal salary arrangement, see John M. Murrin, "Review Essay," *History and Theory* 11 (1972): 262–64.

34. See, generally, Louise P. Kellogg, "The American Colonial Charter," in *American Historical Association, Annual Report* I (1903): 185–341, esp. pp. 284–305.

4

Feudalism, Communalism, and the Yeoman Freeholder

The American Revolution Considered as a Social Accident

THE STAR OF social history has been in the ascendant, especially in the American sky, for several years past. Defined, more precisely than formerly, as the history of the institutional structure of society, it has indicated one way in which historians might move on from the points arrived at by the economic interpretations of the 1920s and 1930s and the intellectual history of the 1940s and 1950s. Political history in particular is being rewritten in terms of social class, ethnic and religious affiliation, and a social psychology that may even restore the family to its old importance for our understanding of the political commonwealth.[1]

From this new social perspective a variety of conventional topics—the democratic and humanitarian movements of the age of Jackson, half-a-dozen seemingly ill-assorted phases of Progressivism, and even that perennial enigma, the Civil War—appear in a new light. It may be the more noteworthy, then, that so far the American Revolution has *not* been similarly reinterpreted. Was the eighteenth-century context so unlike the society of the mid-nineteenth and early twentieth centuries that the great event of that age, the Revolution, cannot be seen as having been generated from within, as Jacksonian egalitarianism or the Civil War were, but rather as being imposed from without? So most historians, like most of the revolutionaries, have believed. Did the Revolution, furthermore, leave

Originally published in *Essays on the American Revolution*, ed. Stephen G. Kurtz and James H. Hutson (Chapel Hill: University of North Carolina Press, 1973), 256–288.

unaltered the direction and the rate of social change? Was colonial society already moving ineluctably, whether a political revolution occurred or
not, into its nineteenth-century patterns?

I

Until very recently few historians argued that the causes of the Revolution
lay in the structure of colonial society. Neither J. Franklin Jameson, when
in 1925 he broached the question of the Revolution as a social movement,
nor Frederick B. Tolles, in reassessing the matter in 1954, paid any attention to the possibility that social causes impelled the political events of
the years 1763 to 1775.[2] It has recently occurred to several historians, however, that the deepest roots of the Revolution may indeed have tapped
the social subsoil of colonial America. Gordon S. Wood has suggested
that a "social crisis within the gentry" of Virginia in the mid-eighteenth
century, sometimes taking the form of excessive independence and dis-
obedience of sons toward parents, may help explain the near unanimity of
that class in support of the political revolution.[3] In his study of Andover,
Massachusetts, Philip J. Greven, Jr., detects a subtle connection between
social change and revolution. An emerging gap between the third and
fourth generations of settlers impelled the colonists to extend to the king
himself "the idea of independence from parental authority." Somehow,
Greven implies, the inner structure of the family had already anticipated
the ideology of Thomas Paine.[4] The crumbling of old communal ties may
have worked to the same end. The practical pluralism and individualism
among the no longer homogeneous townsmen of New England, according
to the variant accounts of Kenneth A. Lockridge and Edward M. Cook,
Jr., were leading to social and political revolution and also, as a kind of
reaction during the conflict, to the patriotic imposition of a forced unanimity.[5] Jack P. Greene contends that Americans of the pre-Revolutionary
generations were suffering from an identity crisis and that independence
pointed a way out of their self-doubt.[6] The gross rhetorical exaggera-
tions by which they expressed their grievances against the mother country, Wood has suggested, were stimulated by a basic reality: "*Something
profoundly unsettling was going on in* [their] society."[7] That something,
according to Edmund S. Morgan, was a fear that old social and economic virtues were being lost in the march of material affluence during

the eighteenth century; hence the colonists' nonimportation and non-consumption agreements of the 1760s and 1770s were aimed not only at gaining redress from Parliament but at self-reformation—doing without luxuries, supplying their own essential wants, and cutting themselves off from the unproductive services of English merchants.[8] As Bernard Bailyn, J. G. A. Pocock, and Gordon Wood have pointed out, this recrudescence of Spartan self-denial invoked not only the Calvinist economic ethic but also old English "country" or commonwealth ideas of classical civic virtue that appeared to shield the colonies from the "corruption" into which the British government was sinking.[9]

For the most part these hypotheses remain in the realm of ingenious conjecture and fragmentary afterthought appended to studies of other eighteenth-century matters. The meagerness of the evidence adduced for them could about as easily lead back to the contrary conclusion that, as Thomas C. Barrow has put it, "such tensions and divisions as did exist within American society were relatively minor and harmless"—and that the Revolution basically was the colonial war for political independence that most historians, like most people of that time, have supposed it was.[10] By comparison with the social tensions and divisions of the nineteenth century, those of the eighteenth, though real enough, recede to a level that may be considered about normal in human affairs.

The Civil War, the great cataclysm of the nineteenth century, can more convincingly be explained in terms of the pervasive social anxiety of that later time, an uneasiness that through a peculiar chain of circumstances and events aggravated every political dispute, made sectional and racial divisions seem intolerable, and so combined to produce an irreconcilable conflict.[11] That war has never been satisfactorily explained, at any rate, in terms simply of economic interest, partisan advantage, or even the social peculiarities of North and South—certainly not by reiterating the abstract constitutional theories upon which the sectional leaders laid such weight. The contrast to the eighteenth century on the last point is especially significant. The question of the proper constitutional relationship of the colonies to the empire seems, especially to a historian of the society of the later United States, to have been a sufficient cause of the political revolution that did occur; the revisionist attentions of social historians and psychologists do not appear to be required.

It is the older question of the social effects of the Revolution, however, that most concerns us here. If it may be said that the Civil War resolved few of the underlying social tensions that had led to it, is it possible that the Revolution, even though it did not spring from such causes, nevertheless had a greater impact upon the structure of society? The general understanding of recent historians has been that it did not. Most of the social effects that Jameson adduced might better be called *economic* effects—changes in the distribution of wealth and in legal patterns of landholding, confiscation of tory estates, the opening of new land, the impetus to industrial development—as well as such changes in political forms as the disestablishment of churches that were already splitting into "denominations." Professor Tolles, in summing up another thirty years' work on the matter, concluded that it had added less proof to Jameson's hypothesis than it had taken away; virtually nothing new on the structure of society had been unearthed. Whoever possessed the wealth of the country when the Revolution was over, the economic class structure remained about what it had been; reforms in landholding were mainly symbolic; the Industrial Revolution awaited a still later generation.

The general understanding of the matter has changed little since Tolles's article. Recent historians of the early national period have implicitly assumed that social data drawn from different decades between 1750 and 1825 can be used quite interchangeably, the basic structure of society having altered so little during that age.[12] The conclusion prevails, evidently, that American society in the half century after 1775 was substantially what it had been in the quarter century before.

II

Like any epoch—certainly any in the history of American society—the century from 1725 to 1825 was far from static. The direction of change, however, was confused and sometimes contradictory. In certain ways economic growth and greater social maturity were making the New World resemble the Old more closely. Long-settled districts were approaching the demographic pattern of Western Europe: a denser population, both urban and rural; more pronounced stratification of economic classes; more specialization of labor; and less vertical mobility than before. At the same time, however, the rapid extension of settlement into the remote backcountry—a new kind of frontier that Frederick Jackson Turner dated from about 1730—continually renewed the earlier sources of mobility and made it difficult to impose the degree of social stability that the earlier seaboard settlements had once enjoyed.[13] As the frontier advanced, the social circumstances of the West, which seemed ever less like those of European tradition, also affected the eastern districts from which the migrants came; after 1825 industrialization and mass immigration further intensified the radical impact of the frontier. In a society thus becoming both more like and more unlike that of Europe, more settled and more unsettled, more complex and less homogeneous, a revolutionary war—even one conducted for the most narrowly political ends—could hardly fail to stimulate certain kinds of change and to inhibit others.

At the least, however glacial the changes in the social structure, the American Revolution marked a major turning point in the perception that Americans had of their society. As colonials they had adhered to English values and conformed to old-country institutions—both often of a rather archaic sort—as closely and as soon as their growing resources of population and wealth permitted. The recurrent tension between this conservative, even reactionary, ideal and the practical liberty and individuality that their new circumstances stimulated is a familiar theme of colonial history—Puritanism against secularism, communalism eroded by economic progress, hierarchic authority challenged by antinomianism. Recently the same sort of conservative-liberal tension has been observed as a central element of the "Jacksonian persuasion" half a century after the Revolution.[14] By 1825 the liberal-individualist side was clearly dominant, and conservative caution recessive, among a people who now thought of themselves as establishing new social models for the Old World to imitate. It is a reasonable hypothesis that the shift from one set of values to the other had been accelerated by the political events of the 1760s and 1770s. From that time on the kind of instability that had been conventionally deplored in colonial society as a sad "declension" from proper standards was instead accepted as setting a new and better model, and standards that were too obviously English were rejected. It was not in commercial affairs alone that Americans cast off the "great reluctance to innovation, so remarkable in old communities," as was observed in 1785, and moved ahead on "a line far beyond that to which they had been accustomed."[15]

This redressing of the conservative-liberal balance affected some parts of the social structure more than others. Some social values and institutions to which the course of events drew attention were explicitly forsworn, while others were just as explicitly rallied around, and the development of still others quietly proceeded no matter how poorly they fit the new circumstances. American society between the Revolution and 1825—in many respects, indeed, right down through the nineteenth century and into the twentieth—was an odd mixture of archaic and modern elements.

This is not surprising. National independence, although sought for the sake of preserving certain accustomed political patterns, required rapid development of new ones. On the other hand, the Revolution provided a radical justification for various archaic elements that were also carried along, consciously or unconsciously, into the nineteenth century. Some of the archaic ideas, as they were incongruously applied to their modern circumstances, inadvertently hastened change more than they retarded it, just as radical ideology sometimes retarded social change rather than advanced it. Confusion necessarily resulted in the minds of historians as well as contemporaries, both native and foreign, between what was truly new on the American scene and what was a vestige of another age. Just as American speech was studded with old English expressions that Englishmen took for fresh (or barbaric) new coinages, some of the archaic elements in American society were in a modern context the most radical.

III

Certain developments in the late colonial era, especially during the generation after 1725, suggest that without the Revolution nineteenth-century America might have become a very different place from that with which we are familiar. If American society in 1825 did not differ sweepingly from the social order of 1725, the Revolution and particularly its idealization of social anachronisms may have been the chief reason. Revolutionary ideology powerfully stimulated a nostalgic attachment to a seventeenth-century simplicity that the eighteenth century had been doing its best to erode. Most notably, perhaps, colonial society had been far closer to a state of practical equality in the seventeenth century than it became in the eighteenth. Except for New England, contemporary critics often associated this lack of social differentiation with acute social disorder. Before 1700 the colonists were more nearly equal, but thought they should be less. They moved steadily toward this goal in the eighteenth century until by the Revolution they were indeed less equal, only to discover that they should be more. In this regard the Revolution challenged what was perhaps the main social trend of the previous half century.

Most colonies in the eighteenth century experienced what European specialists would recognize as a "feudal revival." A conspicuous example is South Carolina's demand for a lifetime "nobility" or upper house in the early 1770s, but since South Carolina planters were much wealthier than other colonial elites, this proposal is less surprising than the absence of other feudal relics in the colony, such as entail.[16] Elsewhere the revival took different forms.

By 1630, after the commercial corporation had demonstrated the unprofitability of founding colonies, proprietary projects on a feudal model dominated virtually all seventeenth-century attempts to plant English settlements in the New World. By the end of the century all of them had failed quite decisively, although in Carolina the proprietary regime struggled on for another twenty years. Lord Baltimore's Maryland, ducal New York, and the Jerseys had been royalized, while William Penn was reduced to pathetic impotence in his own colony on the Delaware, and the Culpepers and their heirs had failed to derive any significant benefit from their claim to the Northern Neck of Virginia. Historians accordingly conclude that feudalism was too anachronistic to survive in the free air of a new world.[17]

The opposite explanation is more compelling. Feudal projects collapsed in the seventeenth century, not because America was too progressive to endure them, but because it was too primitive to sustain them. A feudal order necessarily implies a differentiation of function far beyond the capacity of new societies to create. In every colony the demographic base was much too narrow. Even in New France the rationalized feudal order that Colbert attempted to impose in the Saint Lawrence valley produced an impressive number of paper seigneuries by 1700, but not feudalism in any recognizable sense. Only by the middle of the eighteenth century would the population of New France expand sufficiently to make the seigneurial system profitable—and quite durable thereafter.[18]

In this regard the English colonies were not drastically different from French Canada. Although the seventeenth century had not created a workable feudal regime in a single English colony, it did bequeath its feudal charters and land patents to the next century. Charters and land patents are legal documents that can always be revived, provided someone has sufficient reason to do so. By 1730 the older colonies had become populous enough to make the old feudal claims incredibly lucrative. The data from each colony have long been familiar; taken together, a truly striking pattern emerges.

As late as the 1720s the New York manors were largely untenanted and profitless to their owners. The East Jersey proprietors had abandoned the effort to derive a steady income from their patent.[19] The claims of the Carolina proprietors became almost worthless when Charleston revolted in 1719, and a decade later all but one proprietor—Lord Carteret, later Earl Granville—sold out to the crown.[20] Lord Fairfax, the Culpeper heir, netted only £100 from the Northern Neck in 1721, nothing in 1723, and another £100 in 1724.[21] Years later Pennsylvania still returned perhaps £100 clear profit to the heirs of the first proprietor. Maryland alone was beginning to show signs of a profitable future following the restoration of the proprietary regime shortly after the Hanoverian succession.[22]

Between 1730 and 1745 old claims were revived and consolidated from Carolina to New York. Thomas Penn sailed to Philadelphia to put his affairs in order in 1732, and Lord Baltimore visited Maryland in 1732–1733, where he negotiated a number of financial arrangements highly favorable to himself.[23] Rather than visit the Carolinas, Carteret first relied on the royal governments of the two colonies to collect his quitrents and then, when this arrangement proved disappointing, prevailed on the crown in 1745 to consolidate his claim into a single holding, later called the Granville District, that took in over half the land and about two-thirds of the population of North Carolina.[24] In 1745 Lord Fairfax obtained an exceptionally favorable court decision that enlarged his claim in the Northern Neck to 5,200,000 acres, which soon encompassed twenty-one counties of Virginia.[25]

As in France, the feudal revival in the English colonies employed old legal and social forms for quite single-mindedly modern purposes. Old charters, which at one time had assumed a mutuality of obligations and responsibilities, were revived only because they had become profitable.

In the colonies, as in France, these claims aroused resentment precisely because they divorced the pursuit of profit from any larger sense of community welfare. Historians miss the point when they reject the notion of feudalism in America on the grounds that no one seriously intended to resurrect the Middle Ages. On both sides of the Atlantic the revival ripped feudal relationships out of their original social context and seized what surviving obligations could be enforced for the income they might produce.[26] And, in fact, exploitation of legal privilege became the greatest source of personal wealth in the colonies in the generation before Independence. By the 1760s the largest proprietors—and no one else in all of English America—were receiving colonial revenues comparable to the incomes of the greatest English noblemen and larger than those of the richest London merchants. Indeed the Penn claim was rapidly becoming the most valuable single holding in the Western world.[27]

The feudal revival was as divisive as it was profitable, provoking more social violence after 1745 than perhaps any other problem. Wherever the revival was strong, response to the Revolution was mixed or divided. Pennsylvania and Maryland, where feudal charters conveyed immense political power to the proprietors, both developed royalist movements that hoped to replace proprietary government with a royal regime. By 1755 Franklin in particular had grown utterly disgusted by the Penns' habit of protecting proprietary revenue while ignoring the colony's most urgent needs. His bitter campaign to bring in the crown eventually destroyed the Quaker party and seriously weakened the Revolutionary movement in Pennsylvania.[28] Similarly in Maryland the leaders of both parties showed exceptional reluctance to embrace the Revolution.[29] Practically all of the violence in North Carolina in the twelve years before the Battle of Alamance occurred within the Granville District. The earliest riots were directed against the proprietor's land policy, which remained a grievance throughout the Regulator disturbances. His claim to quitrents deprived the colony of a leading source of revenue and forced it to resort to other taxes that also contributed to the war of the Regulation.[30]

In large part, however, these disputes were due to the fact that the greatest colonial proprietors were absentee landlords. The colonial social structure was not graced with a resident upper class of the eminence that their income and rank could have supported. But there was a second rank of resident proprietors whose position suggests what both the strengths and weaknesses of an American landed aristocracy might have become had the development of such a social class not been cut off after the Revolution. Unlike the absentee Calvert, Carteret, and Penns, Lord Fairfax established his seat in the Northern Neck, where by 1768 he was receiving £4,000 in quitrents, besides revenue from manor rents, land sales, and other sources. The governor and the House of Burgesses had fought the Fairfax claim into the 1740s, but once the crown had determined every disputed point in the baron's favor, the colony accepted him without violence of the sort that occurred elsewhere. Doubtless a major reason for this acquiescence was Fairfax's willingness to become a resident proprietor, an ornament of provincial society. Throughout the Northern Neck large landholders were increasingly turning to leases and rents as a primary source of revenue. For example, Robert Carter of Nomini Hall was able to live exclusively off rents (about £2,250 a year) by 1790. Fairfax was simply the most spectacular example among many, and his physical presence lent a genuine title and real dignity to the social life of the region. George Washington, for one, remained quite loyal to the baron throughout the Revolution.[31]

Residency did not ensure as happy an outcome in New York, where the seventeenth-century manors also were becoming profitable in the middle third of the eighteenth century. Scarsdale, Philipsborough, and Livingston returned between £1,000 and £2,000 a year, Rensselaerswyck probably more, and Cortlandt Manor less.[32] The manor lords would have qualified as middling gentry in England, while their income greatly exceeded that of the provincial nobility of Toulouse.[33] The tenant rising on Livingston Manor in 1753–1754 and the much larger New York tenant revolt of 1766 challenged the manorial system in the most direct way.[34]

In terms of genuine feudalism the revival was thus grossly imperfect, more a matter of economic profit for the proprietor than of mutual obligations between lord and man or landlord and community that might have harmonized the relationship. Where a sense of genuine mutuality did exist, the system sometimes acquired powers of endurance that outlasted the Revolution, but elsewhere it was destroyed. In the Hudson-Mohawk valley it survived both the tenant riots and the Revolution, partly because the manor lords provided some genuine economic benefits for their tenants. The developmental function of manorialism and its ethnic role among Dutch farmers probably helped it to survive there into the 1840s.[35]

Absenteeism was a different matter, especially when it conveyed tremendous political power. Lord Baltimore built the most elaborate and most expensive patronage system in English America out of his proprietary revenues.[36] In Pennsylvania the Proprietary party dominated the council, the closed corporation of the city of Philadelphia, the college, the courts, and most other political offices.[37] The East Jersey proprietors, most of whom lived in Perth Amboy or New York, used their dominance of the council to protect their interests against both the assembly and the tenant rioters of Newark and Elizabethtown.[38] In all of these cases the feudal revival differed from mere land speculation in two respects. It involved a legal or customary claim to the exercise of political power regardless of the wishes or interests of the community as a whole. And rather than profit only from the opening of new lands to settlement, it also imposed its fiscal demands upon older areas without offering any benefits in return. In both respects it distinctly resembled the feudal reaction in Europe far more closely than the good American habit of pure land speculation.

We can only guess what sort of society the feudal revival might have produced had it gone unchecked for another half century. The trend towards tenancy, which helped to legitimate Lord Fairfax, continued after independence in Virginia until by 1830 it had disfranchised about half of the adult white males. Could Virginia have assumed the same revolutionary posture in 1810 or 1830 that it found easy to adopt in 1776?[39] At the very least the destruction of the revival during the Revolution was socially and perhaps politically significant. The growth of mercenary feudalism for another generation or two might *possibly* have divided some colonies beyond the point at which they could have revolted successfully from the Empire, and it might have made a political union of the continent on common principles much more difficult to achieve. But because the Revolution happened when it did, the feudal revival was truly destroyed.

For obvious reasons the absentees lost most completely. The Granville and Calvert proprietorships were confiscated; the Penns were allowed to retain their "manors" or private estates, but the proprietorship itself was abolished at a cost to the commonwealth of £130,000 sterling voted by the legislature.[40] Tory landlords lost their estates in New York, but whigs did not, which suggests that confiscation was designed chiefly to punish political loyalism rather than to create a new egalitarian order. Nevertheless the impact was considerable. The number of freeholders increased significantly, especially in areas that had been heavily tenanted before. Even the few large-scale beneficiaries were usually new men who in one way or another made life difficult for the old landlords.[41] The East Jersey situation was less complex. There the proprietors lost their privileged political position, but they still exist today as a legal entity. They survived because they had already ceased to matter; they had failed to make good their claim to quitrents even before the Revolution broke out.[42]

The geographical limits to the feudal revival are quite instructive. In particular New England and New Englanders displayed a striking immunity to the whole phenomenon. Old charters were also revived around mid-century in Maine and New Hampshire, but no one used them to claim quitrents or to press demands upon older settled regions. Instead their function was developmental, rather similar to the Ohio Company of Virginia in their own day and to numerous speculative enterprises of the nineteenth century with perhaps a greater admixture of responsibility to the community. But when proprietors attempted to impose feudal obligations upon Yankee settlers outside New England, the results were invariably explosive. Almost all the East Jersey tenant rioters of 1745–1754 were Yankees. So apparently were most of New York's rioters of 1745–1766. In each of these cases neighboring Dutch farmers accepted identical feudal impositions with few quarrels. Obviously Yankee behavior requires special explanation.[43]

If a modern land system is one that desymbolizes and disencumbers land in the interest of the freest possible exchange, New England resisted the feudal revival because in several important respects it was rather less modern than the rest of English America. As in Tudor and Stuart England, freehold proclaimed a man's independence by ensuring that he was not subject to the will of another. For New Englanders, consequently, the freehold system helped to bind the town together as a community of consenting individuals. Since the town elected its officers and governed its own affairs through a general meeting of the freeholders (the great majority), it has usually been taken for an early form of the democracy of the nineteenth and twentieth centuries. But if the form seems familiarly modern, it embodied an archaic English tradition.[44]

The early New England town, Kenneth Lockridge has recently argued, was not only a Puritan utopia but also a peasant utopia, a "Utopian Closed Corporate Community," ordering its own affairs by the "common consent of the neighbors" that had been customarily invoked by English villagers of the Middle Ages, though in the New World all the lesser peasant tenures had been transformed into simple freehold.[45] Because it distilled the communal side of medieval peasant experience—with lordship quite deliberately excluded—it could resist feudal claims with furious energy during the middle third of the eighteenth century. John Adams elevated this antagonism to the level of high ideology in his *Dissertation on the Canon and Feudal Law* (1765), which explained New England history as an emancipation from feudal restraints. By contrast, the more atomized pattern of settlement in other colonies failed to generate the communal cohesion and the consistent belief necessary for sustained resistance to the feudal revival. Jefferson, by inventing a mythical contract between the Jamestown settlers and James I, developed his own antifeudal interpretation of Virginia history in 1775, but as he himself admitted, few Virginians agreed with him at the time.[46]

Ultimately the Revolution would announce an ideology of natural rights in the name of which the feudal revival would be all but obliterated, even from historical memory. Yet despite obvious similarities, the nation's triumph was not New England's. By exploiting the fiscal side of lordship the revival had triumphed where communalism was weak. Although, conversely, the social communalism of New England had prevented the feudal revival from making headway there, self-government based upon the joint consent of all the responsible inhabitants of the town had been breaking down in the course of the eighteenth century, as the population grew denser, less homogeneous, more individualistic, and more European. The town meeting still sought the appearance of consensus through a process of accommodation that muted and obscured, as far as possible, the rising level of conflict. In some degree the Revolution accelerated the transformation from truly communal consensus to the explicitly majoritarian democracy of the nineteenth century in which political parties institutionalized and even promoted conflict by appealing to the self-interest or prejudice of the individual voter. The steps in this process after 1775 need to be investigated with the same care that Lockridge and Cook have given to the earlier years, but it is likely that the Revolutionary generation, by declaring political home rule to be the guiding principle of government, inadvertently lost sight of the end that it had served: the maintenance of communal consensus.[47]

Freshly released from bonds of social community as well as of "feudal" lordship, the new democratic individualism harked back to yet a third old English model that had persisted more successfully in eighteenth-century America than in England itself—the yeoman freeholder, a figure most typical of the back-country settlements of Pennsylvania, the new Southwest, and northern New England. Increasingly he would be taken as the archetype of the American everywhere. Instead of peasant communities the new nation preferred to idealize the peasant himself or rather the yeoman of English folk memory: self-reliant, honest, and independent, the classic figure of eighteenth-century English "country" ideology that the American revolutionaries appropriated to describe themselves—and the backbone of Jeffersonian democracy, the common man of Jacksonian rhetoric. The immediate origins of the explicit doctrines both of social egalitarianism and political democracy that were articulated in the post-Revolutionary half century may reasonably be sought in the political revolution declared on the principle that all men are created equal.

IV

How decisive a turning point in the development of the American social structure the Revolution was can only be guessed. It summarily put an end to one archaic element of eighteenth-century society, the feudal revival, and inadvertently turned away from a no less ancient communalism while beginning to exalt a third traditional figure, the virtuous yeoman freeholder, into an ideal detached from its older, more organic social and civic context. Perhaps Alexander Hamilton, like certain English politicians and writers of the eighteenth century, perceived that that old-fashioned ideal was no longer sufficient to govern the modern world of commerce, banks, factories, and specialized professions, but to a growing majority of citizens of the new republic his ideas smacked of the parliamentary and royal "corruption" of civic virtue against which the Revolution had been declared.[48]

The Federalist party found itself in the awkward position of fostering what amounted to traditional "court" policies—a national debt, a bank, executive patronage, an army, an expanded judicial system—in a nation of "country" ideologues. By excluding hereditary orders the Constitution had consciously divorced its balance of governmental powers from any corresponding division of society into estates or orders. Yet somehow, Federalists believed, they had to combine revolutionary ideology with an organic and deferential social order. The new Constitution provided the necessary opportunity. Federalists could truly defend the document as more radical, more republican than the Articles of Confederation, if only because the new House, unlike the old Congress, was directly elected by the people. But since congressional constituencies would be much larger than existing electoral districts within the states, Federalists also expected the new system to return to office "the wise, the rich, and the good"—the sort of man who could count on being generally known throughout a wide geographical area. From this perspective the rise of a disciplined opposition party was socially quite significant because only systematic organization of the electorate could make other kinds of candidates available.[49]

While the national capital remained at Philadelphia, Federalists set a dizzying social pace characterized by splendid new houses, fashionable equipages, frequent balls, dinners, and parties—what Harrison Gray Otis called "the annual fatigue." Only through a conspicuous display of wealth, Federalists seemed to believe, could they legitimate the elite role they had assumed in the government of the republic. In effect the federal government tried to engraft itself upon the existing social order of America's leading city, and for a few years the experiment showed signs of endurance. Nothing of the kind was even conceivable once the government removed itself to the wilderness village of Washington, where under frugal Jeffersonian stewardship it rapidly became "a government out of sight and out of mind." There the divorce of government from distinct social orders, already announced in Revolutionary ideology, became a political reality. Republican virtue eliminated the threat that a Federalist government had posed for the new equality, but the cost was severe. The government found itself embarrassingly irrelevant to the social needs and concerns of America in general.[50]

Thus whatever chance the economic and demographic growth of the eighteenth century had offered for a complex but well-integrated social structure was cut off, not all at once, to be sure, but irreversibly nonetheless with the ultimate decline of the Federalist party and the later failure of the Whig program for governmental direction of an "American system." Economic growth continued in the nineteenth century, of course, but Americans found it excessively awkward to maintain a reasonable degree of harmony, stability, and equity among economic classes and other social groupings while thinking of themselves as so many self-reliant, unconstrained individuals on the yeoman-freeholder model.

To build a modern commercial and industrial economy on that archaic premise was to undermine such yeoman equality as had in fact persisted from colonial to nineteenth-century America. Recent studies leave little doubt that the eighteenth-century trend toward economic stratification continued almost unaffected by the new egalitarianism of 1775 to 1825. We know far more, indeed, about economic class than about any other social category, because of the almost exclusive preoccupation of social historians with it.[51] There has always been a close correlation between economic class and social status in America (though perhaps wealth translated less directly into social standing during the century between 1725 and 1825 than before or after), and the acquisition and distribution of wealth has usually seemed the central social question, though again rather more so since 1825 than before.

Historians have usually taken the question of socioeconomic class, or rather socioeconomic equality, to be central to the existence of political democracy. But they have too easily assumed that the egalitarianism of the oncoming "age of the common man" ought properly to have been based on a general increase of actual equality of wealth and social classlessness. Evidence that not a few ardent egalitarians were in fact rather uncommon men has been regarded as a paradox at best and at worst a blot on the democratic purity of the Jacksonian era. It may be, however, that social egalitarianism was a not very surprising reaction to the irresistible growth of economic and social inequality. The image of a golden age of republican equality, of a society of yeoman freeholders (abstracted from their place among the various interrelated classes of English social tradition and colonial reality), had its greatest appeal at a time when there was solid reason to feel things were going too far the other way.

Historians have only recently begun to make precise calculations of the distribution of wealth before and after the Revolution, and these at widely separated points in time. It seems likely that the long-accepted impression will stand: that, as the wealth of the country increased between 1725 and

1825, so did the extremes in its distribution between rich and poor. In the seaboard cities and in eastern rural districts the upper class of great merchants or landowners was growing much richer, and a lower class of tenant farmers and laborers was getting both poorer and more numerous.[52] The characteristically American middle class of independent farmers, tradesmen, and professional men, however, still outnumbered all the rest in most parts of the country. In newly settled districts close behind the frontier the availability of cheap land fostered a fairly equal division of property for a time, while at the other extreme certain of the oldest areas, where the customarily careless farming methods had worn down the soil, fell back into a lower level of general and individual poverty. In Virginia the whole cycle worked itself out from east to west during the eighteenth century, from the exhausted soil of the tidewater to the settled but still thriving fall-line and piedmont counties and the rapidly developing frontier of western Virginia and Kentucky.[53] Elsewhere too the "long-term tendency seems to have been toward greater inequality, with more marked class distinctions," reversed only temporarily, at certain points, by the economic vicissitudes of the Revolutionary years.[54] As the wealth of the country continued to increase—in the Middle Atlantic states the $213 per capita of 1774 almost doubled by 1850—the actual distribution of wealth grew more uneven wherever the frontier circumstances of the generation of settlement had been outgrown.[55]

By any objective measurement the class structure did not change radically. The growth of more tangible extremes of wealth and poverty in effect gave substance to the eighteenth-century belief in hierarchy that the nineteenth century no longer accepted. The personnel of the upper class of the commercial ports kept changing, most rapidly during and after the Revolution, but the rising merchant families of Boston, New York, or Philadelphia, and of smaller places like Newburyport, slipped quite credibly into the social status—and sometimes the very houses—of those who failed in business or suffered confiscation and exile for loyalty to the crown.[56] Although the redistribution of property that followed confiscation of certain loyalist estates in New York, Maryland, and elsewhere did put much of it in the hands of smaller landholders, the extent of change fell far short of social revolution.[57] The families of the colonial gentry, or the close counterparts who succeeded some of them, not only improved their relative advantage as an economic elite—investing in new western lands and the industries of the early factory age—but maintained their position as the de facto upper class of early nineteenth-century society.[58]

But they were progressively less accepted as a gentry by right. The precise stages whereby the old hierarchic ideal of the English colonists gave way to the new egalitarianism of the Jacksonian persuasion remain obscure, like so much else in the social history of the period. Historians have been more interested in the democratic political applications of egalitarianism than in its specifically social gestation. Although hierarchy was rejected and social equality taken to be the thoroughly modern ideal, the new egalitarianism made a conscious principle out of the widespread practical equality of condition that had prevailed among the small land-owners, independent artisans, and petty businessmen of the simpler age that was now, except in various recently settled frontier districts, being relegated to the past. In effect the archaic English "country" tradition of the virtuous yeoman freeholder was thereby sustained, although it was increasingly commingled with the broader leveling strain that much humbler kinds of Englishmen had voiced from time to time since John Ball in the fourteenth century questioned the authority of the gentle-man's pedigree. Such egalitarianism as had been most explicitly asserted in America down to the Declaration of Independence had had more to do with political parity among constituted governing bodies—of towns, counties, or provinces—than with the social equality of persons. But dur-ing the next half century the claim to the equal right to home rule was explicitly enlarged to include the democratic right of each citizen to social equality as well as to a voice in government.

American egalitarianism eventually assaulted every artificial barrier to equality, not so much to equality of material or social condition as to the individual's equal opportunity to establish superiority over his peers. Perhaps the reason that baseball was rapidly developed out of the archaic English village game of rounders, to become the national pastime of the new republic, was that more than any other sport it symbolized how Americans thought equality ought to work. Every player bats and fields as a conspicuous individual, thus reflecting equality of opportunity, and then his performance is measured to three decimal places in order to sort everybody out according to a precise hierarchy of achievement. As in the national economy, relatively slight statistical differences pay heavily dis-proportionate rewards.

In society at large the number of "artificial" impediments to equal competition was capable of infinite expansion, a possibility that endowed the doctrine of equality with its own powerful, inherent dynamic of reform. The Revolution rejected birth and legal privilege as proper criteria for setting some people apart from others. Later reformers could add education, family connections, wealth, race, and gender to the proscribed list, usually so that Americans could compete ever more furiously and, reformers believed, ever more fairly—for the joy of outdoing their neighbors. So long as government remained all but irrelevant to society and the economy, the pursuit of equality was frustrating and often self-defeating. Only with the reassertion of government in later generations could the doctrine assume a more consistent and effective reformist role.

For a people to think of their society in terms drawn from the objective conditions of a simpler but outdated age is neither unusual nor necessarily harmful. Inherited values shape present circumstances even while being reshaped by them. For Americans to find themselves confronting a new polarization between great wealth and widespread poverty would conceivably have been reason enough to articulate a contrary standard, even if they had never had occasion to hear the egalitarian phrases of the Declaration of Independence. Having declared their political liberty in egalitarian terms, however, they were too easily persuaded, when declaring for social equality, to do so in libertarian terms that made their efforts more symbolic than effectual. Partly because of their Revolutionary heritage Americans could not really face the possibility that their liberty— their freedom to compete—was undermining their equality.

Some notable reforms of the time raised this dilemma. Abolition of entail in Virginia, which J. Franklin Jameson—like Thomas Jefferson— thought a mortal blow to the old order, is now generally understood to have been little more than an egalitarian gesture, since entail had not been required to ensure the existence of great estates in a country where land was easily obtained and usually profitable. But if the abolition of entail had any practical effect in such a country, it was libertarian rather than truly egalitarian.[59] The freedom to seize the speculative opportunities of the market in land had been a main source of the greatest fortunes of colonial days; it was certainly worth more in the nineteenth century than the right to tie up particular tracts of land in perpetuity would have been. It is true that the freedom to speculate helped many ordinary farmers to

acquire a modest competence in one new district after another as settlement advanced across the continent. But after a new district had been
fully settled, liberty from legal restraints on landholding sooner or later
had the opposite effect of concentrating ownership in fewer hands. The
unwelcome growth of permanent tenancy and a fixed class of farm laborers in the midwestern regions of free soil and homesteads, as well as in
the South and East, challenged the egalitarian tradition as the nineteenth
century advanced.[60]

Other reforms of the post-Revolutionary half century also promised
to make men more equal, on the model of the yeoman freeholder, but
instead made them free to become unequal, and on a far grander scale
than was possible through land speculation. During the first half of the
nineteenth century governmental regulation of the economy, hitherto
accepted when required for the general welfare of the commonwealth,
was progressively abandoned, first in practice and finally in principle.
The new, liberal principle of laissez-faire was supposed to be egalitarian
as well; it may have been in some degree a reaction to the steady increase
of inequality among the economic classes of the time. Overt egalitarianism, which came to a head in the Anti-Masonic movement of the late
1820s and overnight made fervent democrats of such recent opponents of
universal suffrage as the gentlemen of the Albany Regency, was directed
in particular against the artificial privileges of state-chartered and state-
regulated monopolies. Yet for Andrew Jackson to strike down the regulatory power of the central Bank of the United States because it represented
aristocracy—personified as it was by an undoubted Philadelphia gentleman, Nicholas Biddle—was to open the way as time went on to far greater
and far less restrained concentrations of economic power. The transporta-
tion revolution, after an initial stage of public capitalization and control,
and the Industrial Revolution from its inception were allowed to proceed
as though an unregulated modern economy would distribute the wealth it
produced as satisfactorily as the simple agricultural and mercantile economy of the colonial past had done—or as parts of the contemporary but
old-fashioned West were still doing. Of course it did not. In the second
half of the nineteenth century the current egalitarian dogma, based upon
the increasingly archaic figure of the yeoman freeholder, helped produce
modern extremes of inequality far beyond anything attained by the pre-
Revolutionary feudal revival.

The sheer size of wealth and the extent of poverty in the latter part of the nineteenth century were not the most untoward results. Men spoke of the new conditions in terms borrowed from the rejected past—of industrial "barons" and a "new feudalism"—but the old feudal balance between baronial obligations and privileges was not easily restored to a dogmatically egalitarian society. The spirit of noblesse oblige persisted among the successors to the colonial merchant gentry, in Boston and Philadelphia if not New York or Chicago, but with diminishing practical force in economic and political affairs.[61] Landed gentlemen established themselves on the mid-western prairies somewhat as Lord Fairfax had done in the Northern Neck, but like the captains of industry they were considered to be only the most conspicuous exemplars of the material success to which the common man aspired, rather than a distinctive social class with special responsibilities to their inferiors.[62] The nineteenth-century elite was increasingly a mere plutocracy, insistent upon the absolute rights of property; the working classes reluctantly but inevitably had to acknowledge that in such a changed situation "capital" and "labor" no longer shared a common interest. In the twentieth century the chief effort of social reformers, seeking to come to grips with this problem, would be to level economic classes up or down to something like the relative equality of material condition of an age now long vanished, rather than to restore that age's forgotten ideal of an equitably related hierarchy among existing social classes.

The stratification of economic classes had been going on, however, since long before the American Revolution. Soon after that time, as the Revolutionary mixture of political egalitarianism and liberalism was extended to a doctrine of social equality, the further development of structural ties between social classes was cut off. In rejecting social hierarchy, as a relic of the feudal past, in favor of the equally archaic and far less recoverable practical equality of a simpler age, the reformers of later generations repeatedly condemned themselves to frustration.

v

The reinvigoration of certain old social institutions and the suppression of others during the Revolutionary era has other implications. Louis Hartz has tried to explain all of American history in terms of the absence of a feudal past. Lacking the old dialectic between feudalism and liberalism that made socialism possible in Europe, America is imprisoned in a liberal present that seems to allow no escape.[63] Hartz derived his perception from the nineteenth century, particularly the Jacksonian era.[64] For that period his emphasis is surely correct. As of 1825 America no longer had a feudal past because the Revolution had put social hierarchy on the road to obloquy and then to oblivion, just when it might have achieved significant dimensions. But he exaggerates his case by reading the phenomenon backward through the whole of American history.

The profundity of Revolutionary thought owed something to the growing relevance, up to that point, of social ideology to the social order and to the perception by 1790 of the limits of that relevance.[65] Conversely the victory of the Revolution over "feudal" hierarchy helps account for the banality of Jacksonian thought, when political and constitutional rhetoric (mostly borrowed from the Revolution itself) seldom bore any meaningful relation to social realities.

This painful gap between political loyalty and social reality became, perhaps, the central tension of the nineteenth century, and it helps to define and to limit the social significance of the American Revolution. Especially in its Jeffersonian variety the Revolution provided a "national" political framework in which very different societies, or remnants of societies, could pretend to share a common loyalty and common interests. So long as the government did nothing important the illusion could last, but whenever it pursued a vigorous policy the nation threatened to fall apart. Hamilton's program antagonized too many interests to endure. Jeffersonian foreign policy after 1807 drove New England to calculate the value of the Union. The Republican program of reconstruction in 1816 was totally dismantled within twenty years and produced a nullification crisis along the way. By loudly doing nothing the Jacksonians restored the Jeffersonian illusion of a harmonious nation, but Polk's active foreign policy destroyed the dream and began the final descent toward actual Civil War.

The Revolution created a national government, but not a national community. The imperatives by which that government survived may even have weakened the sense of community within each of its member societies without providing a convincing substitute. To an extent not easily measured disembodied Revolutionary rhetoric made hard problems difficult to define, much less resolve. Perhaps the ultimate impact of the Revolution was to divorce power from politics and politics from social reality. Not until after the Civil War and an irresolute "Reconstruction" were over would America begin to draw them all together again.

Notes

1. See Eric Hobsbawm, "From Social History to the History of Society," *Daedalus,* C (1971), 20–45.
2. J. Franklin Jameson, *The American Revolution Considered as a Social Movement* (Princeton, 1926); Frederick B. Tolles, "The American Revolution Considered as a Social Movement: A Re-Evaluation," *American Historical Review,* LX (1954–1955), 1–12.
3. Gordon S. Wood, "Rhetoric and Reality in the American Revolution," *William and Mary Quarterly,* 3d Ser., XXIII (1966), 29–30.
4. Philip J. Greven, Jr., *Four Generations: Population, Land, and Family in Colonial Andover, Massachusetts* (Ithaca, N.Y., 1970), 281–282.
5. Kenneth A. Lockridge, *A New England Town, The First Hundred Years: Dedham, Massachusetts, 1636–1736* (New York, 1970), 161–163, 179–180; Edward M. Cook, Jr., "Social Behavior and Changing Values in Dedham, Massachusetts, 1700 to 1775," *WMQ,* 3d Ser., XXVII (1970), 578.
6. Jack P. Greene, "Search for Identity: An Interpretation of the Meaning of Selected Patterns of Social Response in Eighteenth-Century America," *Journal of Social History,* III (1970), 218–220.
7. Wood, "Rhetoric and Reality," *WMQ,* 3d Ser., XXIII (1966), 31. Emphasis added.
8. Edmund S. Morgan, "The Puritan Ethic and the American Revolution," *WMQ,* 3d Ser., XXIV (1967), 8–18.
9. Bernard Bailyn, *The Ideological Origins of the American Revolution* (Cambridge, Mass., 1967); Gordon S. Wood, *The Creation of the American Republic, 1776–1787* (Chapel Hill, 1969); J. G. A. Pocock, "Machiavelli, Harrington, and English Political Ideologies in the Eighteenth Century," *WMQ,* 3d Ser., XXII (1965), 549–583; Pocock, "Virtue and Commerce in the Eighteenth Century," *Journal of Interdisciplinary History,* III (1972–1973), 119–134.
10. Thomas C. Barrow, "The American Revolution as a Colonial War for Independence," *WMQ,* 3d Ser., XXV (1968), 464. Barrow's attempt to link the Revolution to modern struggles for colonial independence has its own pitfall. No recent war for independence has involved colonies as closely tied to the mother country by culture, language, and direct descent as were the original thirteen states. The American Revolution was different and must be explained on different grounds, because it did *not* involve a major ethnic antagonism.

11. Rowland Berthoff, *An Unsettled People: Social Order and Disorder in American History* (New York, 1971), chap. 18.

12. E.g., Sidney H. Aronson, *Status and Kinship in the Higher Civil Service: Standards of Selection in the Administration of John Adams, Thomas Jefferson and Andrew Jackson* (Cambridge, Mass., 1964).

13. Frederick Jackson Turner, *The Frontier in American History* (New York, 1920), chap. 3.

14. Marvin Meyers, *The Jacksonian Persuasion: Politics and Belief* (Stanford, 1957).

15. Robert A. East, *Business Enterprise in the American Revolutionary Era* (New York, 1938), 323.

16. Jack P. Greene, *The Quest for Power: The Lower Houses of Assembly in the Southern Royal Colonies, 1689–1776* (Chapel Hill, 1963), 406–407; Bailyn, *Ideological Origins,* 279–280; Jackson Turner Main, *The Upper House in Revolutionary America, 1763–1788* (Madison, 1967), 18–20. For earlier attacks upon South Carolina's appointive council, see M. Eugene Sirmans, *Colonial South Carolina: A Political History, 1663–1763* (Chapel Hill, 1966), 261, 306.

17. The best example is the general levity with which virtually every history of the colonial period treats Lord Shaftesbury's Fundamental Constitutions of Carolina. For a similar attitude toward early Maryland, see Louis B. Hartz, *The Liberal Tradition in America* (New York, 1955), 64–66.

18. Cf. Sigmund Diamond, "An Experiment in 'Feudalism': French Canada in the Seventeenth Century," *WMQ,* 3d Ser., XVIII (1961), 3–34, with Richard C. Harris, *The Seigneurial System in Early Canada* (Madison, 1966), esp. 63–81.

19. The most recent account is Gary S. Horowitz, "New Jersey Land Riots, 1745–1755" (Ph.D. diss,, Ohio State University, 1966), esp. 39, 48.

20. Edward McCrady, *The History of South Carolina under the Proprietary Government, 1670–1719* (New York, 1897), 645–680; Sirmans, *Colonial South Carolina,* 103–128; Christopher C. Crittenden, "The Surrender of the Charter of Carolina," *North Carolina Historical Review,* I (1924), 383–402; William L. Saunders, ed., *The Colonial Records of North Carolina (1662–1776)* (Raleigh, 1886–1890), III, 32–47.

21. Stuart E. Brown, Jr., *Virginia Baron: The Story of Thomas 6th Lord Fairfax* (Perryville, Va., 1965), 39; Louis B. Wright, ed., *Letters of Robert Carter, 1720–1727: The Commercial Interests of a Virginia Gentleman* (San Marino, Calif., 1940), 69, 108.

22. On the Penn revenues, see Lawrence H. Gipson, *The British Empire before the American Revolution,* rev. ed. (Caldwell, Idaho, and New York, 1936–1969), III, 180. Lord Baltimore was willing to lease his right to quitrents for only £300 sterling per year as late as 1716, but by 1729 he knew that they were quite valuable. Cf. Newton D. Mereness, *Maryland as a Proprietary Province* (New York, 1901), 80, with Charles A. Barker, *The Background of the Revolution in Maryland* (New Haven, 1940), 130–134.

23. Robert Proud, *The History of Pennsylvania, in North America, from the Original Institution and Settlement of that Province* ... (Philadelphia, 1797–1798), II, 206–208; Barker, *Background of the Revolution in Maryland,* 134–144.

24. See G. F. R. Barker in *DNB* s.v. "Carteret, John, Earl Granville"; E. Merton Coulter, "The Granville District," *James Sprunt Historical Studies,* XIII (1913), 33–56.

25. Douglas S. Freeman, *George Washington, A Biography* (New York, 1948–1957), I, 501–510; Brown, *Virginia Baron,* 94–98.

26. Alfred Cobban, *The Social Interpretation of the French Revolution* (Cambridge, 1964), 25–53; George V. Taylor, "Types of Capitalism in Eighteenth-Century France," *English Historical Review,* LXXIX (1964), 478–497; Taylor, "The Paris Bourse on the Eve of the Revolution, 1781–1789," *AHR,* LXVII (1961–1962), 951–977; Taylor, "Non-Capitalist Wealth and the French Revolution," *ibid.,* LXXII (1966–1967), 469–496; Elizabeth L. Eisenstein, "Who Intervened in 1788? A Commentary on *The Coming of the French Revolution,*" *ibid.,* LXXI (1965–1966), 77–103. See also the acrimonious discussion of the problem in Jeffrey Kaplow, Gilbert Shapiro, and Elizabeth L. Eisenstein, "Class in the French Revolution," *ibid.,* LXXII (1966–1967), 497–522. Two excellent discussions of the feudal revival, both broader in scope than the seigneurial reaction and old-regime France, are Penfield Roberts, *The Quest for Security, 1715–1740* (New York, 1947), chap. 3; and R. R. Palmer, *The Age of the Democratic Revolution: A Political History of Europe and America, 1760–1800* (Princeton, 1959–1964), I, chaps. 1–3. Alexis de Tocqueville's observations of a century ago are also quite pertinent. He argued that feudalism had become intolerable in France precisely because it was no longer feudal. Lordship had almost completely disappeared, while feudal relationships in general had been converted to fiscal obligations and advantages that did not correspond at all to the social division between noble and bourgeois. The system was hated because it was mercenary and because of the dependency it symbolized. *The Old Regime and the French Revolution,* trans. Stuart Gilbert (New York, 1955), 22–23. After 50 years of attempts to interpret the French Revolution in terms of a clash between a feudal and a capitalistic order, many historians are now moving quite decisively back toward Tocqueville.

27. Only about 400 English landed families had annual incomes exceeding £4,000 in 1760; a few were as great as the £30,000 to £40,000 of the dukes of Newcastle and Bedford, but the average was around £6,000. By then Lord Baltimore's income from Maryland surpassed £30,000 a year, which was equal to an 18% duty on the exports of the colony. By the 1770s the Penns had probably caught up with the Calverts. Averaging about £10,000 sterling a year in land sales, they increased the quitrents from about £500 in 1732 to over £10,000 by 1774, besides £6,000 from various royalties and a sizable amount from rents on their 80 manors, which contained about 600,000

acres. The Granville District, despite poor management, returned about
£5,000 in quitrents alone by the 1760s.

These English levels of wealth in 1760 have been calculated at two-thirds
of the 1790 levels discussed in G. E. Mingay, *English Landed Society in
the Eighteenth Century* (London, 1963), chaps. 1–2, esp. 10, 20–21, 23. For
Newcastle's fortune, see *ibid.,* 78. For Bedford's, which was about the same
as Baltimore's, see Gladys Scott Thomson, *The Russells in Bloomsbury, 1669–
1771* (London, 1940), 301. On Baltimore's revenues, see Barker, *Background
of the Revolution in Maryland,* 142–144, and his "The Revolutionary
Impulse in Maryland," *Maryland Historical Magazine,* XXXVI (1941),
135. Data on the Penns have been compiled from William R. Shepherd,
History of Proprietary Government in Pennsylvania (New York, 1896), 88,
and from William H. Kain, "The Penn Manorial System and the Manors
of Springetsbury and Maske," *Pennsylvania History,* X (1943), 240. For the
revenue of the Granville District, see Saunders, ed., *N. C. Col. Rec.,* IX,
49, 261, 262. For the sake of useful comparison, all of the above statistics
have been reduced to sterling. In addition, they reveal gross rather than
net income. In England, the net return on land was usually two-thirds to
three-fourths the gross earnings, but for political families it was less. Mingay,
Landed Society, 52–54. Lord Baltimore undoubtedly had the highest
overhead among the great proprietors, and his net income was 35 to 40% of
his gross, or about £13,000 per year, which was still well within the upper
level of England's wealthiest 400 families.

28. James H. Hutson, "Benjamin Franklin and Pennsylvania Politics, 1751–1755:
A Reappraisal," *Pennsylvania Magazine of History and Biography,* XCIII (1969),
303–371; and his "The Campaign to Make Pennsylvania a Royal Province,
1764–1770," *ibid.,* XCIV (1970), 427–463, and XCV (1971), 28–49.

29. More study of both the proprietary and antiproprietary movements
in Maryland is needed, but see Barker, *Background of the Revolution in
Maryland;* Aubrey C. Land, *The Dulanys of Maryland: A Biographical Study
of Daniel Dulany, the Elder (1685–1753), and Daniel Dulany, the Younger
(1722–1797)* (Baltimore, 1955); Bernard C. Steiner, *Life and Administration
of Sir Robert Eden* (Baltimore, 1898); and David C. Skaggs, "Maryland's
Impulse Toward Social Revolution, 1750–1776," *Journal of American History,*
LIV (1967–1968), 771–786.

30. Saunders, ed., *N. C. Col. Rec.,* VII, 513–514, VIII, 524, IX, 262, 358–359.
William K. Boyd, ed., *Some Eighteenth Century Tracts concerning North
Carolina* (Raleigh, 1927), 308–312. See also, Marvin L. Michael Kay,
"Provincial Taxes in North Carolina during the Administrations of Dobbs
and Tryon," *North Carolina Historical Review,* XLII (1965), 440–453; his
"The Payment of Provincial and Local Taxes in North Carolina, 1748–1771,"
WMQ, 3d Ser., XXVI (1969), 218–240; and his "An Analysis of a British
Colony in Late Eighteenth Century America in the Light of Current
American Historiographical Controversy," *Australian Journal of Politics and*

History, II (1965), 170–184. This last piece uses the Regulator controversy to challenge the Hartz thesis about the liberal tradition in America.

31. H. R. McIlwaine, ed., *Journals of the House of Burgesses of Virginia, 1727–1734, 1736–1740* (Richmond, 1910), 82, 83, 92–96, 125, 155; Brown, *Virginia Baron,* 155, 160, *passim*; Willard F. Bliss, "The Rise of Tenancy in Virginia," *Virginia Magazine of History and. Biography,* LVIII (1950), 427–441; Louis Morton, *Robert Carter of Nomini Hall: A Virginia Tobacco Planter of the Eighteenth Century,* 2d ed. (Williamsburg, Va., 1945), 78.

32. Main, *Upper House,* 55; Beatrice G. Reubens, "Preemptive Rights in the Disposition of a Confiscated Estate: Philipsburgh Manor, New York," *WMQ,* 3d Ser., XXII (1965), 440. Because Cortlandt Manor was divided among ten joint proprietors, the income available to any one of them was never very large. Rents apparently varied from about £30 to something over £100 a year, but they did tend to rise over time and leases tended to be made shorter. Sung Bok Kim, "The Manor of Cortlandt and Its Tenants, 1697–1783" (Ph.D. diss., Michigan State University, 1966), 91–92, 120–124, 128–133, 140, 144, *passim.* Iron, a source of income overlooked by Kim, may have been as important as rents. See *New-York Weekly Journal,* Apr. 2, 1744; *New-York Weekly Post-Boy,* June 17, 1745.

33. Mingay, *Landed Society,* 23, again allowing a reduction by one-third to reach the level of 1760; Robert Forster, *The Nobility of Toulouse in the Eighteenth Century: A Social and Economic Study* (Baltimore, 1960), 178–188. French *livres* converted into pounds sterling at a ratio of about 23:1 on the eve of the French Revolution. Arthur Young, *Travels in France during the Years 1787, 1788, and 1789,* ed. Constantia Maxwell (Cambridge, 1929), 405.

34. Oscar Handlin, "The Eastern Frontier of New York," *New York History,* XVIII (1936), 50–75; Irving Mark, *Agrarian Conflicts in Colonial New York, 1711–1775* (New York, 1940).

35. Sung Bok Kim, "A New Look at the Great Landlords of Eighteenth-Century New York," *WMQ,* 3d Ser., XXVII (1970), 581–614; David M. Ellis, *Landlords and Farmers in the Hudson-Mohawk Region, 1790–1850* (Ithaca, N.Y., 1946), esp. 225–312.

36. Barker, *Background of the Revolution in Maryland,* esp. 267–274; Donnell M. Owings. *His Lordship's Patronage: Offices of Profit in Colonial Maryland* (Baltimore, 1953).

37. G. B. Warden, "The Proprietary Group in Pennsylvania, 1754–1764," *WMQ,* 3d Ser., XXI (1964), 367–389.

38. Edgar J. Fisher, *New Jersey as a Royal Province, 1738–1776* (New York, 1911), 58–71.

39. Chilton Williamson, *American Suffrage from Property to Democracy, 1760–1860* (Princeton, 1960), 230, 234.

40. Brown, *Virginia Baron,* 176–191; William Waller Hening, ed., *The Statutes at Large; Being a Collection of All the Laws of Virginia, from the First Session of the Legislature, in the Year 1619* (Richmond and Philadelphia, 1823), XI,

128–129; James T. Mitchell and Henry Flanders, eds., *The Statutes at Large of Pennsylvania from 1682 to 1801* (Harrisburg, 1896–1908), X, 33–39.

41. For an excellent summary of recent research on confiscations in New York, see Alfred F. Young, *The Democratic Republicans of New York: The Origins, 1763–1797* (Chapel Hill, 1967), 62–66.

42. John E. Pomfret, *The New Jersey Proprietors and Their Lands* (Princeton, 1964), 107–120.

43. Horowitz, "New Jersey Land Riots," *passim.* On the ethnic base of the New York riots, see Handlin, "The Eastern Frontier of New York," 58, 73. Roy H. Akagi, *The Town Proprietors of the New England Colonies: A Study of Their Development, Organization, Activities, and Controversies, 1620–1770* (Philadelphia, 1924), chap. 8, is still extremely helpful, especially for comparing New England with other areas in terms of the uses to which ancient patents were put. See also Otis G. Hammond, "The Mason Title and Its Relation to New Hampshire and Massachusetts," American Antiquarian Society, *Proceedings*, N.S., XXVI (1916), 245–263.

44. Michael Zuckerman, "The Social Context of Democracy in Massachusetts," *WMQ,* 3d Ser., XXV (1968), 523–544.

45. Lockridge, *New England Town,* 18–22; Warren O. Ault, "Open-Field Husbandry and the Village Community: A Study of Agrarian By-Laws in Medieval England," American Philosophical Society, *Transactions,* N.S., LV, Pt. 7 (1965), 41.

46. Thomas Jefferson, *A Summary View of the Rights of British America . . .* (Williamsburg, Va., 1774); Merrill Peterson, *Thomas Jefferson and the New Nation: A Biography* (New York, 1970), 71.

47. Lockridge, "Land, Population and the Evolution of New England Society, 1630–1790," *Past and Present,* No. 39 (Apr. 1968), 62–80; Cook, "Social Behavior and Changing Values in Dedham," *WMQ,* 3d Ser XXVII (1970), 546–580.

48. See Isaac Kramnick, *Bolingbroke and His Circle: The Politics of Nostalgia in the Age of Walpole* (Cambridge, Mass., 1968); Gerald Stourzh, *Alexander Hamilton and the Idea of Republican Government* (Stanford, 1970); and Pocock, "Virtue and Commerce," *Jour. Interdis. Hist.,* III (1972–1973), 119–134. Lance G. Banning, "The Quarrel with Federalism: A Study in the Origins and Character of Republican Thought" (Ph.D. diss., Washington University, 1972), traces the impact of country ideology upon the Jeffersonian Republicans in the 1790s.

49. Wood, *Creation of the American Republic,* 471–564; Banning, "Quarrel with Federalism," esp. chap. 5.

50. Cf. Wood, *Creation of the American Republic,* 475–483, 593–615; Ethel E. Rasmusson, "Democratic Environment-Aristocratic Aspiration," *Pennsylvania Magazine of History and Biography,* XC (1966), 155–182; and James Sterling Young, *The Washington Community, 1800–1828* (New York, 1966).

51. E.g., Jackson Turner Main, *The Social Structure of Revolutionary America* (Princeton, 1965), esp. 4–6.

52. E.g., James A. Henretta, "Economic Development and Social Structure in Colonial Boston," *WMQ*, 3d Ser., XXII (1965), 75–92.

53. Jackson Turner Main, "The Distribution of Property in Post-Revolutionary Virginia," *Mississippi Valley Historical Review*, XLI (1954), 241–258.

54. Main, *Social Structure of Revolutionary America*, 286.

55. Alice Hanson Jones, "Wealth Estimates for the American Middle Colonies, 1774," *Economic Development and Cultural Change*, XVIII, No. 4, pt. 2 (1970), 128.

56. East, *Business Enterprise in the American Revolutionary Era*, 222–237; Benjamin W. Labaree, *Patriots and Partisans: The Merchants of Newburyport, 1764–1815* (Cambridge, Mass., 1962), chaps. 4–5.

57. Young, *Democratic Republicans of New York*, 62–66; Philip A. Crowl, *Maryland During and After the Revolution: A Political and Economic Study* (Baltimore, 1943), 54; Richard D. Brown, "The Confiscation and Disposition of Loyalists' Estates in Suffolk County, Massachusetts," *WMQ*, 3d Ser., XXI (1964), 549.

58. Stow Persons, "The Origins of the Gentry," in Robert H. Bremner, ed., *Essays on History and Literature* (Columbus, Ohio, 1966), 83–119.

59. C. Ray Keim, "Primogeniture and Entail in Colonial Virginia," *WMQ*, 3d Ser., XXV (1968), 585–586. It may be, however, that as wealth became more concentrated after the 1780s, entail would have been more useful had the law still allowed it. Even before that time its position is still uncertain. To count the number and percentage of wills creating entails, as Keim has done, is insufficient. Because descent by fee tail was automatic, such an estate would not appear in a will after the first-generation testament that created it. Since entails were cumulative, the counting of wills cannot determine the proportion of estates held in fee tail as against fee simple at any given moment. Certainly for the tidewater, where most entails were located, the system grew in importance between 1705 and the Revolution. Entailed estates were in general the larger ones; the quantity of land so held was greater than indicated by the mere number of entails. We lack comparable English data from which to estimate Virginia's approximation to or deviation from the norm of the mother country. For other colonies the question has never been seriously studied.

60. To some extent 19th-century law had to recognize the practical necessity of certain kinds of concentration of wealth that the Revolutionary generation had rejected. Outside New England colonial law had imposed primogeniture in cases of intestacy, but this provision apparently had little impact because most estates of any size were bequeathed by will. For this reason most scholars now regard its abolition as more symbolic than substantive, despite the explicit egalitarian intent of the reform. By contrast, colonial Massachusetts had permitted primogeniture only through direct

testimentary action. The law required partible inheritance, with a double share to the eldest son, in all intestacy cases. But repeated subdivision of the land had proceeded so far by the end of the 18th century that the courts began to impose primogeniture even on intestate estates. All of the land was awarded to the eldest son, who was required to settle cash on his brothers and sisters. "Massachusetts estates are very rarely divided," Tocqueville observed in the 1830s; "the eldest son generally takes the land, and the others go to seek their fortune in the wilderness." Alexis de Tocqueville, *Democracy in America,* ed. Phillips Bradley (New York, 1945), I, 293.

61. Paul Goodman, "Ethics and Enterprise: The Values of a Boston Elite, 1800–1860," *American Quarterly,* XVIII (1966), 437–451.

62. Paul Wallace Gates, *Frontier Landlords and Pioneer Tenants* (Ithaca, N.Y., 1945).

63. Hartz, *The Liberal Tradition in America*, and his *The Founding of New Societies: Studies in the History of the United States, Latin America, and South Africa, Canada, and Australia* (New York, 1964), 1–122. Cf. the symposium on the Hartz thesis by Hartz, Harry Jaffa, Leonard Krieger, and Marvin Meyers in *Comparative Studies in Society and History, V* (1962–1963), 261–284, 365–377, and the comments by Sydney James, "Colonial Rhode Island and the Beginnings of the Liberal Rationalized State," in Melvin Richter, ed., *Essays in Theory and History: An Approach to the Social Sciences* (Cambridge, Mass., 1970), 167–168.

64. Cf. Louis B. Hartz, *Economic Policy and Democratic Thought: Pennsylvania, 1776–1860* (Cambridge, Mass., 1948).

65. Wood, *Creation of the American Republic,* esp. 383–390, 475–499, 593–615.

5

1776: The Countercyclical Revolution

"I SHALL BURN all my Greek and Latin books," exclaimed the jubilant Horace Walpole in 1762 when he heard of the capture of Martinique; "they are histories of little people. The Romans never conquered the world, till they had conquered three parts of it, and were three hundred years about it; we subdue the globe in three campaigns; and a globe, let me tell you, as big again as it was in their days."[1] In five years beginning in 1758, the British Empire crushed New France, took Guadeloupe and Martinique from France, nearly drove the French out of India, brutally punished the Cherokees for entering the North American war in 1760, and when Spain finally intervened in the struggle in 1762, conquered Havana and Manila before the Peace of Paris ended the fighting in 1763.[2] Nothing in the history of the British people prepared them for so awesome a triumph. And yet, just twelve years later, British soldiers clashed with Massachusetts militia at Lexington and began another world war. Both France and Spain intervened, and by 1783 Britain had to concede the independence of the United States of America.

The irony was overwhelming. It still is. To many contemporaries, including both the duc de Choiseul and the comte de Vergennes (that is, the French foreign minister who negotiated the peace treaty and his successor who gave America the French alliance in 1778), Britain's spectacular triumph over its imperial rivals by 1763 all but guaranteed the revolt of the mainland colonies in the years that followed. With no French or Spanish enemy nearby to threaten them, the colonists would discover,

Originally published in *Revolutionary Currents: Nation Building in the Transatlantic World*, ed. Michael A. Morrison and Melinda S. Zook (Lanham, MD: Rowman and Littlefield, 2004).

both men predicted, that they no longer needed British protection and would soon throw off British rule.[3]

Choiseul and Vergennes saw the Canada cession as a master stroke of French policy. Many loyalists and historians have agreed with them. Had Canada remained French, lamented Governor Thomas Hutchinson of Massachusetts in 1773, "none of the spirit of opposition to the Mother Country would have yet appeared & I think the effects of [the Canada cession] worse than all we had to fear from the French or Indians."[4]

Yet the argument does not hold up under analysis. The mainland colonies remained vulnerable to assault from the sea, and only Britain could give them naval protection. Although the French army had left Canada, the *habitants* remained behind, and the colonists still feared them. Parliament's Quebec Act of 1774 terrified patriots in the British colonies because they understood its potential. It marked a serious effort to placate the French settlers on their own terms on the eve of conflict between Britain and the thirteen colonies. The First Continental Congress denounced the Quebec Act for encouraging the French settlers "to act with hostility against the free Protestant colonies, whenever a wicked ministry shall chuse so to direct them." Once the fighting began, the Second Continental Congress, fearing that the governor of Quebec "is instigating the people of that province and the Indians to fall upon us," launched its own preemptive invasion of Canada in 1775. The patriots escalated their resistance into armed conflict with Britain not because the Gallic Peril had disappeared but despite their recognition that it had revived.[5]

Britain was unable to convert its gigantic triumph over its imperial rivals into a successful postwar policy for North America. That failure is still, after more than two centuries, the enigma at the core of the American Revolution. Unless we can account for it, we still cannot explain why the Revolution happened at all. In my judgment, the scholarship of the past two or three decades, as wonderful and imaginative as much of it has been, has only deepened this central problem. Old explanations, such as the Canada cession and the rise of a sense of American national identity within the British Empire, have collapsed.[6] Other studies have been giving us an empire that was becoming much more tightly integrated in the three or four decades before independence. We can see similar patterns whether we look at transatlantic migration, the late imperial economy,

the rise of evangelical religion, colonial political culture, or the willingness of colonists to embrace a larger British and imperial identity.

The achievement of American independence was a countercyclical
event. It ran against the prevailing integrative tendencies of the century.
The American Revolution was a crisis of imperial *integration* that the
British state could not handle.

I

Beginning around 1730, when the population of the mainland colonies was only about 630,000 settlers and enslaved Africans, transatlantic migration soared to peaks that, in absolute numbers, had never been
achieved before. This volume was probably a higher percentage of the
existing settler population than any colony had known since its founding
generation. About 248,000 enslaved Africans and 284,000 Europeans
landed in the thirteen colonies between 1730 and 1775. When the fighting began in 1775, about 10 percent of the residents had arrived in North
America since 1760. The British Empire had become a remarkably efficient redistributor of people who took advantage of the demand for
labor or the availability of land thousands of miles away. Land in North
Carolina, Pennsylvania, New York, or even Nova Scotia could start thousands of people moving across the ocean on quite short notice—close to
10,000 a year by the early 1770s.

But if transatlantic migration was binding ever more people together
ever more tightly, the whole process could seem like a disaster to some
of those left behind, particularly Irish or Scottish landlords who faced a
serious risk of losing most of their tenants and their rental income. Wills
Hill, Earl of Hillsborough, owned 100,000 acres of land on his Irish
estates and faced constant pressure from emigration. As president of the
Board of Trade, he supported the Proclamation of 1763, which created at
least a temporary barrier to the settlement of most western lands in North
America. He became the first secretary of state for the American colonies
in 1768 and again used all his influence to prevent the creation of new
colonies in the West. When speculators won over even the king to their
Vandalia project, he resigned in frustration in 1772. But the British government did adopt one of his major ideas. It began interviewing emigrants

as a way of gauging the seriousness of the problem and, perhaps, as a prelude to a statutory limitation of emigration from the British Isles.[7]

Similar patterns characterized the late imperial economy. It became much more dynamic and efficient after 1730 or 1740, to the great benefit of most colonial consumers and to the pain of some merchants who found that increased competition could seriously reduce their profit margins. The colonial population doubled about every twenty-five years, which meant an automatic increase in demand for British products. But British imports increased even more rapidly than population in the last three to five decades (depending on the colony) before independence and contributed immensely to the growing refinement of life in the half century before independence. And because growing European demand kept the prices of American exports high, while the prices of imports from Britain were falling, partly in response to the first phase of the industrial revolution, the settlers were, in short, getting more for their money. As Glasgow absorbed an ever larger share of the tobacco trade, Scotland also achieved a level of prosperity it had never known before. To a significant degree, Chesapeake tobacco provided the material base for the Scottish Enlightenment, the most exciting intellectual movement of the era.[8]

II

The Great Awakening and internal colonial politics, for very different reasons, have often been invoked to explain why the Revolution happened. On the surface, both seem to provide compelling arguments. Nearly all evangelicals in the thirteen colonies supported the Revolution. Nearly all loyalists, except in Nova Scotia, rejected revivalism. Similarly, the resistance movement after 1764 had strong support within colonial assemblies. It began by affirming the principle of "no taxation without representation," which expanded to "no legislation without consent" by 1774, both of which were strong affirmations of each colony's right to self-government through its elective assembly.

Yet the Great Awakening never pitted North American churches against their British counterparts across the Atlantic. Nothing comparable to the antebellum split of evangelical churches along sectional lines occurred within the British Empire before the Revolution. Instead, the revivals divided communities within themselves and sent both factions looking for allies in other colonies and across the ocean. Beginning with George Whitefield's spectacular tour of the colonies in 1739–1740, the Awakening brought distant peoples into contact with one another who otherwise might never have heard of each other. The College of New Jersey—a Presbyterian institution and the first colonial college founded specifically to propagate vital piety—paid its own homage to the geographical extent of the revivals by taking its first president from Long Island, its second from New Jersey, its third (Jonathan Edwards) from Congregational Massachusetts, its fourth from Virginia, its fifth from Maryland, and its sixth from Scotland. And even though evangelicals gave overwhelming support to the Revolution, antievangelicals were by no means a loyalist phalanx. They can be found all along the political spectrum of the era from Thomas Paine and Thomas Jefferson on the left, to George Washington and James Madison in the center, and to Joseph Galloway and Thomas Hutchinson on the right. Except in Connecticut and New Jersey, evangelicals seldom achieved positions of political leadership. Antirevivalists directed events on both sides of the revolutionary divide.[9]

Underlying trends in colonial public life show similar patterns and ambiguities. In seventeenth-century Virginia, the orthodox colonies of New England, and the Dutch areas of New York, jury trials for noncapital crimes were rare before the Glorious Revolution. Only in the eighteenth century did the colonies fully embrace the jury ideology that had taken shape in England under the later Stuarts, ably described by Lois G. Schwoerer in this volume.[10] In histories of colonial politics, the most misleading assumption has been that of a teeter-totter. If the assembly was rising, royal government must have been declining. Beyond any doubt the assemblies played an increasing role in provincial life throughout the century. They sat longer, passed more laws, and drew on a more elite segment of the population for their membership. But royal government also became measurably stronger in the middle decades of the century. In every colony except New York, the most effective royal governors served sometime between 1720 and the 1760s. In Virginia, South Carolina, and Georgia, they succeeded through a highly ritualized form of persuasion and flattery that the assembly reciprocated. The Virginia House of Burgesses had only one public quarrel with a royal governor in the forty-five years between 1720 and the Stamp Act of 1765. In New Hampshire,

Massachusetts, New York, and New Jersey, successful governors used patronage and influence to build majorities in the assembly. And even though all the assemblies helped organize resistance to the Stamp Act and the Townshend Acts, many of them stopped well short of revolution after Parliament passed the Coercive Acts in 1774. In the five colonies from New York through Maryland, no legal assembly ever repudiated the Crown. All of them had to be pushed aside by popularly elected provincial congresses. When the Revolution finally came, much of its thrust was directed at the assemblies, not through them.[11]

Even the language of revolution was a fairly recent British import. Seventeenth-century colonists spoke of their "liberties," not of "rights," much less "natural rights," a phrase that John Locke finally turned into a commonplace expression. The language of natural rights took hold quite late in North America, only during the adult years of the resistance leaders of the 1760s. In the colonies it mixed, sometimes uneasily, with that other heritage from the English Commonwealth tradition, the conviction that public life presents an eternal struggle between power and liberty, that power nearly always wins over time, and that corruption is its most effective weapon. For Bernard Bailyn, this "Country" ideology has become the necessary and sufficient explanation for the Revolution. In the colonies, he argues, formal royal prerogatives were stronger than in Britain, where the Crown, for example, no longer vetoed bills or dismissed judges. But the governors' informal powers, especially their patronage, were never sufficient to manage the assemblies as effectively as Sir Robert Walpole controlled Parliament. This gap between formal and informal constitutions was filled by angry factions who denounced the corruption of royal officials. As early as the 1730s, Bailyn believes, the colonists were primed for revolution. Parliament had only to provide the stimulus to set the process in motion.[12]

The Declaration of Independence did unite the language of natural rights with a formal indictment of George III for a systematic conspiracy to undermine liberty in the colonies, mostly through corruption. Without this pervasive fear, the Revolution of 1776 would not have happened. But for most of the provincial era, the languages of politics had functioned quite differently. Natural rights and English rights were interchangeable terms until the early or mid-1770s. The colonists believed that the English constitution embodied their natural rights.[13]

When the language of corruption was invoked, it often reflected a governor's strength, not, as Bailyn's argument assumes, his weakness. In northern colonies those who attacked corruption were opposition leaders unable to win majority support in the legislature, such as Lewis Morris during the John Peter Zenger affair in New York in the 1730s or the Boston opposition to Governor William Shirley in the late 1740s. In other words, this language replicated its role in British politics in the age of Sir Robert Walpole, who dominated the government between 1721 and 1742. In southern colonies, this "Country" paradigm was not even oppositional after the 1720s. Rather, both governors and planters believed that their colonies had achieved an ideal constitutional balance, and they used the tension between power and liberty to celebrate their own accomplishment, a government without corruption that achieved its goals through mutual trust and cooperation. Maryland's governor, by contrast, had more patronage than any other colonial executive. It never gave him the political effectiveness or stability that Virginia, South Carolina, and Georgia achieved through their stylized politics of harmony.[14]

The Seven Years' War, or what Lawrence Henry Gipson called the Great War for the Empire, brought these integrative tendencies to a culmination. After Britain's very rocky start through 1757, William Pitt took charge of the war effort, sustained about 30,000 redcoats in America, and raised about 20,000 provincial troops for each campaign from 1758 until the fall of Montreal in 1760. The mainland colonies then raised thousands more for the West Indian campaigns of 1761 and 1762. So massive and successful was this overall effort that both Old Lights and New Lights discovered millennial significance in the global triumph of British liberty. The Presbyterian Church, rent by a schism over the revivals in 1741, healed the breach at the height of the war in 1758. When George III succeeded his grandfather as king in 1760, his North American subjects responded warmly to his call for the restoration of virtue and piety to public life. Throughout North America, the colonists gloried in their British identity.[15]

III

We are back where we started. The British Empire by 1763 achieved a level of integration it had never known before, and the result was equally unprecedented—total victory over New France. Yet even though the colonies had been anglicizing their societies for decades, important differences remained between them and the mother country. The most significant involved the household. The English practice of primogeniture had never taken deep hold in America. The head of the household expected to pass his own status down to all his sons and to enable all his daughters to marry men of comparable standing in the community. This pattern dated back to the reforms of the London Company, which made landholding a reasonable ambition for most Virginia settlers after 1618, and Plymouth also made land available to male settlers from the 1620s. Compared with Britain, North America had been a paradise for younger sons for a century and a half. But after about 1750, many households, even if they added a craft to their main occupation of farming, had difficulty sustaining this level of opportunity. Some fathers responded by privileging sons over daughters and older sons over younger ones. In Virginia most tidewater land had been entailed by the 1760s—that is, the owner could not divide the estate for sale in separate parcels or bequeath it to more than one heir, although he could set up other sons on land somewhere else. At this level the basic anglicizing tendencies of the century had to seem like a foreclosure of opportunity to many settlers.[16]

Ceaseless expansion became the American answer to this dilemma, and Indians paid the heaviest price for the ambitions of ordinary settlers. And yet the demand for expansion does not get us very far in trying to explain the onset of the revolution against Britain. The British did slow the process, more for speculators than for actual settlers, and the eagerness of settlers (or squatters) to move west probably helped radicalize great planters who began to despair of the Crown's willingness to grant titles to lands that they claimed. But after Hillsborough's resignation as American secretary in 1772, the British government was also moving toward the settlement of the Ohio valley. The Revolution erupted because of confrontations along the eastern seaboard, not in the West, although tensions there also contributed to the alienation of affection that fatally undermined British authority.[17]

We are left with the oldest tool available to historians for explaining anything: narrative. We have to tell the story of the three imperial crises that undermined the British Empire despite all the advantages it had won by 1763. The Stamp Act Crisis of 1764–1766 began when George Grenville, the prime minister, tried to address the empire's needs for defense and revenue. In the process he polarized the very real needs of the empire with the traditional rights of the colonists, especially the right to be taxed only through the consent of their assemblies. After Grenville rejected the relevance of this argument, colonial mobs nullified the Stamp Act by compelling the stamp distributors in each colony to resign.

The colonists blamed Grenville's ministry, not Parliament or the Crown, for the crisis, and they rejoiced heartily when George III replaced Grenville with the new ministry of the Marquess of Rockingham in the summer of 1765. Rockingham decided that repeal was the only alternative to a civil war in North America, but he needed a better argument than colonial riots to build a parliamentary majority for repeal. Even before news of colonial nonimportation agreements reached London, he encouraged British merchants and manufacturers to petition for repeal on the grounds that the Grenville program had deranged their trade. This argument then persuaded the colonists that their own nonimportation agreements had been decisive in converting the ministry to repeal, a misconception that would again make nonimportation central to resistance to Britain from 1768 to 1775 as well as from 1806 to 1812. Apparently no one stopped to reflect that the Stamp Act itself, once stamps became unavailable, imposed nonexportation on the colonies for several months. Merchants refused to send ships to sea lest they be confiscated for lack of stamped clearance papers after they reached their destinations. The crisis ended when Parliament repealed the Stamp Act, which had levied taxes on legal documents, pamphlets, and newspapers; but Parliament only amended the Sugar Act of 1764 by lowering the duty on imported molasses from three pence to one penny per gallon while extending the tax to British West Indian as well as foreign molasses. That duty, disguised in the statute's preamble as a regulation of trade, brought in more than £30,000 per year until Lexington.[18]

The colonists believed that they had vindicated their rights as Englishmen. But the resolution of the crisis revealed another gap, this one structural, that hardly anyone but Benjamin Franklin understood. In the debate over the Stamp Act, both sides had rejected the distinction between "internal" taxes, such as excises on the consumption of goods or stamp duties on legal documents, and "external" taxes, or port duties imposed on oceanic commerce. Grenville never doubted that Parliament could lay duties on colonial trade, something that it had been doing since 1673, and he argued that if it possessed that power, it could impose internal taxes as well. Colonial spokesmen denied that Parliament could impose any duties for revenue, either internal or external, but they acknowledged that Parliament could levy port duties for the regulation of trade. Most colonial spokesmen did concede the *power* of Parliament to do all three, but they insisted that Parliament's exercise of the power to tax would deprive them of their rights as Englishmen. The Sons of Liberty, by taking to the streets and nullifying the Stamp Act before it could go into effect, demonstrated—violently but effectively—that whatever Parliament's claim of right, it lacked the power to collect an internal tax. As the Revenue Act of 1766 also demonstrated, it certainly did have that power over American trade, whether or not the colonists conceded the right. Significantly, hardly anybody objected strenuously to the penny duty on molasses. Most merchants saw it as an opportunity to do within the law what they had been doing through smuggling ever since the Molasses Act of 1733.

In short, the Stamp Act crisis was debated along an ideological axis of legislation (the regulation of trade, a power that was conceded to Parliament) versus taxation (which was denied). But the crisis was resolved along the internal-external axis, which both sides claimed was meaningless (see figure 5.1). The Stamp Act was repudiated, but the duty on molasses became more lucrative than ever. Only Benjamin Franklin grasped how the empire had actually been working for the previous century. As he told the House of Commons in 1766, "[T]he sea is yours; you maintain, by your fleets, the safety of navigation in it, and keep it clear of pirates; you may have therefore a natural and equitable right to some toll or duty on merchandizes carried through that part of your dominions, towards defraying the expence you are at in ships to maintain the safety of that carriage." He also thought that elementary prudence would prevent Parliament from abusing this power. Excessive duties would kill trade, not increase revenue. The Townshend Crisis (1767–1770) would change his mind about the underlying decency and wisdom of British imperial policy.[19]

IV

Imperial authority was indeed recovering after repeal of the Stamp Act, but then Charles Townshend launched the second imperial crisis

Internal taxes (1765)
  Stamp Act
	External taxes (1767–1770)
	  Sugar Act (1764)
	  Revenue Act of 1766
	  Townshend Revenue Act (1767)

Ideology

Internal legislation (1774)
  The Massachusetts Government
  Act showed that this quadrant
  was the most sacred one
  to the colonists
	External legislation (1776)
	  The Navigation Acts made this
	  quadrant the most sacred one
	  to the British.

Geography

In this figure, the horizontal axis represents ideology, or something in people's minds—for the colonists, the effort to achieve consistency by distinguishing between parliamentary legislation (permissible) and parliamentary taxation (illegitimate). The vertical axis stands for something physical and real, the coastline of North America, which marked the internal–external dichotomy in the debates of the period. To most contemporaries, this dichotomy seemed a matter of expediency, not principle. In fact, it marked the power axis of the empire, the boundary of *effective* parliamentary action. Parliament could exercise power over oceanic commerce. It never succeeded in extending that power to the internal affairs of the colonies.

Note that while the Stamp Act was contested in terms of the taxation–legislation dichotomy, the crisis was resolved along the internal–external axis. The colonists stopped rioting when the Stamp Act was repealed, even though the Sugar Act remained in place and, as amended by the Revenue Act of 1766, became much more blatantly a revenue measure, not a regulation of trade.

Note also that the intersection of the two axes creates four quadrants that can also reveal what the primary issue became in each successive crisis—internal taxation in 1765–1766, external taxation from 1767 to 1770, and internal legislation in 1774–1775. Only with independence did the colonists repudiate the Navigation Acts (external legislation), under which they had lived for more than a century.

Figure 5.1   Geography and Ideology in the Coming of the Revolution

when he persuaded Parliament to pass the Townshend Revenue Act in 1767. It addressed no real problem. It created many new ones. It did not pretend to meet the empire's serious need for revenue to support an army in the West. It took off excises in England that brought in twice as much revenue as Townshend expected to gain from the new duties that he imposed on tea, lead, glass, painters' colors, and paper, to be collected in American ports. That revenue would be used primarily to pay the salaries of colonial governors and judges in northern royal colonies, thus eliminating any dependence they still had on the assemblies. Parliament also created the American Board of Customs

Commissioners. In a choice that suggested his desire for a confrontation, Townshend located the headquarters of the new board in Boston, the most violent North American city during the Stamp Act riots, rather than in centrally located Philadelphia, which had been much quieter in 1765.

The colonists reacted much more slowly to the Townshend Revenue Act than they had to the Stamp Act. John Dickinson and other writers realized that whatever Townshend's real objectives had been (he died suddenly in September 1767 before his legislation took effect), it did mark a direct challenge to government by consent in the colonies, but effective resistance to an "external tax" proved difficult to organize. The Massachusetts House of Representatives sent a circular letter to the other assemblies in February 1768 urging a concerted resistance, but not much happened. The southern colonies already paid fixed salaries to their governors and were much less alarmed than Massachusetts by the new use of parliamentary revenue under the Townshend Act. Many merchants balked at the call for another round of nonimportation, and effective agreements did not take hold in the major northern ports until early 1769, more than a year after the Revenue Act went into effect, and then only in response to subsequent British provocations.

If the new measures had been prudently managed, the ministry could probably have gotten through the next few years without creating a serious intercolonial crisis. But in March 1768, raucous (though nonviolent) demonstrations in Boston on the anniversary of the Stamp Act's repeal frightened the Customs Commissioners into a demand for military support, and the violent riot in June that followed the seizure of John Hancock's sloop *Liberty* for smuggling led to a second call for troops. Hillsborough turned these minor incidents into a major crisis. He ordered the Massachusetts House to rescind its circular letter, forbade any other assembly to receive it favorably, and dispatched four regiments of redcoats to Boston. In this way local incidents mushroomed into a confrontation involving all the mainland colonies. Reacting to favorable responses to the circular letter, the governor in every royal province was forced to dissolve his assembly until government by consent really did seem threatened by 1769. The confrontation between the army and Boston led to violence and the deaths of five civilians when soldiers fired in self-defense on an angry crowd on March 5, 1770. As Franklin had warned in 1766 when asked whether soldiers could enforce the Stamp Act, "They will not find a rebellion; they may indeed make one."[20]

Lord North broke up colonial resistance by repealing all the Townshend duties except the one on tea, which had, in fact, provided over 70 percent of the revenue collected under the act. Although British tea continued to be boycotted, the broader nonimportation agreements fell apart by the end of 1770, and colonial spokesmen harshly condemned those colonies, such as Rhode Island and New York, that were first to capitulate. As gratifying as these outbursts must have been to imperial officials, another trend was more significant. Nobody celebrated. The Sons of Liberty knew they had lost a major encounter. The simultaneous failure of the Wilkite reform movement in England, in which about a fourth of the voters signed petitions calling for new parliamentary elections, persuaded many observers that government by consent was indeed under siege throughout the empire.[21]

The real significance of the Townshend Crisis is that it never ended and that it made a conspiracy thesis quite credible to American settlers. Sober colonists now suspected that Parliament itself, not just one particular ministry, was deeply corrupt and still planning to deprive them of their liberties. Why else would it insist on retaining the tea tax? Many colonists were also losing confidence in the integrity of the king, who never responded to any of their petitions. The most significant casualty during the second imperial crisis was the erosion of the mutual confidence, or what colonists called the "affection," that had bound the largely voluntaristic societies of North America together with the hierarchical kingdom of Great Britain into an effective empire. The *Gaspée* affair of 1772, in which Rhode Islanders destroyed a marauding customs vessel, illustrated how far mutual trust had disintegrated by then. When Britain tried to identify the perpetrators and ship them to England to stand trial for their lives, no one in Rhode Island would name them, and even more ominously for imperial harmony, twelve colonies—all but Pennsylvania—created legislative committees of correspondence to keep in touch with one another and *anticipate* the next assault of the British government on colonial liberties. The coming of the Revolution is really a story of growing colonial disaffection, the destruction of the one bond that had held very different societies together despite the inability of nearly all leaders to explain adequately how the imperial system actually worked.[22]

V

In 1773, Lord North revised his colonial policy around a seemingly sensible but disastrously mistaken assumption. Nobody, he reasoned, would start a revolution if the government *lowered* the price of tea in the colonies. In response to a major credit crisis and the possible bankruptcy of the East India Company, Britain's largest corporation, the company, seconded by Franklin, asked North to repeal the Townshend duty in America and thus open the whole continent to British tea. North rejected that suggestion in favor of something more clever. He repealed the remaining import duties on the company's tea within Britain but kept the Townshend duty in America. That change would permit the company to undersell smuggled Dutch tea in both Britain and the colonies. The Tea Act also granted the company and its small number of consignees a monopoly on shipping the tea to America and selling it there to consumers.

These monopolistic features gave the Sons of Liberty the leverage they needed to nullify the act. They did not have to try to police the entire waterfront to enforce nonimportation, as during the Townshend Crisis. They could concentrate their attention on the small number of vessels carrying the tea. They pressured consignees to resign and forced the specially chartered tea ships to depart without landing their cargoes. These tactics worked everywhere but Boston, where Governor Thomas Hutchinson protected the consignees in Castle William in Boston harbor and then refused to grant clearance papers to the tea ships. On the night before the duties would have to be paid, the patriots dumped 342 chests of tea into Boston harbor rather than allow cheap but dutied tea to get loose among Massachusetts consumers and thus establish a precedent for broader parliamentary taxation of the colonies.[23]

Parliament responded with the Coercive Acts. The Boston Port Act, passed in March 1774 and implemented on June 1, closed the port of Boston (including Charlestown) until the town paid for the tea. Britain enforced it ruthlessly and, obviously, the Royal Navy had the power to do so. By the end of June numerous public calls had been issued for a Continental Congress to meet in Philadelphia in September, and it was already clear that any such congress would adopt major trade sanctions against Britain. But then the Massachusetts Government Act, passed in May and implemented in August, transformed the charter government of Massachusetts without the colonists' consent, mostly by making the

Council, or upper house, appointive instead of elective and by restrict-ing the powers of town meetings. The result was massive refusal to obey. Jurors would not take oaths under the new arrangements, and county conventions met to close the royal law courts and take charge of local affairs.

Because the new governor, General Sir Thomas Gage, refused to recog-nize the traditional House of Representatives that had gathered in Salem, the towns elected their own Provincial Congress, which was already con-vening in Concord, and it created its own Committee of Public Safety as its informal executive body. North's ministry assumed that Gage and his soldiers would be able to intimidate the whole province of Massachusetts Bay. Instead the colonists confined his power to the town of Boston. Taxes went to the Provincial Congress in Concord, not to Gage in Boston. Each county's militia purged itself of untrustworthy officers and accepted leadership from Concord. Stunned, Gage warned North in September that he would need 20,000 redcoats to carry out his mission. He was discovering that the alternative to government by consent was not a more authoritarian and effective structure under the Crown but rather the utter disintegration of British authority in the colony. In January, North replied by dispatching some reinforcements and by ordering Gage to send an expedition to Concord. The Revolutionary War broke out not over the "external" legislation of the Port Act but in a hopeless attempt to enforce another inland measure, the Massachusetts Government Act.[24]

Once the fighting began and the king rejected even the very moderate Olive Branch Petition of the Second Continental Congress, the conspir-acy theses prevalent on both sides of the Atlantic turned into self-fulfilling prophecies. The king believed that the colonists had been plotting inde-pendence at least since 1765. The colonists concluded that the 30,000 redcoats and Hessians heading for America proved that the British state was determined to crush their liberties. The last bond of empire to yield was the underlying colonial affection for the British people, who stood condemned in American eyes by their acquiescence in the war and in the king's use of foreign mercenaries. As Thomas Jefferson put it in a passage that did not make the final draft of the Declaration of Independence,

[T]hese facts have given the last stab to agonizing affection; and manly spirit bids us to renou[n]ce forever these unfeeling brethren. [W]e

must endeavor to forget our former love for them, and to hold them,
as we hold the rest of mankind, enemies in war, in peace friends. [W]e
might have been a free & a great people together; but a communication
of grandeur and of freedom, it seems, is below their dignity. [B]e it so,
since they will have it. [T]he road to happiness and to glory is open to
us too; we will climb it apart from them and acquiesce in the necessity
which denounces our eternal separation.[25]

The colonies declared their independence in July, and the British then
inflicted on them the bloodiest war in their history to that time. Even two
centuries later, the Revolution has been exceeded only by the Civil War in
the percentage of casualties suffered by its participants.[26]

VI

The coming of the Revolution is mainly a story of growing popular disaffection. But that pattern does not explain the new political order that
arose after independence. To become effective republics, the newly independent states would have to experience internal revolutions that would
redefine their public lives in remarkable ways. By 1776 the British made the
colonists choose "whether they would be men and not English or whether
they would be English and not men," as Edmund S. Morgan has nicely
put it.[27] The transition from the rights of Englishmen to the rights of man
meant a rejection of the British model of constitutionalism and had truly
revolutionary implications. The earliest state constitutions, however, did
seem to create something like sovereign legislatures within their borders,
even as they groped to find some adequate way to institutionalize what
they were beginning to call the separation of powers. At first, in nearly
every state, the legislature itself defined the fundamental rights of its citizens, even though, as critics pointed out, any subsequent legislature could
then repeal or change them. Rights defined through conventional legislation were not "fundamental" because they could be repealed at any time.

The Massachusetts Constitution of 1780 found an answer to this
dilemma. It was drafted by a convention elected only for that purpose,
and the constitution was then ratified by the citizens assembled in their
town meetings. This procedure drew a sharp distinction between the
sovereign people, who alone had the power to make a constitution, and
the legislature elected under that constitution. In 1787 the Philadelphia

Convention extended that process to the emerging American nation when it insisted that the new Federal Constitution be ratified by state conventions summoned only for that purpose. Popular sovereignty thus took hold as the underlying myth that still organizes public life in the United States.[28]

In France, as William H. Sewell Jr. demonstrates in chapter 3, the Revolution very nearly became the nation, which defined itself as a passionate repudiation of the past. Americans, by contrast, did not reject the Gregorian calendar or the boundaries of their states as they had been laid out under British colonial rule. In Eric Van Young's terms, they launched the most successful creole revolution of the era, an accomplishment made possible because, unlike their Latin American counterparts, they seldom had to listen to the voices of indigenous peoples or of their own enslaved Africans. The muted protests of these "others" enabled the settlers to participate fully in the transatlantic revolution that soon spread from North America to France. But unlike the French, the American public did not even debate the nation or the shape it ought to assume until the ratification struggle that followed the Philadelphia Convention of 1787. In the United States the Revolution was a military struggle for independence that inspired republican experiments at the state level, but a sense of American national identity emerged only gradually, mostly as a consequence of independence and a recognition, especially among Federalists, that if the Union collapsed, the results could be catastrophic. Americans set about defining their national identity because most of them realized that they were not yet a nation. Why else would some men, two decades after the ratification struggle, have organized an Association of American Patriots for the Purpose of Forming a National Character?[29]

Two aspects of America's countercyclical revolution remain surprising. First, it did remarkably little long-term damage to Great Britain, which soon discovered that it could retain most of the economic benefits of the old imperial system without assuming the costs of defense. Second, although Americans had lived under British rule for a century and a half almost without even contemplating independence, once they repudiated George III, they did not look back. There has never been a serious movement since 1776 to restore monarchy in the United States, and no central government of the United States has ever claimed the powers of a sovereign parliament. From the perspective of most Indians, the new republic was more imperial than the old empire. The Revolution generated irresistible pressure to open the West to settlement and vastly expanded the public role of ordinary householders. But among the victors in the revolutionary struggle, the biggest gainers were middling white householders who won an unprecedented share of public power. The lower houses of the legislature grew much larger and became open to men of modest wealth, the suffrage expanded, and, as the political parties took hold nationally after 1790, voter turnout sometimes reached extraordinary levels.[30]

In the twelve years after ratification, the Federalist Party tried to turn the American republic into a purified version of the British state by funding the national debt at par, chartering the Bank of the United States (modeled on the Bank of England) to handle government finance, and creating a professional army and navy. Their Democratic-Republican opponents denounced them as mad anglophiles who would probably restore monarchy if they could, a charge that all but a few Federalists denied in good conscience. But only after the so-called revolution of 1800, which brought Jefferson and the Democratic-Republicans to power on the national level, did the American Revolutionary Settlement take permanent hold. Jefferson reduced the army and navy to token strength, set about paying off the national debt (without repudiating it), and rejoiced when the charter of the Bank of the United States expired in 1811. The Louisiana Purchase, meanwhile, doubled the land area of the nation.

Jefferson's republic became the embodiment of American exceptionalism. Jeffersonians rejected active participation in Europe's balance of power. They set out to achieve hegemony within North America, not in the conventional European manner of building enormous armies and fleets sustained by a huge burden of taxation but by encouraging American citizens to take physical possession of the continent from the Atlantic to the Pacific, to the terror of its Indian occupants and of the republic's Mexican neighbors. (Canadians fared better because they still had British protection.) The Monroe Doctrine extended these ambitions to the entire Western Hemisphere. No other society has ever tried anything of the kind.[31]

In 1838, young Abraham Lincoln, in his first major public address, spelled out some of the implications of this achievement:

All the armies of Europe, Asia, and Africa combined, with all the treasure of the earth (our own excepted) in their military chest; with a

Buonaparte for a commander, could not by force, take a drink from the Ohio, or make a track on the Blue Ridge, in a trial of a thousand years.

. . . If destruction be our lot, we must ourselves be its author and finisher. As a nation of freemen, we must live through all time, or die by suicide.[32]

The success of the United States made the republic unique and probably gave it the ability to hold the loyalties of its citizens through its most severe crisis, the Civil War. One wonders how often Lincoln recalled these words during that struggle.

But American exceptionalism has also had a price. No other society has ever been able to imitate it. Others can borrow from our constitutions and bills of rights and have often combined them with some version of parliamentary government derived from Britain. But no one else has ever aspired to hegemony over an entire hemisphere, sustained without a serious military establishment only through the everyday economic activities of its citizens. That accomplishment became the most distinctive legacy of 1776 and, for most Americans, defined their national identity until the world wars of the twentieth century forced the United States to create an army, navy, and air force that could match any others on the planet. The long-term consequences of this transformation are still unfolding. Most spokesmen for the revolutionary generation would warn us to be on guard. Global empire and liberty do not easily reinforce one another.

Notes

1. Horace Walpole to George Montague, March 22, 1762, *The Yale Edition of Horace Walpole's Correspondence,* ed. W. S. Lewis et al., 43 vols. (New Haven, Conn.: Yale University Press, 1937–1983), 10:22.
2. To regain Havana, Spain ceded Florida to Britain and agreed to pay an enormous ransom for Manila. Britain returned Guadeloupe and Martinique to France.
3. For the prophecies of Choiseul and Vergennes, see Edward Channing, *A History of the United States,* 6 vols. (New York: Macmillan, 1905–1925), 2: 602–3.
4. See especially Lawrence Henry Gipson, "The American Revolution as an Aftermath of the Great War for the Empire, 1754–1763," *Political Science Quarterly* 65 (March 1950): 86–104, esp. 104.
5. For a fuller discussion, see John M. Murrin, "The French and Indian War, the American Revolution, and the Counterfactual Hypothesis: Reflections on Lawrence Henry Gipson and John Shy," *Reviews in American History* 1 (September 1973): 307–18. The quotations are from "The Association"

(October 1774) and the "Declaration of the Causes and Necessities of Taking Up Arms" (July 1775), *Journals of the Continental Congress, 1774–1789,* ed. Worthington Chauncey Ford, 34 vols. (Washington, D.C.: U.S. Government Printing Office, 1904–1937), 1:76; 2: 152.

6. See my "A Roof without Walls: The Dilemma of American National Identity," in *Beyond Confederation: Origins of the Constitution and American National Identity,* ed. Richard Beeman, Stephen Botein, and Edward C. Carter II (Chapel Hill: University of North Carolina Press, 1987), 333–48, and T. H. Breen, "Ideology and Nationalism on the Eve of the American Revolution: More Revisions in Need of Revising," *Journal of American History* 84 (June 1997): 13–39.

7. Aaron Fogleman, "Migrations to the Thirteen North American Colonies, 1700–1775: New Estimates," *Journal of Interdisciplinary History* 22 (spring 1992): 691–709, esp. table 1 on p. 698; Bernard Bailyn, *Voyagers to the West: A Passage in the Peopling of America on the Eve of the Revolution* (New York: Knopf, 1986), esp. 29–36 on Hillsborough; and Bernard Bailyn and Philip D. Morgan, eds., *Strangers within the Realm: Cultural Margins of the First British Empire* (Chapel Hill: University of North Carolina Press, 1991).

8. Some of the most relevant studies, within a huge literature, are James F. Shepherd and Gary M. Walton, *Shipping, Maritime Trade, and the Economic Development of Colonial North America* (Cambridge: Cambridge University Press, 1972); John W. Tyler, *Smugglers and Patriots: Boston Merchants and the Advent of the American Revolution* (Boston: Northeastern University Press, 1986); Thomas M. Doerflinger, *A Vigorous Spirit of Enterprise: Merchants and Economic Development in Revolutionary Philadelphia* (Chapel Hill: University of North Carolina Press, 1986); T. H. Breen, " 'Baubles of Britain': The American and Consumer Revolutions of the Eighteenth Century," *Past and Present* 119 (May 1988): 73–104; Cary Carson, Ronald Hoffman, and Peter J. Albert, eds., *Of Consuming Interests: The Style of Life in the Eighteenth Century* (Charlottesville: University Press of Virginia, 1992); Richard L. Bushman, *The Refinement of America: Persons, Houses, Cities* (New York: Knopf, 1992); Jacob M. Price, "The Rise of Glasgow in the Chesapeake Tobacco Trade, 1707–1775," *William and Mary Quarterly* 11 (April 1954): 179–99; Istvan Hont and Michael Ignatieff, eds. *Wealth and Virtue: The Shaping of Political Economy in the Scottish Enlightenment* (New York: Cambridge University Press, 1983); Richard B. Sher and Jeffrey R. Smitten, eds., *Scotland and America in the Age of Enlightenment* (Princeton, N.J.: Princeton University Press, 1990); and Ned C. Landsman, *From Colonials to Provincials: American Thought and Culture, 1680–1760* (New York: Twayne, 1997).

9. For a fuller discussion, see John M. Murrin, "No Awakening, No Revolution? More Counterfactual Speculations," *Reviews in American History* 11 (June 1983): 161–71.

10. See Lois G. Schwoerer, chapter 1 in this volume. The founders of West New Jersey and Pennsylvania shared the jury ideology described by Schwoerer. William Penn contributed to it in a major way. For the older colonies, see John M. Murrin and A. G. Roeber, "Trial by Jury: The Virginia Paradox," in *The Bill of Rights: A Lively Heritage,* ed. John Kukla (Richmond: Virginia State Library and Archives, 1987), 108–29, and John M. Murrin, "Magistrates, Sinners, and a Precarious Liberty: Trial by Jury in Seventeenth-Century New England," in *Saints and Revolutionaries: Essays on Early American History,* ed. David Hall, John M. Murrin, and Thad W. Tate (New York: Norton, 1984), 152–206, and "English Rights as Ethnic Aggression: The English Conquest, the Charter of Liberties of 1683, and Leisler's Rebellion in New York," in *Authority and Resistance in Early New York,* ed. William Pencak and Conrad Edick Wright (New York: New-York Historical Society, 1988), 56–94. My own research into the court records of nine New England counties for anywhere between three and eight decades after the Glorious Revolution shows that jury trials for noncapital crimes became routine by the early eighteenth century and that acquittal rates rose sharply above what they had been during the Puritan era. For the pattern in eighteenth-century New York, see Julius Goebel Jr. and T. Raymond Naughton, *Law Enforcement in Colonial New York: A Study in Criminal Procedure (1664–1776)* (New York: Commonwealth Fund, 1944).

11. The classic arguments for the rise of the assembly and the decline of royal government were made by Leonard W. Labaree, *Royal Government in America* (New Haven, Conn.: Yale University Press, 1930), and Jack P. Greene, *The Quest for Power: The Lower Houses of Assembly in the Southern Royal Colonies, 1689–1776* (Chapel Hill: University of North Carolina Press, 1963). For the growing impact of royal governors, see John M. Murrin, "Political Development," in *Colonial British America: Essays in the New History of the Early Modern Era,* ed. Jack P Greene and J. R. Pole (Baltimore: The Johns Hopkins University Press, 1984), 408–56.

12. See James H. Hutson, "The Emergence of the Modern Concept of a Right in America: The Contribution of Michel Villey," *American Journal of Jurisprudence* 39 (1994): 185–224; John M. Murrin, "From Liberties to Rights: The Struggle in Colonial Massachusetts," in *The Bill of Rights and the States: The Colonial and Revolutionary Origins of American Liberties,* ed. Patrick Conley and John P. Kaminski (Madison, Wis.: Madison House, 1992), 63–99; T. H. Breen, "The Lockean Moment: The Language of Rights on the Eve of the American Revolution," (lecture, University of Oxford, May 15, 2001); and Bernard Bailyn, *The Ideological Origins of the American Revolution* (Cambridge, Mass.: Belknap Press, 1967), and *The Origins of American Politics* (New York: Knopf, 1968).

13. Jeremy Stern, in a Princeton dissertation (still in progress) on the Townshend Crisis in Massachusetts, is paying close attention to the radicalization of language, including the shift toward an emphasis on John Locke and natural rights.

14. For a fuller discussion of political culture in the colonics, see Jack P. Greene, "Political Mimesis: A Consideration of the Historical and Cultural Roots of Legislative Behavior in the British Colonies in the Eighteenth Century," with a comment by Bernard Bailyn and a reply by Greene, *American Historical Review* 75 (December 1969): 337–67, and Murrin, "Political Development," in Greene and Pole, eds., *Colonial British America,* 408–56. Two excellent studies of northern governors are Jere R. Daniell, "Politics in New Hampshire under Governor Benning Wentworth, 1741–1767," *William and Mary Quarterly* 23 (January 1966): 76–105, and John A. Schutz, *William Shirley, King's Governor of Massachusetts* (Chapel Hill: University of North Carolina Press, 1961). For "Country" politics in southern colonies, see David Alan Williams, "Anglo-Virginia Politics, 1690–1735," in *Anglo-American Political Relations, 1675–1775,* ed. Alison G. Olson and Richard M. Brown (New Brunswick, N.J.: Rutgers University Press, 1970), 76–91; Robert M. Weir, "'The Harmony We Were Famous For': An Interpretation of Pre-revolutionary South Carolina Politics," *William and Mary Quarterly* 26 (October 1969): 473–501; and W. W. Abbot, *The Royal Governors of Georgia, 1754–1775* (Chapel Hill: University of North Carolina Press, 1959). For a spectacular glimpse of the ruthless and dysfunctional tone of Maryland politics, see Cecilius Calvert to Governor Horatio Sharpe, March 17, 1761, *Archives of Maryland,* ed. William Hand Browne et al., 72 vols. (Baltimore: Maryland Historical Society, 1883–1972), 14: 1–13.

15. For a superb study of the conflict, see Fred Anderson, *Crucible of War: The Seven Year' War and the Fate of Empire in British North America, 1754–1766* (New York Knopf, 2000). His earlier book, *A People's Army: Massachusetts Soldiers and Society in the Seven Years' War* (Chapel Hill: University of North Carolina Press, 1984), is primarily a study of 1756, when tensions between British officers and provincial soldiers reached their peak. Harold E. Selesky, *War and Society in Colonial Connecticut* (New Haven, Conn.: Yale University Press, 1990), emphasizes the growing professionalism of provincial soldiers as the war progressed, including their willingness to reenlist. For millennialism and imperial patriotism, see Nathan O. Hatch, *The Sacred Cause of Liberty: Republican Thought and the Millennium in Revolutionary New England* (New Haven, Conn.: Yale University Press, 1977). Eleven sermons were published in the colonies to celebrate the accession of George III. Dozens more celebrated the capture of Louisbourg, Quebec, and Montreal and the Peace of Paris of 1763.

16. See especially Toby L. Ditz, "Ownership and Obligation: Inheritance and Patriarchal Households in Connecticut, 1750–1820," *William and Mary Quarterly* 47 (April 1990): 235–65; Gloria L. Main, "Inequality in Early America: The Evidence from Probate Records of Massachusetts and Maryland," *Journal of Interdisciplinary History* 7 (spring 1977): 559–81; Gordon S. Wood, *The Radicalism of the American Revolution* (New York Knopf, 1992), esp. chap. 3; and Holly Brewer, "Entailing Aristocracy in

Colonial Virginia: 'Ancient Feudal Restraints' and Revolutionary Reform," *William and Mary Quarterly* 54 (April 1997): 307–46.

17. Marc Egnal, *A Mighty Empire: The Origins of the American Revolution* (Ithaca, N.Y.: Cornell University Press, 1988), tries to link revolutionaries with expansion and loyalists with opposition to expansion. In my judgment, his argument is too ideological. Eric Hinderaker, *Elusive Empires: Constructing Colonialism in the Ohio Valley, 1673–1800* (New York: Cambridge University Press, 1997), is a brilliant contrast of French, British, and American imperialism in the Ohio Valley. See also Woody Holton, "The Ohio Indians and the Coming of the American Revolution in Virginia," *Journal of Southern History* 60 (August 1994): 453–78, and, more generally, *Forced Founders: Indians, Debtors, Slaves and the Making of the American Revolution in Virginia* (Chapel Hill: University of North Carolina Press, 1999).

18. P. D. G. Thomas, *British Politics and the Stamp Act Crisis: The First Phase of the American Revolution* (Oxford: Clarendon Press, 1975); Paul Langford, *The First Rockingham Administration, 1765–1766* (Oxford: Oxford University Press, 1973); Jean-Yves LeSaux, "Commerce and Consent: Edmund Burke's Imperial Vision and the American Revolution" (Ph.D. diss., Princeton University, 1992). LeSaux shows that, although all British spokesmen accepted parliamentary sovereignty, they could mean very different things when they invoked it.

19. The best study is still Edmund S. Morgan and Helen M. Morgan, *The Stamp Act Crisis: Prologue to Revolution,* 3rd ed. (Chapel Hill: University of North Carolina Press, 1995). For the Franklin quotation, see Edmund S. Morgan, ed., *Prologue to Revolution: Sources and Documents on the Stamp Act Crisis, 1764–1766* (Chapel Hill: University of North Carolina Press, 1959), 145.

20. Morgan, *Prologue to Revolution,* 144.

21. George Rudé, *Wilkes and Liberty: A Social Study of 1763 to 1774* (Oxford: Clarendon Press, 1962); P. D. G. Thomas, *John Wilkes: A Friend to Liberty* (Oxford: Clarendon Press, 1996).

22. Easily the best narrative history of these events is Merrill Jensen, *The Founding of a Nation: A History of the American Revolution, 1763–1776* (New York: Oxford University Press, 1968), 186–433. Pauline Maier, *From Resistance to Revolution: Colonial Radicals and the Development of American Opposition to Britain, 1765–1776* (New York: Knopf, 1972), is a very perceptive study of the process of disaffection, which was a much stronger word in the eighteenth century than it is today. See also Pauline Maier, "John Wilkes and American Disillusionment with Britain," *William and Mary Quarterly* 20 (July 1963): 373–95, and "Coming to Terms with Samuel Adams," *American Historical Review* 81 (February 1976): 12–30. Richard D. Brown, *Revolutionary Politics in Massachusetts: The Boston Committee of Correspondence and the Towns, 1772–1774* (Cambridge, Mass.: Harvard University Press, 1970), is an essential study of the cumulative process of disaffection.

23. The standard study is Benjamin W. Labaree, *The Boston Tea Party* (New York: Oxford University Press, 1964).

24. David Ammerman, *In the Common Cause: American Response to the Coercive Acts of 1774* (Charlottesville: University Press of Virginia, 1974); David Hackett Fischer, *Paul Revere's Ride* (New York: Oxford University Press, 1994).

25. Pauline Maier, *American Scripture: Making the Declaration of Independence* (New York: Knopf, 1997), 240–41.

26. Howard H. Peckham, *The Toll of Independence: Engagements and Battle Casualties of the American Revolution* (Chicago: University of Chicago Press, 1974), esp. 131–34.

27. Morgan and Morgan, *The Stamp Act Crisis,* 119.

28. Edmund S. Morgan, *Inventing the People: The Rise of Popular Sovereignty in England and America* (New York: Norton, 1988). For a superb, brief account of the development of American constitutionalism in these years, see Robert R. Palmer, *The Age of the Democratic Revolution: A Political History of Europe and America, 1760–1800,* 2 vols. (Princeton, N.J.: Princeton University Press, 1959–1964), 1:213–35.

29. See William H. Sewell Jr., chapter 3 in this volume, and Eric Van Young, chapter 4 in this volume. See also Isaac Kramnick, "The 'Great National Discussion': The Discourse of National Politics in 1787," *William and Mary Quarterly* 45 (January 1988): 3–32, and, for the Association of American Patriots, Joyce Appleby, *Inheriting the Revolution; The First Generation of Americans* (Cambridge, Mass.: Belknap Press, 2000), 196. For a subtle argument that American leaders understood the importance of the Union but that hardly anybody made its survival his top priority, see James E. Lewis Jr., *The American Union and the Problem of Neighborhood: The United States and the Collapse of the Spanish Empire, 1783–1829* (Chapel Hill: University of North Carolina Press, 1998).

30. Gordon S. Wood, *The Creation of the American Republic, 1776–1787* (Chapel Hill: University of North Carolina Press, 1969); Jackson Turner Main, "Government by the People: The American Revolution and the Democratization of the Legislatures," *William and Mary Quarterly* 23 (July 1966): 354–67; Stanley Elkins and Eric McKitrick, *The Age of Federalism: The Early American Republic* (New York: Oxford University Press, 1993).

31. For fuller discussions of the American Revolution Settlement and of American exceptionalism, see John M. Murrin, "The Great Inversion, or, Court versus Country: A Comparison of the Revolution Settlements in England (1688–1721) and America (1776–1816)," in *Three British Revolutions: 1641, 1688, 1776,* ed. J. G. A. Pocock (Princeton, N.J.: Princeton University Press, 1980), 368–453, and "The Jeffersonian Triumph and American Exceptionalism," *Journal of the Early Republic* 20 (spring 2000): 1–25.

32. "Address before the Young Men's Lyceum of Springfield, Illinois, January 27, 1838," In *The Collected Works of Abraham Lincoln,* ed. Roy P. Basler et al., 11 vols. (New Brunswick, N.J.: Rutgers University Press, 1953–1990), 1: 109.

PART III
Defining the Republic

6

A Roof without Walls

The Dilemma of American National Identity

THE UNITED STATES Constitution, as we have come to realize, provided an innovative answer to the legal problem of sovereignty within a federal system. This difficulty had destroyed the British Empire by 1776, and by 1787 it seemed likely to reduce the Congress of the United States to impotence. The Federalists solved this dilemma by applying on a continental scale the new principles of revolutionary constitutionalism that the states had explored and developed between 1776 and 1780, the year in which the Massachusetts Constitution completed the model. To be fully legitimate, a constitution had to be drafted by a special convention and ratified by the people. By so institutionalizing the premise that the people alone are sovereign, and not government at any level, Americans made it possible for a sovereign citizenry to delegate some powers to the states, others to the central government. We still live happily, more or less, with the benefits of this discovery.[1]

But the Constitution was also a more tentative answer to a broader cultural problem. It established what Francis Hopkinson called a "new roof" over an American union of extremely diverse states. Opponents of the Constitution often warned that "the several parts of the roof were so framed as to mutually strengthen and support each other," he contemptuously declared, "and therefore, there was great reason to fear that the whole might stand independent of the walls." With heavy logic, he refuted this possibility.[2]

Originally published in *Beyond Confederation: Origins of the Constitution and American Identity*, Richard Beeman, Stephen Botein, Edward C. Carter II, eds. (Chapel Hill, University of North Carolina Press, 1987).

Hopkinson had the right image but the wrong alignment. The Federalists, not their opponents, were building a roof without walls.

I

The American Revolution was not the logical culmination of a broadening and deepening sense of separate national identity emerging among the settlers of North America. The sprawling American continents had taken a remarkably homogeneous people, the Indians, and divided them into hundreds of distinct societies over thousands of years. America was quite capable of doing the same to Europeans. The seventeenth century created, within English America alone, not one new civilization on this side of the Atlantic, but many distinct colonies that differed as dramatically from one another as any of them from England. Even the Revolution would establish, not one new nation, but two distinct polities: the United States and Canada. A century later the Civil War nearly added a third. The Latin America wars for independence produced twenty-two nations from a few vice-royalties.

For the English, the Atlantic functioned much as a prism in the seventeenth century, separating the stream of immigrants into a broad spectrum of settlements from the Caribbean to New England. Most colonies shared many important traits with immediate neighbors (Massachusetts with Connecticut, Maryland with Virginia, St. Kitts with Barbados), but differences became cumulative as one advanced farther along the spectrum. At the extremes—Barbados and Massachusetts, for instance—the colonies had almost nothing in common.

Historical demography suggests the larger pattern. For complex reasons that included climate and settler motivation, the farther north one went, the greater that life expectancy generally became, the higher the percentage of women in the colony, and the sooner population growth by natural increase set in. The extent of population mixture also followed the spectrum. New Englanders really were English. The Middle Atlantic colonies threw together most of the peoples of northwestern Europe. The Chesapeake added a significant African population, which would expand dramatically from the 1690s on. Africans eventually outnumbered Europeans by two to one in South Carolina and by much greater ratios in the islands. Climate and demography also affected local economies.

Apart from the fur trade, few settlers north of Maryland engaged in economic activities strange to Europeans. As rapidly as possible, they even
converted to European crops (without abandoning maize), grown mostly
through family labor. But the staple colonies specialized in the growth
and export through unfree labor of non-European crops, especially
tobacco and sugar. The West Indies did not even try to raise enough food
to feed the settlers and their servants and slaves.[3]

Government and religion also followed the spectrum. At the province level. New England gloried in its corporate autonomy, which Rhode
Island and Connecticut would retain until the Revolution. Royal government, by contrast, really defined itself in the Caribbean during the
Restoration era. On the mainland south of New England, most settlers
lived under proprietary governments that eventually became royal, but
Virginia had been royal since 1624, and Maryland and Pennsylvania
regained their proprietary forms after losing them for a time following the
Glorious Revolution. In local government, the New England town—a
variation of the traditional English village—spread no farther south than
East Jersey. English counties, not villages, became the dominant form of
local organization from West Jersey through North Carolina, and parishes prevailed in South Carolina and the islands. In general, the farther
north one traveled, the higher became the percentage of local resources
that settlers were willing to spend on religion. Formally, the Old World
established church, the Church of England, became the New World
establishment everywhere from Maryland south by 1710. In the Middle
Atlantic region, dissent and establishment fought to a standstill, with toleration the big winner. In New England except for Rhode Island, Old
World dissent became New World establishment.[4]

Some uniformities different from England's did emerge to bridge these
cultural chasms. Except in the smaller sugar islands, all of the colonies
enjoyed a more widespread distribution and ownership of land. No colony successfully reproduced a hereditary aristocracy. Indeed, younger
sons enjoyed liberties in North America hard to match in any European
society. Similarly, England's complex legal system was everywhere simplified and except in Quaker communities, the settlers also adopted a ferocious style of waging war. For Europe's more limited struggles among
trained armies, they substituted people's wars of total subjection and even
annihilation. Their methods were deliberately terroristic. They, not the

Indians, began the systematic slaughter of women and children, often as targets of choice. Finally, the English language became more uniform in America than in England simply because no colony was able to replicate the mother country's rich variety of local dialects.[5]

Nevertheless, the overall differences stand out more starkly than the similarities. The spectrum of seventeenth-century settlement produced, not one, but many Americas, and the passage of time threatened to drive them farther apart, not closer together. Most of what they retained in common—language, Protestantism, acquisitiveness, basic political institutions—derived from their shared English heritage, however institutionally skewed, and not from their novel encounters with the continent of North America.

II

Between the Glorious Revolution of 1688–1689 and the Peace of Paris of 1763, the colonies grew more alike in several respects. As newer generations adjusted to climate, life expectancy improved south of Pennsylvania, population became self-sustaining, and family patterns grew more conventional. Warfare retained its original brutality in conflicts with Indians, but it too Europeanized as the primary enemy became the settlers and soldiers of other European empires. The widespread imposition of royal government through the 1720s gave public life structural similarities it had lacked in the seventeenth century.

As these examples suggest, British North America in fundamental ways became more European, more English, in the eighteenth century. The growth of cities, the spread of printing and newspapers, the rise of the professions, and the emulation of British political culture all encouraged this trend. But the colonies did not all change in the same way. New England anglicized at the core. On the fringes of the social order, it retained much of its original uniqueness, such as the Puritan Sabbath and annual election sermons. The southern colonies anglicized on the fringes while remaining unique at the core, which now more than ever was characterized by plantations and slave labor. A planter's economic base had no English counterpart, but his daily behavior closely imitated gentry standards. In the Middle Atlantic region, where emulation of England always had ethnic and class overtones, the pattern was less clear.[6]

A few examples will have to suffice in illustrating this process. New England increasingly replicated basic European institutions. Southern provinces, by contrast, imported much of what they needed and did not acquire the same capacity to produce their own. Thus, for instance, every college but one was north of Maryland in 1775. New England trained virtually all of its own clergy, lawyers, and physicians. By contrast, no native-born South Carolinian (and only a few dozen Virginians out of the several hundred men who took parishes in the colony) became Anglican clergymen. All of South Carolina's bar and much of Virginia's was trained in England. Similarly, New Englanders wrote their own poetry, much of it bad, while Maryland imported poets, a few of them quite good (such as Richard Lewis).[7]

Perhaps the change was most conspicuous in public life. In the seventeenth century many colony founders had tried quite consciously to depart from and improve upon English norms. They attempted to build a city upon a hill in Puritan Massachusetts, a viable autocracy in ducal New York, a holy experiment of brotherly love in Quaker Pennsylvania, a rejuvenated feudal order in Maryland, and an aristocratic utopia in Carolina. But from about the second quarter of the eighteenth century, colonial spokesmen expressed ever-increasing admiration for the existing British constitution as the human wonder of the age. Improvement upon it seemed scarcely imaginable. North American settlers read British political writers, absorbed their view of the world, and tried to shape their provincial governments into smaller but convincing replicas of the metropolitan example.[8]

One conspicuous consequence was imperial patriotism. The generation in power from 1739 to 1763 fought two global wars and helped to win the greatest overseas victories that Britain had ever seized. Despite frequent disputes in many colonies, royal government achieved greater practical success in America than at any other time in its history to 1776. Colonial expressions of loyalty to Britain became far more frequent, emotional, intense, and eloquent than in earlier years. To the extent that the settlers were self-conscious nationalists, they saw themselves as part of an expanding British nation and empire. Loyalty to colony meant loyalty to Britain. The two were expected to reinforce one another.[9]

Occasionally a new vision of a glorious future for the American continent would appear in this rhetoric, but almost without exception these writers confined their exuberance to an Anglo-American context. North America would thrive with Britain, Nathaniel Ames's almanacs excitedly told New Englanders. Because population grew faster in America than in Europe, mused Benjamin Franklin, the colonies would one day surpass the mother country, and perhaps crown and Parliament would cross the ocean to these shores.[10]

In other words, political loyalties to an entity called America scarcely yet existed and could not match the intensity with which settlers revered either their smaller provinces or the larger empire. Despite the frequent worries voiced in the British press or expressed by British placemen in America, native-born North Americans showed no interest in political union, much less independence. Every colony involved rejected the Albany Plan of Union of 1754 regardless of the manifest military peril from New France.

This reality was far from obvious to the British. They, not the settlers, imagined the possibility of an independent America. Imposing new patterns of uniformity on colonies that they had to govern routinely, few London officials grasped the extent or significance of local differences three thousand miles away. The British worried about the whole because they did not understand the parts, and they reified their concerns into a totality they called America. Debate over the Canada cession focused these anxieties more sharply than ever before and also revealed that British writers almost took it for granted that one day the American colonies would demand and get their independence. Wise policy required that Britain avert this result for as long as possible.

In a word, America was Britain's idea. Maybe it was even Britain's dream, but if so, it soon became her nightmare. Every countermeasure taken to avert the horror seemed only to bring it closer. Nothing is more ironic in the entire span of early American history than the way in which Britain finally persuaded her North American settlers to embrace a national destiny that virtually none of them desired before the crisis of 1764–1776.[11]

There was, in short, nothing inevitable about the creation and triumph of the United States. Rather, the American nation was a by-product that at first nobody wanted. The British believed that they were doing everything they could to avoid such a thing. The settlers until almost the last moment denied that they had anything of the kind in mind. Only British oppression, they insisted, could drive them from the empire.[12]

At one level the Revolution was thus the culminating moment in the process of anglicization. The colonists resisted British policy, they explained with increasing irritation and anger, because London would not let them live as Englishmen. They demanded only the common rights of Englishmen, such as no taxation without representation and trial by jury, and not unique privileges for Americans. (At the same time, they did believe that the availability of land in North America gave them unique benefits unavailable to fellow subjects at home.) Britain demanded that North Americans assume their fair share of common imperial obligations and embarked on a reform program after 1763 that was designed to centralize and rationalize the empire. Beginning with the Stamp Act crisis of 1764–1766, London thus polarized the needs of the whole and the rights of the parts. She was never able to put them together again.

Precisely because public life in America was so thoroughly British, the colonists resisted Britain with all the available weapons of eighteenth-century politics—ideology, law, petitions, assembly resolves, grassroots political organizations, disciplined crowd violence. Until 1774, when the Continental Congress finally provided an American institutional focus for general resistance, patriot leaders looked to the radical opposition movement in London as the logical center of their own. Not surprisingly, until the Congress met, more of its members had visited London than Philadelphia. The Revolution, in short, was a crisis of political integration and centralization that Britain could not master. Britain could not control politically the forces that were drawing the parts of the empire closer together. That failure left patriots on this side of the ocean alone with America. They had shown that they would fight and even confederate to protect the rights of the parts. They had yet to discover whether they could create enough sense of common identity to provide for the needs of the whole. The challenge was exhilarating—and terrifying.[13,14]

III

Perhaps we can now appreciate the dilemma of American national identity. To the extent that North Americans were more alike by 1760 than they had been in 1690 or 1660, Britain had been the major focus of unity and the engine of change. To repudiate Britain meant jeopardizing what the settlers had in common while stressing what made them different from one another. Older patriots quickly sensed the danger. If goaded into the attempt, the colonies would indeed be able to win their independence, John Dickinson assured William Pitt in 1765. "But what, sir, must be the Consequences of that Success? A Multitude of Commonwealths, Crimes, and Calamities, of mutual jealousies. Hatreds, Wars and Devastations; till at last the exhausted Provinces shall sink into Slavery under the yoke of some fortunate Conqueror." Younger patriots were more confident about America. They welcomed the chance to become fabled heroes in their ironic quest to prove that the British had been right about America all along and that their own doubts and hesitations were unworthy of their lofty cause. At his Yale commencement of 1770, John Trumbull predicted the eventual supremacy of America in the arts and sciences, called the colonies a nation, and exulted in the deluge of blood that would accompany this transition to greatness.

> See where her Heroes mark their glorious way.
> Arm'd for the fight and blazing on the day
> Blood stains their steps; and o'er the conquering plain,
> 'Mid fighting thousands and 'mid thousands slain.
> Their eager swords promiscuous carnage blend.
> And ghastly deaths their raging course attend.
> Her mighty pow'r the subject world shall see;
> For laurel'd Conquest waits her high decree.

The colonists would inherit from Britain, not just their own continent, but the world. America's fleets would "Bid ev'ry realm, that hears the trump of fame,/Quake at the distant terror of her name." Trumbull hardly needed to announce the moral, but he did anyway. Although the process would take some centuries to complete, America's triumphs would hide "in brightness of superior day/The fainting gleam of Britain's setting ray."[15]

This bloodcurdling rhetoric probably concealed real anxieties. Any task that sanguinary—that worthy of heroes—was quite daunting. Not only would an American national identity have to be forged in a brutal war with the world's mightiest maritime power, but the settlers would have to do so without the usual requisites of nationhood. Sir Lewis Namier has contrasted two basic types of European nationalism from the eighteenth century to the present. Both reduce to a question of human loyalties. To what social collectivity do people choose or wish to be loyal? One pattern was traditional and, at root, institutional. England was a nation because it possessed reasonably well defined boundaries and a continuity of monarchical rule for about nine hundred years. The crown had created Parliament, which became both a reinforcing and a competing focus for loyalties as the two, together with their public, defined England's distinct political culture in the seventeenth century. Switzerland provided Namier with another example. This mountainous republic forged a common institutional identity among its several cantons despite their division into three languages and two major religions.

The other model, just beginning to find important spokesmen in late eighteenth-century Germany, was linguistic nationalism. Among a people who shared no common institutional links, language seemed an obvious focus for loyalty. Even though the boundaries between competing languages were by no means clear-cut, this type of nationalism would come to dominate Central and Eastern Europe in the nineteenth and twentieth centuries. Whereas institutional nationalism had the potential to absorb waves of reform without internal upheaval, linguistic nationalism recognized no obvious geographical boundaries and had to replace existing political institutions with new ones to achieve full expression. Although it began with warm sentiments of benign humanitarianism, it was far more likely to become militaristic and destructive, and by the twentieth century it could be deflected into overt racism whenever it seemed necessary to distinguish true Germans, for example, from outsiders who had merely mastered the language over several generations.[16]

The most fascinating and troubling feature about the American case is that neither model could work here. The American continent could boast no common historic institutions other than crown and Parliament. It had acquired no shared history outside its British context. Likewise, the American settlers possessed only one language in common: English. In both cases, the logic of national identity pointed back to Britain, to counterrevolution, to a repudiation of the bizarre events of 1776. From this perspective, the loyalists were the true nationalists. Many older patriots implicitly agreed, at least to the extent that they too equated nationhood with the institutionalization of centralized power. To them centralization meant a severe challenge to liberty, a threat to the Revolution itself. Yet all

patriots understood that, unless they could unite and fight together effectively, they would lose the war. Their early answer to this dilemma was virtue. Americans had it; the British had lost it. Virtue, or patriotism, would
inspire the settlers to sacrifice their private interests, even their lives, for
the general welfare.[17]

As the struggle progressed into a seemingly endless war and the North
Americans (often for the first time) came into intimate contact with each
other, this conviction wore thin. The shock of recognition was uncomfortable and disturbing, for it was just as likely to expose differences as
similarities. It revealed, in effect, the underlying spectrum of settlement.
Too often the Americans discovered that they really did not like each
other very much, but that they needed common trust to survive. Mutual
suspicion and fascination jostled for preeminence in the hearts of patriots. The language of virtue may have intensified the sense of hostility, for it
became all too easy to explain any annoying cultural differences as someone else's lack of virtue and commitment. The terms of opprobrium that
Americans hurled at each other may even have contained more venom
than did the anti-British polemics of the period, many of which reflected
the anguish of an ancient and real affection now inexplicably betrayed.

The most conspicuous fault line divided New Englanders from everyone else, although other antagonisms surfaced as well. Yankees could
not conceal their sense of moral superiority, which often seemed rankly
hypocritical to observers from other regions. "We Pennsylvanians act as
if we believe that God made of one blood all families of the earth," complained William Maclay; "but the Eastern people seem to think that he
made none but New England folks."[18] One New York merchant, Gerard
G. Beekman, thought that nearly everyone in Connecticut "has proved
to be d . . . d ungreatfull cheating fellows." Thirteen years later he was still
denouncing "the best of them out of that damd Cuntry" for defaulting
on their debts."[19] Lewis Morris, Jr., could not even keep a similar sense of
disgust out of his last will and testament in 1762. He ordered that his son
Gouverneur Morris (the later patriot) receive

> the best Education that is to be had in Europe or America but my
> Express Will and Directions are that he be never sent for that pur-
> pose to the Colony of Connecticut least he should imbibe in his youth
> that low Craft and cunning so Incident to the People of that Country,

which is so interwoven in their constitutions that all their art cannot disguise it from the World tho' many of them under the sanctified Garb of Religion have Endeavored to Impose themselves on the World for honest Men?[20]

When John Adams passed through New York City in 1774, he heard Yankees castigated as "Goths and Vandalls," infamous for their "Levelling Spirit." He retaliated in the privacy of his diary by speculating on the shocking lack of gentility and good breeding among the New York elite. To Abigail Adams, Virginia riflemen seemed every bit as loathsome and barbaric as British propaganda claimed.[21]

Sometimes regional hatreds became severe enough to reduce the northern department of the Continental army to near impotence. Yankees showed such complete distrust of New York's General Philip Schuyler that he virtually lost the ability to command. Soldiers from other parts of America, reported Captain Alexander Graydon of Pennsylvania, retaliated in kind. They regarded the eastern men as "contemptible in the extreme," in part because their officers were too egalitarian. In 1776 a court-martial acquitted a Maryland officer accused of showing disrespect to a New England general. "In so contemptible a light were the New England men regarded," explained Graydon, who sat on the court, "that it was scarcely held possible to conceive a case, which could be construed into a reprehensible disrespect of them.[22]

IV

American national identity was, in short, an unexpected, impromptu, artificial, and therefore extremely fragile creation of the Revolution. Its social roots were much weaker than those that brought forth the Confederate States of America in 1861, and yet the Confederacy was successfully crushed by military force.[23]

At first Congress tried to govern through consensus and unanimity. That effort always created strain, and it finally broke down in 1777–1778. Thereafter no one could be certain whether the American union could long outlast the war. In June 1783 a mutiny in the Pennsylvania line drove Congress from Philadelphia. The angry delegates gathered in the small crossroads village of Princeton, New Jersey, where they spent an anxious

four months in uncomfortable surroundings. They found that they had
to contemplate the fate of the Union. Could the United States survive
with Congress on the move and its executive departments somewhere
else? Charles Thomson, secretary to Congress since 1774, doubted that
the Union could endure without British military pressure to hold the several parts together. This worry obsessed him for months.[24] By 1786 New
England delegates were talking openly of disunion and partial confederacies, and this idea finally appeared in the newspapers in early 1787.[25]

Instead, a convention of distinguished delegates met in Philadelphia
that summer. It drafted a Constitution radically different from the
Articles of Confederation. By mid-1788 enough states ratified the plan to
launch the new government in April 1789. This victory followed a titanic
struggle in which the Constitution had almost been defeated by popularly chosen conventions in nearly every large state. Among the small
states, New Hampshire and Rhode Island also seemed generally hostile.

Ratification marked a victory for American nationalism, as folklore has
always told us, but it also perpetuated political conflict, which continued
without pause into the new era. Most patriots equated union with harmony and were quite upset by the turmoil of the 1790s. The only union
they could maintain was accompanied by intense political strife, a pattern of contention that did, however, observe certain boundaries. It had
limits.[26]

The actions of the Washington administration in its first few years
seemed to vindicate the gloomiest predictions of the Antifederalists, but
these proud patriots did not respond by denouncing the Constitution.
Instead, they began the process of deifying it. They converted it into an
absolute standard and denounced their opponents for every deviation
from its sublime mandates. In effect they returned to their anchorage in
British political culture to find a harbor in which their ship might float.
They converted the Constitution into a modern and revolutionary counterpart for Britain's ancient constitution. To keep the central government
going at all, they embraced the venerable antagonism between court and
country, corruption and virtue, ministerial ambition and legislative integrity. The Federalists claimed only to be implementing the government
created by the Constitution. Their Jeffersonian opponents insisted that
they, in turn, were merely calling the government to proper constitutional
account. But they both accepted the Constitution as their standard, a

process that kept the system going and converted its architects into something like popular demigods within a generation.[27]

The lesson taught by the first American party system was curious in the extreme. Americans would accept a central government only if it seldom acted like one. The British Empire had crumbled while trying to subordinate the rights of the parts to the needs of the whole. The Continental Congress had brought American union to the edge of disintegration by protecting the rights of the parts at the expense of common needs. The Constitution seemed to provide an exit from this dilemma, a way of instilling energy in government while showing genuine respect for revolutionary principles. But it did not work quite that way.

Vigorous policies by the central government always threatened to expose the underlying differences that could still tear America apart. The spectrum of settlement had been muted, warped, and overlaid with new hues, but it was still there. Thus, although everyone soon agreed that the new government was a structural improvement on the Articles, it exercised very few substantive powers in practice that people had not been happy to allocate to the old Congress. In a word, the Constitution became a substitute for any deeper kind of national identity. American nationalism is distinct because, for nearly its first century, it was narrowly and peculiarly constitutional. People knew that without the Constitution there would be no America.[28]

In the architecture of nationhood, the United States had achieved something quite remarkable. Francis Hopkinson to the contrary, Americans had erected their constitutional roof before they put up the national walls. Hovering there over a divided people, it aroused wonder and awe, even ecstasy. Early historians rewrote the past to make the Constitution the culminating event of their story.[29] Some of the Republic's most brilliant legal minds wrote interminable multivolume commentaries on its manifold virtues and unmatched wisdom. Orators plundered the language in search of fitting praise. Someone may even have put the document to music.[30] This spirit of amazement, this frenzy of self-congratulation, owed its intensity to the terrible fear that the roof could come crashing down at almost any time. Indeed, the national walls have taken much longer to build.

The very different Americas of the seventeenth century had survived into the nineteenth after repudiating the Britain from whom they had acquired their most conspicuous common features in the eighteenth. While the Republic's self-announced progenitors, New England and Virginia, fought out their differences into the Civil War, the middle states quietly eloped with the nation, giving her their most distinctive features: acceptance of pluralism, frank pursuit of self-interest, and legitimation of competing factions.

The Constitution alone could not do the job, but the job could not be done at all without it. The Constitution was to the nation a more successful version of what the Halfway Covenant had once been to the Puritans, a way of buying time. Under the shade of this lofty frame of government, the shared sacrifices of the Revolutionary War could become interstate and intergenerational memories that bound people together in new ways.[31] Ordinary citizens could create interregional economic links that simply were not there as late as 1790, until a national economy could finally supplant the old imperial one. Like the Halfway Covenant, the Constitution was an ingenious contrivance that enabled a precarious experiment to continue for another generation or two with the hope that the salvation unobtainable in the present might bless the land in better times.[32]

Notes

1. Gordon S. Wood, *The Creation of the American Republic, 1776–1787* (Chapel Hill, N.C., 1969).

2. In Paul M. Zall, ed., *Comical Spirit of Seventy-Six. The Humor of Francis Hopkinson* (San Marino, Calif., 1976), 186–194, esp. 190.

3. For strong examples of this extensive demographic literature, see the essays in Stanley N. Katz and John M. Murrin, eds., *Colonial America: Essays in Politics and Social Development*, 3d ed. (New York, 1983), 122–162, 177–203, 290–313; and in Thad W. Tate and David L. Ammerman, eds. *The Chesapeake in the Seventeenth Century: Essays on Anglo-American Society* (Chapel Hill, N.C., 1979), 96–182. See also Richard S. Dunn, *Sugar and Slaves: The Rise of the Planter Class in the English West Indies, 1624–1713* (Chapel Hill, N.C., 1972), esp. 300–334.

4. John M. Murrin, "Political Development," in Jack P. Greene and J. R Pole, eds., *Colonial British America: Essays in the New History of the Early Modern Era* (Baltimore, 1984), 408–456. John M. Murrin, Mary R. Murrin, and Gregory E. Dowd are engaged in a study, still in progress, that will enumerate colonial clergymen, colony by colony and year by year. The data show that the ratio of clergy to people generally rose from south to north, which also provides a rough index of each society's financial support for organized religion.

5. Daniel J. Boorstin provides a good starting point on language in *The Americans: The Colonial Experience* (New York, 1958), chaps. 41–43. For an excellent introduction to early legal history, see David H. Flaherty, ed., *Essays in the History of Early American Law* (Chapel Hill, N.C., 1969). On war, see John Shy, *A People Numerous and Armed: Reflections on the Military Struggle for American Independence* (New York, 1976), 225–254; Edmund S. Morgan, *American Slavery, American Freedom: The Ordeal of Colonial Virginia* (New York, 1975), 73–74; Francis Jennings, *The Invasion of America: Indians, Colonialism, and the Cant of Conquest* (Chapel Hill, N.C., 1975), esp. chaps. 9, 13; and Allen W Trelease, Indi*an Affairs in Colonial New York: The Seventeenth Century* (Ithaca, N.Y., 1960), 60–85.

6. The process of anglicization in the Middle Colonies is too complex to pursue here, but an adequate account would have to examine and compare the different ways that particular ethnic groups were assimilated into the larger culture. For example, see Randall H. Balmer, "Dutch Religion in an English World: Political Upheaval and Ethnic Conflict in the Middle Colonies" (Ph.D. diss., Princeton University, 1985). Balmer argues that New York City Dutch settlers cultivated close ties with the classis of Amsterdam and retained a rather sentimental attachment for the Dutch language while intermarrying with Anglicans and assimilating to upper-class English standards. The Jersey Dutch rejected both the authority of Amsterdam and elite English norms. They adjusted to an English world by going evangelical and aligning with the Presbyterians. Ned C. Landsman's Scots who settled in central New Jersey were commercially active and largely succeeded in capturing and defining the Presbyterian church. In the process they forged a new Scottish-American identity, which, like that of the Jersey Dutch, was linked to revivalism. But Ulster Scots who settled in Pennsylvania's Susquehanna Valley were less commercial and were antirevival. See Landsman, *Scotland and Its First American Colony, 1683–1765* (Princeton, N.J., 1985); and Elizabeth I. Nybakken, "New Light on the Old Side: Irish Influences on Colonial Presbyterianism," *Journal of American History*, LXVIII (1981–1982), 813–832.

7. John M. Murrin, "The Legal Transformation: The Bench and Bar of Eighteenth Century Massachusetts," in Katz and Murrin, eds., *Colonial America*, 540–572, illustrates this process.

8. For a survey, see Murrin, "Political Development," in Greene and Pole, eds., *Colonial British America*, 408–456.

9. Max Savelle, "Nationalism and Other Loyalties in the American Revolution," *American Historical Review*, LXVII (1961–1962), 901–923; Paul A. Varg, "The Advent of Nationalism, 1758–1776," *American Quarterly*, XVI (1964), 169–181; Judith A. Wilson, "My Country Is My Colony: A Study in Anglo-American Patriotism, 1739–1760," *Historian*, XXX (1967–1968), 333–349; Nathan O. Hatch, "The Origins of Civil Millennialism in America: New England Clergymen, War with France, and the Revolution," *William and Mary Quarterly*, 3d Ser., XXXI (1974), 407–430.

10. Sam Briggs, ed., *The Essays, Humor, and Poems of Nathaniel Ames, Father and Son.* (Cleveland, Ohio, 1891), esp. 284–286, 308–311, 313, 324–325; Benjamin Franklin, *Observations concerning the Increase of Mankind* (1755), in Leonard W. Labaree et al., eds., *The Papers of Benjamin Franklin* (New Haven, Conn., 1959–), IV, 227–234.

11. See J. M. Bumsted, " 'Things in the Womb of Time': Ideas of American Independence, 1633 to 1763," *WMQ*, 3d Ser., XXXI (1974), 533–564. Close examination of Bumsted's sources will show that this was a debate among Europeans, including British placemen and travelers in America. Only an occasional native-born colonist participated, often with some bewilderment about why this dialogue was taking place at all.

12. For a classic statement, see Benjamin Franklin, *The Interest of Great Britain Considered, with Regard to Her Colonies, and the Acquisition of Canada and Guadeloupe* (1760), in Labaree et al., eds., *The Papers of Benjamin Franklin*, IX, esp. 90–91. For a shrewd analysis of the role that Independence did play for a major patriot in his strategy of resistance, see Pauline Maier, "Coming to Terms with Samuel Adams," *AHR*, LXXXI (1976), 12–37.

13. See, generally, Pauline Maier, *From Resistance to Revolution: Colonial Radicals and the Development of American Opposition to Britain, 1765–1776* (New York, 1972); David Ammerman, *In the Common Cause: American Response to the Coercive Acts of 1774* (Charlottesville, Va., 1974); H. James Henderson, *Party Politics in the Continental Congress* (New York, 1974).

14. Dickinson to Pitt, Dec. 21, 1765, in Edmund S. Morgan, ed., *Prologue to Revolution: Sources and Documents on the Stamp Act Crisis, 1764–1766* (Chapel Hill, N.C., 1959), 119.

15. John Trumbull, *An Essay on the Use and Advantages of the Fine Arts . . .* (New Haven, Conn., 1770), 3–6, 11–12, 14.

16. Sir Lewis Namier, "Nationality and Liberty," in Namier, *Vanished Supremacies: Essays on European History, 1812–1918* (New York, 1963), 31–53.

17. For recent efforts to understand the patriots in generational terms, see Pauline Maier, *The Old Revolutionaries: Political Lives in the Age of Samuel Adams* (New York, 1980), esp. chap. 6; and Peter C. Hoffer, *Revolution and Regeneration: Life Cycle and the Historical Vision of the Generation of 1776* (Athens, Ga., 1983), which studies younger revolutionaries.

18. Edgar S. Maclay, ed., *Journal of William Maclay, United States Senator from Pennsylvania 1789–1791* (New York, 1890), 210.

19. Quoted in Philip L. White, *The Beekmans of New York in Politics and Commerce, 1647–1877* (New York, 1956), 223–224.

20. Quoted in Max M. Mintz, *Gouverneur Morris and the American Revolution* (Norman, Okla., 1970), 15.

21. L. H. Butterfield et al., eds., *Diary and Autobiography of John Adams* (Cambridge, Mass., 1961), II, 107, 109; Abigail to John Adams, Mar. 31, 1776, in L. H. Butterfield et al., eds., *Adams Family Correspondence* (Cambridge, Mass., 1963–), I, 369. Abigail asked whether the common people of Virginia

were "not like the uncivilized Natives Brittain represents us to be?" The rest
of the letter shows that she believed they were.

22. See, generally, Don R. Gerlach, *Philip Schuyler and the American Revolution in New York, 1733–1777* (Lincoln, Nebr., 1964). For the quotations, see Alexander Graydon, *Memoirs of His Own Time, with Reminiscences of the Men and Events of the Revolution*, ed. John Stockton Littell (Philadelphia, 1846), 158, 179; see also 147–149.

23. For a fuller discussion, see John M. Murrin, "War, Revolution, and Nation Making: The American Revolution versus the Civil War," in Murrin, ed., *Violence and Voluntarism: War and Society in America from the Aztecs to the Civil War* (forthcoming, Philadelphia, 1987).

24. Eugene R Sheridan and John M. Murrin, eds., *Congress at Princeton, Being the Letters of Charles Thomson to Hannah Thomson, June to October 1783* (Princeton, N.J., 1985), 19, 29–30, 66–67, 73, 83, 86, 91–92.

25. Edmund C. Burnett, ed., *Letters of Members of the Continental Congress* (Washington, DC, 1921–1936), VIII, 247–248, 282, 415–416, 533, for some of the major correspondence on this subject. The first public call for separate confederacies appeared in Boston's *Independent Chronicle*, Feb. 15, 1787. Cf. William Winslow Crosskey and William Jeffrey, Jr., *Politics and the Constitution in the History of the United States, Vol. III, The Political Background of the Federal Convention* (Chicago, 1980), 395.

26. See, generally, Richard Hofstadter, *The Idea of a Party System: The Rise of Legitimate Opposition in the United States, 1780–1840* (Berkeley, Calif, 1969).

27. Lance Banning, "Republican Ideology and the Triumph of the Constitution, 1789 to 1793," WMQ, 3d Ser., XXXI (1974), 167–188.

28. For fuller discussions, see John M. Murrin, "The Great Inversion, or Court versus Country: A Comparison of the Revolution Settlements in England (1688–1721) and America (1776–1816)," in J.G.A. Pocock, ed., *Three British Revolutions: 1641, 1688, 1776* (Princeton, N.J., 1980), 368–453; and Lance Banning, *The Jeffersonian Persuasion: Evolution of a Party Ideology* (Ithaca, N.Y., 1978).

29. Peter C. Hoffer, "The Constitutional Crisis and the Rise of a Nationalistic View of History in America, 1786–1788," *New York History*, LII (1971), 305–323.

30. See Edward S. Corwin, *Court over Constitution: A Study of Judicial Review as an Instrument of Popular Government* (Princeton, N.J., 1938), 229–230 n. This incident was probably an example of Confederate humor, not a real event.

31. Charles Royster, "Founding a Nation in Blood: Military Conflict and American Nationality," in Ronald Hoffman and Peter J. Albert, eds., *Arms and Independence The Military Character of the American Revolution* (Charlottesville, Va., 1984), 25–49.

32. Kenneth M. Stampp, *The Imperiled Union: Essays on the Background of the Civil War* (New York, 1980), 3–36, shows how tentative the idea of a perpetual union really was.

7

Fundamental Values, the Founding Fathers, and the Constitution

"WE FORMED OUR Constitution without any acknowledgement of God," President Timothy Dwight told his Yale audience as the War of 1812 loomed threateningly over the community. "The Convention, by which it was formed, never asked, even once, his direction, or his blessing upon their labours. Thus we commenced our national existence under the present system, without God." Dwight traveled a great deal and knew personally some of the delegates to the Philadelphia Convention. Very likely one of them told him about the day on which the Fathers of the Constitution refused to invoke God in any form.[1]

During one of the stormiest moments of the Constitutional Convention, Benjamin Franklin tried to break the impasse between large-state and small-state advocates that threatened to paralyze the proceedings. Why, he asked on June 28, 1787, had the members "not hitherto once thought of humbly applying to the Father of lights to illuminate our understandings?" During the prolonged crisis with Great Britain that had led to Independence, the First and Second Continental Congresses had routinely opened their proceedings with public prayers, he noted. He did not point out that the Rev. Jacob Duché, the principal chaplain to Congress in those years, had somewhat spoiled the overall effect by becoming a loyalist. Instead, Franklin insisted that the United States had already benefited from "frequent instances of a Superintending providence in our favor." *"God governs in the affairs of men,"* he proclaimed

Originally published in *To Form a More Perfect Union: The Critical Ideas of the Constitution*, ed. Herman Beltz, Ronald Hoffman, and Peter J. Albert (Charlottesville: University Press of Virginia, 1992), 1–37.

emphatically. He therefore moved "that henceforth prayers imploring the assistance of Heaven, and its blessings on our deliberations, be held in this Assembly every morning before we proceed to business, and that one or more of the Clergy of this City be requested to officiate in that service."[2]

The motion drew a second from Roger Sherman of Connecticut, one of two born-again Christians at the Convention, although his modern biographer, Christopher Collier, considers him a "political" New Light— someone, that is, who knew that joining the New Light coalition could be a prerequisite to a successful public career and who probably persuaded his neighbors (this point remains unclear) that he had experienced the conversion required of a full church member.[3]

What happened after Franklin and Sherman urged the Founding Fathers to invoke God? Alexander Hamilton, we know, opposed the motion. However proper such a gesture might have been at the outset of the Convention, he argued, it was imprudent "at this late day" because it might indicate to the broader public: "that the embarrassments and dissentions within the convention, had suggested this measure." So James Madison recorded at the time.[4] According to the much later and highly problematic recollections of the youngest delegate at the gathering, Jonathan Dayton of New Jersey, Hamilton accompanied his objections with a highly irreverent speech. We shall probably never know whether Hamilton said anything of the kind at that particular moment, but the sentiments attributed to him by Dayton are quite compatible with the convictions of an admirer of David Hume, the skeptical Scottish philosopher whose writings Hamilton had devoured early in his military career.[5]

According to Dayton, Hamilton "commenced a high-strained eulogium on the assemblage of *wisdom, talent,* and *experience,* which the Convention embraced" and expressed his confidence in the delegates and their abilities. They, he declared, *"were competent* to transact the business which had been entrusted to their care." They "were equal to every exigence which might occur; and . . . therefore he did not see the necessity of calling in *foreign aid!"*[6] After considerable discussion, opponents of the proposal avoided voting explicitly on prayer or God by carrying a motion to adjourn instead.

This controversy is far more revealing than most brief political exchanges. Not only is God never mentioned in the text of the United States Constitution (an omission that has distressed believers ever since), but the delegates deliberately avoided invoking him throughout the four long months of the Convention. As Franklin's notes tersely summarized, "The Convention, except three or four persons, thought Prayers unnecessary."[7] Other than himself, Sherman, probably Dayton, and Edmund Randolph of Virginia, prayer attracted no backers.

This lack of support does not explain why the delegates opposed it. Their motives varied. The "true cause of the omission could not be mistaken," observed North Carolina's Hugh Williamson. "The Convention had no funds."[8] This obstacle may have seemed insuperable to him in 1787, but it had not deterred the First Continental Congress, an earlier body of delegates with no formal budget, from engaging Duché in 1774. George Washington and other members were wealthy enough to donate small stipends had they so desired. According to Madison, "several others" shared Hamilton's practical objection that to bring in a chaplain a month into the convention's proceedings would generate "alarm out of doors" about "the state of things within." Randolph offered an ingenious compromise. Because the Fourth of July was approaching, nobody could object if the Convention asked a clergyman to preach a sermon appropriate to the occasion. After the Fourth, the delegates could begin all daily proceedings with prayers, and no one would notice that a transition had occurred. Franklin seconded this substitute motion, but it failed to get any more support than his original proposal.[9]

Beyond any doubt, the Founding Fathers emphatically refused to pray together while they were drafting the fundamental charter of the new nation. We cannot tell how many of the fifty-five delegates were present for this debate, but the probable minimum is nineteen, and there is no inherent reason to assume that June 28 attracted fewer than the normal average of about thirty delegates present on a given day, unless Luther Martin's interminable oratory of June 27–28 drove from the room even those who showed up on the morning of the twenty-eighth. Prayer lost by at least four to one, and the margin may have been seven to one or even greater. The Constitution's failure to invoke God was no mere oversight. In that respect the document faithfully mirrored the attitudes of the delegates who wrote it.[10]

Today we like to think of the Revolutionary generation as a quiet repository for fundamental values, for our most cherished principles. When we get into trouble, we can turn to the Founders for guidance and certainty. Somehow we have grown more confused than they ever were. But as the prayer incident reveals, the Founders had no one set of principles that everyone could share. At a time when even Congress retained a chaplain and shared public prayers, the delegates refused to pray at all. Theirs was a world in upheaval, not a safe haven for basic truths. Even the fundamentals were changing. As the eighteenth century roared to its conclusion in the maelstrom of the French Revolution. Americans—much like Europeans—divided ferociously over *which* fundamental values they embraced.

Before turning to the broader question of the clash of value systems, perhaps we should look closely at a specific example of what this kind of conflict could involve. What, for instance, did "original intent" mean to the generation that drafted and implemented the Constitution? The question has obvious relevance to our time. During the administration of Ronald Reagan, Attorney General Edwin Meese, Judge Robert H. Bork, and other conservative spokesmen frequently asserted that the courts have gone astray by overinterpreting the Constitution. As a corrective, they insisted, we ought to rein ourselves in by returning to the original intent of the Founders. Disciplined by their restraint, modern judges will not make law. They will administer existing law according to the narrow intent of the Constitution itself.

The demand for original intent has obvious validity—at some levels, anyway. In interpreting the First Amendment, for instance, any court would have to agree that the phrase "Congress shall make no law respecting an establishment of religion" means something fundamentally different from "Congress shall make laws respecting an establishment of religion." The prohibition was real then and still is now.

Problems arise only in cases of disputed meaning. When we disagree about what the Constitution mandates, permits, or prohibits, how do we determine what the Founders intended? The common sense of the matter today is that we should turn to the records of the Federal Convention to learn what individual delegates said about particular clauses. But even if we can agree on the validity of this method, it will not always address our concerns. The records of the Convention are corrupt, incomplete, or vague on many issues, making them an extremely perilous arbiter.[11] And uncertainties sometimes remain in cases where the record itself may be perfectly clear.

One example should illustrate the point. Article I, Section 8 empowers Congress "to raise and support Armies," "to provide and maintain a Navy," and "to make Rules for the Government and Regulation of the land and naval Forces." Article II, Section 9 names the president as "Commander in Chief of the Army and Navy of the United States." The Constitution never uses more general terms, such as the modern phrase, the "armed forces" of the United States. It speaks explicitly of the army, the navy, and also the state militias. Any serious application of the doctrine of original intent ought therefore to conclude that the National Defense Act of 1947 is unconstitutional because it created an armed force unknown to the Constitution and unintended by the Founders, namely, the United States Air Force. The obvious response—that the Founders never dreamed of the existence of an air force—has served us well for over forty years, even though the first successful balloon flight across the English Channel, a highly publicized event, occurred in 1783, and French Revolutionary armies were about to convert hot air balloons to military purposes.[12] While still a member of Congress in 1784, Thomas Jefferson described the early experiments in considerable detail. "The uses of this discovery," he explained, would probably include "traversing . . . countries possessed by an enemy" and "conveying intelligence into a besieged place, or perhaps enterprizing on it, reconnoitring an army, &c."[13] Jefferson has been accused of many things, but creative military imagination is not one of them. If the military uses of balloons occurred instantly to him, no doubt the idea crossed the minds of informed delegates with considerable military experience, such as Washington and Hamilton. In their idle moments they may well have fantasized about an air force coming into being someday, but if so they did not write about these musings, and they experienced no need to empower the new government to create such an arm.

To take a very different issue, the delegates lived in a world in which nearly all blacks were still slaves except for a growing minority that had acquired freedom. The process of emancipation had gained real momentum in the North and still had power in the upper South in the 1780s. But a great majority of blacks would remain slaves until 1865. The Revolutionary generation's sense of civil rights for a mostly enslaved African-American population could hardly be adequate for our age in which all blacks are legally free and equal, a possibility that then must have seemed about as remote as the creation of an air force. Several governments in the South, for example, required the reenslavement of emancipated blacks who failed to leave their state by a certain deadline. Free blacks were free, but hardly as free as whites.

Yet those who demand a return to original intent have problems only with the courts' extension of civil rights, not with their tolerance of the Air Force. This selectivity should tell us that a specific social agenda, far more than a passion for constitutional objectivity, energizes the call for original intent. Civil rights advocates can point to their very powerful bulwarks in the Thirteenth, Fourteenth, and Fifteenth amendments. No comparable constitutional guarantee yet sustains the Air Force.

So far this discussion has said nothing about what the Founders themselves meant by original intent. Interestingly, although they disagreed sharply among themselves, they all rejected the Meese-Bork doctrine. To them original intent could *not* mean referral to the records of the Philadelphia Convention to clarify their understanding of disputed clauses. For half a century under the new Constitution, there was no full text to refer to because Madison refused to publish his notes during his lifetime. He died in 1836, and his notes first appeared in print in 1840. He insisted on this delay precisely so that no one could cite his records in the way that modern conservatives now propose to use them. As he explained to one inquirer in 1821 (the year that Robert Yates's very incomplete notes appeared, silently altered in many particulars by their anonymous editor, Edmond Genet), he withheld publication "till the Constitution should be well settled by practice, and till a knowledge of the controversial part of the proceedings of its framers could be turned to no improper account." His reasoning was explicit. "As a guide in expounding and applying the provisions of the Constitution, the debates and incidental decisions of the Convention can have no authoritative character."[14]

On its face, Madison's logic seems strange, even perverse to us, but it made sense in the eighteenth century and well into the nineteenth. Legislatures and conventions kept journals of proceedings (all formal motions, amendments, votes, and committee assignments) and preserved the precise texts of the measures that they passed, but they did not even attempt to record debates. Those that survive are all unofficial. They reflect the initiative of some particular individual, who may have misunderstood what someone else said, deliberately misrepresented him, or simply omitted a good part of the argument. Some early reporters for the state ratifying conventions and the first federal Congress were alcoholic or doodled aimlessly in the margin while the debates droned on. Madison's own notes, detailed as they are, still compress speeches of several hours' duration into a few paragraphs.[15] Even if we decide to accept the accuracy of these accounts, they only tell us what one man thought, not why the majority voted as it did or what that majority assumed it was doing.

If original intent did not signify to the Founders what our common sense suggests it should have, what did they mean by the phrase? As H. Jefferson Powell has demonstrated, they split into two broad camps, each captained by an author of *The Federalist Papers*, Hamilton and Madison. Underlying their arguments was an ingrained sense of textual criticism derived ultimately from Protestant readings of the Bible. The central injunction remained to stick close to the text. Commentaries or glosses on the text are no substitute for the original and can be dangerous.

But what if the text itself is unclear? Did the Constitution empower Congress to incorporate the Bank of the United States, or did it not? Hamilton said yes. Madison and Jefferson said no. Arguing as a lawyer steeped in English common law, Hamilton insisted that one construed a Constitution the way a court interpreted a statute. The preamble identified whatever evil the measure was trying to correct and indicated in what way doubtful phrases should be understood. In the case of the United States Constitution, the "general welfare" clause would thus give Congress broad discretionary powers, particularly when coupled with the "necessary and proper" clause in Article I, Section 8.[16] This meaning of original intent was soon taken up by Chief Justice John Marshall, but it attracted much dissent.

Jefferson called for a strict-constructionist reading of the Constitution when he urged Washington to veto the bank bill, but only later in the decade would Madison provide a formidable justification for a narrow interpretation of all grants of power to the federal government.[17] A constitution, he insisted, differs from a statute. The majority that drafts a statute also gives it life, but those who draft a constitution have no power to implement it. Only the people can do that through the process of ratification. The real question is not what the drafters thought they were writing, but what the people believed they were implementing. Only the texts of the ratification resolutions—but not accounts of debates in the ratification conventions, which are even more imperfect and inadequate than those for the Philadelphia Convention—can tell us what the Constitution means. Those who ratified the Constitution intended to create a more limited government than either Hamilton or Madison (in their *Federalist Papers,* for instance) fought for in 1787–88, and their will must prevail.

By the 1820s most politicians accepted Madison's argument, even though the Marshall Court remained broadly Hamiltonian. From the Nullification Crisis of 1830–33 until the Civil War, the two views continued in sharp conflict, but Hamilton and Marshall gained strength in the North and finally emerged victorious at Appomattox. The Thirteenth, Fourteenth, and Fifteenth amendments restricted the latitude of the states still further and helped to guarantee that the Hamiltonian understanding of original intent would become the mainstream of American law, making possible even the judicial activism of the Warren Court. A return to the Madison doctrine would now require a repudiation of the Civil War and its constitutional achievements. Even Madison would concede that the opinion of the people, expressed in its most solemn form as a constitutional amendment, must override earlier opinions by the public on the same subject. As matters now stand, the Meese-Bork position requires the repudiation of the only opinion of the Founders themselves on original intent that has had any validity for more than a century without even returning to the only alternative that they ever recognized as viable.[18]

Eighteenth-century differences over original intent suggest a larger problem about fundamental values. Although all the Founders probably believed that such values exist, they did not agree on what they are or how to find them. Instead, contemporaries had to choose among several competing value systems, each with brilliant articulation in the high thought of the day. Humans being what they are, few chose one set of values to the complete exclusion of all others. Most people absorbed strands from more than one source and did their best to reconcile the tensions that their efforts created. In that respect they were not much different from ourselves, except perhaps in their conviction that fundamental values could somehow be identified and affirmed. That question itself now divides, rather than unites us. Situational ethics and moral relativism had not yet found formidable defenders, although the eighteenth century did produce a generous share of religious skeptics who often embodied an incipient form of moral relativism.

The tensions among these systems were real, even if most contemporaries—in America, at least—struggled to reduce rather than magnify them. In general those who lived in the last half of the eighteenth century had to choose among six rival sets of fundamental values: Calvinist orthodoxy, Anglican moralism. civic humanism, early classical liberalism, Scottish moral sense and commonsense philosophy, and the artisanal radicalism best exposited by Thomas Paine.[19]

In North America, strict Christian orthodoxy meant some variant of Calvinism with its commitment to predestination, justification by faith alone, and the primacy of revelation over reason. Calvinists insisted that all men deserve damnation and can do absolutely nothing on their own to avert that terrible sentence. Only God can save them, and they have no chance at all until they realize beyond all equivocation that they have no chance at all, that their best deeds stink in the nostrils of the Lord. All Protestants (and most Catholics, for that matter) were confident that there can be no ultimate conflict between reason and revelation. What God tells us through creation or nature cannot contradict what he has specifically revealed. What separated the orthodox from others on this issue is what they did when they encountered apparent discrepancies. The orthodox began with Scripture and rethought their rationalistic arguments until the two were again harmonious. Their position was anything but obsolete between 1750 and 1800 when Jonathan Edwards and his followers produced the most consistent and persuasive body of Calvinist theology ever generated in North America. To many contemporaries, Edwardsian theology was the most exciting and compelling thought of the age. The unorthodox, by contrast, began to challenge Scripture in the light of reason, an enterprise that Voltaire in particular pursued with zeal, malice, and devastating wit.[20]

Anglican moralism, or latitudinarian theology, took shape in England as an explicit critique of Calvinist orthodoxy. Its most popular manifestation was, beyond any doubt, Richard Allestree's *The Whole Duty of Man,* first published in London in 1658 and often reprinted, a work of practical piety that appeared in nearly every major private library in the colonial South and quite often in small ones as well. Only the Bible, *The Book of Common Prayer*, and various catechisms were more widely owned in colonies that had an Anglican establishment. The elegant writings of Archbishop John Tillotson ably developed the main points of latitudinarianism. Tillotson almost equaled *The Whole Duty of Man* in popularity in the southern colonies and also won many admirers in New England, particularly at Harvard College, after 1700. These Anglicans rejected Calvinist predestination, stressed the careful performance of religious and ethical duties, and assured believers that God would indeed forgive them for any remaining transgressions provided they repented and sincerely begged his pardon. Although Anglicanism was America's most rapidly declining religion by the 1780s, more delegates at the Philadelphia Convention shared that background than any other faith. Most southern planters and lawyers and such northerners as Benjamin Franklin, Gouverneur Morris, and William Samuel Johnson had been strongly affected by latitudinarianism.[21]

Civic humanism (or country ideology, or republicanism), to the degree that it can be traced to Polybius and Cicero, was older even than Christianity, but it had no significant impact on Great Britain until the last half of the seventeenth century or on North America until the second quarter of the eighteenth. To civic humanists the primary concern of man was not salvation but serving the public in a political capacity. There his preoccupation ought to be the preservation of liberty, which those who wield power are forever trying to destroy. In the modern world this attack was usually indirect—through corruption—not head-on through a military coup or other explicit application of force. In the entire history of the world, liberty had seldom held out long against power. In the eighteenth century, only the English and their American colonists could make it thrive. They identified a "mixed and balanced" constitution as essential to Britain's success, and the key to that balance was the "virtue" or "patriotism" of the individual citizen, particularly as embodied in the lower house of the legislature.

This ideology was intensely masculine. Virtue meant the voluntary subordination of one's self-interest to the public good. The supreme act of patriotism was, of course, the sacrifice of one's life for his country. Only autonomous adult males—those not subject to the will of another—could be virtuous. Anyone who was subordinate to someone else's will—women, slaves, children, economic dependents—could not be entrusted with the liberties of a free society. In its most cautious formulation, civic humanism confined liberty to the independent country gentry and the institutions they could control.[22]

England's first civic humanists were self-conscious anti-Calvinists, and the implicit tensions between Protestant orthodoxy, whether Calvinist or Anglican, and civic humanism remained conspicuous. At the psychological level they could be overwhelming. The true Christian, a model of humility, must recognize his (or her) utter worthlessness. The patriot glories in the pride of his (there can be no her) virtue. A committed Christian could become a patriot and make the supreme sacrifice, but men who began as patriots first could not easily accept the full demands—emotional and intellectual—of Calvinist orthodoxy. When John Randolph of Roanoke experienced a severe religious crisis during the War of 1812, he could think of no way to love his neighbors and return good for evil except by retiring from public life for several years and living almost as a hermit. His was but an extreme example of a tension that could afflict any politicized man who had not already committed himself to a Christian denomination.[23]

The fourth option, early classical liberalism, derived from John Locke, particularly his *Second Treatise of Government*, published just after the Glorious Revolution, and was much amplified by Adam Smith's monumental *An Inquiry into the Nature and Causes of the Wealth of Nations*, which appeared in 1776. According to Locke, all humans have rights that antedate history and are even anterior to organized society. The acquisition and protection of property became to him a fundamental reason for creating societies and governments, and a government that refused to protect this right lost all legitimacy. As reworked by Smith and other Scots, the emphasis on natural rights receded but the justification of acquisitiveness increased in importance. Early liberalism worried many contemporaries because it seemed to provide a license for greed and threatened to reduce the common good to a mere sum of individual interests prudently pursued. "That *Man* is designed for *Society*," warned evangelical Calvinist Gilbert Tennent, "appears from the original *Constitution* of the human *Nature*." He feared that men "will be tempted, against the *Law* of *Nature*, to seek a *single* and independent State, in order to secure their *Ease* and *Safety*," an urge that to him violated the "mutual *Love*" that is "the *Band* and *Cement*" of society. To Tennent obligation preceded right, and the very notion of a state of nature seemed morally repugnant.[24]

Smith's arguments were always much more sophisticated than such a criticism implied, and he was far more concerned to liberate the economic energies of ordinary people than to reward the rich with still-greater wealth. But many orthodox Christians saw liberalism as a defense of the sin of greed, and civic humanists had to take alarm at the threat of corruption that any legitimation of acquisitiveness entailed. This question appeared far more urgent in the United States (where voters outnumbered college graduates by many hundreds to one and a high percentage of voters could hold office) than in Scotland (which had several times more college graduates than voters). In Smith's homeland, increasing the wealth and power of the kingdom through the private enrichment of thousands of individual families seemed just about the only civic act open to ordinary men.

The fifth set of fundamental values came out of the Scottish Enlightenment and tried hard to synthesize the other options into one compelling whole. Francis Hutcheson, who shared Locke's passion for natural rights, worried that Locke, by grounding these rights in the ability of ordinary men in a state of nature to deduce their mutual obligations by unaided reason, had hopelessly overintellectualized the process. On Locke's terms only a small elite would ever discover that they had natural rights to protect. Hutcheson's answer to this difficulty was moral sense philosophy. All humans, he insisted, possess an inherent moral sense that tells them without any need to reflect on the subject that certain acts are abominable and others benevolent. Orthodox critics worried that Hutcheson, a Presbyterian minister from Ireland who became professor of moral philosophy at the University of Glasgow, made the moral sense so powerful that it left little room for Original Sin. Hutcheson had to survive a heresy trial to win respectability. His arguments found a broad audience in Scotland, where he became the first academic to lecture in English and thus attracted great numbers of hearers from the community at large. His influence spread to America through excited disciples, such as Francis Allison, and reluctant converts, such as John Witherspoon, a critic of Hutcheson in Scotland who nonetheless appropriated nearly all of his moral philosophy into his own lectures when he became president of the College of New Jersey.[25]

The Scottish Enlightenment reached its most skeptical and daring phase in the writings of David Hume, a political moderate who denied that reason can prove the existence of God, challenged Locke's whole notion of a state of nature and natural rights, and strongly questioned the civic humanist reading of history. Where country ideologues saw only decline in the movement from the "Gothic constitutions" of the Middle Ages to the absolute states of Europe in the eighteenth century, Hume detected improvement in civility and wealth and refused to take alarm at the acquisitive habits of ordinary people. His successors, the moderate literati of Edinburgh and other university cities in Scotland, invented common-sense philosophy to give Protestantism a firm base in human reason, took over Hutcheson's moral sense, but extended Hume's attack on Locke's state of nature. At its peak, the Scottish Enlightenment became intensely historical, seeking answers to human problems in the recorded experiences of human societies.

To a remarkable extent, the Scots invented the social sciences. Hume and William Robertson became outstanding critical historians. Smith's *Wealth of Nations* inspired the modern discipline of economics. Adam Ferguson asked the kind of questions that have become central to sociology. Hume's essay "That Politics May Be Reduced to a Science" launched an endeavor that modern political science continues. These efforts and the more philosophical inquiries of Thomas Reid and Dugald Stewart all found admirers in America, where Scottish moral sense and common-sense philosophy banished all rivals in the colleges through most of the nineteenth century.[26]

For all of its synthesizing instincts, the Scottish Enlightenment could not escape dilemmas of choice. Hume's skepticism always lurked in the background, capable of ensnaring curious students under the most conscientious Protestant teachers. The Scots' emphasis on historical process weakened without repudiating the doctrine of Original Sin. To the gentlemen of Edinburgh, Adam's fall no longer seemed to explain much about their world. This tendency provoked chronic quarrels between the moderate literati, who by mid-century dominated the patronage structure of the kirk, and evangelicals, who also looked to America for allies and found them in the Edwardsians. Witherspoon became distinctive because, not only did he appropriate most of the arguments of the moderates, including their demand for complete religious toleration, but he also remained an evangelical who insisted on the need for religious conversion. Despite his efforts, his students at Princeton increasingly absorbed the secular side of the Scottish Enlightenment at the expense of the theological. The college, a major training ground for ministers before Independence, produced few of them after the war.[27]

A sixth set of values, artisanal radicalism, was much less fully developed as a coherent system through the 1780s. But in the next decade Paine became its most eloquent spokesman, and it found numerous adherents among artisans and backcountry farmers. Until it built explicitly upon the labor theory of value (also traceable to John Locke) in the 1790s, its power to delegitimate the pretensions of others greatly exceeded its ability to legitimate its own claims. Paine's *Common Sense* (1776) demolished forever in America the foundations of hereditary monarchy and aristocracy without eliminating the civic humanist commitment to the common good and to checks and balances. New York City artisans, Philadelphia's radical militia, and such spokesmen for the Pennsylvania interior as William Findley scored brilliant successes in deflating the claims of specific opponents to disinterested benevolence, but by 1790 their own model of a simple unicameral constitution dependent entirely on the people had lost decisively to more complex forms that derived from civic humanism as modified for American society. By equating their artisanal skills with landed wealth as a basis for personal independence and political virtue in American society, radicals appropriated civic humanist values to their own purposes rather than repudiate them entirely. They also enjoyed using angry Protestant rhetoric to bring the elite down a notch or two, although most American churches remained close to conventional orthodox attitudes toward the social order. But with the widespread dissemination of Paine's more systematic writings in the 1790s, the labor theory of value achieved an astonishing impact in Britain and a still greater influence in America. In the 1760s, political spokesmen had often portrayed themselves as disinterested men of leisure. By 1820 any American who hoped to retain an audience had to earn his own living.[28]

In a word, the tensions among these systems could be muted, but they refused to disappear. On some occasions and for some purposes, individuals could overcome the inherent obstacles and draw upon several different systems to create a powerfully persuasive argument. On other occasions people had to make painful choices between them. Jefferson provides marvelous examples of both kinds. The Declaration of Independence put together into a compelling whole central aspects of three of these competing systems. But his effort to grapple with the morality of slavery forced him to choose which value was more fundamental and for whom.

The Declaration of Independence is Lockean in its appeal to natural rights, equality, and the right to revolution. Although Jefferson changed Locke's trinity of life, liberty, and property into life, liberty, and "the pursuit of happiness," he may even have derived that intriguing phrase from Locke's *Essay Concerning Human Understanding*. Sufficiently exposed to Scottish historicity to feel uncomfortable with the state of nature, he usually subordinated the right to property to the more fundamental right of each person to migrate from the society in which he was born. If a man moved to a place with vacant and unclaimed land, he could occupy it himself and thereby establish good title. In effect the migration argument provided him with a functional substitute for the state of nature. It gave him something which really existed in historical time and which acquired impressive explanatory power for North America. Jefferson probably also shared Jean-Jacques Burlamaqui's reservations about making property a natural right. Historically, as eighteenth-century jurists well understood, governments have defined what property is, and the law of property has varied considerably from one society to another. Like many of his contemporaries, Jefferson could accept property as a very basic civil right, defined by government but not anterior to it, provided government adopted uniform rules and enforced them impartially. After 1776 he did not often resort to natural rights arguments.[29]

The civic humanist portion of the Declaration—the indictment of George III—is the longest section of the text. The complaints against swarms of officeholders, the corruption of the colonial judiciary by undermining its independence, and the use of a standing army without colonial consent are vintage items from this tradition. Many of the others could come from both a Lockean or a civic humanist perspective, although the Declaration never explicitly mentions a social contract that the king has violated. Instead it insists that George III "has abdicated Government here, by declaring us out of his Protection and waging War against us"—a rather more legalistic position and perhaps a deliberate echo of Parliament's own position in the Glorious Revolution of 1688 and 1689 when it declared that James II had abdicated his throne by fleeing to France.

Scottish common sense appears in the appeal to "self-evident" truths, and Scottish moral sense emerges in Jefferson's discussion of the relationship between the British and American peoples. In a passage that Jefferson wrote and Congress deleted, he declared that the insensitivity of the British people to American appeals has "given the last stab to agonizing affection." Americans must reject these "unfeeling brethren" who, like their king, had flunked the moral test of empire. "We must endeavor to forget our former love for them, and to hold them as we hold the rest of mankind [—]enemies in war, in peace friends," he added. "We might have been a free and a great people together; but a communication of grandeur & of freedom it seems is below their dignity. Be it so, since they will have it. The road to happiness & to glory is open to us too."[30]

Although the Declaration does invoke "nature's God," it is in no sense an orthodox Calvinist document. Jefferson made no appeal to that tradition in preparing his argument for Independence. Nor did he in any explicit way draw upon Anglican moralism. But American culture soon supplied what he withheld. In all probability, cosmopolitan gentlemen of latitudinarian tastes favored it in disproportionate numbers. Clergymen from a Calvinist tradition rapidly appropriated the full Puritan heritage to explain Independence as a providential act by a people in special covenant with God. This emphasis often acquired a millennial dimension as well.[31]

The Declaration's continuing success as a justification for American nationhood stems largely from Jefferson's ability to combine arguments drawn from widely diverse systems. What did not persuade one person might convince someone else. Orthodox Americans quickly sanctified it in a way that Jefferson had not imagined doing. But he had far less success coping with slavery.

Jefferson considered slavery a violation of natural rights. The king's protection of the slave trade against colonial attempts to abolish it, the Virginian claimed in 1774, placed the interests of "a few British corsairs" above "the rights of human nature deeply wounded by this infamous practice." One of his rejected passages in the Declaration of Independence made a similar argument. Scottish moral sense theory only strengthened this conviction, for it gave Jefferson a way of affirming the moral equality of people whom he could never acknowledge as his intellectual peers. Yet unlike George Washington, Patrick Henry, Robert Carter of Nomini Hall, Richard Randolph, and other Virginia patriots, he never emancipated his own slaves. Until his death in 1826, he kept several hundred people in bondage.[32]

Jefferson justified his slaveholding in civic humanist terms. Throughout his life he felt a horror of debt that makes sense only in the language of country ideology. Debt could destroy his or any Virginia planter's capacity to function as an autonomous and virtuous citizen. The connection between debt and slavery became explicit in an agonized letter that he wrote in 1787:

> The torment of mind I endure till the moment shall arrive when I shall not owe a shilling on earth is such really as to render life of little value. I cannot decide to sell my lands, I have sold too much of them already, and they are the only sure provision for my children. Nor would I willingly sell the slaves as long as there remains any prospect of paying my debts with their labour. In this I am governed solely by views to their happiness which will render it worth their while to use extraordinary cautions for some time to enable me to put them on an easier footing, which I will do the moment they have paid the debts from the estate, two thirds of which have been contracted by purchasing them.[33]

To protect his personal independence, Jefferson came close to blaming his slaves for their condition. It was their fault that he ran into debt buying them. They should be grateful for the opportunity to work harder to pay off that obligation and not be sold. Yet in the 1790s Jefferson had to sell about fifty slaves to satisfy his creditors. He struggled conscientiously not to break up families in the process, but his definition of family did not always coincide with theirs. The subsequent resentment and grumbling from the quarters seemed offensive to his refined sensibilities. Slaves refused to understand why a future president of the United States sometimes felt the need to protect his civic humanist identity at the expense of their Lockean rights.[34]

The conflict of values in the eighteenth century was starkly real, and it affected the Constitution. In different ways civic humanism, classical liberalism, and the Scottish Enlightenment all challenged Calvinist orthodoxy and, to a lesser degree, Anglican moralism. Religious leaders responded by appropriating parts of each. But as the prayer incident reveals, Christian orthodoxy in any form was in short supply at the Philadelphia Convention.

The Founding Fathers did their best to minimize these antagonisms. Franklin, John Adams, and Jefferson all claimed to be Christians. They all thought of themselves as religious men. Franklin routinely said family prayers in his household and in the decade before Independence worked with Sir Francis Dashwood to revise *The Book of Common Prayer* in a rationalist direction. Young John Adams graduated from Harvard College expecting to become a clergyman, but then he veered into law because of particular religious scruples. Jefferson put enormous amounts of time and energy into compiling two religious works that he called "The Philosophy of Jesus" and "The Life and Morals of Jesus." First he selected the passages of the New Testament that he considered morally edifying, mostly from Matthew and Luke. Then he took the best Greek, Latin, French, and English versions of the Bible and put them together as parallel texts for each passage. He, of course, decided which passages to include and which to omit.[35]

All three—as well as Madison, Washington, and other patriot leaders—claimed to be Christians. And yet the truly orthodox quite rightly wondered about the nature of their Christian commitment, except in the case of Washington, whose lack of fervor, distaste for dogma, inability to invoke the word "Christ," and refusal to receive the sacraments seems never to have attracted adverse comment. When Franklin died in 1790, rumors flew throughout Philadelphia. Had he expired with calm resignation? Had he made any formal profession of Christian beliefs? In his case the discrepancies among contemporary witnesses are minor. Franklin affirmed no set of doctrines, but he remained a Christian moralist who believed, or felt that he ought to believe, in an afterlife. Yet popular reports of his skepticism would not vanish. The Constitution, proclaimed *The American Annual Register . . . for the Year 1796*, "betrays as much indifference about religion, as if it had been exclusively penned by Benjamin Franklin himself. It is well known that the doctor believed *nothing*. He was by far the greatest philosopher of whom America can boast. Yet all the world knew that this great man disbelieved Christianity."[36]

Jefferson's "infidelity" finally became a major issue during the presidential campaign of 1800, but he refused to go public with his religious convictions. His decision was prudent, for in some parts of the country he could still have been arrested for blasphemy. Unable to accept the virgin birth, he believed that Jesus was not only the world's greatest moral teacher but also its most important bastard. In advising young Peter Carr about his education in 1787, Jefferson gave him two options about Jesus.

Carr could agree with those "who say he was begotten by god, born of a virgin, suspended and reversed the laws of nature at will, and ascended bodily into heaven." Or Carr could decide that Jesus "was a man, of illegitimate birth, of a benevolent heart, enthusiastic mind, who set out without pretensions to divinity, ended in believing them, and was punished capitally for sedition according to the Roman law." But Jefferson did not give Carr much real choice in deciding between these alternatives. Everyone, Jefferson insisted, ought to "read the bible . . . as you would read Livy or Tacitus." Reason alone must "call to her tribunal every fact, every opinion." "Do not be frightened from this enquiry by any fear of it's [*sic*] consequences," Jefferson added, even if "it ends in a belief that there is no god," because "you are answerable not for the lightness but the uprightness of the decision."[37]

Jefferson may not have been an ethical relativist in quite the twentieth-century sense, but on religious and even social questions he came rather close. Like most other Founders, he optimistically favored broad toleration because he hoped that human reason could improve on the confusion and bigotry that competing orthodoxies had brought to mankind. Reason, not revelation, was primary. Humans still had much to learn about social ethics, and he was convinced that what was morally proper in one society could even be utterly wrong in another. The criterion, he explained, is utility, "Men living in different countries, under different circumstances, different habits and regimens, may have different utilities; the same act, therefore, may be useful, and consequently virtuous in one country which is injurious and vicious in another differently circumstanced."[38]

John Adams aroused less controversy among the orthodox, but his religious convictions were not that different from Jefferson's. "Twenty times, in the course of my late Reading, have I been on the point of breaking out, 'This would be the best of all possible Worlds, if there were no Religion in it!!!'" he wrote Jefferson in 1817. "But in this exclamati[on] I should have been as fanatical as Bryant or Cleverly. Without Religion this World would be Something not fit to be mentioned in polite Company, I mean Hell." These remarks seem to be a preface to an affirmation of Original Sin, but Adams took his argument in quite a different direction. "So far from believing in the total and universal depravity of human Nature; I believe there is no Individual totally depraved. The most abandoned Scoundrel that ever existed, never Yet Wholly extinguished his Conscience, and while Conscience remains there is some Religion."[39] In other words, Adams could affirm Christianity only if Scottish moral sense triumphed over orthodoxy. He refused to subordinate his judgment to anyone else's doctrine or theology, and insisted that he must decide for himself what was or was not orthodox. Like Jefferson, he could not bring himself to accept the divinity of Jesus.

How did this conflict of values connect with the drafting of the Constitution? Of course Jefferson and Adams were both abroad in 1787 and not even at the Convention, but the two men had an important indirect impact on the drafting and acceptance of the Constitution. Through four long months of deliberations, the delegates moved from a prototype that resembled the Virginia constitution of 1776, to which Jefferson had made important contributions, toward one that looked much more like the Massachusetts constitution of 1780, of which Adams was the principal author.[40] When it became clear that the federal Constitution could not be ratified unless the federalists agreed to add a bill of rights, Jefferson employed all his powers of persuasion in urging Madison to respond positively and creatively to this demand.[41] The views of both Jefferson and Adams are quite relevant to the achievements of 1787–88.

The Framers were not atheists. They all affirmed some degree of Christian commitment. But they were not orthodox, either—not many of them, anyway. Forced to choose between orthodoxy and enlightenment, nearly all of them evaluated the word of God by the reason of man, not human reason by the word of God.

The two chief architects of the Constitution, James Madison and James Wilson, had both been heavily influenced by the Scottish Enlightenment, including Hume. Madison as a young man studied Hebrew for a year with John Witherspoon at Princeton, which probably indicates that he seriously considered a ministerial career. As late as 1778 he still defended Calvinist predestination, but as an adult he never joined a Church and was much more successful than Jefferson in keeping his religious opinions private. Other than an acceptance of a divinely sanctioned higher law, it is hard to know what he still believed by the 1780s, but he was no longer an orthodox Calvinist.[42] Wilson, like young John Adams, had rejected the clerical career for which his family had sent him to college. He, too, chose the bar instead. His law lectures place him close to the moderate literati of Edinburgh, fully committed to moral sense philosophy and unwilling to concede any real conflict between it and revelation. The Scriptures, he told his students, "are addressed to rational and moral agents, capable of previously knowing the rights of men, and the tendencies of actions; of approving what is good, and of disapproving what is evil." In other words, the Scriptures "support, confirm, and corroborate, but do not supercede the operations of reason and the moral sense."[43]

Madison, Wilson, and the other delegates at Philadelphia set themselves a daunting task, the creation of a government that—through checks and balances, the separation of powers, and a viable division of legitimate authority between state and national levels—would contain within itself a potential for indefinite endurance. Madison no longer believed, as had many of his countrymen in 1776, that the American people were more virtuous than others. Americans could be as greedy and repulsive as anyone else. Although he too hoped for elementary decency and integrity from average citizens, Madison thought the Framers must devise a government that would behave more virtuously than the people at large. By pitting faction against faction in an enlarged republic run by gentlemen, no majority faction was likely to emerge, and minority factions could fairly easily be controlled through the majority principle. The Constitution thus became a device for establishing a republican government over a population of liberals. Ordinary people would still pursue their self-interest every day, but government would try to accomplish something grander, the common good. Although every national politician was potentially factional on questions that concerned his own or his constituents' interests, no harm would follow unless this minority somehow became a majority. "In the extended republic of the United States, and among the great variety of interests, parties and sects which it embraces," Madison affirmed, "a coalition of a majority of the whole society could seldom take place on any other principles than those of justice and the general good."[44] He hoped that he had created what a later commentator called "a machine that would go of itself."[45]

In the language of today's television evangelists, the Founders drafted a secular humanist text. The Constitution meets all the essential criteria of today's angry preachers, even though "secular humanism" was not a phrase used by the Founders.[46] The Constitution is not Christian in any doctrinal sense. Throughout their deliberations, the Founders consciously rejected any appeal for divine aid and neglected even to mention God in their completed text. This omission was all the more striking because Congress had invoked "the Great Governor of the world" in the Articles of Confederation, and most state constitutions or bills of rights had used at least a similar metaphor for God somewhere in the document.[47]

Nor does the Constitution rest on any broad consensus about Original Sin, a favorite method of Christianizing the document today. Few Founders held orthodox views on that question. Humans, they assumed, are easily corruptible, not irremediably corrupt from conception. I exaggerate just a little in suggesting that, to the Founders, Original Sin, if it existed at all, was a disability that afflicted other people. The men of the Revolution were forever affirming their own disinterestedness and the purity of their motives while denouncing the corruption of their political opponents. As the machine metaphor powerfully suggests, the Constitution is a purely human answer to human problems within history.

These attributes, and the ethical relativism that the Founders shared in an incipient form, are the criteria for secular humanism as defined by the Evangelical Right today.[48] The consequences may be serious. A few years ago William B. Hand, chief justice of the United States District Court for the Southern District of Alabama, declared secular humanism a religion and banned from the public schools all books that, in his opinion, embraced such convictions, including several dangerous home economics textbooks which point out that divorce occurs often these days. He was quickly overturned by a higher court, but if his judgment should ever prevail, and if my analysis is correct, the obvious conclusion is a trifle unsettling. It ought to be unconstitutional to teach the Constitution in American public schools.

Perhaps I should stop there, but the American people did not, and neither shall I. The Constitution did not long remain a distillation of secular humanism, eighteenth-century style. Although the Revolutionary era probably marked the low point in church attendance throughout American history, average citizens were more likely to be orthodox than the Founders, and they soon invested the document with their own religious values and aspirations. What had happened earlier to the Declaration now occurred with the Constitution. The culture Christianized it. Because nothing in the Constitution is inherently anti-Christian, that process began early and achieved considerable but always incomplete success.

No incident better displays this process than what the public learned about Franklin's motion for public prayers at the Convention. The notes of Robert Yates were published in 1821. They give a brief account of what happened. Franklin first acknowledged the difficulties the delegates faced. "As a sparrow does not fall without Divine permission," he asked, "can we suppose that governments can be erected without his will? We shall, I am afraid, be disgraced through little party views. I move *that we have prayers every morning*." Without explaining why, Yates added in a separate one-line paragraph: "Adjourned till to-morrow morning." He did not specifically record that Franklin's motion never carried.[49]

The Yates entry was ambiguous enough to encourage the public to believe what it wished, especially once the ghost of Jonathan Dayton provided encouragement. Around 1815 he had recounted his version of the event to William Steele, who reported it to his son Jonathan D. Steele in 1825, a year after Dayton's death. Steele's version badly garbled what happened. How much of the blame was his and how much was Dayton's we shall never know.

When Franklin finished his speech on behalf of prayer, "never," asserted Dayton, "did I behold a countenance at once so *dignified* and *delighted* as was that of Washington . . . ! Nor were the members of the Convention, generally less affected." While Hamilton attacked the invocation of foreign aid, "Washington fixed his eye upon the speaker, with a mixture of *surprise* and *indignation*." The delegates shared Washington's scorn, for "no one deigned to *reply*, or take the smallest notice of the speaker, but the motion for appointing a chaplain was instantly seconded and carried; whether under the *silent disapprobation* of Mr. H——, or his *solitary negative*, I do not recollect." The Convention then adjourned for the weekend, which Dayton made a part of Franklin's motion. It met on Monday with tempers calmed and a chaplain present, and after prayers it quickly passed the Connecticut Compromise.[50]

Steele's account of Dayton's version of what happened reached the public on August 26, 1826, about seven weeks after the deaths of Jefferson and Adams on the fiftieth anniversary of the Declaration had quite dramatically confirmed to nearly all contemporaries God's overt approval of the American republic. (Former president James Monroe confirmed this tradition by dying on July 4, 1831, but Madison had to pay for his misdeeds. As the last Founder to die, he did not quite make it to July 4 when his time came in 1836. Instead, he expired on June 28, the anniversary of the occasion when he and fellow delegates had defeated prayer at the Philadelphia Convention.) Although Madison denied the accuracy of the Dayton version in private letters, no adequate account became available before Madison's notes were published in 1840.[51] Until then the American people had every reason to believe that the delegates used prayer to solve their most ferocious dispute.

The process of sanctifying the Constitution began with its adoption and has continued ever since. The most common method has been the creation and invocation of a "civil religion," a language representing the lowest common denominator of religious values that most of the public can accept. It permits government officials to invoke God's aid and guidance in a way that comforts and sometimes inspires an audience. At moments of strife or danger, the old Puritan rhetoric of a chosen people can also emerge, and so can the jeremiad when a manifest need to repent and reform seems at hand. At first Federalists, Whigs, and Republicans were rather more comfortable with these devices than were Jeffersonian and Jacksonian Democrats. As the nineteenth century progressed, Whigs and Republicans also tried to give America's civil religion a much more explicit Protestant evangelical content. By the age of William Jennings Bryan and Woodrow Wilson, even many Democrats had joined in, but overt evangelicalism was much more likely to divide than to unite the polity.[52]

What then became of the conflict of values that had helped to generate the Constitution? The competing systems were by no means unique to the United States, but the way that the republic resolved its disagreements about fundamental values probably was. In Britain, for example, early classical liberals knew that they were not orthodox Christians. Although Locke managed to combine much of Anglican doctrine with his own Unitarian convictions, Hume was a skeptic, and the mature Adam Smith may have been an atheist, as were such prominent utilitarians and liberals as Jeremy Bentham and John Stuart Mill. Civic humanism, still a powerful force in Britain during the American Revolution, weakened rapidly thereafter, while Scottish philosophy continued to find adherents even as it lost its base in Edinburgh and became more widely diffused throughout the kingdom.[53]

The United States displays no such pattern. Probably because of the close association between classical liberalism and religious infidelity, almost no American thinkers proclaimed themselves committed liberals. Americans were so proud of their progressive Revolution that virtually no one accepted the label of conservative. The liberal-conservative dichotomy did not become a prominent part of the language of politics, I suspect, until the middle decades of the twentieth century. Wealthy Mahlon Dickerson provides an amusing example of this absence and what it meant. A lifelong Jeffersonian and Jacksonian officeholder who served as senator and secretary of the navy for extended periods, he heard a rumor in 1838 that some people were calling him a "conservative." Though nearly seventy, he spent an exhausting day prowling the state to track down and quash this horrid slander. To him both liberals and conservatives were British, and he rejected nearly everything about the British political system.[54]

Yet as Madison knew as early as *Federalist* No. 10, liberal behavior was quite conspicuous in the United States. In the nineteenth century it became more characteristic of America than of any other society in the world. In its most overt entrepreneurial forms it won enthusiastic support among evangelicals. Liberal values and behavior, if not the philosophical system of liberalism, made converts of the orthodox in America.

To an unusual degree, Americans resolved these tensions through role-playing. The typical liberal was the head of a household trying to feed his family and if possible get rich through intense involvement in the market. Yet he expected his political leaders to be statesmen who, while looking after his local interests, would fight corruption and stand for the public good. Civic humanism continued to provide the conscience of American public life, as the nation's obsession with corruption reveals. The truest Christian was, of course, the American mother in an age that saw the churches drastically feminized. Whether republicans or liberals, nearly all men in the nineteenth century still insisted that women must remain humble and serve others—their parents first and later their husbands and children. Most women probably agreed or at least learned to be resigned to their role, but increasing numbers of them either resisted or used this public acknowledgment of their selfless virtue to demand improved legal and political rights. Scottish commonsense and moral sense philosophy also survived in the United States for most of the nineteenth century, at least in the colleges where the faculty continued to assure generations of students that Scottish thought retained the power to reconcile reason and revelation.

Much of American uniqueness lies in the nation's refusal to admit that the differences in these systems are as fundamental as the values each affirms. The pluralism of the republic has extended, not just to ethnic and religious diversity, but to its basic value systems as well. The main line of political development has pitted a largely nonevangelical Jeffersonian-Jacksonian coalition against a disproportionately evangelical Whig-Republican alignment that has usually derived some kind of reform agenda from its commitment to liberal entrepreneurial values and born-again piety. This compound remains highly unstable but has also been extremely persistent. It can rarely control the country for long, but it never goes away. Two hundred years later it is still battling to reduce the republic and its secular humanist Constitution to a Christianized homogeneity.[55]

The purpose of the Founders was startlingly different from what the Evangelical Right hopes to impose on America. Without the contributions of eighteenth-century secular humanists, the American republic would never have become what it is today. If the original intent of the Founding Fathers survives into the coming century, secular humanism will continue to interact with other value systems in constantly reshaping the nation.

Notes

1. Timothy Dwight. *A Discourse, in Two Parts, Delivered July 23, 1812, on the Public Fast, in the chapel of Yale College*, 2d. ed. (Boston, 1813), p. 24. My thanks to Harry S. Stout for bringing this sermon to my attention. Dwight may have learned about the prayer incident at the Philadelphia Convention from Connecticut delegates Oliver Ellsworth, a personal friend, or Roger Sherman, a participant in the debate and a New Haven resident when Dwight attended Yale as a student. For Dwight's eulogies ol the two men, see his *Travels in New England and New York*, ed. Barbara Solomon, 4 vols. (Cambridge, Mass. 1969), 1:219–21, 4:210–11.
2. Max Farrand, ed., *The Records of the Federal Convention of 1787*, rev. ed., 4 vols. (New Haven, 1937), 1:450–52. On Jacob Duché, see Edmund Cody Burnett, *The Continental Congress* (New York, 1941), pp. 38–40, 252–53.
3. Christopher Collier, *Roger Sherman's Connecticut: Yankee Politics and the American Revolution* (Middletown, Conn., 1971), pp. 36–37, 325. The other evangelical at the Convention was Richard Bassett of Delaware, a good friend and supporter of Francis Asbury, the first Methodist bishop in the United States. Bassett voted frequently at the Convention, but he served on no committees, and there is no record that he ever spoke. He later became

a fairly prominent Federalist politician. See the *Dictionary of American Biography* and, for a hagiographic sketch, Robert E. Pattison, "The Life and Character of Richard Bassett," *Papers of the Historical Society of Delaware* 29 (1900).

4. Farrand, ed., *Records of the Convention*, 1:452.
5. John C. Miller, *Alexander Hamilton: Portrait in Paradox* (New York, 1959), pp. 46–47. Miller questions the authenticity of Dayton's version of what Hamilton said mostly because it suggests an uncharacteristic disrespect for Franklin (see p. 175n).
6. Farrand, ed., *Records of the Convention*, 3:471–72.
7. Ibid., 1:452n.
8. Ibid., p. 452.
9. Ibid.
10. Fifteen delegates presided, spoke, or took notes on the proceedings of Thursday, June 28, which were abbreviated because of the early adjournment. These fifteen men represented nine states, but eleven states were present for a vote the next day. Few delegates would have timed an arrival at or return to the Convention for a Friday. Thus probably at least four other delegates were around for Thursday's debates. But I cannot account for one discrepancy. Early in Thursday's proceedings, Dayton asked that a vote be postponed because Gov. William Livingston would be absent until the next day. Until he returned, New Jersey would be unrepresented. This claim indicates that Dayton alone represented New Jersey at that moment. But William Paterson's notes cover June 28 in detail, even if they are in the handwriting of another New Jersey delegate, David Brearley. See ibid., pp. 444–79, for the two days. For Dayton's request, see p. 445. For Luther Martin's endless, oratory on June 27–28, see 3:271–72.
11. See James H. Hutson, "The Creation of the Constitution: The Integrity of the Documentary Record," *Texas Law Review* 65 (1986–87):1–39.
12. For the 1783 flight, see Charles C. Gillispie, *The Montgolfier Brothers and the Invention of Aviation, 1783–1784* (Princeton, 1983), and Mary Beth Norton, *The British-Americans: The Loyalist Exiles in England, 1774–1789* (Boston, 1972), pp. 91–92. Bernard and Fawn M. Brodie, *From Crossbow to H-Bomb*, rev. ed. (Bloomington, Ind., 1973), pp. 109–10, briefly describe early wartime uses of this invention.
13. Thomas Jefferson to Philip Turpin, Apr. 28, 1784, in Julian P. Boyd et al., eds., *The papers of Thomas Jefferson*, 24 vols. to date (Princeton, 1950-), 7:134–37.
14. James Madison to Thomas Ritchie, Sept. 15, 1821, *Letters and Other Writings of James Madison, Fourth President of the United States*, 4 vols. (Philadelphia, 1865), 3:228. On Yates's notes, see Hutson, "Creation of the Constitution," pp. 9–12.
15. For example, on June 27 Luther Martin of Maryland spoke, according to Robert Yates, "upwards of three hours." Yates's account of this effort runs just over three pages. Madison summarized Martin in a page and a half (Farrand, ed., *Records of the Convention,* 1: 436–41. The quotation is on p. 438).

16. Alexander Hamilton's opinion on the constitutionality of the bank, dated Feb. 23, 1791, is in Harald C. Syrett et al., eds., *The Papers of Alexander Hamilton,* 27 vols. (New York, 1961–87), 8:63–134.

17. See Jefferson's opinion on the constitutionality of the bank, Feb. 15, 1791, in Boyd et al., eds., *Papers of Jefferson,* 19:275–82; Irving Brant, *James Madison,* vol. 3, *James Madison: Father of the Constitution, 1787–1800* (Indianapolis, 1930), pp. 436–37.

18. My discussion of this issue rests heavily on H. Jefferson Powell's outstanding essay "The Original Understanding of Original Intent," *Harvard Law Review* 98 (1984–85):885–948.

19. For a somewhat different taxonomy of value systems, see Isaac Kramnick's important essay "The 'Great National Discussion': The Discourse of Politics, in 1787," *William and Mary Quarterly,* 3d ser. 45 (1988):3–32. Kramnick is analyzing ideas about government and politics. My concern is more with the structured ethical systems available to the Revolutionary generation.

    Other highly developed systems of values also existed in the early republic but had too few adherents to exert much impact beyond their own members, although civic humanism, classical liberalism, and the Scottish Enlightenment undoubtedly affected them in various ways. Examples include Roman Catholicism, Judaism, the Shaker religion, and various strands of German pietism. None of them will he discussed in this essay.

20. Of an enormous literature, see Perry Miller, *Jonathan Edwards* (New York, 1949), and Voltaire, *Philosophical Dictionary,* trans. and ed. Peter Gay (New York, 1962), esp. pp. 58–72, 230–32, 237–44, 248–53, 328–32, 400–405.

21. John Spurr, "'Latitudinarianism' and the Restoration Church," *Historical Journal* 31 (1988):61–82; Norman Fiering, "The First American Enlightenment: Tillotson, Leverett, and Philosophical Anglicanism," *New England Quarterly* 54 (1981):307–44; Richard Beale Davis, *Intellectual Life in the Colonial South, 1585–1763* vols. (Knoxville, Tenn., 1978), 2:580–81, 715, and chap 4. I have used the 1763 Edinburgh edition of *The Whole Duty of Man.* No doubt some estate inventories did not distinguish between that work and *The New Whole Duty of Man* (London 1747 and subsequent editions). *The New Whole Duty* differed from the original primarily in identifying deists rather than Puritans as the principal danger to the Church of England. It thus insisted strongly on certain points of doctrine that the former volume had generally avoided.

22. Within an extensive literature, the most important study of the Anglo-American origins and development of this tradition is J. G. A. Pocock, *The Machiavellian Moment: Florentine Political Thought and the Atlantic Republican Tradition* (Princeton, 1975). For American developments specifically, see Bernard Bailyn, *The Ideological Origins of the American Revolution* (Cambridge, Mass., 1967); Gordon S. Wood, *The Creation of the American Republic, 1776–1787* (Chapel Hill, 1969); Lance G Banning, *The Jeffersonian Persuasion: Evolution of a Parts Ideology* (Ithaca, N.Y.,

1978); and John M. Murrin, "The Great Inversion, or Court versus Country: A Comparison of the Revolution Settlements in England (1688–1721) and America (1776–1816)," in J. G. A. Pocock, ed., *Three British Revolutions: 1641, 1688, 1776* (Princeton, 1980), pp. 368–453.

23. For the anti-Calvinist origins of civic humanism in England, see Blair Worden, "Classical Republicanism and the Puritan Revolution," in Hugh Lloyd-Jones et al., eds., *History and Imagination: Essays in Hanor of H. R. Trevor-Roper* (New York, 1981), pp. 182–200. For a fuller discussion of Randolph in this context, see J. Jefferson Looney and Ruth L. Woodward, *Princetonians, 1791–1794 A Biographical Dictionary*, ed. John M. Murrin Princeton, 1991), pp. 88–102. More generally, see Mark Valeri, "The New Divinity and the American Revolution." *William and Mary Quarterly* 3d ser. 46 (1989):741–69; and Ruth H. Bloch, "The Gendered Meanings of Virtue in Revolutionary, America," *Signs* 13 (1987): 37–58.

24. For the argument that America was far more liberal than civic humanist, see Joyce Appleby, *Capitalism and a New Social Order: The Republican Vision of the 1790s* (New York, 1984), and, for the colonial period, Jack P. Greene, *Pursuits of Happiness: The Social Development of Early Modern British Colonies and the Formation of American Culture* (Chapel Hill, 1988). For discussions of this theme, see John Ashworth, "The Jeffersonians: Classical Republicans or Liberal Capitalists?" *Journal of American Studies* 18 (1984):425–35; Lance G. Banning, "Jeffersonian Ideology Revisited: Liberal and Classical Ideas in the New American Republic." *William und Mary Quarterly*, 3d ser. 43 (1986), 3–19; Joyce Appleby, "Republicanism in Old and New Contexts," *William and Mary Quarterly*, 3d ser. 43 (1986):20–34; John M. Murrin, "Can Liberals Be Patriots? Natural Right, Virtue, and Moral Sense in the America of George Mason and Thomas Jefferson," in Robert P. Davidow, ed., *Natural Rights and Natural Law: The Legacy of George Mason* (Fairfax, Va., 1986), pp. 35–65; and James T. Kloppenberg, "The Virtues of Liberalism: Christianity, Republicanism, and Ethics in Early American Discourse," *Journal of American History* 74 (1987–88):9–33. For the civic consciousness of the Scottish Enlightenment in general and Adam Smith in particular, see the exceptionally strong set of essays in Istvan Hont and Michael Ignatieff, eds., *Wealth and Virtue: The Shaping of Political Economy in the Scottish Enlightenment* (Cambridge, 1983). See also John Robertson, *The Scottish Enlightenment and the Militia Issue* (Edinburgh, 1985). For the quotation, see Gilbert Tennent, *Brotherly Love Recommended, by the Argument of the Love of Christ: A Sermon Preached at Philadelphia January 1747–8 . . .* (Philadelphia, 1748), p. 3. (My thanks to Wilson Carey McWilliams for bringing this passage to my attention.) For Jonathan Edwards's similar anxieties about acquisitiveness, see the covenant that he persuaded his Northampton congregation to adopt in March 1741/42, in Perry Miller el al., eds., *The Works of Jonathan Edwards*, 9 vols. to date (New Haven, 1957–), 4: 550–54; and for a discussion, see

Mark Valeri, "The Economic Thought of Jonathan Edwards," *Church History* 60 (1991): 37–54.

25. See Peter Jones, "The Scottish Professoriate and the Polite Academy," in Hont and Ignatieff, eds., *Wealth and Virtue*, pp. 89–117; David F. Norton, "Francis Hutcheson in America," *Studies in voltaire and the Eighteenth Century* 154 (1976): 1547–118; John Witherspoon, *Lectures on Moral Philosophy*, ed. Jack Scott (Newark, Del., 1982), esp. Scott's Introduction; Ned C. Landsman, "Witherspoon and the Problem of Provincial Identity in Scottish Evangelical Culture," in Richard B. Sher and Jeffrey K. Smitten, eds., *Scotland and America in the Age of the Enlightenment* (Princeton, 1990), pp. 29–45; Garry Wills, *Inventing America: Jefferson's Declaration of Independence* (New York, 1978), esp. pp. 167–319; Ronald Hamowy, "Jefferson and the Scottish Enlightenment; A Critique of Garry Wills's *Inventing America: Jefferson's Declaration of Independence,*" *William and Mary Quarterly*, 3d ser. 36 (1979):503–23. Hamowy powerfully challenges Wills's specific claim for Hutcheson's impact on Jefferson and the Declaration, but the man's widespread influence on educated Americans is undeniable.

26. The best introduction to tins subject is Richard B. Sher's fine book *Church and University in the Scottish Enlightenment* (Princeton, 1985). See also Mark A. Noll, "Common Sense Traditions and American Evangelical Thought," *American Quarterly* 37 (1985):215–38; and Douglas Sloan, *The Scottish Enlightenment and the American College Ideal* (New York, 1971).

27. See Mark A. Noll, *Princeton and the Republic, 1768–1822: The Search for a Christian Enlightenment* (Princeton, 1989). and John M Murrin, "Christianity, Enlightenment, and Revolution: Hard Choices al the College of New Jersey after Independence," *Princeton University Library Chronicle* 50 (1989):221–61. This essay is superseded by Murrin, introduction to Looney and Woodward, *Princetonians*, pp. xvii–lviii.

28. Important studies include E. P. Thompson, *The Making of the English Working Class* (London, 1963); Margaret and James Jacob, eds., *The Origins of Anglo-American Radicalism* (London, 1984): Gary B. Nash, *The Urban Crucible: Social Change, Political Consciousness, and the Origins of the American Revolution* (Cambridge, Mass., 1979); Bernard Friedman, "The Shaping of the Radical Consciousness in Provincial New York," *Journal of American History* 56 (1969–70):781–801; Steven Rosswurm, "The Philadelphia Militia, 1775–1783," in Ronald Hoffman and Peter J. Albert, eds., *Arms and Independence: The Military Character of the American Revolution* (Charlottesville, 1984), pp. 75–118; Gordon S. Wood, "Interests and Disinterestedness in the Making of the Constitution," in Richard Beeman, Stephan Botein, and Edward C. Carter II, eds., *Beyond Confederation: Origins of the Constitution and American National Identity* (Chapel Hill, 1987), pp. 69–109; Isaac Kramnick, "Republican Revisionism Revisited," *American Historical Review* 87 (1982):629–84; Gary B. Nash, "The American Clergy and the French Revolution," *William and Mary Quarterly*, 3d ser. 22 (1965):392–412; and Sean Wilentz, *Chants*

Democratic: New York City and the Rise of the American Working Class, 1788–1850 (New York, 1984), pp. 23–103.

29. An important recent study is Richard K. Matthews, *The Radical Politics of Thomas Jefferson: A Revisionist View* (Lawrence, Kans., 1984), esp. pp. 19–29. For the migration argument, see Jefferson's *A Summary View of the Rights of British America* (1774), in Boyd et al., eds., *Papers of Jefferson*, 1:121–23. For Locke's use of the idea of the pursuit of happiness, see John Locke, *An Essay concerning Human Understanding,* ed. Alexander Campbell Fraser, 2 vols. (Oxford, 1894), 1:341. (My thanks to Thomas L. Pangle for alerting me to this possibility.) The connection between Locke, Burlamaqui, and Jefferson is explored in Morton White, *The Philosophy of the American Revolution* (New York, 1978). For a revealing discussion of the actual restraints upon property in eighteenth-century America, see Forrest McDonald, *Novus Ordo Seclorum: The Intellectual Origins of the Constitution* (Lawrence, Kans., 1985), pp. 9–55. See also Boyd et al., eds., *Papers of Jefferson*, 21:452, index entry under "Rights, natural," an exercise suggested to me by my colleague Daniel Rodgers. For the larger context of the Founders' attempts to tame the radical potential in natural rights theory, see Daniel T. Rodgers, *Contested Truths: Keywords in American Politics since Independence* (New York, 1987), chap. 2.

30. Boyd et al., eds., *Papers of Jefferson,* 1:315–19, 413–33, esp. pp. 319 and 431, for the various drafts of the Declaration, the quotation omitted from the final version, and the abdication passage.

31. See generally John F. Berens, *Providence & Patriotism in Early America, 1640–1815* (Charlottesville, 1978). On the tendency of cosmopolitan gentlemen to support the Constitution, see Jackson Turner Main, *Political Parties before the Constitution* (Chapel Hill, 1973).

32. See Jefferson, *A Summary View* and "Notes on Proceedings in the Continental Congress," June 1–Aug. 7, 1775, in Boyd et al., eds., *Papers of Jefferson,* 1:130, 317–18; Wills, *Inventing America,* pp. 218–28.

33. Jefferson to Nicholas Lewis, July 29, 1787, in Boyd et al., eds., *Papers of Jefferson,* 11:640. In quoting this passage, William Cohen renders "cautions" as "exertions." See his "Thomas Jefferson and the Problem of Slavery," *Journal of American History* 56 (1969–70):516. The original manuscript is blurred and a case can be made for either reading, but Boyd's is more plausible, according to Eugene R. Sheridan, associate editor, the *Papers of Thomas Jefferson*, Princeton University.

34. Cohen, "Jefferson and Slavery," pp. 503–26.

35. See Alfred Owen Aldridge, *Benjamin Franklin and Nature's God* (Durham, N.C., 1967), chap. 13; Lyman H. Butterfield, ed., *Diary and Autobiography of John Adams,* 4 vols. (Cambridge, Mass., 1961), esp. 1:42–43, 73; Eugene R. Sheridan, Introduction to Dickinson W. Adams and Ruth W. Lester, eds., *Jefferson's Extracts from the Gospels: "The Philosophy of Jesus" and "The Life and Morals of Jesus"* (Princeton, 1983), pp. 3–42.

36. Aldridge, *Franklin and Nature's God,* pp. 264–69, esp. p. 268 (quotation).

37. Constance B. Schulz, " 'Of Bigotry in politics and Religion': Jefferson's Religion, the Federalist Press, and the Syllabus," *Virginia Magazine of History and Biography* 91 (1983):73–91; Jefferson to Peter Carr, Aug. 10, 1787, Boyd et al., eds., *Papers of Jefferson*, 12: 15–17. Jefferson never changed his mind about the illegitimacy of Jesus. "And the day will come when the mystical generation or Jesus, by the supreme being as his father in the womb of a virgin," Jefferson wrote John Adams on Apr. 11. 1823, "will be classed with the fable of the generation of Minerva in the brain of Jupiter" (in Lester J. Cappon, ed., *The Adams-Jefferson Letters: The Complete Correspondence between Thomas Jefferson and Abigail and John Adams*, 2 vols. [Chapel Hill. 1959], 2:594).

38. Jefferson to Thomas Law, June 13, 1814, Thomas Jefferson, *Writings*, ed. Merrill D. Peterson (New York, 1984), p. 1338.

39. Adams to Jefferson, Apr. 19, 1817, Cappon, ed., *Adams-Jefferson Letters*, 2:509.

40. For a fuller discussion of this point, see John M. Murrin, "1787: The Invention of American Federalism," in David E. Narrett and Joyce S. Goldenberg, eds., *Essays on Liberty and Federalism: The Shaping of the U.S. Constitution* (College Station, Tex., 1988), pp. 20–47.

41. The relevant portions of this correspondence have been collected in Alpheus Thomas Mason, ed., *The States' Rights Debate: Antifederalism and the Constitution*, 2d ed. (New York, 1972), pp. 170–88.

42. Madison's explicit defense of Calvinism is no longer extant, but much of its contents can be inferred from the recipient's reply. See Samuel Stanhope Smith to Madison, Nov. 1777–Aug. 1778, William T. Hutchinson et al., eds., *The Papers of James Madison*, 19 vols. to date (Chicago and Charlottesville, 1962-), 1:194–212. See also Ralph L. Ketcham, "James Madison and Religion—A New Hypothesis," *Journal of the Presbyterian Historical Society* 38 (1960):65–90; idem, "James Madison and the Nature of Man," *Journal of the History of Ideas* 19 (1958):62–76. Ketcham reads more positive religions affirmations into his sources than I can find. Madison would not have remained so secretive about his convictions, or lack of them, unless he feared exposure.

43. Charles Page Smith, *James Wilson, Founding Father, 1742–1798* (Chapel Hill, 1956), p. 17; Robert Green McCloskey, ed., *The Works of James Wilson*, 2 vols. (Cambridge, Mass., 1967), 1:144. Compare Stephen A. Conrad, "Polite Foundation: Citizenship and Common Sense in James Wilson's Republican Theory," *Supreme Court Review, 1984*, ed. Philip B. Kurland et al. (Chicago, 1984), pp. 359–88. See also Daniel Walker Howe, "Why the Scottish Enlightenment Was Useful to the Framers of the American Constitution," *Comparative Studies in Society and History* 31 (1989): 572–87.

44. *Federalist* No. 51 in Jacob E. Cooke, ed., *The Federalist* (Middletown, Conn., 1961), pp. 352–53. Too often *Federalist* No. 10 is taken as Madison's celebration of liberal America. This passage from No. 51 indicates the republican context in which his acceptance of liberal behavior belongs.

45. See generally Michael Kammen, *A Machine That Would Go of Itself: The Constitution in American Culture* (New York, 1987), p. 18. The phrase comes

from James Russell Lowell's 1888 celebration of the Founders' achievement, but the metaphor of a machine began much earlier (pp. 17–19).

46. However, men of the Enlightenment often called themselves "the parly of humanity." See Peter Gay, *The Party of Humanity: Essays in the French Enlightenment* (Princeton, 1959).

47. For a fuller discussion, see John M. Murrin, "Religion and Politics in America from the first Settlements to the Civil War," in Mark A. Noll, ed., *Religion and American Politics from the Colonial Period to the 1980s* (New York, 1990), pp. 19–43, esp. pp. 29–30. For the Articles of Confederation, see Samuel Eliot Morison, ed., *Sources and Documents Illustrating the American Revolution, 1764–1788, and the Formation of the Federal Constitution,* 2d ed. (Oxford, 1929), p. 186, Art. 13.

48. So a number of TV evangelists have declared in numerous television sermons, although I have not taken notes while watching them and cannot cite any particular one.

49. Farrand, ed., *Records of the Convention*, 1:457–58.

50. Ibid., 3:467–73, esp. pp. 471–72.

51. Madison to Jared Sparks, Apr. 8, 1831; Madison to Thomas S. Grimke, Jan. 6, 1834, ibid., pp. 499–500, 531.

52. Catherine L. Albanese, *Sons of the Fathers: The Civil Religion of the American Revolution* (Philadelphia, 1976); John F. Wilson, *Public Religion in American Culture* (Philadelphia, 1979).

53. Locke's religiosity, once widely doubted, has been generally accepted since the publication of D. G. James, *The Life of Reason: Hobbes, Locke, Bolingbroke* (London, 1949). On Smith, see John Dunn, "From Applied Theology to Social Analysis: The Break between John Locke and the Scottish Enlightenment," in Hont and Ignatieff, eds., *Wealth and Virtue,* p. 120. For later utilitarians and liberals, see Elie Halévy. *The Growth of Philosophic Radicalism,* trans. Mary Morris (Boston, 1955). For a fine study of the indirect ways in which civic humanism continued to affect nineteenth-century British thinkers, see J. W. Burrow, *Whigs and Liberals: Continuity and Change in English Political Thought* (Oxford, 1988).

54. Mahlon Dickerson, entry for Aug. 20, 1838, Diary, July 16, 1832–Aug. 26, 1845, typescript copy, p. 104, Mahlon Dickerson Papers, New Jersey Historical Society, Newark

55. For these purposes, perhaps the best single introduction to nineteenth-century American political culture is Paul A. Johnson, *A Shop-keeper's Millennium: Society and Revivals in Rochester, New York, 1815–1837* (New York, 1978). On the transformation of American Protestantism, see Nathan O. Hatch, *The Democratization of American Christianity* (New Haven, 1989).

8

The Making and Unmaking of
an American Ruling Class

UNLIKE EUROPE, THE United States in the mid-nineteenth century had no visible ruling class. The most prominent old families and the wealthiest men in the country seldom held high office or controlled major policy decisions, nor were their children any more likely than they to exercise public power. Although white laboring men who worked for wages had no chance to hold office and blacks, women, and paupers could not even vote, formal political power had shifted dramatically from the top toward the middle of society.

Most Americans take this situation for granted. They should not. The American colonies seldom lacked ambitious men eager to establish their own claim to rule. The seventeenth century treated them rudely, but for much of the eighteenth the thrust of political and social change favored their goals. The Revolution both challenged and invigorated their aspirations, but they finally failed. They prospered—but they did not govern.

This essay, after describing the devices that England's ruling class used to establish and maintain its dominance, traces similar efforts in the colonies, especially Virginia, Massachusetts, New York, and Pennsylvania. Their founders took it for granted that a sharp boundary ought to separate rulers from the ruled, but none of them could replicate the English system in the seventeenth century. Between 1690 and 1760 this gap between their aspirations and political realities narrowed greatly. The richest and most prestigious families increasingly monopolized high office. At no time in American history have wealth, power, and status coincided more closely. The thrust of social and economic change seemed strongly in their favor

Originally published in *Beyond the American Revolution: Explorations in the History of American Radicalism*, ed. Alfred F. Young (DeKalb, IL: Northern Illinois University Press, 1993), 28–79.

until they confronted an unexpected challenge from the British imperial state and its highly developed ruling class. Upper-class colonists in public life had to choose between loyalty to Britain at the cost of popular disfavor, and active resistance to Britain, which meant appealing to and building upon the discontent of ordinary people. Once elite patriots accepted independence, they had to discover whether they still possessed the political resources to control public life in their states. As it became clear that they did not, many of them turned to the continental level to build the leverage they would need to become a *national* ruling class. This struggle turned into one of the most momentous and contested issues of the 1790s. The triumph of the Jeffersonian Republicans over the Federalists after 1800 decisively undermined the effort to establish a national ruling class. Public office went increasingly to middling men, not the very rich.

We are not discussing what to Karl Marx was the greatest transformation in class relations in modern times, the separation of ownership from the means of production and the social and political changes that followed from that shift. We are analyzing the dynamics of class relations before that transition occurred, a problem that has fascinated Marxists, neo-Marxists, and non-Marxists. We are also trying hard not to reify a subject that was always in motion. E. P. Thompson said it well in 1963: "The [class] relationship must always be embodied in real people and in a real context. . . . And class happens when some men, as a result of common experiences (inherited or shared), feel and articulate the identity of their interests as between themselves, and as against other men whose interests are different from (and usually opposed to) theirs." Nor should we expect identical systems to occur in different societies. "Consciousness of class arises in the same way in different times and places," he added, "but never in *just* the same way."[1]

Before proceeding, we need to provide a few basic definitions. *Ruling class* refers to a class that dominates both the socio-economic sphere (or civil society in Marxian terminology) and the political sphere (i.e., the State). A ruling class in the fullest sense of the term exercises direct control over the most powerful agencies of government. Thus it not only rules by means of hegemony but also exercises and controls sovereignty. Put more simply, in a country with a ruling class, the people who own the place also govern it. "It is not a new idea," wrote John Jay in 1810, "that those who own the country are the most fit persons to participate in the government of it."[2]

In preindustrial England, families with the greatest wealth and dignity dominated public life. Components of this ruling class included *aristocrats* with hereditary estates and titles (duke, marquess, earl, viscount, and baron) and the *gentry,* families below the aristocracy with enough landed wealth to live off their rental income. Together, aristocrats and gentry controlled Parliament—indisputably the most powerful institution in the English government by the eighteenth century. In exercising power, they obtained advice and major services from other prominent persons, such as merchants, bankers, and lawyers. These people in turn usually called themselves *gentlemen,* an imprecise but much used word that suggested someone of cultivation and wealth who did not have to work with his hands. (The gentry, unless they had a higher title such as baronet or knight, also called themselves gentlemen, but most gentlemen ranked below the gentry.) Merchants and professionals served the ruling class in important ways, but few really belonged to it.[3]

In the colonies we speak not of a ruling class (or separate ruling classes) but instead of *upper classes* and *elites.* These terms are less precise yet still useful. By *upper class* we mean roughly the wealthiest five percent of provincial society, men who in various ways had distinguished themselves from most of their neighbors. Components of the upper classes differed somewhat from one colony to another but included planters with more than twenty servants or slaves, other landlords with large holdings, the richest merchants, and, eventually, many lawyers. By *elite* we mean the men who held the most important political offices in a colony, including seats in the provincial assembly. In the eighteenth century, as we shall explain, the colonial elites were increasingly comprised of upper-class individuals. Yet because they remained subject to the supreme political authority of Crown and Parliament, we do not consider the various colonial elites to have been genuine ruling classes. From this perspective, it might indeed have taken a revolution to transform separate colonial elites into a consolidated ruling class.

The Remaking of the English Ruling Class

Throughout the period between the founding of the American colonies and their successful revolution against Great Britain, every European society had a visible ruling class. Usually the wealth of these families came from landed estates. They had formal aristocratic titles, they acquired the cultural and political skills necessary to manage existing governments, and they expected to pass on their status to their descendants. Every viable ruling class also had to have ways of recruiting small numbers of outsiders into its circle, if only because in every generation a fair percentage of dominant families failed to maintain the male line. But the boundary between rulers and ruled was sharp.

"Nothing appears more surprising to those who consider human affairs with a philosophical eye, than the easiness with which the many are governed by the few; and the implicit submission, with which men resign their own sentiments and passions to those of their rulers," wrote David Hume in the mid-eighteenth century. "When we inquire by what means this wonder is effected, we shall find that, as Force is always on the side of the governed, the governors have nothing to support them but opinion."[4] Hume described what a later generation would call deference, a system of social relationships in which men of inferior resources (family, wealth, education, or all three) willingly defer to the judgment of their superiors in matters of public concern. When deference functioned well, yeomen routinely voted for the largest landholder in their part of the county, as did tradesmen for wealthy merchants in the cities. Nonvoters willingly obeyed the laws passed by their superiors.[5]

But deference was not the only means available to command assent. The state also used influence and, when all else failed, naked force, either legal or military. Those in power could win support from below by distributing favors—patronage, honors, pensions, contracts—among people who might otherwise resist their policies. Recipients of major posts—for example, an army colonel or a commissioner of the board of customs—had lesser favors to bestow on people below them, the whole system constituting a network of *clientage,* which also had its counterpart in the more private world of ascending household economies. Every British ministry in the eighteenth century routinely used large doses of these forms of influence to maintain its majority in the House of Commons.[6]

Like other European states of the same period, the British government tried to maintain a monopoly of violence, first by disarming 90 percent of the population, and—especially after 1660—by building a standing army. Every government relied, in short, on a mix of deference, influence, and force. In England the British government depended primarily on deference and influence, but it was willing to employ force when the stakes were high. It passed the Riot Act in 1715 to make force readily available to local magistrates. The Black Act of 1723 turned the judicial system into a ruthless engine for crushing poachers. Some of the government's efforts to stamp out smugglers resembled small wars against coastal communities. Finally, under threat of the French Revolution, the British state used the law quite mercilessly to smash the radical egalitarians of the 1790s. In Scotland after the union with England in 1707, the emphasis was on influence and force rather than deference, for which few active opportunities were available. Voters there were rarer than college graduates, and the state did not even encourage the creation of a militia of Protestant gentlemen eager to demonstrate their loyalty to the regime. Instead, the Jacobite risings of 1715 and 1745 met savage repression by the British Army. Ireland's aristocracy and gentry relied even more blatantly on the routine use of soldiers to secure obedience. England, Scotland, and Ireland each had a ruling class, in other words, but they dominated their societies in different ways.[7]

Even in England the full system took time to develop. Much of it did not yet exist when the first colonies were founded between 1607 and 1640. The crown had no standing army and very limited patronage to bestow. It governed mostly through the willing services of landed aristocrats and greater gentry, men who could be alienated. It had few resources beyond the network of deference and clientage built into an aristocratic social order. A major rift within this ruling class, especially over a subject as sensitive as religion, could unravel the system that gave those who governed power over others.

Rulers, in short, could be challenged. Between 1640 and 1660 Parliament went to war with King Charles I, executed him in 1649, abolished the House of Lords, and established a commonwealth for eleven years. Real power soon passed to Oliver Cromwell, a puritan general who never lost a battle and who spent the last decade of his life trying to reconcile traditional notions of a proper ruling class with puritan demands that only the godly hold office. Less exalted Englishmen, such as the Levellers and Diggers, demanded a much more radical restructuring of English society. Cromwell's efforts failed even before his death in 1658, and less than two years later the Restoration of Charles II brought back government by king, lords, and commons. The rest of the seventeenth century would show that to achieve stability the aristocrats who governed had to broaden their social base to include most of the gentry.[8]

By 1688 England's ruling class was secure enough to drive out King James II, a Catholic, and invite in the Protestant William of Orange from the Netherlands and make him King William III, all without serious political or social disruption. This Glorious Revolution guaranteed that the House of Commons, a bastion of gentry power, would finally become essential to the entire governing process. It has met every year since 1689, and from 1721 to 1742 Sir Robert Walpole demonstrated that a commoner as prime minister could be far more effective than a lord. Throughout the period the British state became much bigger, greatly expanding the patronage and military force available to the governing few. So long as he had well over a hundred offices to distribute among eager MPs, a prime minister who sat in the Commons was seldom outvoted by any bloc of opposition forces. The British state that the colonists encountered by 1760 was thus quite a different phenomenon from the one the founding generations had known in the first half of the seventeenth century.[9]

Where There's a Will, There's Not Always a Colonial Way

The people who settled colonial America were used to a visible cleavage between the governed and those who rule. They were not accustomed to the routine use of military force in civil government, nor after the very early years did they bring many soldiers with them. Most settlers probably thought that their provincial societies ought to embody the distinction between rulers and the ruled in much the same way that England did before 1640, which meant an emphasis on deference and influence rather than force. They expected a high correlation between status, wealth, and power among the men in office.

Largely through circumstance but partly through choice, no such system took firm hold in the seventeenth century. Only in the eighteenth century would most colonies begin to achieve something resembling a European division of responsibility between rulers and ruled. Nowhere was this process complete, even in the eighteenth century, but it went further in Virginia than anywhere else. Massachusetts, which challenged the English formula in fascinating ways during its period of puritan rule, moved toward a more conventional English system in the eighteenth century, but it did not develop an elite as confident as the planter gentry of Virginia or as capable of passing on its status to its descendants. The gentry, merchants, and lawyers of colonial New York were much more successful at monopolizing high offices, but along the way they encountered frequent resistance to their claims, both from within and from below. Pennsylvania did not lack for gentlemen after about 1720, but their ability to rule was always precarious. A comparison of these four colonies, with occasional glances at others, should illuminate both the potential for creating upper-class political elites in America and the limitations inherent in the process.

Titled aristocrats and landed gentry did not come to America. The few who crossed the ocean seldom stayed. The Crown, the various lord proprietors (such as the successive Lords Baltimore in Maryland or William Penn and his descendants in Pennsylvania), and the corporations that founded colonies (such as the Virginia Company of London and the Massachusetts Bay Company) had to give power to individuals further down the English social scale. They turned to men who had in some way distinguished themselves from ordinary settlers, to those who were in the process of becoming provincial upper classes, or elites. Virginia's largest planters certainly qualified. So did the patroons and manor lords of the Hudson Valley and the wealthiest merchants of Boston, New York City, and Philadelphia. Men with a full or partial college education were also exceptional. The younger sons of minor English gentry, just outside the ruling class in England, had an excellent chance to become justices of the peace, assemblymen, or even members of the governor's council in America. But except in New England, seventeenth-century America offered few chances for education or other refinements. A founder's success in acquiring wealth and office did not guarantee that his sons would possess the same advantages. Early death, of father or sons, often magnified these difficulties.[10]

This necessity to recruit officeholders in America from below the top echelons of the English social hierarchy had important consequences, some of them permanent. Many of the men who acquired office in early America were the younger sons of English gentry or merchants. They showed little inclination to impose primogeniture and entail (the legal devices that sustained the privileges of eldest sons) upon their new societies. Compared with Europe, the English colonies were from the start a paradise for younger sons. That change took root so deeply that it has never been seriously challenged.[11] In like manner the absence of a standing army in most colonies for most of the colonial era compelled the government to insist (except in Quaker societies) that the settlers arm themselves. In no American province did the government establish the monopoly of violence that Europe took for granted by the eighteenth century, and firearms were always and still are more widely available in America than in other Western countries.[12]

The legitimacy of the newcomers' claim to power rested on two sources. One was approval by government and therefore by the English state. The other was willing acceptance by the community they served. Often it was difficult to get both. Legitimacy then remained perilous and could be challenged. This kind of tension made it nearly impossible before the Glorious Revolution of 1688–89 to find men whose right to govern was accepted on both sides of the ocean and who could be confident that their sons would enjoy the same status.[13]

Virginia

The Convergence of Upper Class and Elite

Virginia illustrates all of these problems and the process by which most of them were overcome. A political elite acceptable to both the Crown and to ordinary settlers did not take hold for several generations. Only during the forty years after 1690 or 1700 did the major officeholders of the colony begin to look much more like a traditional ruling class. These men were the economic, political, and social leaders of their society, and everyone knew it.

Virginia in the very early years had many true gentlemen, but when they met disease and death instead of quick wealth, the survivors retreated to England. Power fell to an ambitious group of men who prospered during the tobacco boom of the 1620s, but few of them lived long enough to pass on their advantages to their sons or produced sons who survived long enough to inherit their fathers' status. Instead, at a time when perhaps 85 percent of the Europeans who went to Virginia arrived as indentured servants, the major offices in the colony went to a new wave of free immigrants that contained the first Blands, Byrds, Carters, Harrisons, Jeffersons, Lees, Randolphs, and Washingtons. Often younger sons of minor gentry or London merchant families, they understood political power, and from the 1640s to the 1670s they began to monopolize appointments to the county courts and elections to the House of Burgesses. They had the resources to begin purchasing servants or slaves, and access to power also helped them to acquire large tracts of land. They probably thought of themselves as the first generation of a secure ruling elite for Virginia, at least until Bacon's Rebellion taught them a disturbing lesson in 1676.[14]

Nathaniel Bacon's success revealed the weakness of deference and the brittleness of public authority in Virginia. Several months into a costly war with the Susquehannock Indians, Bacon denounced the governor's reliance on expensive forts (good only for defense) and offered to lead unpaid volunteers in offensive campaigns against neighboring tribes, hostile or neutral. When small planters (those with few or no servants) sided overwhelmingly with Bacon against not only the governor but also a reforming House of Burgesses, the government collapsed during the summer and had to be restored in the autumn months through the armed might of the London tobacco fleet. The upheaval terrified the men around the governor, Sir William Berkeley, and made them far more conscious of their upper-class identity. They castigated the rebels as "an insulting rabble . . . who account the Law their manacles, and like swine turn all into disorder & become insolent [and] abuse all in authority." Bacon, in a famous appeal, mocked the social pretensions of his opponents. They were, he charged, "unworthy favourites and juggling parasites," mere "sponges" who had "sucked up the public treasure." Himself a gentleman by birth, Bacon assured his followers that the governor's men had no better social qualifications than many of the rebels. But this appeal to class resentments never became an explicit class struggle, a demand to destroy a ruling class. Instead, Bacon denied that Virginia had one.[15]

Over the next half century the men who governed Virginia's counties and dominated both houses of its legislature became something much closer to a typical ruling class. By 1700 they already showed considerable success in passing on their wealth and their offices to their sons. By then planters with twenty or more slaves dominated the council. By the 1720s and 1730s big planters also controlled the House of Burgesses, the county courts, and the vestries in those parts of the colony that had passed beyond the frontier stage. The line between small and large planter was not easily bridged. Few could cross it through savings, hard work, or the annual profits from tobacco, but British newcomers who brought capital or education with them could still enter the governing elite.[16]

By the eighteenth century the bastion of power for great planters was the county court, buttressed by the Anglican vestry. Both were co-optive bodies. When vacancies arose, in other words, the existing members decided who would fill them, and the governor merely ratified the result with a formal appointment. With very few exceptions, a planter had to be named by his peers to the county court before he could stand for the House of Burgesses, and the men elevated to the council usually had prior experience in the lower house. Each county also had numerous lesser offices ranging from lowly fence viewers to more exalted grand jurors and, the only position that paid well, tobacco inspectors. The justices distributed these posts among the small planters, apparently with an even hand. Planters who voted were likely to receive some post or other. Modern scholarship has still not determined whether these appointments reflected a general pattern of deference or whether they concealed a system of clientage and influence that linked particular small planters to individual justices. Very likely some combination of both prevailed in different proportions from one county to another, but deference probably outweighed influence in most.[17]

As the great planters built their impressive houses after about 1720, indulged in genteel culture and recreations, and passed on their advantages to their children with ever-less effort, few could doubt that those who governed in Virginia had become an easily recognizable group of interrelated planter dynasties. Except for the coercive relationship that bound slaves to their masters, the system seldom relied upon force. Small planters accepted rule by great planters with little thought of ever creating an alternative system. Virginia had become a participatory oligarchy in which both small and great planters understood their social and political roles.[18]

Virginia's governing elite increasingly resembled England's ruling class but never fully replicated it. Some differences remained critical—the labor systems of the two societies, the commercial origins of most of the colony's first families, the continuing ability of the elite to provide for younger sons, and the relative absence of ties of patronage between great planters and the governor. Successful governors earned support among the burgesses through persuasion, not patronage. For half a century the system worked quite well, long enough to convince the great planters that they deserved to rule.[19]

New England

From Godly Rule to Upper-class Empowerment

Just as colonial Virginia provided opportunities to rule for people who would have had no such claim in England, early New England also explored social and political possibilities not open in the mother country. The puritans expected to be governed by godly laymen. The gentry among them, such as John Winthrop, intended to limit the active exercise of political power to godly gentlemen. Less exalted puritans fought to gain a share of that power. As religious motivation lost intensity after 1689, a much more secular elite began to emerge. In the eighteenth century these men made formidable gains. The underlying trend was toward the consolidation of power in fewer hands, although the men in office still had to satisfy both the Crown above them and the people below. In 1760 they were not yet a fully secure governing elite, but they had traveled a long way in that direction since the seventeenth century, and the momentum of historical change seemed strongly in their favor.

The most bracing political innovation in seventeenth-century New England was a largely successful effort to create a stable political system built as much upon individual piety as upon social class. The puritan colonies institutionalized what Cromwell had tried only briefly and then abandoned, government by the godly. The leaders of this effort hoped to minimize the difference between what they were actually doing and what they had known in England. John Winthrop, Thomas Dudley, Sir Richard Saltonstall, Theophilus Eaton, and a few other founders were conspicuous "saints" (that is, their neighbors agreed that they had had a valid conversion experience) and also came from at least the outer edges of England's ruling class. Winthrop, Dudley, and Saltonstall all founded political dynasties that exercised power in Massachusetts and Connecticut into the eighteenth century. They expected to make most of the important political decisions for their colonies themselves. They never established that degree of control.[20]

In the 1630s several English puritan aristocrats sought assurances that, if they migrated to New England, they and their heirs would be guaranteed the right to hold high office. John Cotton, speaking for the men already in power, tried to reassure Lord Viscount Saye and Sele that he and his friends were indeed welcome and that Massachusetts would be an aristocracy, not a democracy. But Cotton appealed to scripture in refusing a guarantee of hereditary rule. He could not yield on the main concern of his inquirer, and the puritan lords never did migrate to New England.[21]

Winthrop preferred to have laws made by a small group of "magistrates" elected by the people each year but, in all likelihood, retained in office for life. Puritan voters continually demanded a bigger role for themselves and major restrictions upon the magistrates. Drawing upon the Massachusetts Bay Company charter, they insisted upon electing a House of Deputies to meet four times a year with the magistrates, who in turn emerged as the upper house of the legislature by the 1640s. Winthrop thought of the magistrates as the governing few and the deputies as among the governed, but the deputies would not accept this distinction. They won for themselves an essential share of the power to make laws, and they used it to pass a Body of Liberties in 1641 and a fuller law code in 1648 to restrict the discretionary powers of the magistrates. Neither text had the approval of any authority in England.[22]

After the Restoration, the king became far more threatening to New England's autonomy. Even a charter might not help, as Massachusetts discovered when the Crown revoked the patent of the Massachusetts Bay Company in 1684. From 1686 to 1689 James II ruled Massachusetts through an appointive governor, council, and court system. The House of Deputies was abolished. By 1688 the Crown had merged all of the New England colonies, New York, and East and West New Jersey into a much larger province called the Dominion of New England. Governor Sir Edmund Andros had no intention of confining power to God's elect. He brought into office a number of merchants and other gentlemen who had been excluded on religious grounds before 1686, but by 1689 even many of the newcomers, initially intrigued by the prospect of becoming North America's first intercolonial ruling elite, had grown weary of the autocratic Dominion government. In the wake of England's Glorious Revolution, Boston had one of its own in April 1689 and overthrew the Andros regime. To ensure broad popular support, Massachusetts created several hundred new freemen or voters, in effect abrogating the old government's requirement that they be church members. The era of strict puritan rule was over. In 1691 a new royal charter imposed an appointive governor and justices upon Massachusetts, restored the assembly, and accepted property qualifications, not orthodoxy, as the proper way to limit suffrage.[23]

One result was a drastic change in the people holding office. Few deputies under the old charter became representatives under the new. Partly a generational shift and partly a repudiation of the men who had failed to resist the Dominion of New England adequately, this transformation led to frequent turnover of representatives and considerable uncertainty in government. For two generations godly rule had provided a workable substitute for a conventional ruling class. The province now had to discover whether it could devise a way to do without either or whether it could generate its own ruling families acceptable both to the voters and to British authorities.[24]

In the 1690s about half the representatives in any given assembly were newcomers to the house. By the 1760s that proportion had plummeted to one out of seven. In the 1690s the governor's appointees as justices of the peace (a royal patronage position in Massachusetts in a way that it was not in Virginia) were usually seen as intruders by their towns and seldom elected to the house. By the early 1760s about two-thirds of the representatives were justices, most of whom supported administration policy most of the time. Because the number of offices grew much more slowly than the population, the men who held office stood out more conspicuously over time. And this phenomenon had a pronounced dynastic effect. In two-thirds of the towns that participated actively in provincial politics, four families controlled the office of representative at least two-thirds of the time. In a third of the politically active towns, two families held that post at least half the time. At the highest levels of provincial politics by mid-century, a few families—notably the interrelated Hutchinsons and Olivers—began to act as though Massachusetts owed them its most prestigious appointments, to the great annoyance of such ambitious but less distinguished rivals as the Otises and the Hancocks.[25]

Deference certainly explains much of the success of this emerging elite, but by no means all of it. Far more than in Virginia, royal government in Massachusetts also relied upon influence. Even though their income from fees was never great, those who received appointments from the Crown (the most common were justices and militia officers) and secured election to the legislature were expected to support the governor's policies. But when they voted for highly unpopular measures, the voters could punish them. In times of crisis (the land bank dispute of 1740–41, the controversy over specie resumption after 1748, the excise crisis of 1754), some justices defected to the opposition, and the overall percentage of justices in the house fell sharply, only to climb to greater heights a few years later. The new secular elite had grown accustomed to exercising considerable power, but by 1760 it was still not strong enough to take its position for granted. Even the best families, although they normally got their way, could be challenged. In the hothouse politics of the town of Boston, they usually were.[26]

The Mid-Atlantic

The Challenge of Cultural Diversity

The Mid-Atlantic colonies represented still other variations on the same theme. Upper classes emerged in New York and Pennsylvania who laid claim to office on the basis of wealth and family prestige. But ethnic and religious tensions made it difficult to create traditional deference systems that would work effectively across these cultural barriers. These antagonisms almost guaranteed that there would be political conflict within elites, and they greatly complicated the relationship between the elites and ordinary settlers. New York and Pennsylvania devised quite different solutions to these problems.

New York stood out from the rest of North America in one particular. Both under Dutch and English rule it had a small military garrison. Its governors could contemplate the use of overt force in a way that neighboring executives could not. Until about 1700 this threat had a real if unmeasurable impact on public life. Even more characteristic of early New York politics was ethnic conflict, often cast in religious terms. Dutch settlers resented their English conquerors and looked to Calvinism and the Dutch Reformed Church to preserve their way of life. Every English governor, by contrast, hoped to win the cooperation of the most prominent Dutch merchants and landowners. Many of these men accepted public office, and some began to intermarry with the conquerors, a process that threatened to alienate other Dutchmen.[27]

These antagonisms exploded during Jacob Leisler's revolt of 1689, the New York counterpart to the Glorious Revolution in England and Boston. Fearful that Dominion officials in New York would find some way to turn the colony over to Roman Catholic supporters of James II, the Leislerians took control of the fort guarding New York Harbor and, in the months that followed, the whole province. As a group they were heavily Dutch and less prominent and less wealthy than their opponents, but Leislerians typically expressed their anger in religious rather than class terms. For their part, Anti-Leislerians were much more likely to invoke primitive class rhetoric to strip the rebels of any pretension to legitimacy. Leisler, complained Nicholas Bayard, raised "the rabble" against the colony's duly constituted government. To their enemies, Leislerians were "all men of meane birth and sordid Educacon and desperate Fortunes"; all "ye men of best repute for Religion Estates & Integrity" opposed Leisler's regime. As in Virginia, a popular upheaval made upper-class men far more conscious of their social status and far more aware of their vulnerability as a political elite. They responded with indignation. Largely because the Dutch Leislerians could find no effective way to present their case in London to a Dutch king of England, the old elite controlled the appointment of a new governor, returned to New York, and hanged Leisler for treason in 1691.[28]

The resulting hatreds did not subside until the early eighteenth century. As ethnic antagonisms cooled, New York emerged with a pluralistic but intermarried elite that closely controlled access to major offices despite frequent quarrels within the group. After about 1730 the gigantic manorial estates of the Hudson Valley finally began to return good profits, and their owners established regular and close relations with wealthy merchants and prominent lawyers in New York City. Landlord domination of political office went quite far. Of the 137 men who sat in the assembly or the council, acquired a seat on the highest court or practiced law before it, or served as attorney general or register or principal surrogate of the Supreme Court between 1750 and independence, 110 (80.3%) either owned more than a thousand acres or were closely related to someone who did.[29]

Landlord domination of the countryside could generate radicalism in the city by the 1760s. New York's assembly remained quite small—twenty-seven members for most of the eighteenth century. When two landlord factions vied for control, the four seats in New York City often held the balance, and the capital was too large for any one group to dominate for long. The DeLanceys, whose urban links were mostly to commerce, urged voters not to be gulled by the rival Livingstons, whose city spokesmen were mostly lawyers. The Livingstons in turn warned artisans that merchants sought only their own profit and would gladly undersell local crafts with imported English products.[30]

The elite, in short, stimulated class awareness in the city and did a great deal to undermine traditional deference. They sought power to gain access to the influence it brought them. That effort weakened them in some respects, while strengthening them in others. Urban voters began to regard their social superiors with a considerable amount of cynicism. They usually voted against incumbents, only to see the new winners come to terms with the governor in support of unpopular policies.

Pennsylvania's diverse upper class developed still a different pattern. Even more clearly than New York, the colony sustained rival and mutually exclusive elites, one Quaker, the other non-Quaker. In the course of the eighteenth century, the Quakers came to dominate legislative office, while non-Quakers increasingly monopolized executive and judicial posts. Neither alone could become a true ruling class, and politics prevented their convergence. They did not intermarry.

The system took two generations to emerge. Quaker domination of public life through the 1720s permitted frequent factional struggles among members of the Society of Friends. But as Quakers became an ever-smaller minority within the region, they could no longer afford open division. Between 1730 and 1770, wealthy and intermarried Quakers grew less exclusive and less powerful. A highly coherent Quaker Party took shape which controlled the assembly throughout this period, but it evolved from a tight coalition of wealthy Quaker families—the Logans, Pembertons and Norrises stood out—into a more secularized organization led by such non-Quakers as Benjamin Franklin and Joseph Galloway, men who were willing to respect Quaker scruples but could also negotiate with the Crown in an era of nearly continuous warfare.[31]

The rising non-Quaker gentry—including the Allen, Chew, Hamilton, Shippen, and Willing dynasties—developed in a different direction. Descended from men of established wealth, they emerged as a coherent bloc in the 1730s and 1740s. Capitalizing on the Penn family's defection from the Society of Friends, they captured just about every important office controlled by the proprietors after mid-century—the governor's council, the Supreme Court, the land office, the Philadelphia city corporation, and the College of Philadelphia. Helping themselves to generous shares of proprietary lands, many of them gradually withdrew from trade in a bid to become true gentry. They increasingly intermarried, and found relaxation and amusement only with one another. During the frontier crises of 1755 and 1764, they appealed openly to Scots-Irish Presbyterian and German Lutheran and Reformed voters in an effort to win control of the assembly. They failed, partly because eastern Quaker counties were overrepresented at the frontier's expense, partly also because the proprietary elite had no firm social ties to the people they courted.[32]

In short, the proprietary gentry, for all of their wealth, prestige, exclusiveness, and sense of cohesion, never gained control of the legislative process. Although the aspirations were there, these upper-class families were a ruling elite only in a limited sense. Their inability to win elections suggests, at best, weak links of deference between them and the artisans and farmers of Pennsylvania. Their monopoly of high office gave them great potential influence, but they had little impact on a Quaker assembly, few of whose members were interested in military rank, war contracts, or even judicial appointments that would require them to administer oaths.

The governing elites of New York and Pennsylvania differed from both Virginia's and New England's in another important particular. Their prestige and influence crossed colonial boundaries, a phenomenon that became characteristic of the Mid-Atlantic region.[33] Lewis Morris and James Alexander held high office in both New York and New Jersey. Robert Hunter Morris became chief justice of New Jersey and governor of Pennsylvania. John Kinsey served as speaker of the house in both New Jersey and Pennsylvania. This pattern continued into the Revolution. William Livingston achieved political prominence in New York, then moved to New Jersey shortly before independence, and was there elected governor every year from 1776 until his death in 1790. John Dickinson acted as chief executive for Pennsylvania and Delaware at different times. Thomas McKean, who began his public life in Delaware, eventually became governor of Pennsylvania. Gouverneur Morris, who started in New York, represented Pennsylvania in the Constitutional Convention. Although no systematic study of this phenomenon has ever been made, numerous other examples could be cited involving such families as the Smiths of Burlington and Philadelphia, the Antills, Edsalls, Chews, Tilghmans, and Coxes.

Only in this region did prominent families think of themselves as an intercolonial governing class even before independence. They did so, in all probability, because the ethnic and religious groups that made up the region paid little heed to formal colonial boundaries. Jersey Quakers gathered with Pennsylvania Quakers at the yearly meeting of the Society of Friends, while the Dutch long outweighed all rivals in the Hudson Valley and in Bergen County, New Jersey.[34] Scots settled in the Mohawk Valley of New York, at Perth Amboy and its hinterland in New Jersey, and in Pennsylvania, and the Scots-Irish were also widely dispersed through the Mid-Atlantic colonies and the southern back-country.[35] The Presbyterian Church was always an intercolonial insti-tution, even when it split into Old Side and New Side synods between 1741 and 1758, the first remaining in Philadelphia, the second locating in New York.[36] So from its founding was the College of New Jersey, organized by Presbyterians in the 1740s primarily to meet the church's needs throughout the region, in parts of New England, and increasingly in the upper South as well.[37] Status acquired in one place could carry over to another.

Toward a Ruling Class by 1763?

Achievements and Limits

On the eve of the revolutionary struggle, how did the colonial elites com-pare with the English ruling class? The answer to that question depends in good part on understanding how the larger system of class relation-ships in the colonies compared with Britain's. North America was much more rural and had no set of men as wealthy as the families that governed England. England had no class of laborers as exploited as the slaves in America. The most affluent 1 percent in England probably controlled over 40 percent of the wealth, and the richest 5 percent owned over 70 percent of the kingdom's land and personal property. In the colonies the yeomanry—roughly 60 percent of white householders—controlled 70 percent of the land. The wealthiest 5 percent in colonial society claimed only 30 percent. The most distinctive feature of the colonies was the relative economic autonomy of the middling orders. Thus colonial society had a lower basement and a lower ceiling than England, and it also had far more people crowded into the middle. Yet as the decades passed, the upper classes were becoming more exclusive, more distinctive, and more successful at capturing and holding office.[38]

Relations with social inferiors affected the ability of elites to govern. Virginia's great planters had successfully neutralized overt class conflict by enslaving the people who did most of the physical work in their society and by granting real social privileges to all whites. The officeholders of Massachusetts always faced greater potential opposition from politically alert and increasingly literate middling settlers. The competing upper-class factions of New York often frustrated one another's ambitions, although the DeLancey family did very well for itself in the third quarter of the century. Pennsylvania's rival elites never coalesced, and never dared make many political demands on ordinary settlers. In no province were clientage networks as dense as in Britain, for the goal of family autonomy remained a highly plausible target throughout the large stratum of middling persons. Thus no colony had an upper class as secure as Britain's, but in every colony the men in power by 1760 had more convincing credentials for becoming a traditional ruling class than had been true in 1690. Wealth, power, and status were converging in ways that might eventually have created one or more ruling classes in North America.[39]

Wealth and status earned in the private sphere needed some kind of public sanction to become a right to rule in North America, and the king's representatives in the provinces usually decided who received these favors. The system of titles used throughout the continent by the mid-eighteenth century reflected this hierarchy. Only the governor was addressed as "Your Excellency." In royal colonies he was appointed directly by the Crown, and in Maryland and Pennsylvania by the lord proprietor. Only Rhode Island and Connecticut retained direct election of their chief executives. Members of the council, also royal appointees in most colonies, were called "Honorable" as were justices of a colony's supreme court and the county courts of common pleas. Justices of the peace bore the title "Esquire." Military officers went by their militia rank and, of course, tended to move upwards in the normal course of the life cycle, but not every lieutenant could expect to rise to colonel. Most men seem to have used for the rest of their life the highest title they had ever claimed, even after resigning a civil or military commission. As in England, the title "gentleman" had almost no legal meaning and was used by many individuals, some of whom doubtless had few claims to any such distinction. Between the death of the founding generation and the 1750s, few men appropriated the title in Connecticut, which had no royal governor or court, but it was widespread in Massachusetts and other royal provinces.[40]

Even in Virginia the need to seek Crown approval limited the ability of the planters to become a ruling class. They did not control the ultimate sources of political power in their society. On the other hand, the very existence of the governor's royal court in a province stimulated emulation of Britain's ruling class and roused the continuing ambition among the colonial elite to become more than they were at any particular moment.

For all of their differences, the separate provincial elites shared two common traits. The most conspicuous was similar tastes in consumption— Georgian architecture and furnishings, the latest clothing fashions from London, an interest in similar reading materials—all of which tended to set them apart from less-refined settlers. The other characteristic was an ambiguous relationship to British authority, which they used to ratify their social and political pretensions but which nearly all of them had some experience in resisting on one occasion or another. After 1760 Crown and Parliament would increasingly force the colonial elites to choose whether to rally social inferiors to resist British demands, or retain Britain's good favor at the risk of losing popular acceptance in their colonies.[41]

Revolution

Between Parliament and People

Between the close of the Seven Years' War and the outbreak of the American Revolution, some segments of the colonial elites began to transform themselves into a ruling class capable of governing North America without the support of Whitehall. At first, most of them probably thought of themselves more as part of a local than a continental ruling class, but the imperatives of resistance before independence, and political survival after, broadened their awareness and their ambitions. They were repelling assaults on their prerogatives by the British ruling class, and at the moment of independence in 1776, they probably enjoyed the confidence of most white male Americans. At that point they were not at all certain whether to concentrate their energy at the state or the continental level. In turning to the people at large for support in the struggle against British authority in their own states, the elites promoted a process of political mobilization that acquired its own momentum and proved hard to control. Hence even as they fought off the imperial threat from above, they faced a new democratic challenge from below.

It is highly conceivable that Anglo-American history could have followed a different course. In 1764 Sir Francis Bernard, the royal governor of Massachusetts, proposed the creation of an American "*Nobility* appointed by the *King* for life" as a way to recognize and reinforce the status and authority of the colonial elites. But after the Seven Years' War, London officials adopted a contrary approach. Confronted with the costs of managing an empire of global proportions, they sought to augment the power of the metropolitan ruling class at the colonial elites' expense. The combination of Sugar, Stamp, and Currency Acts passed by Parliament in 1764–65 represented a direct attack on both the elites' economic interests and their political authority.[42]

To rebuff this attack, the elites joined together as never before in protesting Parliament's actions as a violation of the rules of empire. To be sure, there were important differences over questions of strategy and substance. The Virginia House of Burgesses divided almost evenly over Patrick Henry's resolutions boldly challenging parliamentary taxation on grounds of principle. The Hutchinson faction in Massachusetts advocated petitions framed in terms of customary "privileges" rather than constitutional "rights." Yet the intercolonial Stamp Act Congress which met in New York in October 1765 took only two weeks to agree on a basic line of defense, one that reserved to colonial legislatures the exclusive authority to tax the settlers.[43]

The achievement of unity among colonial elites did not, by itself, cause the metropolitan ruling class to relent. Without the action of urban mobs who blocked implementation of the Stamp Act in the fall of 1765, Parliament would probably not even have given serious consideration to the demand for repeal.[44]

Scholars disagree over the extent to which urban crowds acted under upper-class direction during the Stamp Act crisis. Although street organizers such as Ebenezer MacIntosh in Boston and Alexander McDougall in New York City evidently enjoyed the patronage of wealthy sponsors, urban mobs on several occasions clearly exceeded the wishes of their social betters in the resistance movement. After the gutting of Thomas

Hutchinson's Boston mansion, for example, Josiah Quincy, Jr., decried "the fury and instability of the populace" and reaffirmed his faith in "that glorious medium, the British Constitution" as a source of protection against anarchy as well as tyranny.[45]

In retrospect, however, what appears most notable about the Stamp Act riots is how the fears and resentments of the participants were focused rather narrowly on stamp distributors and their sympathizers, not on the rich or powerful in general. In mobilizing against the Stamp Act, urban crowds defended not only the principle of home rule, but also the prerogatives of many of those who ruled at home. Some men, such as Thomas Hutchinson in Massachusetts, suffered a loss of prestige that they would never be able to recover. But in New York both the Livingstons and the DeLanceys took sufficiently dramatic stands against the Stamp Act to retain credibility. In Virginia the widespread elite reluctance to encourage resistance quite evaporated between May and September 1765. Philadelphia's Quaker elite, eager to replace proprietary with royal government, permitted protest but discouraged resistance, which proprietary leaders helped to provoke.[46]

Repeal of the Stamp Act in the spring of 1766 represented a major victory for the colonial elites, who had upheld their authority by emphasizing the shared rights and interests of all colonists—or at least of all free adult white males. Yet concurrent disturbances in the countryside suggest the enormous risks run by the elites when they turned to the populace at large for support. Developments in New York provide a case in point. While residents of New York City celebrated the news of repeal, thousands of tenants and squatters in the Hudson Valley rioted in protest against the manorial claims of several of the colony's largest landlords. Not surprisingly, although the Livingstons and other lordly sorts had eagerly joined the fight against the Stamp Act, they raised no cry of tyranny when the royal governor ordered British soldiers to suppress the land riots. In this instance, the use of military force worked. But it also highlighted the weakness of deference and influence as mechanisms of social control in rural New York.[47]

During the decade between the Stamp Act crisis and the Declaration of Independence, the colonial elites divided internally over how best to protect their interests in the face of renewed efforts by the British ruling class to reduce their power and status. On one side were loyalists (or

Tories) who accepted colonial subordination as a prerequisite for social and political stability; on the other side were patriots (or Whigs) who dared to risk disorder for the sake of preserving, and enhancing, American autonomy. Although a full explanation of why the elites of some colonies were overwhelmingly patriots, while those of other colonies contained a sizable number of loyalists, remains elusive, there seems to have been a general pattern to elite allegiances. In many colonies, at least, the ultimate division over independence followed longstanding partisan lines and was anticipated by conflicting responses to the Townshend Acts.[48]

Whereas the Stamp Act had served to bring together various elite factions in mutual opposition to British policy, the more limited challenges embodied in the Townshend Acts tended to drive these groups apart. The external character of the Townshend duties (as distinct from the direct or internal tax imposed by the Stamp Act) as well as the intention of using their revenues to pay the salaries of high government officials meant that members of "court" factions already aligned politically with the governors had less to lose and something to gain from the legislation. Thus the Hutchinsons and Olivers in Massachusetts and, after their electoral triumph in 1769, the DeLanceys in New York openly defended the legitimacy of the Townshend Acts. The Quaker Party in Pennsylvania again hesitated to encourage overt resistance. There was no "Townshend Acts Congress." and nonimportation agreements were only belatedly achieved and partially enforced. Yet colonial rhetoric escalated as members of "country" parties already aligned politically against the governors increasingly dominated the leadership of the resistance movement. Well schooled in the logic of English opposition thought, these radical Whigs attacked imperial policy not only as a violation of the rules of empire but also as a ministerial conspiracy to reduce the colonists to abject slavery.[49]

Partial repeal of the Townshend duties eased tensions temporarily, but fear took control on both sides of the Atlantic after passage of the Tea Act in 1773. It prompted the Boston Tea Party, which led in turn to the Boston Port Act, the Massachusetts Government Act, and other efforts to single out Massachusetts for punishment. Instead, these Coercive (or Intolerable) Acts made the plight of Massachusetts the common cause of colonists across the continent. The consensus that developed in 1774–75 was broader than that of 1765–66. While court factions within the elites tended to fall away, for the first time a large proportion of the yeomanry joined actively in resistance to British authority.[50]

Colonial outrage over the Coercive Acts led to the creation of an institutional framework for leadership by an intercolonial patriot elite—the Continental Congress—and the restructuring of authority at all levels of society. By initially entrusting the enforcement of its directives to local committees and provincial congresses and conventions, Congress acknowledged that it lacked the police powers of a full-fledged ruling body. Yet its prestige exceeded its might, and it rapidly expanded its executive functions. Between 1774 and 1776, in a process that might be termed "reciprocal legitimation," the various levels of the patriot counter-regime conferred authority on each other, while organizing the populace at large first to support a trade embargo, then to fight a war, and eventually to endorse independence. At the apex rested Congress, which ought to be conceptualized, not as an American legislature or counterpart to Parliament, but as a plural executive for the continent, a substitute for the imperial Crown.[51]

From a continental perspective, the process appears remarkably smooth. No comprehensive analysis of congressional membership is available, but a survey of the delegates who served between 1774 and 1776 reveals that three-fifths boasted prior experience in provincial assemblies—a rough indication of the elite status most had in common.[52] As the imperial crisis intensified, militant and moderate delegates alike recognized the need for compromise and cooperation to survive against the British threat. The year-long delay between the creation of the Continental Army and the Declaration of Independence reflected this central concern for unity. Despite the continuing reservations of some delegates, the final break with Great Britain proved relatively simple to make: the overthrow of imperial authority did not require the physical elimination of the king or the metropolitan ruling class.[53] In 1765 the colonial elites had looked to those below them on the social scale for validation of their authority in the face of the challenge launched from abroad and above. In 1776 the wisdom of their strategy seemed confirmed when ordinary settlers overwhelmingly accepted the judgment of Congress about which regime in which colony was legitimate. Congress had indeed replaced George III, a truly revolutionary event.

Yet the continental perspective can be misleading. As resistance developed into war, and war into massive revolution and independence, many members of Congress left to take up other duties. Some, like George Washington and Benjamin Franklin, accepted military commands or diplomatic posts in continental service. Many others, such as Patrick Henry and Samuel Adams, returned to their states and resumed their roles as local rather than "national" leaders. By the late 1770s even congressmen often complained that their body could not hold a sufficient corps of talented men. To the extent that an interstate ruling elite was beginning to appear in these years, its center was more in the officer corps of the Continental Army than in Congress.[54]

Within the states, the transition from resistance to Revolution often created great turmoil. Especially in provinces where a high proportion of the colonial elite remained loyal to the Crown, well-to-do patriots out of necessity welcomed "new men" from lower social ranks into positions of power. These newcomers possessed their own interests and pursued their own agendas, generating controversy and conflict within the patriot movement.[55]

Nowhere were the results more dramatic than in Pennsylvania, where the resistance movement discredited virtually the entire Quaker Party (except Franklin) and many proprietary leaders as well. Men of humbler origins quickly rose to prominence. Beginning as lesser partners in Philadelphia's patriot coalition, artisans after 1774 jumped to positions of command within successive committees of resistance. By early 1776 mechanics comprised fully 40 percent of Philadelphia's committeemen— more than the proportion of merchants and lawyers combined. When John Dickinson and other prominent Pennsylvania patriots hesitated to cut all ties with Britain, artisan leaders went their own way and pressed energetically for independence.[56]

In seizing the revolutionary initiative, artisans repudiated deference both in practice and in principle. A letter circulated by the Philadelphia militia during the summer of 1776 articulated the mechanics' position. When choosing delegates to draft a state constitution, the militiamen warned, "great and over-grown rich Men will be improper to be trusted, they will be too apt to be framing Distinctions in Society because they will reap the Benefits of such Distinctions." This was not a call for the redistribution of private wealth, but a demand for the restructuring of the social order by choosing political decision-makers from outside the upper class.[57]

In selecting delegates to Pennsylvania's constitutional convention, voters followed the militiamen's advice and elected men without impressive wealth or elite connections. The delegates in turn drafted a constitution conferring the right to vote and hold office on all adult male taxpayers and providing for a unicameral assembly, annually elected and open to public view. Yet the convention declined to endorse the principle of an "agrarian law" to prevent the concentration of property. In a market economy devoid of business corporations, the fear of tyranny focused on the abuse of political prerogatives rather than on exploitation by capital in the private sphere. Democratic control of government seemed an adequate solution to the problem.[58]

Simultaneously the surviving leaders of the proprietary party began to regroup within an Anticonstitutionalist or "Republican" opposition (opposed, that is, to the radical constitution of 1776). They proved quite adroit at mobilizing various discontented groups, including even Quakers and other pacifists, against the radicals. For the first time the two old elites, proprietary and Quaker, showed signs of merging. They would soon begin thinking in national terms as well.[59]

Revolution

The Expanding Challenge of Popular Upheaval

The upheaval in Pennsylvania in 1776 foreshadowed conflicts that would vex Americans for the next dozen years and both hinder and promote, in different ways, the formation of a national ruling class. The challenge from below came with greater force and coherence than ever before, but it also gave a new urgency to elite efforts to unite and regain control of public affairs. As a diverse population struggled with Thomas Paine's challenge "to begin the world over again," lines of cleavage appeared at all levels of the polity. Upper-class patriots struggled among themselves for dominance in the Continental Congress, while they were repeatedly challenged from below in state legislatures. However, with the drafting and ratification of the Constitution in 1787–88, prospects for the creation of a national ruling class acquired unprecedented plausibility as Federalists sought to establish a central government with the power and prestige to bring order out of tumult.

In combining to oppose the British ruling class, patriot leaders had overcome longstanding intercolonial prejudices, but they could not erase differences of economic interest, social organization, and cultural tradition. Hence it took the state legislatures four years to ratify the Articles of Confederation, a document that resembled a treaty for mutual defense more than a framework for national government. Nor did the shared experience of the War for Independence solidify ties among the state elites. As a result, the Continental Congress emerged from the war more divided and less respected than when it entered the struggle. So weak was the chain of authority in 1783 that Congress fled Philadelphia to escape harassment by soldiers demanding back pay. When they regrouped in Princeton, New Jersey, many delegates doubted that the American Union could long survive the end of the war which had called it into existence.[60]

Within Congress, disputes over financial, frontier, and foreign policy reflected and reinforced a spirit of sectional antagonism. Analyses of Congressional voting behavior during and after the Revolution reveal an evolving pattern of geographically based parties. During the late 1770s North (or East) opposed South, usually successfully. Then in the early 1780s a newly formed Mid-Atlantic bloc of reluctant revolutionaries turned ardent nationalists took charge. Since they were the heirs of the only colonial elites with extensive intercolonial experience, their nationalism was not surprising. But they lost both their control of Congress and their internal cohesion with the advent of peace. By the mid-1780s Southerners battled Northerners over questions of commercial reform and westward expansion. The split over John Jay's treaty negotiations with Spain in 1786 generated open talk of dividing the United States into two or more separate confederacies.[61]

Meanwhile, challenges to elite control within the states came from two distinct quarters: artisans and laborers in urban centers on the one hand, and farmers, especially in the backcountry, on the other. In general, both groups rallied to the support of elite patriots at the beginning of the Revolution, but each group grew disaffected as the War for Independence dragged on and dragged it down. While the economic impact of the war is difficult to quantify, one recent effort suggests that, on average, Americans' personal income fell dramatically over the course of the conflict. After the war British policy prevented the revival of conventional trading patterns. Consequently, the return of peace produced neither prosperity nor consensus.[62]

Major seaports were among the first areas to suffer the war's negative economic consequences, including enemy occupation, inflation, unemployment, and food shortages. Crowds gathered not only to toss Tories out of town but to seize the property of genteel Whigs suspected of engrossing necessities in a time of collective emergency. From Boston to Charleston the patriot coalition threatened to dissolve along class lines. After the war urban artisans organized to demand government intervention on their behalf. In New York City, for instance, they founded the General Society of Mechanics and Tradesmen and nominated their own candidates for state offices. In Boston they formed the Association of Tradesmen and Manufacturers and lobbied successfully for a state protective tariff. By such means the "mechanic interest" asserted its autonomy and, usually without resort to riots, put political pressure on the patriot elite.[63]

A greater but separate challenge to elite control came from the countryside. Early in the war many of the economic dislocations that fueled tensions in the cities worked to the benefit of farmers in the hinterlands. Domestic food shortages brought higher prices for surplus crops. Inflated paper currency made it easier to pay taxes, which were also more fairly apportioned than before in most states when reforms in the mode of property assessment transferred a greater part of the total burden onto the rich. As a result, farmers found the early rewards of independence enticing—perhaps too enticing for their long-term good.[64]

For upper-class patriots, tax reform was part of "the price of Revolution" they had to pay to retain the allegiance of the rural majority. Many Whig grandees also bought government securities to help finance the war effort, sometimes risking their personal fortunes for the common welfare. Once victory seemed assured, however, wealthy creditors throughout America called for full funding of state and national debts, hard money, and heavy taxes to make good on public obligations as soon as possible. When depression set in shortly after the war's conclusion, they also demanded speedy repayment of private debts in specie, partly because many of them owed large sums to British merchants.[65]

Backcountry farmers reacted to these demands with alarm. Having become increasingly alert to market opportunities during the war, rural producers in the flush of peace and victory took advantage of easy credit to purchase substantial quantities of foreign imports. Given the general shortage of specie in postwar America, large payments due in coin threatened widespread financial ruin in the countryside. Disillusioned by the record of elite leadership, rural voters overcame deferential habits and began to exercise their democratic rights. Exploiting electoral changes wrought by the new state constitutions, farmers from interior regions increasingly chose persons like themselves to represent them in the state legislatures. The result was a series of political confrontations within state governments across the continent over questions of monetary policy, taxes, and debt relief—and eventually the outbreak of Shays's Rebellion in Massachusetts.[66]

Not coincidentally, Pennsylvania, with its highly democratic political framework, was the first state to introduce paper money as legal tender during the postwar crisis. By contrast, in Virginia, where the gentry retained political control, the assembly never gave paper money serious consideration, although it did delay collection of, and then lower, taxes. New York followed a middle course. By the mid-eighties a yeoman-based legislative bloc tied to Governor George Clinton had put the likes of Robert R. Livingston, Gouvernour Morris, and John Jay on the defensive in state politics. Yet descendants of New York's colonial elite remained influential in the upper house. Three times the New York Assembly passed a paper money bill only to have the Senate reject it. Finally, on the fourth attempt, the Senate gave way, and New York issued paper currency usable for tax purposes and certain private debts.[67]

The rebellion in Massachusetts reveals both the utility and futility of influence as a means of upper-class rule in postwar America. Although farmers comprised nearly half of the lower house and almost one third of the upper house in the 1780s, the Massachusetts General Court refused time and again either to issue paper money or to provide alternative means of tax or debt relief. The key to this puzzle lies in the dynamics of governmental patronage. Most officeholders who served in the legislature shared the upper class's interest in upholding public credit and private contracts. Together they stood firm against agrarian calls for help.[68]

Government intransigence prompted rural insurgence, especially in western communities in which prewar deference networks had disintegrated. What began as a series of courthouse riots developed, during the fall of 1786, into a concerted armed revolt. Having exhausted other means of political control, Governor James Bowdoin and his council opted for the application of brute force. After efforts to raise troops under congressional auspices came to naught, Boston merchants in January 1787 agreed to finance a special state army to crush the rebellion. The soldiers did their job, and before winter was out, law and order—but not harmony—were restored across the state.[69]

Had Boston's artisans rallied to the cause of rural debtors, the outcome might have been different. But Boston's mechanics remained loyal to the government during the crisis. Although they, too, suffered severely from the dislocations of the postwar economy, the memory of wartime inflation and food shortages prompted a distrust of paper money and, more generally, of the motives of the "landed interest." In Massachusetts, as elsewhere, artisans and farmers challenged the patriot elite separately, but not as a united front.[70]

The Federal Constitution and the Making of an American Ruling Class

Faced with this dual threat from below and concerned to resolve conflicts among themselves at the top, upper-class patriots more than ever before turned to national consolidation as a solution to political and social disorder. Most of the fifty-five delegates who gathered at Philadelphia during the summer of 1787 to draft the federal Constitution fit this description. Two-thirds were rich, and three-fifths were well-born or well-married. A large majority had participated in earlier continental conclaves: three had attended the Stamp Act Congress, eight had signed the Declaration of Independence, and forty-two had served in the Continental Congress. Twenty-two saw military service during the Revolution, including George Washington, two other generals, and three members of his staff.[71] Yet who the delegates were was less important than what they tried to do. With a keen sense of urgency, they sought to create a political structure capable of appeasing the concerns of urban artisans, reducing the power of backcountry farmers, and promoting the development of a national ruling class that would "think continentally," rather than in sectional, state, or regional terms.[72]

Few delegates were prepared to endorse Alexander Hamilton's call for a national political hierarchy capped by a chief executive and senate serving for life—a plan self-consciously modeled on the British Constitution and also reminiscent of the proposal made a quarter century before by Sir Francis Bernard for the creation of an American nobility with lifetime titles.[73] Nobody called for the introduction of hereditary privilege. But most delegates agreed on the need to curb "the excess of democracy," as Elbridge Gerry put it, that seemed to plague the state legislatures. He favored a requirement of popular elections in the federal government only "if it were so qualified that men of honor & character might not be unwilling to be joined in the appointments." "The people," agreed Roger Sherman, "[immediately] should have as little to do as may be about the Government. They want information and are constantly likely to be misled." In tracing the source of "the evils under which the U. S. laboured," Edmund Randolph affirmed that "every man had found it in the turbulence and follies of democracy." Comfortable with the secrecy in which they debated, delegates could speak their minds about the people.[74]

Working from James Madison's blueprint, the delegates designed a central government whose republican architecture would be supported by the pillars of deference, influence, and force. They intended to strengthen all three. Although the drafting process itself was marked by sharp contention, the final document reflected a broad consensus over who should rule at home. Thus the question of how to select and apportion the Senate generated great debate, yet delegates on opposing sides shared John Dickinson's conviction that it should "consist of the most distinguished characters, distinguished for their rank in life and weight in property, and bearing as strong a likeness to the British House of Lords as possible." When Charles Pinckney questioned whether conditions in the United States were conducive "to the rapid distinction of ranks," Madison responded in the affirmative. "In all civilized Countries," he explained, "the people fall into different classes hav[in]g a real or supposed difference of interests." While he acknowledged that America was more egalitarian than European nations, he insisted that "we cannot however be regarded even at this time as one homogeneous mass," and he predicted that in the future both social inequality and class resentment would increase. "No agrarian attempts [i.e., efforts to pass legislation limiting property holdings] have yet been made in the Country," he warned, "but symptoms of a leveling spirit . . . have sufficiently appeared in . . . certain quarters to give notice of the future danger." By this logic, a high-toned Senate was not only feasible, it was necessary to preserve liberty and justice in a stratified republic.[75]

Just as significant as the framers' preference for a high-toned Senate was their plan for a compact lower house. Notwithstanding their last-minute decision to raise the maximum number of representatives from one per forty thousand inhabitants to one per thirty thousand, the body was designed to be small—65 members at the start, virtually the same size as the assemblies of New York and Pennsylvania, and considerably smaller than the Virginia House, much less the Massachusetts assembly, which numbered over 200 members in 1787. By Madison's own reckoning, the ratio of one representative to thirty thousand inhabitants approximated that achieved in the British House of Commons—with the large proportion of MPs from pocket boroughs excepted. Embedded in this calculation was a strategy for reestablishing a safe political distance between the people and those who governed in their name.[76]

Madison explained this strategy elegantly in *The Federalist* no. 10. On the one hand, the large size of electoral districts would favor the selection of "men who possess the most attractive merit, and the most diffusive and established characters." Only men of reputation—the upper class— would be known to all voters throughout a large district of 30,000 people, which was about twice the size of Boston or Baltimore. On the other hand, the large size of the republic would inhibit the formation of an "unjust and interested majority" bent on subverting the rights of others, especially their right to property. Madison assumed that deference would prevail so long as voters chose representatives on the basis of their general reputation, not the particular interests they advocated. He did not justify upper-class rule for its own sake, but he insisted that the enlightened few could better judge the public good and protect private liberty than the impassioned many. Since the foremost danger came from below during the 1780s (in the form of "a rage for paper money, for an abolition of debts"), the solution lay in shifting power to those above.[77]

At the same time that they sought to revive deferential politics, the framers of the Constitution intended to give the federal government enough power to rule the United States as a single nation-state, rather than as a league of sovereign units. Although they made no attempt to eliminate the separate state governments, they did wish to establish a central regime capable of subordinating sectional and localistic interests to the national good. The Constitution gave the federal government independent means both to raise revenue and enforce its will. By conferring upon Congress (in conjunction with the president) the authority not only to levy imposts and direct taxes, but also to create an executive bureaucracy, a standing army, and even a nationally coordinated militia, the framers provided the basis for a stronger concentration of influence and force than Parliament had had at its disposal within America when attempting to reform the colonies after 1763.[78]

Yet the framers also realized that the means for transferring power to a high-toned central government had to rest upon the people's broad commitment to popular sovereignty. The convention had to draw upon the revolutionary experience of ordinary citizens at the state level. It had to build upon active consent. "Notwithstanding the oppression & injustice experienced among us from democracy," George Mason reminded his fellow delegates early in the proceedings, "the genius of the people is in favor of it, and the genius of the people must be consulted." The delegates could create a government capable of using effective force, but they could not use force to impose such a government. Legitimacy required popular ratification.[79]

The ratification struggle revealed that while not everyone accepted Madison's diagnosis, proponents and opponents of the document alike understood the elitist implications of his remedy. Most ominous from the Antifederalist point of view was the prospect that rule by the enlightened few would devolve into an aristocratic oligarchy along European lines. As young John Quincy Adams noted in his diary: "If the Constitution be adopted it will be a grand point in favor of the aristocratic party: there are to be no titles of nobility; there will be great distinctions; and those distinctions will soon be hereditary, and we shall consequently have nobles, but no titles."[80] What to the Federalists was a framework for responsible self-government seemed to their antagonists a program for class oppression.

Central to the dispute was the question of what sort of men should rule a republic. Whereas Madison argued for entrusting power primarily to those at the apex of the social order, Antifederalist Melancton Smith of New York contended that "those in middling circumstances have less temptation; they are inclined by habit, and the company with whom they associate, to set bounds to their passions and appetites." "When the interest of this part of the community is pursued, the public good is pursued," Smith explained, "because the body of every nation consists of this class, and because the interests of both the rich and the poor are involved in that of the middling class." Hence members of the "middling class" ought to predominate in a republican legislature—as indeed they increasingly did within the states.[81]

Notwithstanding the popular appeal of such Antifederalist logic, the Federalists won the contest over ratification. They did so in part because the dual threat from below never coalesced into a single force. Backcountry farmers proved highly suspicious of the Constitution, but urban artisans responded warmly to the prospect of a national government strong enough to promote economic growth. More generally, the Federalists out-organized their foes and made further concessions—such as the promise of a Bill of Rights—when these proved necessary.[82]

The framers, in short, believed that they had found a way to secure popular consent for the establishment of a genuine ruling class in which they, of course, would play a prominent role. Few of them realized that they had also created a system that could give ordinary citizens a far more active voice in continental affairs than any of them had ever had before. Over the short term, Madison's understanding prevailed. Over the long run, however, Melancton Smith's vision would be largely realized— ironically, with Madison's help.

The Unmaking of an American Ruling Class

Initially it appeared that the Constitution would produce the sort of political leadership the framers desired. The First Congress had a distinctly more elite cast to it than contemporary state legislatures. Nearly half of its members hailed from prominent colonial families, most were rich, and only a small minority were practicing farmers.[83] This pattern persisted through the federal government's first decade of operation, especially after the capital moved back to Philadelphia, where ambitious public figures from every state had numerous opportunities to socialize and even intermarry with the nationalizing elite of the nation's largest city. Their efforts suggest that real potential existed for the consolidation of a national ruling class based primarily on wealth and breeding.[84]

But contrary to colonial tendencies and Antifederalist fears, the federal Congress did not evolve into a hereditary oligarchy akin to the British Parliament. Partisan conflicts during the 1790s prevented the integration of the patriot elites and stimulated new efforts to mobilize the citizenry at large against established authority. The defeat of the Federalists in 1800 marked an end of the trend toward centralized government by a national ruling class. It also signalled the effective convergence, as in 1774–76, of artisans and farmers under the same party banner.

The very effort to solidify a continental ruling class began its unmaking. As the first secretary of the treasury, Alexander Hamilton sought to accomplish indirectly through federal fiscal policy what he could not do directly through the institutional framework of the Constitution. Again he turned to Great Britain for his example and proposed a program true to English precedent. If he could not have a chief executive and Senate serving for life, at least he would have a substantial national treasury to pay for energetic government and to promote unity within the top echelons of society. Full funding of the federal debt, assumption of the state debts, and the creation of a national bank promised to tie wealthy creditors throughout the country to the federal government, while affording them added economic leverage within their respective states. The purport of Hamilton's program, in brief, was to use the influence of the federal government to speed the transition of state elites into a national ruling class.[85]

Hamilton did not anticipate that his program would generate fierce contention rather than mutual cooperation among state elites. Like the Continental Congress before it, the federal Congress during the early 1790s divided sharply along sectional lines. The cleavage was rooted in differing upper-class interests. Harder hit by the war and more inclined to speculate in western lands and slaves than in government securities, southern planters had less to gain from Hamilton's funding program than northern merchants, especially the 150 or so who were the windfall winners in the assumption sweepstakes.[86] Similarly, southern congressmen perceived in the national bank and Hamilton's friendly policy toward Great Britain a design to sacrifice the welfare of the landed interest to that of the commercial, and to pass control of the government from proper representatives to northern stock jobbers.[87] By 1794 the efforts of the Constitution's framers to balance "the two great divisions of Northern & Southern interests" had seemingly come to naught. Instead, the process was already under way whereby, for the first time in the history of the republic, the elite of one section was learning how to undermine the bonds of deference and influence that supported the elite in another section. Reasonably secure as rulers within their own states, southern planters, often working through radical English and Irish émigré journalists, discovered how to appeal directly to farmers and artisans in the Mid-Atlantic states against their Federalist officeholders. For the time being, Federalist New England remained largely immune to these efforts.[88]

Thanks in good measure to Madison, the battle over Hamilton's fiscal program developed into a broad-based partisan rivalry. Having attempted through the Constitution to filter out the passions of the multitudes and reestablish elite predominance in government, Madison in the early 1790s dramatically switched course and moved to mobilize the multitudes against the Federalist administration he had helped to put in place. Not that he was as inconsistent in his positions as Hamilton alleged. To Madison's mind, the primary threat to the public good in the 1790s was quite different from what it had been in the 1780s. Then the peril had come from unjust majorities dominating various state governments; now the danger consisted of an unjust sectional minority manipulating the national government. "If a faction consists of less than a majority," Madison had noted in *Federalist* no. 10, "relief is supplied by the republican principle, which enables the majority to defeat its sinister views by a regular vote."[89] With Thomas Jefferson as his great collaborator, Madison set about organizing the Republican party in order to rally a virtuous (as opposed to factious) majority of voters nationwide to rescue the country from subversion by Hamilton and his corrupt cabal.[90]

In the South, Republicans found plenty of allies among the state elites. Consequently, although a number of prominent southerners remained loyal to the Federalist cause, the growth of Republican opposition there in the 1790s tended to reinvigorate rather than subvert deferential attitudes.[91]

In the North, however, the rise of the Republican party had democratic implications. In New England and the Mid-Atlantic states, Republican leadership quite often went to men who lacked elite credentials. It also included many upwardly mobile merchants and manufacturers, some of whom became quite wealthy, whose personal prospects were threatened by Hamilton's program. Northern Jeffersonians challenged the better-established Federalists by appealing to the economic interests and social resentments of artisans and farmers. Writing in the Philadelphia press in the fall of 1792, Madison outlined the strategy. He portrayed the Federalists as men "more partial to the opulent than to the other classes of society" who hoped that "the government itself may by degrees be narrowed into fewer hands, and approximated to an hereditary form." "[H]aving debauched themselves into a persuasion that mankind are incapable of governing themselves," he charged, "it follows with them, of course, that government can be carried on only by the pageantry of rank, the influence of money and emoluments, and the terror of military force."[92]

Federalists denounced Republicans in equally virulent terms. Against the backdrop of the French Revolution and the outbreak of war in Europe, Hamilton and his supporters interpreted the Republican challenge as a fundamental assault on the political stability of the new nation. They railed against the dangers of Jacobinism and mobocracy, and savaged the Democratic-Republican societies for assuming the right to agitate against the policies of the nation's duly elected rulers.[93] Turning provisions of the Constitution to their advantage, the Federalists employed influence to promote their cause. As Hamilton had explained some years before, "the reason of allowing Congress to appoint its own officers of the Customs, collectors of the taxes and military officers of every rank is to create in the interior of each State, a mass of influence in favor of the Federal Government." Once in power he put this strategy into practice. A study of the civil service during the 1790s demonstrates that partisan considerations played a critical part in the choice of customs officers, postmasters, and other lower-echelon federal officials. These men in turn helped build the Federalist party at the local level.[94]

When deference and influence proved inadequate to uphold federal authority, the Federalists resorted to coercion. By calling out a massive army to crush the Whiskey Rebellion in 1794, the Washington administration aimed not only to enforce the excise tax on liquor in western Pennsylvania, but also to demonstrate the capacity of the national government to command obedience over the full domain of the United States. By passing the Alien and Sedition Acts in 1798, congressional Federalists sought not only to protect the nation from foreign provocateurs during a war scare but also to silence the Republican press. In both cases, the Federalists followed the example of the British ruling class in aggressively suppressing domestic dissent.[95]

If the Federalists had won an enduring victory, they most probably would have built something like another England in America. But they failed. Why? The question defies a simple answer and has received little scholarly attention in recent years. Any explanation must be tentative.

The Mid-Atlantic nationalists do seem to have made their biggest mistakes in their home territory. Their triumph in Pennsylvania politics from the mid-1780s into the mid-1790s depended upon the ability of former proprietary men to merge with and represent Quakers and German sectarians who, as the wartime victims of Constitutionalist disfranchisement policies, helped give the Federalists (Anticonstitutionalists in state politics) a solid popular majority. The use of force against whiskey rebels and later against John Fries's tax rioters broke the still-fragile deferential links between Federalist leaders and their voting base. In England force was usually an emergency expedient called upon to restore the more peaceful devices of deference and influence. In Pennsylvania it killed both, at least for the Federalists. By the late 1790s the struggle for that state was all but over, with the Jeffersonian Republicans as huge winners, despite the continuing threat of a French war.[96]

Of course Pennsylvania was not the nation, or even the whole Mid-Atlantic region, but in a country tightly balanced between Federalist New England and the Jeffersonian South, it counted heavily. Elsewhere, the Republican party's expansive democratic appeal contributed greatly to Federalism's defeat at the polls in 1800, and yet the first party system was more than a contest between democracy and aristocracy, even in the North. Federalists enjoyed popular support where their fiscal and commercial policies produced concrete economic benefits, particularly in New England. While they alienated large numbers of urban artisans in Mid-Atlantic cities during the 1790s, they made significant inroads among frontiersmen and some farmers who had opposed ratification of the Constitution. New York, New Jersey, and Delaware all became closely contested battlegrounds, with New York proving decisive.[97]

To a large extent, the fate of the Federalists after the Whiskey Rebellion rested on European developments over which they had little control, but to which they might have responded more adroitly. Although widespread outrage at Jay's Treaty put their pro-British foreign policy to the test in 1795, three years later the groundswell of patriot fervor after the XYZ Affair presented the Federalists with an enormous opportunity. Had President John Adams asked for an official declaration of war against France in 1798 (as Hamilton and other Federalist leaders desired), the Federalists might have been able to discredit their opponents for good in most northern states and even in parts of the South, much as the Republicans later used the War of 1812 to destroy Federalist credibility. But after arousing passionate Republican opposition through his support of the Alien and Sedition Acts, Adams pursued a more pacific course, one that left the Federalists deeply divided and opened the way for Republican victory in 1800.[98]

Reflections

Private Wealth and Public Power in Republican America

Republican ascendancy after 1800 had profound implications. Thomas Jefferson in his first inaugural address proclaimed that henceforth, in principle, the majority would rule. More important, in practice he and his party set about shrinking the scope and functions of the federal government. As a result, during his first term in office the momentum toward political centralization was reversed, and power began to shift from the national level back to the states, where the ratio of legislative representatives to the general population was much higher than in Congress. Although this trend was interrupted by the Embargo of 1807–9 and the War of 1812, it was resumed with the "Era of Good Feelings." By the 1820s state governments were taking the lead in shaping economic and social policy.[99] "The federal government is hardly concerned with anything but foreign affairs," Alexis de Tocqueville concluded after his tour of the United States in 1831–32; "it is the state governments which really control American society." He was right.[100]

With the resurgence of state authority in the early nineteenth century, political power moved down the social scale, much as it had during the revolutionary era. When Tocqueville decried "the tyranny of the majority," he was referring to the operation of state governments, not the national regime. Modern studies on the composition of state legislatures indicate that men of moderate circumstance predominated in these assemblies.[101] Contrary to the hopes of the Constitution's framers, Melancton Smith's vision of middle-class democracy was largely realized by the Age of Jackson, although a few southern states held out longer than others. Nowhere else in the Western world was political power more sharply separated from wealth and breeding. Tocqueville saw that pattern quite clearly. "In the United States," he wrote, "it is men of moderate pretensions who engage in the twists and turns of politics. Men of parts and vaulting ambition generally avoid power to pursue wealth."[102]

The main theme of this essay has been that this result represented a fundamental break with the pre-revolutionary pattern of political development. In the seventeenth century, hardly anyone doubted that those who governed should be set apart from the people they ruled, although demographic and economic circumstances inhibited the emergence of stable colonial elites. During the first half of the eighteenth century, as colonies became more socially complex, upper-class families established their right to rule at the provincial level, deliberately emulating as much as possible aristocratic English norms. Within the imperial context, however, the colonial elites remained clearly inferior to the increasingly cohesive ruling class of the mother country. When the metropolitan ruling class sought to curb longstanding colonial rights and privileges after the Seven Years' War, the colonial elites had no alternatives but to yield or turn to those below them on the social scale for help in resisting this challenge to their authority. They proved successful in rallying mass support, but once mobilized, urban artisans and backcountry farmers began to press new demands of their own. By the end of the conflict, congressional authority was on the wane at the continental level, and in the mid-1780s patriot elites also found themselves losing control of public policy to men of middling status within the states.

Through the creation of a stronger central government, the framers of the Constitution sought to reverse the decline in the political prospects of America's upper classes. Federalists envisioned a national regime dominated by "the wise, the rich, and the good," as Hamilton put it, and thus endowed with sufficient prestige and power to command popular loyalty and obedience. But conflicts between elites of different states and regions prevented the consolidation of a national ruling class in the 1790s. Neither deference, influence, nor force could stop the Jeffersonian victory in the "Revolution of 1800."

Because of the Jeffersonians the divergence from English precedent became decisive. After 1800 power shifted away from the national government and toward the state legislatures comprised of middling men. Tocqueville, whatever his faults, grasped this basic democratic fact of American life. Men of great wealth and breeding did not disappear from American society. Indeed, they grew far richer than their predecessors had ever been, but they acquired no hegemony over politics. Few of them even held office. This pattern took firm hold before the United States transformed itself from a society of autonomous producers into one of employers and employees, and the consequences, though less conspicuous now than in 1850, are still highly visible.

The Jeffersonian revolution even transformed the meaning of corruption in American politics. Both before and right after the Revolution, the fear of corruption concentrated on the possibility that the executive would undermine the legislature and seduce assemblymen or private citizens through the favors it could offer. The public sphere always seemed capable of destroying the integrity of the private. In the nineteenth century corruption increasingly came to mean that private wealth might undermine the integrity of the public sphere. Influence peddling no longer implied an initiative from government. It meant that wealthy citizens would be able to buy favors from less affluent officials. That anxiety remains a central concern of American politics, the price that the republic has learned to pay for the way that it has divorced its political and economic hierarchies.[103]

As the nineteenth century unfolded, and as the Marxian transition to a nation of owners and wage laborers took firm hold, the Jeffersonian revolution began to acquire new ironies. Rich Americans acquired fortunes that matched Europe's grandest. Yet they still did not govern, a situation that shocked one onlooker, British Prime Minister William E. Gladstone. He learned in 1877 that railroad baron Cornelius Vanderbilt had left to his son the world's first $100-million industrial fortune (equal to more than a third of the entire federal budget). Wealth on so gigantic a scale ought not to exist accompanied by no "obligation to society," Gladstone declared. "The government ought to take it away from him, as it is too dangerous a power for one man to have." Yet William Vanderbilt doubled that fortune before his own death eight years later, and John D. Rockefeller had amassed $900 million—more than double the federal budget—when he retired in 1897. By then the families of Rockefeller and Andrew Carnegie alone had amassed fortunes that approached 10 percent of the gross national product of the entire country, which was $14.6 billion. None of these men held office in the United States or answered to any kind of political constituency. Yet their routine business decisions altered the lives of thousands of their countrymen and seriously affected millions more. By then it was a distinctive American pattern—enormous economic power without political accountability.[104]

As every subsequent reform movement has asked, citizens had to wonder what to make of America's political economy. Had the Revolution destroyed the ruling class? Or had it created a system in which the wealthiest families had finally learned how to rule without the need to govern? Had the influence of private citizens upon government overwhelmed the authority of government over powerful citizens? And had a new kind of corruption become a routine and essential part of that process? In a capitalist society that generates huge extremes of wealth and want, democracy is ever at risk.

Notes

1. E. P. Thompson, *The Making of the English Working Class* (London, 1963), 9, 10.
2. Tom Bottomore, ed., *A Dictionary of Marxist Thought* (Cambridge, Mass., 1983), s.v. "ruling class"; John Jay to William Wilberforce, 25 October 1810, quoted in Dixon Ryan Fox, *The Decline of Aristocracy in the Politics of New York, 1801–1840* (New York, 1919), 9.
3. See Lawrence Stone and Jeanne C. Fawtier Stone, *An Open Elite? England, 1540–1880* (Oxford, 1984), especially chaps. 6–7. See also E. P. Thompson, "Eighteenth-Century English Society: Class Struggle without Class?" *Social History* 3(1976): 133–65.
4. David Hume, *Essays and Treatises on Several Subjects* [1742], new ed. (Edinburgh, 1825), 1: 27 By "Force" in this context, Hume meant that the governed always outnumber their governors. If really determined to resist, they would succeed.
5. See J. G. A. Pocock, "The Classical Theory of Deference," *American Historical Review* 81(1976): 516–23.
6. Modern analysis of this system began with Sir Lewis B. Namier, *The Structure of Politics at the Accession of George III,* 2d ed. (London. 1957).

See also his *Crossroads of Power: Essays on Eighteenth-century England* (London, 1962).

7. Of the vast literature on England, perhaps the best place to begin is with Lawrence Stone, *The Crisis of the Aristocracy, 1558–1641* (Oxford, 1965), especially chap. 5; and J. H. Plumb, *The Growth of Political Stability: England, 1675–1725* (Boston, 1967). See also J.R. Western, *The English Militia in the Eighteenth Century: The Story of a Political Issue, 1660–1802* (London, 1965); E. P. Thompson, *Whigs and Hunters: The Origin of the Black Act* (New York, 1975), Douglas Hay et al., *Albton's Fatal Tree: Crime and Society in Eighteenth-Century England* (New York, 1975); and Albert Goodwin, *The Friends of Liberty: The English Democratic Movement in the Age of the French Revolution* (Cambridge, Mass., 1979), especially chaps. 8–10. For Scotland, compare Bruce Lenman, *The Jacobite Risings in Britain, 1689–1746* (London, 1980) with John Robertson, *The Scottish Enlightenment and the Militia Issue* (Edinburgh, 1985). For the Irish contrast, see John Phillip Reid, *In a Defiant Stance: The Conditions of Law in Massachusetts Bay, the Irish Comparison, and the Coming of the American Revolution* (University Park, Pa., 1977), especially chaps. 13–14; and Francis Godwin James, *Ireland in the Empire, 1688–1770: A History of Ireland from the Williamite Wars to the Eve of the American Revolution* (Cambridge, Mass., 1973).

8. For a survey that is both recent and balanced see Derek Hirst, *Authority and Conflict: England, 1603–1658* (Cambridge, Mass., 1986).

9. See J. R. Western, *Monarchy and Revolution: The English State in the 1680s* (London, 1972); J. R. Jones, *The Revolution of 1688 in England* (New York, 1972); John Brewer, *The Sinews of Power: War, Money, and the English State, 1688–1783* (New York, 1989); and, for the dynamics of opposition, Linda Colley, *In Defiance of Oligarchy: The Tory Party, 1714–60* (Cambridge, Eng., 1982).

10. Serious analysis of these problems began with Bernard Bailyn, "Politics and Social Structure in Virginia," in James Morton Smith, ed., *Seventeenth-Century America: Essays in Colonial History* (Chapel Hill, N.C., 1959), 90–115.

11. Easily the most thoughtful study of this process is Martin H. Quitt, "Immigrant Origins of the Virginia Gentry: A Study of Cultural Transmission and Innovation" *William and Mary Quarterly,* 3d series (hereafter cited as *WMQ*), 45(1988): 629–55.

12. No study has yet been made analyzing the significance of an armed population in colonial America at a time when ordinary people in Europe were being systematically disarmed, but this contrast is basic to several major interpretations of military events in early America. See especially Richard Slotkin, *Regeneration through Violence: The Mythology of the American Frontier, 1600–1860* (Middletown, Conn., 1973); John E. Ferling, *A Wilderness of Miseries: War and Warriors in Early America* (Westport, Conn., 1980); William L. Shea, *The Virginia Militia in the Seventeenth Century* (Baton Rouge, La., 1983); and Fred Anderson, *A People's Army: Massachusetts Soldiers and Society in the Seven Years' War* (Chapel Hill, N.C., 1984).

13. See Kenneth A. Lockridge, *Settlement and Unsettlement in Early America* (New York, 1981).

14. In a rich literature the most powerful single book is Edmund S. Morgan, *American Slavery, American Freedom: The Ordeal of Colonial Virginia* (New York, 1975). See also Thad W. Tate and David L. Ammerman, eds., *The Chesapeake in the Seventeenth Century: Essays on Anglo-American Society* (Chapel Hill, N.C., 1979).

15. "Virginia's Deploured Condition," Massachusetts Historical Society, *Collections*, 4th series, 9(1871): 176; Bacon's manifesto of 1676, in Merrill Jensen, ed., *American Colonial Documents to 1776,* vol. 9 of *English Historical Documents,* ed. David C. Douglas (New York, 1962), 581–82.

16. See Martin H. Quitt, *Virginia House of Burgesses, 1660–1706: The Social, Educational, and Economic Bases of Political Power* (New York, 1989); David Alan Williams, *Political Alignments in Colonial Virginia Politics, 1698–1750* (New York, 1989); Aubrey C. Land, "Economic Behavior in a Planting Society: The Eighteenth-Century Chesapeake," *Journal of Southern History* 33(1967): 471–85, especially 482; and Jack P. Greene, "Foundations of Political Power in the Virginia House of Burgesses, 1720–1776," *WMQ* 16(1959): 485–506.

17. See David Alan Williams, "The Small Farmer in Eighteenth-Century Virginia Politics," *Agricultural History* 43(1969): 91–101; Robert J. Dinkin, *Voting in Provincial America: A Study of Elections in the Thirteen Colonies, 1689–1776* (Westport, Conn., 1977), especially 194, 198; and Robert E. Brown and B. Katherine Brown, *Virginia, 1705–1786: Aristocracy or Democracy?* (East Lansing, Mich., 1964), chap. 9.

18. See Allan Kulikoff, *Tobacco and Slaves: The Development of Southern Cultures in the Chesapeake, 1680–1800* (Chapel Hill, N.C., 1986).

19. See Thad W. Tate, "The Coming of the Revolution in Virginia: Britain's Challenge to Virginia's Ruling Class," *WMQ* 19(1962): 323–43.

20. For the centrality of the conversion experience to life in early New England, see Edmund S. Morgan, *Visible Saints: The History of a Puritan Idea* (New York, 1963). See also Richard S. Dunn, *From Puritans to Yankees: The Winthrop Dynasty in Colonial New England, 1630–1717* (Princeton, 1962); William A. Polf, "Puritan Gentlemen: The Dudleys of Massachusetts, 1576–1686" (Ph.D. diss., Syracuse University, 1973); and on Governor Eaton of New Haven, Gail Sussman Marcus, "'Due Execution of the Generall Rules of Righteousnesse': Criminal Procedure in New Haven Town and Colony, 1638–1658," in David D. Hall, John M. Murrin, and Thad W. Tate, eds., *Saints and Revolutionaries: Essays on Early American History* (New York, 1984), 99–137.

21. For this exchange see Edmund S. Morgan, ed., *Puritan Political Ideas, 1558–1794* (Indianapolis, 1965), 160–73.

22. See Edmund S. Morgan, *The Puritan Dilemma: The Story of John Winthrop* (Boston, 1958); and Robert E. Wall, Jr., *Massachusetts Bay: The Crucial Decade, 1640–1650* (New Haven, 1972).

23. See especially Richard R. Johnson, *Adjustment to Empire: The New England Colonies, 1675–1715* (New Brunswick, N.J., 1981).

24. The most important recent studies of Massachusetts politics in this period are Robert M. Zemsky, *Merchants, Farmers, and River Gods: An Essay on Eighteenth-Century American Politics* (Boston, 1971); William Pencak, *War, Politics & Revolution in Provincial Massachusetts* (Boston, 1981); and Richard L. Bushman, *King and People in Provincial Massachusetts* (Chapel Hill, N.C., 1985).

25. See Edward M. Cook, Jr., *The Fathers of the Towns: Leadership and Community Structure in Eighteenth-Century New England* (Baltimore, 1976); and John M. Murrin, "Review Essay," *History and Theory* 11(1972): especially 245–72.

26. For the period before 1715 the percentage of justices in the assembly (anyone listed as "Esquire") has been tabulated from *Acts and Resolves, Public and Private, of the Province of Massachusetts Bay* . . . (Boston, 1869–1922), vols. 7–9; for 1715 through 1774 we have used the first 50 volumes of *Journals of the House of Representatives of Massachusetts Bay,* reprint edition by the Massachusetts Historical Society (Boston, 1919–81). John J. Waters, Jr., and John A. Schutz, "Patterns of Massachusetts Colonial Politics: The Writs of Assistance and the Rivalry between the Otis and Hutchinson Families," *WMQ* 24(1967): 543–67 is a fine case study. See also Gary B. Nash, "The Transformation of Urban Politics, 1700–1760," in his *Race, Class, and Politics: Essays on American Colonial and Revolutionary Society* (Urbana, Ill., 1986), 140–70.

27. The best general histories of New York in this period are Robert C. Ritchie, *The Duke's Province: A Study of New York Politics and Society, 1664–1691* (Chapel Hill, N.C., 1977); and Joyce D. Goodfriend, *Before the Melting Pot: Society and Culture in Colonial New York City, 1664–1730* (Princeton, 1992). On more specific points see Stanley M. Pargellis, "The Four Independent Companies of New York," in *Essays in Colonial History Presented to Charles McLean Andrews by His Students* (New Haven, 1931), 96–123; Randall H. Balmer, *A Perfect Babel of Confusion: Dutch Religion and English Culture in the Middle Colonies* (New York, 1989); John M. Murrin, "English Rights as Ethnic Aggression: The English Conquest, the Charter of Liberties of 1683, and Leisler's Rebellion in New York," in William Pencak and Conrad Edick Wright, eds., *Authority and Resistance in Early New York* (New York, 1988), 56–94; and Murrin, "The Menacing Shadow of Louis XIV and the Rage of Jacob Leisler: The Constitutional Ordeal of Seventeenth-Century New York," in Stephen L. Schechter and Richard B. Bernstein, eds., *New York and the Union: Contributions to the American Constitutional Experience* (Albany, N.Y., 1990), 29–71.

28. See Minutes of the Council, 4 June 1689, New-York Historical Society, *Collections* 1(1868): 269–70; and Nicholas Bayard and William Nicolls, "Answer to Blagge's Memorial," in E. B. O'Callaghan, ed., *The Documentary*

History of the State of New York, octavo ed. (Albany, N.Y., 1849–51), 2:388, 390.

29. See generally Sung Bok Kim, *Landlord and Tenant in Colonial New York: Manorial Society, 1664–1775* (Chapel Hill, N.C., 1978). For the statistics on officeholding see Irving Mark, *Agrarian Conflicts in Colonial New York, 1711–1775,* 2d ed. (New York, 1965), 85–94.

30. See especially Roger Champagne, "Family Politics versus Constitutional Principles: The New York Assembly Elections of 1768 and 1769," *WMQ* 20(1963): 57–73.

31. See Gary B. Nash, *Quakers and Politics: Pennsylvania, 1681–1726* (Princeton, 1968); Thomas Wendel, "The Keith-Lloyd Alliance: Factional and Coalition Politics in Colonial Pennsylvania," *Pennsylvania Magazine of History and Biography* 92(1968): 289–305; Alan Tully, *William Penn's Legacy: Politics and Social Structure in Provincial Pennsylvania, 1726–1755* (Baltimore, 1977); and Richard Alan Ryerson, "Portrait of a Colonial Oligarchy: The Quaker Elite in the Pennsylvania Assembly, 1729–1776," in Bruce C. Daniels, ed., *Power and Status: Officeholding in Colonial America* (Middletown, Conn., 1986), 106–35.

32. See especially G. B. Warden, "The Proprietary Group in Pennsylvania, 1754–1764," *WMQ* 21(1964): 367–89; Stephen J. Brobeck, "Changes in the Composition of Philadelphia Elite Groups, 1756–1790" (Ph.D. diss., University of Pennsylvania, 1976); and Brobeck, "Revolutionary Change in Colonial Philadelphia: The Brief Life of the Proprietary Gentry," *WMQ* 33(1976): 410–34.

33. On Middle Colony regionalism and politics see Wayne Bodle, "The 'Myth of the Middle Colonies' Reconsidered: The Process of Regionalization in Early America," *Pennsylvania Magazine of History and Biography* 113(1989): 527–48.

34. For prominent studies of Quaker reform with an intercolonial emphasis, see Sydney V. James, *A People among Peoples: Quaker Benevolence in Eighteenth-Century America* (Cambridge, Mass., 1963); and Jean R. Soderlund, *Quakers & Slavery: A Divided Spirit* (Princeton, 1985). Jack D. Marietta, *The Reformation of American Quakerism, 1748–1783* (Philadelphia, 1984), is, by contrast, confined to events in Pennsylvania. Balmer, *Perfect Babel,* contrasts Dutch religious behavior in New York and New Jersey.

35. See Ned C. Landsman, *Scotland and Its First American Colony, 1683–1765* (Princeton, 1985); and Elizabeth I. Nybakken, "New Light on the Old Side: Irish Influences on Colonial Presbyterianism," *Journal of American History* 68(1981–82): 813–32.

36. See Leonard J. Trinterud, *The Forming of an American Tradition: A Reexamination of Colonial Presbyterianism* (Philadelphia, 1949).

37. See Thomas J. Wertenbaker, *Princeton, 1746–1896* (Princeton, 1946), chaps. 1–3.

38. On wealth distribution compare John A. James, "Personal Wealth Distribution in Late Eighteenth-Century Britain," *Economic History Review,* 2d series, 41(1988): 543–65, especially 559–60; Alice Hanson Jones, *Wealth of a Nation to Be: The American Colonies on the Eve of the Revolution* (New York, 1980), chaps 6–7; Hermann Wellenreuther, "A View of the Socio-Economic Structures of England and the British Colonies on the Eve of the American Revolution," in Erich Angermann, Marie-Luise Frings, and Hermann Wellenreuther, eds., *New Wine in Old Skins: A Comparative View of Socio-Political Structures and Values Affecting the American Revolution* (Stuttgart, 1976), 16–19; Gary B. Nash, *The Urban Crucible: Social Change, Political Consciousness, and the Origins of the American Revolution* (Cambridge, Mass., 1979), 4; Jackson Turner Main, *The Social Structure of Revolutionary America* (Princeton, 1965); and James A. Henretta, "Wealth and Social Structure," in Jack P. Greene and J. R. Pole, eds., *Colonial British America: Essays in the New History of the Early Modern Era* (Baltimore, 1984), 175–88, 281–83.

   On elite success in holding power see generally Jack P. Greene, "Legislative Turnover in British America, 1696 to 1775: A Quantitative Analysis," *WMQ* 38(1981): 442–63; Greene, "The Growth of Political Stability: An Interpretation of Political Development in the Anglo-American Colonies, 1660–1760," in John Parker and Carol Urness, eds., *The American Revolution: A Heritage of Change* (Minneapolis, 1975), 26–52; and Colin Bonwick, "The American Revolution as a Social Movement Revisited," *Journal of American Studies* 20(1986): 355–73.

39. For a recent synthesis of an enormous literature emphasizing both the emergence of colonial elites and the significance of family autonomy, see Jack P. Greene, *Pursuits of Happiness: The Social Development of Early Modern British Colonies and the Formation of American Culture* (Chapel Hill, N.C., 1988).

40. This discussion of titles derives mostly from our reading of public records. For Connecticut's exceptional pattern see Jackson Turner Main, "New Views on the Colonial Past: From the Regional Perspective," paper presented at the annual meeting of the Organization of American Historians (Minneapolis, April 1985), 1.

41. Richard L. Bushman, "American High Styles and Vernacular Cultures," in Greene and Pole, eds., *Colonial British America,* 345–83; and John M. Murrin, "Political Development," in ibid., 408–56 summarize the relevant literature.

42. See Francis Bernard, "Principles of Law and Polity, Applied to the Government of the British Colonies in America" (1764), nos. 86–89, in Jack P. Greene, ed., *Colonies to Nation, 1763–1789: A Documentary History of the American Revolution* (New York, 1975), 11; Edmund S. Morgan and Helen M. Morgan, *The Stamp Act Crisis: Prologue to Revolution* (Chapel Hill, N.C., 1953), chaps. 2–5; and John L. Bullion, *A Great and Necessary Measure: George Grenville and the Genesis of the Stamp Act, 1763–1765* (Columbia, Mo., 1982).

43. Morgan and Morgan, *Stamp Act Crisis,* chap. 7.
44. See ibid., chap. 16; P. D. G. Thomas, *British Politics and the Stamp Act Crisis: The First Phase of the American Revolution* (Oxford, 1975); and Paul Langford, *The First Rockingham Administration, 1765–1766* (New York, 1973).
45. Greene, ed., *Colonies to Nation,* 63. For differing interpretations of Stamp Act crowds, see Morgan and Morgan, *Stamp Act Crisis,* chaps 8–9, 11: and Pauline Maier, *From Resistance to Revolution: Colonial Radicals and the Development of American Opposition to Britain, 1765–1776* (New York, 1972), chaps. 3–4; and Nash, *Urban Crucible,* chap. 11.
46. See Morgan and Morgan, *Stamp Act Crisis,* chaps. 9–10, 12–14. See also Patricia U. Bonomi, *A Factious People: Politics and Society in Colonial New York* (New York, 1971), chap. 7; James H. Hutson, *Pennsylvania Politics, 1746–1770: The Movement for Royal Government and Its Consequences* (Princeton, 1972); and Benjamin H. Newcomb, *Franklin and Galloway: A Political Partnership* (New Haven, 1972), especially chaps. 4–5.
47. Kim, *Landlord and Tenant,* chap. 8; and Edward Countryman. *A People in Revolution: The American Revolution and Political Society in New York, 1760–1790* (Baltimore, 1981), chap. 2, discuss this episode from the point of view of landlords and rioters, respectively.
48. Recent studies that identify the formative character of the Townshend Crisis include John W. Tyler, *Smugglers and Patriots: Boston Merchants and the Advent of the American Revolution* (Boston, 1986), chaps. 3–4; and Thomas M. Doerflinger, *A Vigorous Spirit of Enterprise: Merchants and Economic Development in Revolutionary Philadelphia* (Chapel Hill, N.C., 1986), 189–99; Doerflinger, "Philadelphia Merchants and the Logic of Moderation, 1760–1775," *WMQ* 40(1983): 197–226. For a provocative analysis that locates the roots of revolutionary allegiance in earlier partisan alignments, see Marc Egnal, *A Mighty Empire: The Origins of the American Revolution* (Ithaca, N.Y., 1988). James Kirby Martin, *Men in Rebellion: Higher Governmental Leaders and the Coming of the American Revolution* (New York, 1973) explores social and political factors that influenced the pattern of loyalties within the provincial elites.
49. Merrill Jensen, *The Founding of a Nation: A History of the American Revolution, 1763–1776* (New York, 1968), chaps. 8–14, is an outstanding narrative history of the Townshend Crisis. For the evolving ideology of resistance see Maier, *From Resistance to Revolution,* especially chaps. 5–7.
50. See Benjamin W. Labaree, *The Boston Tea Party* (New York, 1964); Ira D. Gruber, "The American Revolution as a Conspiracy: The British View," *WMQ* 26(1969): 360–72; Bernard Bailyn, *The Ideological Origins of the American Revolution* (Cambridge, Mass., 1967), especially 144–59; and David Ammerman, *In the Common Cause: American Response to the Coercive Acts of 1774* (Charlottesville, Va., 1974).
51. See Jerrilyn Greene Marston, *King and Congress: The Transfer of Political Legitimacy, 1774–1776* (Princeton, 1987).

52. Compilation based mainly on data in *Biographical Directory of the American Congress, 1774–1989*. For a useful analysis of the signers of the Declaration of Independence, see Richard D. Brown, "The Founding Fathers of 1776 and 1787: A Collective View," *WMQ* 33(1976): 465–80.

53. See Jack N. Rakove, *The Beginnings of National Politics: An Interpretive History of the Continental Congress* (New York, 1974), chaps. 3–5.

54. See Arnold M. Pavlovsky, " 'Between Hawk and Buzzard': Congress as Perceived by Its Members, 1775–1783," *Pennsylvania Magazine of History and Biography* 101(1977): 349–64; and Edwin G. Burrows, "Military Experience and the Origins of Federalism and Antifederalism," in Jacob Judd and Irwin H. Polishook, eds., *Aspects of Early New York Society and Politics* (Tarrytown, N.Y., 1974), 83–92.

55. Richard A. Ryerson, *The Revolution Is Now Begun: The Radical Committees of Philadelphia, 1765–1776* (Philadelphia, 1978), 248.

56. See ibid., especially chaps. 2–3, 8–9; and Charles S. Olton, *Artisans for Independence: Philadelphia Mechanics and the American Revolution* (Syracuse, N.Y., 1975), chaps. 4–6.

57. See Steven R. Rosswurm, *Arms, Country, and Class: The Philadelphia Militia and the "Lower Sort" during the American Revolution* (New Brunswick, N.J., 1987), especially 101.

58. See Eric Foner, *Tom Paine and Revolutionary America* (New York, 1976), chap. 4.

59. See Douglas M. Arnold, *A Republican Revolution: Ideology and Politics in Pennsylvania, 1776–1790* (New York, 1989); and Owen S. Ireland, "The Crux of Politics: Religion and Party in Pennsylvania," *WMQ* 42(1985): 453–75.

60. See Rakove, *Beginnings of National Politics*. For the fear of disunion, see Eugene R. Sheridan and John M. Murrin, eds., *Congress at Princeton, Being the Letters of Charles Thomson to Hannah Thomson, June–October 1783* (Princeton, 1985), especially 19, 29–31.

61. See H. James Henderson, *Party Politics in the Continental Congress* (New York, 1974); Joseph L. Davis, *Sectionalism in American Politics, 1774–1787* (Madison, 1977); and Drew R. McCoy, "James Madison and Visions of American Nationality in the Confederation Period: A Regional Perspective," in Richard Beeman, Stephen Botein, and Edward C. Carter II, eds., *Beyond Confederation: Origins of the Constitution and American National Identity* (Chapel Hill, N.C., 1987), 226–58.

62. See John J. McCusker and Russell R. Menard, *The Economy of British America, 1607–1789* (Chapel Hill, N.C., 1985), chap. 17.

63. On economic conditions and class tensions in the cities, see Dirk Hoerder, *Crowd Action in Revolutionary Massachusetts, 1765–1780* (New York, 1977), chaps. 13–14; Nancy Fisher Chudacoff, "The Revolution and the Town: Providence, 1775–1783," *Rhode Island History* 35(Aug. 1977): 71–90; Foner, *Tom Paine*, chap. 5; James K. Alexander, "The Fort Wilson Incident of 1779: A Case Study of the Revolutionary Crowd," *WMQ* 31(1974): 589–612; and Richard Walsh, *Charleston's Sons of Liberty: A Study of the Artisans, 1763–1789* (Columbia, S.C., 1959), 77–87. On artisanal organization after the

war, see Staughton Lynd, "The Mechanics in New York Politics, 1774–1788," *Labor History* 5(1964): 235–41; and Gary J. Kornblith, "From Artisans to Businessmen: Master Mechanics in New England, 1789–1850" (Ph.D. diss., Princeton University, 1983) 1:56–67.

64. See Robert A. Becker, *Revolution, Reform, and the Politics of American Taxation* (Baton Rouge, La., 1980), pt. 2; Ronald Hoffman, *A Spirit of Dissension: Economy, Politics, and the Revolution in Maryland* (Baltimore, 1973), chap. 9; Stephen E. Patterson, *Political Parties in Revolutionary Massachusetts* (Madison, Wis., 1973), chaps. 6–7; and Robert A. Gross, *The Minutemen and Their World* (New York, 1976), 141–42.

65. See Hoffman, *Spirit of Dissension,* chap. 10 and p. 210 (quotation); Jackson Turner Main, *Political Parties before the Constitution* (Chapel Hill, N.C., 1973), 49–62, and chaps. 4–11; Norman K. Risjord, *Chesapeake Politics, 1781–1800* (New York, 1978), chap. 4; and David P. Szatmary, *Shays' Rebellion: The Making of an Agrarian Insurrection* (Amherst, Mass., 1980), chap. 2.

66. Thus the proportion of farmers (excluding large landowners) in the New York Assembly rose from 25 percent in 1769 to 42 percent in 1785, and the proportion of farmers in Virginia's lower house increased from 13 percent in 1773 to 26 percent in 1785. In Pennsylvania farmers comprised 37 percent of the men elected to the assembly between 1780 and 1788, and in Massachusetts they constituted 47 percent of those elected to the lower house between 1784 and 1788. See Jackson Turner Main, "Government by the People: The American Revolution and the Democratization of the Legislatures," *WMQ* 23(1966): 391–407; Main, *Political Parties,* 93 (table 4.2), 175 (table 7.1). For changes in the composition of the upper houses, see Main, *The Upper House in Revolutionary America, 1763–1788* (Madison, Wis., 1967).

67. See Merrill Jensen, *The New Nation: A History of the United States during the Articles of Confederation* (New York, 1950), chap. 16.

68. See Van Beck Hall, *Politics without Parties: Massachusetts, 1780–1791* (Pittsburgh, 1972), chaps. 2–4.

69. See ibid., chaps. 6–7; Szatmary, *Shays' Rebellion,* chaps. 4–6; and Robert J. Taylor, *Western Massachusetts in the Revolution* (Providence, R.I., 1954), chaps. 6–7. For an important study of how Shays's Rebellion related to deference patterns, see John L. Brooke, "To the Quiet of the People: Revolutionary Settlements and Civil Unrest in Western Massachusetts, 1774–1789," *WMQ* 46(1989): 425–62. Brooke points out that the most indebted communities were not the ones to take up arms.

70. Szatmary, *Shays' Rebellion,* 86.

71. On the background of the delegates see Forrest McDonald, *We the People: The Economic Origins of the Constitution* (Chicago, 1958), chap. 3; and Richard B. Morris, *The Forging of the Union, 1781–1789* (New York, 1987), 268–75.

72. Of the vast literature on the framing of the Federal Constitution, the most useful studies for the purposes of the present essay have been Gordon S. Wood,

The Creation of the American Republic, 1776–1787 (Chapel Hill, N.C., 1969), pt. 5; Wood, "Interests and Disinterestedness in the Making of the Constitution," in Beeman et al., eds., *Beyond Confederation,* 69–109; Alfred F. Young, "Conservatism, the Constitution, and the 'Spirit of Accomodation,' " in Robert A. Goldwin and William A. Schambra, eds., *How Democratic Is the Constitution?* (Washington, D.C., 1980), 117–47; Forrest McDonald, *Novus Ordo Seclorum: The Intellectual Origins of the Constitution* (Lawrence, Kans., 1985); and Isaac Kramnick, "The 'Great National Discussion': The Discourse of Politics in 1787," *WMQ* 45(1988): 3–32.

73. For the Hamilton Plan see Max Farrand, ed., *The Records of the Federal Convention of 1787,* rev. ed. (New Haven, 1937) 1: 282–311.

74. Ibid., 1: 48, 50, 51. The bracketed word in the Sherman quotation is an insertion Madison made in his Convention notes years later. Its effect is to align Sherman against direct elections of representatives, but not the indirect elections used under the Articles of Confederation.

75. Ibid., 1:150(Dickinson), 400(Pinckney), and 422–23(Madison).

76. See Jacob E. Cooke, ed., *The Federalist* (Middletown, Conn., 1961), no. 56, especially 382–83.

77. See ibid., 56–65. For a recent analysis of Madison's views see Edmund S. Morgan, *Inventing the People: The Rise of Popular Sovereignty in England and America* (New York, 1988), chap. 11.

78. On the framers' vision of a national military establishment, see Lawrence Delbert Cress, *Citizens in Arms: The Army and Militia in American Society to the War of 1812* (Chapel Hill, N.C., 1982), chap. 6. For what Richard H. Kohn calls the founders' "murder of the militia system" in the early 1790s, see his *Eagle and Sword: The Beginnings of the Military Establishment in America* (New York, 1975), chap. 7.

79. See Young, " 'Spirit of Accommodation,' "; and John M. Murrin, "1787: The Invention of American Federalism," in David E. Narrett and Joyce S. Goldberg, eds., *Essays on Liberty and Federalism: The Shaping of the U. S. Constitution* (College Station, Tex., 1988), 20–47. For Mason's speech, see Farrand, ed., *Records of Federal Convention* 1: 101.

80. David Grayson Allen et al., eds., *Diary of John Quincy Adams* (Cambridge, Mass., 1981), 2: 302–3. The fullest compilation of Antifederalist writings is Herbert J. Storing, ed., *The Complete Anti-Federalist,* 7 vols. (Chicago, 1981).

81. Jonathan Elliot, ed., *The Debates in the Several State Conventions on the Adoption of the Federal Constitution, as Recommended by the General Convention at Philadelphia in 1787,* 2d ed. (Washington, D.C., 1854) 2: 247–48. See also Alfred F. Young, *The Democratic Republicans of New York: The Origins, 1763–1797* (Chapel Hill, N.C., 1967), 103–5.

82. The intensity and complexity of the ratification struggle is best conveyed by Merrill Jensen et al., eds., *The Documentary History of the Ratification of the Constitution* (Madison, Wis., 1976–). For a fine narrative see Robert Allen Rutland, *The Ordeal of the Constitution: The Antifederalists and the*

Ratification Struggle of 1787–1788 (Norman, Okla., 1966). For an analysis of how little Madison thought he was conceding with the Bill of Rights that he and the First Congress drafted, see Kenneth R. Bowling, "'A Tub to the Whale': The Founding Fathers and Adoption of the Federal Bill of Rights," *Journal of the Early Republic* 8(1988): 223–51.

83. See Jack N. Rakove, "The Structure of Politics at the Accession of George Washington," in Beeman et al., eds., *Beyond Confederation,* 276–79; and *Biographical Directory of the Amerian Congress, 1774–1989.*

84. See Ethel E. Rasmussen, "Democratic Environment—Aristocratic Aspiration," *Pennsylvania Magazine of History and Biography* 90(1966): 155–82.

85. See Gerald Stourzh, *Alexander Hamilton and the Idea of Republican Government* (Stanford, Calif., 1970), 87–91; Lance Banning, *The Jeffersonian Persuasion: Evolution of a Party Ideology* (Ithaca, N. Y., 1978), 128–41; E. James Ferguson, "Political Economy, Public Liberty, and the Formation of the Constitution," *WMQ* 40(1983): 404–8; and John R. Nelson, Jr., *Liberty and Property: Political Economy and Policymaking in the New Nation, 1789–1812* (Baltimore, 1987), chap. 2.

86. See E. James Ferguson, *The Power of the Purse: A History of American Public Finance, 1776–1790* (Chapel Hill, N.C., 1961), 251–86, 335–36; and Whitney K. Bates, "Northern Speculators and Southern Debts: 1790," *WMQ* 19(1962): 30–48, especially table 12.

87. See Banning, *Jeffersonian Persuasion,* chap. 5; Drew R. McCoy, *The Elusive Republic: Political Economy in Jeffersonian America* (Chapel Hill, N.C., 1980), chap. 6; Richard Buel, Jr., *Securing the Revolution: Ideology in American Politics, 1789–1815* (Ithaca, N.Y., 1972); chap. 1; and Robert E. Shalhope, *John Taylor of Caroline, Pastoral Republican* (Columbia, S.C., 1980), chap. 2.

88. See Mary P Ryan, "Party Formation in the United States Congress, 1789 to 1796: A Quantitative Approach," *WMQ* 28(1971): 523–42; H. James Henderson, "Quantitative Aproaches to Party Formation in the United States Congress: A Comment," *WMQ* 30(1973): 307–24; Henderson, *Party Politics,* chap. 15; and Michael Durey, "Thomas Paine's Apostles: Radical Émigrés and the Triumph of Jeffersonian Republicanism," *WMQ* 44(1987): 661–88. The quotation is from Farrand, ed., *Records of Federal Convention* 2:450.

89. Cooke, ed., *Federalist,* 60; see also Lance Banning, "The Hamiltonian Madison: A Reconsideration," *Virginia Magazine of History and Biography* 92(1984): 3–28.

90. See Noble E. Cunningham, *The Jeffersonian Republicans: The Formation of Party Organization, 1789–1801* (Chapel Hill, N.C., 1957), chaps. 1–4; and McCoy, *Elusive Republic,* chaps. 6–7.

91. See Nelson, *Liberty and Property,* 76; Norman K. Risjord and Gordon Denboer, "The Evolution of Political Parties in Virginia," *Journal of*

American History 60(1973–74): 961–84; Lisle A. Rose, *Prologue to Democracy: The Federalists in the South, 1789–1800* (Lexington, Ky., 1968); and Richard R. Beeman, *The Old Dominion and the New Nation, 1788–1801* (Lexington, Ky., 1972).

92. See Paul Goodman, "Social Status of Party Leadership: The House of Representatives, 1797–1804," *WMQ,* 25(1968): 465–74; Goodman, *The Democratic-Republicans of Massachusetts: Politics in a Young Republic* (Cambridge, Mass., 1964); and Joyce Appleby, *Capitalism and a New Social Order: The Republican Vision of the 1790s* (New York, 1984), chap 4. The quotations are from Madison, "A Candid State of Parties" *National Gazette,* 22 September 1792, in William T. Hutchinson et al., eds., *The Papers of James Madison* (Chicago, 1962–) 13:371.

93. See Marshall Smelser, "The Jacobin Frenzy: Federalism and the Menace of Liberty, Equality, and Fraternity," *Review of Politics* 13(1951): 457–82; John R. Howe, Jr., "Republican Thought and the Political Violence of the 1790s," *American Quarterly* 19(1967): 147–65; and Buel, *Securing Revolution,* 97–105.

94. See Carl E. Prince, *The Federalists and the Origins of the U.S. Civil Service* (New York, 1977). The quotation is from "The Continentalist," no. 6, *New-York Packet,* 4 July 1782, in Harold C. Syrett et al., eds., *The Papers of Alexander Hamilton* (New York, 1961–81) 3:105.

95. See Thomas P. Slaughter, *The Whiskey Rebellion: Frontier Epilogue to the American Revolution* (New York, 1986), chap. 12; and Manning J. Dauer, *The Adams Federalists* (Baltimore, 1953), chap. 10.

96. See Owen S. Ireland, "The Ethnic-Religious Counter-Revolution in Pennsylvania, 1784–1786" (paper presented at the Philadelphia Center for Early American Studies, 22 January 1988); Ireland, "The People's Triumph: The Federalist Majority in Pennsylvania, 1787–1788," *Pennsylvania History* 56(1989): 93–113; Roland M. Baumann, "Philadelphia's Manufacturers and the Excise Taxes of 1794: The Forging of the Jeffersonian Coalition," *Pennsylvania Magazine of History and Biography* 106(1982): 3–39; and Kenneth W. Keller, "Rural Politics and the Collapse of Pennsylvania Federalism," *American Philosophical Society Transactions* 72, pt. 6 (1982).

97. See David Hackett Fischer, *The Revolution of American Conservatism: The Federalist Party in the Era of Jeffersonian Democracy* (New York, 1965), 201–26; Hall, *Politics without Parties,* chap. 11; Young, *Democratic Republicans,* especially chap. 12; Nelson, *Liberty and Property,* chaps. 6–7; Carl E. Prince, *New Jersey's Jeffersonian Republicans: The Genesis of an Early Party Machine, 1789–1817* (Chapel Hill, N.C., 1964); and John A. Munroe, *Federalist Delaware, 1775–1815* (New Brunswick, N.J., 1954).

98. See Jerald A. Combs, *The Jay Treaty: Political Battleground of the Founding Fathers* (Berkeley, Calif., 1970); Dauer, *Adams Federalists,* chaps. 9–16; Stephen G. Kurtz, *The Presidency of John Adams: The Collapse of Federalism, 1795–1800* (Philadelphia, 1957); and Jacob E. Cooke, "Country above Party: John Adams and the 1799 Mission to France," in Edmund P. Willis,

ed., *Fame and the Founding Fathers: Papers and Comments presented at the Nineteenth Conference on Early American History, March 25–26, 1966* (Bethlehem, Pa., 1967), 53–77.

99. See John M. Murrin, "The Great Inversion, or Court versus Country: A Comparison of the Revolution Settlements in England (1688–1721) and America (1776–1816)," in J. G. A. Pocock, ed., *Three British Revolutions: 1641, 1688, 1776* (Princeton, 1980), 423–25; Carter Goodrich, *Government Promotion of American Canals and Railroads, 1800–1890* (New York, 1960), chaps. 1–3; Stuart Bruchey, *The Roots of American Economic Growth, 1607–1861: An Essay in Social Causation* (New York, 1968), chap. 6; and Robert H. Wiebe, *The Opening of American Society: From the Adoption of the Constitution to the Eve of Disunion* (New York, 1984), especially chap. 10.

100. Alexis de Tocqueville, *Democracy in America,* ed. J. P. Mayer, trans. George Lawrence (Garden City, N.Y., 1966, 1969) 1:246n.

101. Ibid., 1:260n. For data on the social and economic backgrounds of state legislators during the early and middle decades of the nineteenth century, see Harold Joseph Counihan, "North Carolina, 1815–1836; State and Local Perspectives on the Age of Jackson" (Ph.D. diss., University of North Carolina at Chapel Hill, 1971), 19–24; Horace B. Davis, "The Occupations of Massachusetts Legislators, 1790–1950," *New England Quarterly* 24(1951): 89–100; Philip Shriver Klein, *Pennsylvania Politics, 1817–1832: A Game without Rules* (Philadelphia, 1974), 26–29; Peter D. Levine, *The Behavior of State Legislative Parties in the Jacksonian Era: New Jersey, 1829–1844* (Rutherford, N.J., 1977), chap. 3; J. Mills Thornton III, *Politics and Power in a Slave Society: Alabama, 1800–1860* (Baton Rouge, La., 1978), chap. 2; Ralph A. Wooster, *The People in Power: Courthouse to Statehouse in the Lower South, 1850–1860* (Knoxville, Tenn., 1969), chap. 1; and Wooster, *Politicians, Planters, and Plain Folk: Courthouse and Statehouse in the Upper South, 1850–1860* (Knoxville, Tenn., 1975), chap. 1. In a challenge to Tocqueville's portrait of the United States as an egalitarian society, Edward Pessen has documented a large upper-class presence in the municipal governments of Boston, Brooklyn, New York, and Philadelphia. He ignores the composition of state governments, however. *Riches, Class, and Power before the Civil War* (Lexington, Mass., 1973), especially chap. 13. Philip H. Burch, Jr., also neglects the state level of government in his lengthy *Elites in American History,* 3 vols. (New York, 1981).

102. Tocqueville, *Democracy in America* 1:205. Compare 1:198.

103. For the very real reluctance to come to terms with this transition in the early republic, see John M. Murrin, "Escaping Perfidious Albion: Federalism, Fear of Aristocracy, and the Democratization of Corruption in Post-Revolutionary America," in Richard K. Matthews, ed., *Virtue, Corruption, and Self-Interest* (Bethlehem, Penn., forthcoming).

104. Matthew Josephson, *The Robber Barons* (New York, 1934), 183, 184 (italics removed); and Robert A. Divine et al., *America Past and Present,* brief ed. (Glenview, Ill., 1986), 298. For the federal budget see U.S. Bureau of the Census, *Historical Statistics of the United States, Colonial Times to 1970* (Washington, D.C., 1975) 2: 1104.

9

Escaping Perfidious Albion

Federalism, Fear of Aristocracy, and the Democratization of Corruption in Postrevolutionary America

THE AMERICAN REVOLUTION, to a profound degree, was a reaction to the perceived threat of British corruption. Yet in the nineteenth century, as British politics evolved into a stable parliamentary system that pitted liberal and conservative parties against one another, corruption all but disappeared as a political issue. In the United States, anxiety about corruption, instead of receding in the republic designed to destroy it, acquired unprecedented force in American public life, sometimes almost enough to overwhelm all other concerns.[1]

This essay examines the American half of this transformation. It is frankly exploratory and makes no claim to comprehensiveness. It does not even attempt in any systematic way to determine how "real"—as opposed to rhetorical—the problem of corruption was. It does try to suggest why this concern became so overriding in the aftermath of the American Revolution. It offers a brief history of a metaphor, "corruption," concentrating on the decades between the middle third of the eighteenth century and the age of Jefferson. During that period, something less than a century, the language of corruption became an extremely sensitive barometer for measuring the hopes, aspirations, and anxieties expressed in American public life. The problem of corruption moved from the margins of political discourse to become a major preoccupation of the Revolutionary era. George III and his Parliament of placemen were

Originally published in *Virtue, Corruption, and Self-Interest: Political Values in the Eighteenth Century* (Bethlehem, PA: Lehigh University Press, 1994), 103–147.

trying, insisted the patriots, to deprive the American colonies of rights and privileges that they had exercised for generations. The bracing constitutional transformations that swept across both the states and the nation after independence did address these concerns. By banning officeholders from seats in the legislature, the founders of the republic believed that they had an answer for the predominant form of corruption in eighteenth century Britain. But the issue would not die. Instead it intensified dramatically after 1790. In the fierce struggles between Federalists and Democratic Republicans, corruption became nothing less than a national obsession.

Particularly in Pennsylvania, radical Democrats, who had won overwhelming superiority during Thomas Jefferson's presidency, began to denounce one another in language that Federalists had used against them and that they had once reserved for Federalists. They truly believed that in their victory over Federalism they had destroyed an incipient and thoroughly corrupt ruling class. Pennsylvania became to them the most spectacular proof in world history that ordinary people could govern themselves without depending upon an elite based on birth and wealth. But they were far less successful in finding ways to determine which particular ordinary republicans ought to exercise public power over the rest. Those deprived of office accused officeholders of corruption, of attempting to set themselves apart as a new aristocracy or ruling class. In the process, the rhetoric of corruption emerged as the common grammar of politics, so overwhelming that it became difficult to discuss public questions in any other language. The age of Jefferson bequeathed to the United States an obsession with corruption that still deeply colors the way we think about politics.

Far from destroying the British paradigm, the Jeffersonians applied it to the United States at both the state and national levels and then democratized it and dramatically expanded its application. They denounced public officials for using patronage to undermine the integrity of the legislature and thus of the broader society. Every method that they invented for selecting political candidates—ward meetings, legislative caucuses, and party conventions—quickly became, in the eyes of the excluded, a device through which some self-interested faction was attempting to impose its will upon a virtuous people. The appropriate reform in this progression of institutional change always became an effort to rouse the people to action and to develop a more participatory forum for making these decisions. The momentum of this rhetoric accelerated from the dynamic assumptions that there is a *people* as well as a common good, and that the people can identify that common good and defeat corrupt individuals and groups set on undermining it. In this form the language of corruption became a constant ritual of reaffirmation. Always harkening back to the Revolution, political rhetoric located corruption in officeholders and ambitious persons or interests, not the public at large, which remained a vast reservoir of virtue.

In this sense the language of corruption often became a way of discussing issues and fears that a later generation would define as class conflict. That this discourse remained indirect and oblique is hardly surprising. In neither Britain nor France did anything like a Marxian perspective on class take hold until after 1850. In Britain the fear of corrupt state power long inhibited the formation of ideas that pitted laborers against their employers. Reform of the constitution, not the relations of production, defined the radical agenda through the Chartist and anti–Corn Law agitations of the 1840s. In France continuing struggle against Old Regime privilege had a similar effect on radicals, who still hoped to unite all producers—both employers and their workers—against a common enemy. In the United States the idea of a virtuous people as an essential bulwark of the republic led, perhaps even more inexorably, to an emphasis on corruption. But this issue took a sharply different form in America from what it assumed in Britain. Americans celebrated their constitutions and forms of government as the most advanced in the world. They located corruption, not in the structures of government and society, but in the ambitions and deeds of particular groups and individuals.[2]

Rather less often, Jeffersonians glimpsed a newer and even more disturbing possibility. In a society that no longer had a ruling class, the very rich would usually be out of office. Public officials, while not impoverished, would often be men of rather modest resources. Could the wealthy few undermine less wealthy officials by offering them economic favors? In Britain, the political system threatened to contaminate the social order. In republican America, would society corrupt politics? In a land that encouraged all free adult males to pursue wealth and happiness, were the people themselves inherently prone to corruption? Was that danger the real meaning of the American Revolution? When Jeffersonians confronted this possibility, their language grew apocalyptic. They had no answer to the problem. And they bequeathed this dilemma to their successors.

I

So completely reified has the concept of corruption become in the United States that we forget that it is a metaphor and that the use of the metaphor has a history with a beginning and a pattern of change and development, if not yet an ending. If a public official accepts money in exchange for making a particular decision, nothing inherent in the transaction invokes the imagery of something decaying or dying. To make that leap, individuals need another and much broader assumption. They must think of their government or the state as a living entity, a "body politic" that can, perhaps must, experience a cycle of life from birth to maturity, then decay, death, and "corruption." In England, according to the *Oxford English Dictionary*, the earliest political use of the word *corruption* dates from 1393 and described a partial judge. The term took centuries to move beyond the judicial system. During the reign of Henry VIII, for example, the practice of lavish gift giving accompanied most social and political engagements. Gentlemen would have considered it demeaning, perhaps even "corrupt," to give or receive money instead of wine, game, hawks, hunting dogs, and other presents. Everybody understood that what was distributed affected who got ahead and what was decided in the public sphere. No rhetoric of corruption emerged to challenge these practices.[3] The notorious 1621 impeachment trial of Lord Chancellor Francis Bacon, Viscount St. Albans, almost certainly marked a sharp transitional point between the judicial and the political. Increasing anxiety about the corruption of the Stuart court did much to undermine the legitimacy of the monarchy by the 1640s, but only in the last quarter of the seventeenth century, when the language of civic humanism emerged as an extremely effective way for the "country" to criticize the "Court," did "corruption" become a routine and indispensable way of discussing and understanding public events.[4] The Glorious Revolution of 1688–89 and the cycle of Anglo-French wars that it inaugurated vastly magnified the patronage and the revenues available to the English state and seemed almost to guarantee the ability of the Court to hold its working majority in the House of Commons. England had become a body politic in which virtue and patriotism struggled ceaselessly against corruption and decay, especially during the long ministry of Sir Robert Walpole (1721–42).[5]

For more than a century after the founding of Jamestown, the settlers in England's North American colonies seldom invoked corruption as a way of explaining political events. Examples of its use are scattered and desultory. For instance, in 1643 the governor and council of Virginia complained that depositions for court cases "are frequently taken in a private manner, and it may be oftentime, . . .much corruption is used to the great danger and prejudice of the adverse party." As in medieval England, the word described an abuse of the judicial system, and the remedy seemed simple. All depositions had to be sworn in open court.[6] Without using the word *corruption,* Nathaniel Bacon—a very recent immigrant from England—came close to the concept it was beginning to signify there when he denounced the "cabal" of "great men" who had risen under Governor Sir William Berkeley. "Now let us . . . see what sponges have sucked up the public treasure, and whether it has not been contrived away by unworthy favourites and juggling parasites whose tottering fortunes have been repaired and supported at the public charge," declared his manifesto of 1676. But even Bacon never moved beyond an accusation of greed to a broader theory of politics in which corruption could unbalance the colony's "constitution," a word that no participant invoked, so far as I can recall.[7] Nor did the Baconians leave much of a legacy. In the 1680s English navy officers and customs officials gave the colony what one historian has called "a golden fleecing" without stimulating any broad public concern about patterns of corruption.[8]

Early New Englanders were much fonder of the word, but they confined it to a religious and personal context. John Cotton was typical. "Here is the distemper of our natures," he warned, "that we cannot tell how to use liberty, but we shall very readily corrupt ourselves: Oh the bottomless depth of sandy earth! of a corrupt spirit, that breaks over all bounds." The problem had nothing to do with politics. It was personal. In like manner, Roger Williams was saying far more about religion than politics when he declared that "outward Civill peace cannot stand where Religion is corrupted."[9] In all probability the word *corruption* conveyed a biblical message to New Englanders before it signified anything else. They probably read or heard dozens of times such passages as 1 Corinthians

15:53: "For this corruptible must put on incorruption, and this mortal must put on immortality."

If anything, the Puritan acceptance of the covenant insulated individuals against a broadly political understanding of corruption. God punished the community for the sins of individuals or the failure of magistrates to correct those sins. Men who accused John Winthrop of arbitrary and tyrannical behavior worried, not because he was too harsh on anyone in particular, but because he seemed too lenient in disciplining sinners and thus might bring the wrath of God upon the land.[10] When the Massachusetts General Court enacted a broad reform program in 1675, it paid no attention to governmental structure or practices. Instead, it attacked such evils as the "manifest pride" that prompted some men to wear "long haire, like woemens haire, . . . either their owne or others hairemade into perewiggs," and the laxity that permitted toleration of Quakers, idleness, tavern haunting, and young men and women "riding from toune to toune . . . upon pretence of going to lecture," all of which had brought the punishment of King Philip's War upon the colony.[11] Even when New Englanders overthrew the autocratic government of Sir Edmund Andros and the Dominion of New England in 1689, their many justifications of the rising did not go beyond condemnation of his "Absolute and Arbitrary" commission and of the "Crew of abject Persons fetched from New York, to be the Tools of the Adversary, standing at our right hand," all of whom had been "*Horseleeches* . . . sucking on us." The greed of their tormentors never quite turned into the bigger question of corruption in politics.[12]

The middle colonies offered variations on similar themes. Those who rallied to Jacob Leisler's revolution that overthrew the Dominion of New England in New York loathed the rapacity of their opponents but never attached this resentment to any theory of corruption.[13] William Penn, although he moved easily in the circles of the English Whig party which led the way in defining the ideological significance of corruption, saw matters differently on that question. As his famous 1682 preface to the First Frame of Government put it: "*Governments* rather depende upon *Men,* then *Men* upon *Governments.* Let *Men* be *good,* and the *Government* can't be *bad;* if it be *ill.* they will cure it: but if *men* be *bad,* let the *Government* be never so *good,* they will endeavour to warp and spoil it to their Turn." So believed the man who spent more time than any other colony founder in devising a proper form of government for his province. In the end, personal morality mattered more than constitutional structures.[14]

II

The civic humanist concern for corruption crossed the ocean slowly and appeared in different colonies at widely separated times in the first half of the eighteenth century. Virginia led the way. There, Lieutenant Governor Alexander Spotswood (1710–22) persuaded the legislature to pass a tobacco inspection act that created forty lucrative inspectorships (worth about £1000 per year each), most of which he then distributed among members of the House of Burgesses. Then Queen Anne let him down by dying suddenly in 1714, thus forcing Spotswood to call new elections in which his placemen were massacred by the voters and in many cases replaced by small planters who had not even served as justices of the peace. The radical demands of the 1715 assembly prompted Spotswood to dissolve it with one of the most insulting speeches a colonial governor ever delivered to a legal assembly. For the next three years he ruled without one, but when he finally called for new elections in 1718, the opposition attacked him in explicit civic humanist language. Even though their handwritten election tract did not use the word *corruption,* it did not have to, for it developed the English context of that idea quite fully. It asked voters to remember "how the Governour with his Creatures and favourites trampled down the Libertys and propertys of the people and the Rights and privelidges of the house of Burgesses, which at the opening of the assembly he promised to protect and afterwards refused to Assist them because his creatures was the persons Questioned, who Judas like would sell their saviour and Country for an Interest a Smile or fear."[15] Virginia planters embraced country ideology. They strongly resisted all efforts by their governors to use patronage to dominate the assembly. But because royal governors abandoned those efforts and turned instead to effective methods of persuasion, the concern for corruption soon yielded priority to a highly stylized rhetoric of harmony, particularly during the long and successful administration of Sir William Gooch. A strikingly similar pattern took hold in South Carolina during the 1730s and in Georgia during the 1750s.[16]

In the middle colonies, country ideology appealed to opposition groups too weak to win a majority in the assembly. The Lewis Morris faction in New York created John Peter Zenger's *New York Weekly Journal* as North America's first political newspaper while trying to force Governor William Cosby (1732–36) to call a general election. Instead, Cosby indicted Zenger for seditious libel, and the Morrisites made their argument for the governor's corruption in a public courtroom, but Cosby never did dissolve the assembly.[17] Twenty years later, at a time when the Livingston family enjoyed even less success against their Delancey rivals, William Livingston edited and published *The Independent Reflector,* an able opposition paper that deftly exploited civic humanist themes.[18] Pennsylvania was much stranger. There, civic humanist values may have been invoked more often by the administration or proprietary party than by the Quaker party that dominated the assembly. Rector William Smith, for example, frequently complained that the assembly had become so powerful that the constitution was utterly unbalanced in favor of the popular side. He denounced the "artifices by which the villains of the political world, both small and great, generally mislead the easy multitude who entrust them with power"—a process that could end, he warned, in Caesarism. When Julius Caesar cultivated popularity, "Rome gave him an army and that army gave him . . . Rome."[19] The need to defend a proper balance could thus locate corruption at the top, as in New York, or detect its spread from the bottom up, as in Pennsylvania where Smith identified the assembly itself as the principal offender.

New England was slower than any other region to take up this rhetoric, perhaps because of the insulating effect of covenant theology. In England the money question instantly became a magnet that pulled in the entire ideological complex of values that isolated corruption as the central danger to the polity. New Englanders argued incessantly about paper money and depreciation from 1714 into the 1750s. Scarcely a hint of the civic humanist paradigm appeared before the late 1740s, but then it began to win adherents. Governor William Shirley (174156) became so effective at controlling the Massachusetts General Court that his Boston opponents founded *The Independent Advertiser* in 1747 to warn the voters that Shirley's patronage had already undermined the independence of the legislature. As if to prove the point, the House of Representatives in 1749 expelled James Allen, leader of the minority opposition and a patron of young Samuel Adams. In 1754 aggrieved Bostonians published pamphlet after pamphlet attacking an excise tax favored by the farming majority in the General Court because it would shift the tax burden from land onto imported liquors. The protestors drew heavily upon the successful English resistance to Sir Robert Walpole's excise proposal of 1733, but in Massachusetts they lost. The excise passed, the General Court jailed the printer Daniel Fowle for contempt, and he eventually took his press to New Hampshire, where he had to endure an even more deeply entrenched regime of royal patronage under Governor Benning Wentworth.[20]

The civic humanist fear of corruption penetrated Virginia before 1720 and the rest of North America during the middle third of the century, but it was not yet the powerful paradigm of politics that it had become in the Britain of 1760. There, even young King George III and his tutor and first minister, John Stuart, fourth earl of Bute, believed that the kingdom had entered the last throes of degeneracy and corruption, that the government itself "remains compos'd of the most abandon'd men that ever had those offices" (1762), that if "these mirmidons of the blackest kind" held power for just a few more years (as of 1757), "any invader with a handful of men might place himself on the throne and establish despotism here," and that Bute was the only honest man in the entire kingdom.[21]

North American settlers did not yet experience any anxieties as acute as George III's. In all likelihood a majority of planters in Virginia and South Carolina accepted the value system of civic humanism, but they generally believed that their governments had corruption well under control. In northern colonies, those who participated in public life became exposed to these ideas somewhere between the 1730s and 1750s, but in every case studied so far, these concerns were expressed by a political minority unable to win assembly support. When a colonial assembly challenged a governor, the debate became a legalistic and technical argument about precedents, privileges, and prerogatives.[22] Corruption was not the issue, although sometimes a printer such as Daniel Fowle could amuse himself if not gain revenge for his humiliations. On 2 December 1765 his *Portsmouth Mercury* published a satirical piece that claimed to be a letter from "Intian Jo." To understand it, the reader should know that the title "Esquire" or its colloquial version "Squire" belonged to every justice of the peace, an office that was an important patronage position in Massachusetts and New Hampshire.[23]

I was tuder day at Sq____re ****** Hee keep fery cood Tafern as crate many uder Sq____res do an i . . . trank cood syter til i was bliged to co out to p____s, it was dark nite, an i cood se no pody but myself, but sune I herd a Man cri out hoo, hoo, wat u doin, wat u doin____ I sade, ho comes dere? he sade tis i; ho is dat intian Jo? yes i sade tis i tu, ho are u? he sade my name is Sq____re ****** dont u no i was latly made J____P ____ how cums u to p____s on me____o trange i sade Sq____re, wen i was litel poy, dare was but to or tree J____P____al round de cuntry, fery cood men, make al men trade of 'em, now poor intian Jo can't go to p____s widout p____ s____g on J____P____an Sq____res.

Fowle could do little to discomfort the Wentworth regime even during the Stamp Act crisis, but at least he could lament the multiplication of offices.

III

The American Revolution was one of history's greatest reversals. It ran against the prevailing momentum of change between 1730 or 1740 and 1765 and even beyond, all of which was toward greater imperial integration with the colonists as willing participants in the process. This pattern characterized commerce, migration, religion, provincial politics, and wartime cooperation. Imperial trade grew even more rapidly after 1740 than colonial population, which doubled every twenty-five years. The colonial appetite for British products was beginning to seem boundless.[24] The Atlantic was also becoming an ever more efficient distributor of labor from the British Isles to the colonies. Notice of the availability of new lands in North Carolina, Pennsylvania, New York, or Nova Scotia could set thousands of individuals and families in motion within a year or two, heading for America and sometimes threatening to depopulate considerable portions of Scotland or Ireland in the process.[25] Even the First Great Awakening was far more an Atlantic than a North American event, tied together by George Whitefield's seven trips to America and the corresponding societies and newspapers that kept Scotland and London, for example, informed about the progress of revivals in New England or New Jersey.[26] In politics the most successful royal governors that most mainland colonies ever had came during or after the 1740s and 1750s: James

Glen (174356) in South Carolina, Arthur Dobbs (175465) and William Tryon (176571) in North Carolina, Sir William Gooch (172749) and Francis Fauquier (175868) in Virginia, Jonathan Belcher (174757) and William Franklin (176376) in New Jersey, William Shirley (174156) in Massachusetts, and Benning Wentworth (174167) in New Hampshire.[27] Patterns of warfare show the same trend. Despite severe friction between 1754 and 1757, Britain and the mainland colonies achieved an utterly unprecedented level of cooperation in the later years of the Great War for the Empire, and the result was equally unprecedented—total victory over New France by 1763.[28]

Just twelve years after the Peace of Paris, Massachusetts farmers took up arms against the British army, and fifteen months after the fighting started the Thirteen Colonies declared their independence from Great Britain. In 1763 virtually no North American settler expected, much less favored, revolution or independence. By contrast, Englishmen and Scots had been predicting such a development for decades, and the fear of colonial independence—spreading with considerable intensity from one crisis to the next—definitely helped to shape British policy but almost exclusively in counterproductive ways.[29] The insistence on establishing Parliament's claim to tax America, consistently maintained from 1764 until 1778, persuaded the colonists that powerful men in Britain were indeed plotting against their established liberties. That the pattern endured despite frequent changes of government only magnified this perception, just as the determination of the settlers to resist first the stamp tax and then the milder Townshend duties confirmed and strengthened the British fear that colonial conspirators really were plotting independence. In this atmosphere, competing conspiracy theses became, in both cases, self-fulfilling prophecies. The actions of the British army in 1775 and 1776 did not bode at all well for colonial liberties, and Congress did meet this challenge by declaring the colonies independent. By 1776 those who had been crying conspiracy on both sides of the Atlantic had every reason to congratulate themselves on their perspicacity.[30] In this atmosphere, the civic humanist understanding of corruption moved at last from the periphery of public consciousness into the center simply because it provided a satisfactory explanation for what was happening. During the Stamp Act crisis of 1765–66, it was still fairly marginal, and when invoked it was used most of the time, not as a structural explanation for events throughout the empire, but as a way to discredit colonists tainted by the Stamp Act, such as Jared Ingersoll of Connecticut.[31] Nine years later, in the extended debate between John Adams ("Novanglus") and Daniel Leonard ("Massachusettensis"), each party had a fully developed conspiracy thesis that embraced both sides of the ocean and gave corruption an indispensable role. So, of course, did Thomas Jefferson's Declaration of Independence in its lengthy indictment of George III, whose entire reign "is a history of repeated injuries and usurpations, all having in direct object the establishment of an absolute Tyranny over these States."[32]

From 1765 to 1776 the only sure protection against the malign conspiratorial forces of transatlantic corruption had been an appeal to the virtue and righteous wrath of the people. Parliament did not even agree to read the resolutions passed by every colonial assembly denouncing the Stamp Act. To the acute distress of the colonial elites in these bodies, they found themselves impotent against Britain—unless they appealed to the people out of doors. Angry crowds, not the assemblies, nullified the Stamp Act and compelled the home government to listen, respond, and finally repeal the tax.[33] Crowds also drove the British army from Boston in 1770, nullified the Tea Act in 1773, and began the war in April 1775.

In every colony or state, elite settlers who refused to go loyalist had to grope toward a new relationship with the *demos,* the people. Much of what both sides did had no firm precedent in the colonial past. Americans had to innovate, and they found the experience exhilarating. 'Tis not the concern of a day, a year, or an age," proclaimed Thomas Paine in 1776; "posterity are virtually involved in the contest, and will be more or less affected even to the end of time by the proceedings now. Now is the seed time of Continental union, faith, and honor."[34] Even the much more moderate James Madison celebrated American willingness to innovate. The American people "accomplished a revolution which has no parallel in the annals of human society," he announced in 1787. "They reared the fabrics of governments which have no model on the face of the globe."[35] Not everyone agreed, of course. As Alexander Hamilton announced to the Philadelphia Convention in 1787, the problems afflicting the Confederation almost made him "despair that a Republican Govt. could be established over so great an extent." He also knew that "it would be unwise to propose one of any other form." As Madison reported, Hamilton then made clear what he meant: "In his private opinion he had no scruple in declaring, supported as he was by the opinions of so many of the wise & good, that the British Govt. was the best in the world: and that he doubted much whether any thing short of it would do in America."[36]

Between them, Paine, Madison, and Hamilton defined the radical Republican, moderate Republican, and Federalist bands of the American political spectrum in the generation after 1790, especially in Pennsylvania, the state that became the Union's most daring experiment in radical republicanism. All of them would have to define their position on political corruption, and all of them related that question to whether the United States possessed, or ought to possess, a ruling class.[37]

Paine, Madison, and Hamilton all supported ratification of the federal Constitution, but on other troubling issues Madison and Hamilton, in 1787, were much closer to each other than either was to Paine. All three claimed to hate corruption, but they did not always mean the same thing by it. All accepted the main device built into the Constitution to prevent the emergence of a "court" party in America. Article 1, section 6 barred any officeholder of the United States from sitting in either house of Congress.

Hamilton admired the "influence" or patronage that made parliamentary government effective in Britain and lamented its weakness in the United States. By *"influence,"* he told the delegates at the Philadelphia Convention, "he did not mean corruption, but a dispensation of those regular honors & emoluments, which produce an attachment to the Govt."[38] As secretary of the treasury under George Washington, he would take giant steps to imitate the British model without actually appointing sitting congressmen to office. He clearly hoped to strengthen the federal government by attracting to its service the "wise & good," men of family, wealth, education, and experience. Such men could invest in the national and state debts and later buy stock in the Bank of the United States. The Jeffersonian opposition had no difficulty recognizing the Walpolean strategy behind this pattern and soon denounced these arrangements as the spread of British corruption to America.[39]

When James Madison cooperated with Hamilton in writing *The Federalist,* the two men had not yet discovered any major differences in their approaches to national politics. Madison too expected the Constitution to create a ruling class in America, but his reasoning was much more nuanced, and he did not consider British "influence" an acceptable method of government. With Hamilton, he agreed that most men will follow their self-interest most of the time. In other words, the United States had become a liberal society dedicated to the individual pursuit of happiness. But Madison still hoped to create a "republican" government for the nation—a government so structured that it would almost have to embrace the common good, not special interests. In *The Federalist* 10 he argued that an expanded republic would be more stable and much better governed than a small one. In a society as huge as the United States, local interests would almost never be able to become a legislative majority. He saluted the republican result in *The Federalist* 51 when he argued that "a coalition of the whole society could seldom take place on any other principles than those of justice and the general good."[40] He also believed that the individuals making disinterested decisions at the national level would be gentlemen—"men who possess most wisdom to discern, and most virtue to pursue the common good of the society." The creation of election districts with 30,000 voters almost seemed to guarantee that only men of reputation and standing could put together a following over that large an area.[41]

Madison's constitutional career was a search for the right combination of checks and balances to preserve liberty over time. Paine, by contrast, was a radical because he rejected Britain's "mixed and balanced constitution" as inherently corrupt, "the base remains of two ancient tyrannies [monarchy and aristocracy] compounded with some new Republican materials."[42] He looked with suspicion at any check upon government other than the people themselves. Madison was a moderate because he still believed in balanced government, now transformed into the separation of powers. He was a revolutionary because he understood that in the United States a constitutional balance could not rest upon hereditary social orders. Like Jefferson, he warmly supported the two largest upheavals of his lifetime, the American and French revolutions. Also like Jefferson (but unlike the moderate Federalist John Adams), he drew the line at Haiti and did everything in his power to contain or crush the Caribbean republic created in the 1790s by rebellious slaves.[43]

As the new government got under way in the spring of 1789, and as the capital moved back to Philadelphia from New York later that year, the politics of the United States and the Commonwealth of Pennsylvania combined and coalesced over a dizzying succession of issues.

The emerging Jeffersonian opposition denounced Hamilton's fiscal policies as a corrupt menace to the survival of republicanism, the prostitution of the public sphere to the unlimited greed of speculators. Then the French Revolution intensified everyone's concern for the questions at issue, with Federalists siding increasingly with Britain partly out of genuine sympathy but also out of a growing dread of French radicalism and a fear that conflict with Britain would destroy Hamilton's funding program, which to succeed required the continuing collection of duties on British imports. The Whiskey Rebellion, the Quasi-War with France, and the Federalist "reign of terror" of 1798–1801 brought public passions to an amazing peak and in the process transformed the politics of Pennsylvania—and hence the nation.[44]

IV

In 1776 Pennsylvania revolutionaries overthrew, not just George III and Parliament, but also their proprietary governor and legal assembly. A convention drafted a radical constitution with a unicameral legislature and a plural executive and also began to govern in the name of the people while banning from the political process anybody who refused to take an oath accepting the new order. The radicals became known as the Constitutionalist party. In fact, however, many Pennsylvanians loathed the Constitution of 1776. Quakers and German pacifists could not embrace violent revolution. Most supporters of the old proprietary party considered the new order madly egalitarian. Those who could bring themselves to accept the required oath began to agitate for constitutional change within the system. At first they were called Anticonstitutionalists, that is, opponents of the Constitution of 1776, but before long they began to describe themselves as Pennsylvania's Republican party. While the politics of proscription continued in force, voter turnout was quite low and reform prospects remained dim. The return of peace improved Anticonstitutionalist chances enormously, and they rapidly grew in strength in the 1780s as pacifists and ex-loyalists were reabsorbed into the polity. By the late 1780s the Republicans had gained a solid majority within the electorate.[45]

Indeed, Pennsylvania was the only large state in the Union in which a clear majority of voters favored ratification of the federal Constitution in 1787 and 1788. Within Philadelphia the partisan cleavage largely followed economic and class lines. In the countryside, the prevailing split was ethnic and religious. Republicans, who became Federalists in national politics, were likely to be English Episcopalians or Quakers and German sectarians. Constitutionalists, who emerged as Antifederalists and later Jeffersonians at the national level, were disproportionately Irish, Scots-Irish Presbyterians, and German Lutherans and Reformed. In 1789–90 the Federalists were able to use their majority in the assembly to summon a convention and draft a new state constitution, closely modeled on the federal example. It created a bicameral legislature with an annually elected house of representatives and a small senate serving staggered four-year terms, a strong executive (modeled on the presidency of the United States) with vast patronage powers elected for a three-year period and allowed to serve up to three consecutive terms, and an independent judiciary, although the governor could remove a judge from office if so requested by a vote of two-thirds of both houses. All taxpayers could vote, as could their sons if of age—a major concession to Anticonstitutionalists. Federal and state officeholders could not sit in the legislature. A bill of rights contained strong guarantees of the right to worship freely, assemble, and criticize public men and institutions. The Federalists gained control of the state government in 1790 and kept their governor, Thomas Mifflin, in office until 1799. As the decade unfolded, their opponents reorganized as Democratic-Republicans under Thomas Jefferson's banner. They appealed successfully to the growing Irish and German Catholic immigrant vote in Philadelphia, and in the late 1790s made dramatic gains among German sectarians in rural counties.[46]

As the French Revolution spread into American waters, the conflict between Federalists and Democratic-Republicans increasingly became a debate over who should rule in America, with the charge of corruption as a major weapon on both sides. The Democratic Society of Philadelphia, an organization widely copied throughout the entire country, warned its fellow citizens "that the progress of British influence in the United States has endangered our happiness and Independence, that it has operated to make us tributary to Great Britain, and to engender systems and corruptions baneful to Liberty." "So indifatigable [sic] are the aristocratical faction among us, in disseminating principles unfriendly to the rights of man—at the same time so artful as to envelop their machinations with the garb of Patriotism," they cried several months later, "that . . . unless vigilence, union and firmness mark the conduct of all real friends to equal

Liberty, their combinations and schemes will have their desired effect." "The germ of an odious Aristocracy is planted among us—it has taken root,—and has indeed already produced fruit worthy of the parent stock," they declared at the end of 1794. "If it be imprudent to eradicate this baneful exotic, let us at least unite in checking its growth." This theme constantly reappeared in Democratic pronouncements in almost endless variations throughout the Jeffersonian era.[47]

Federalists denounced the Democratic-Republican societies as conspiratorial cabals determined to undermine a legitimate popular government. President Washington castigated "certain self-created societies" in his annual message to Congress in November 1794, and in his farewell address even argued that "the spirit of party" might have a legitimate place in a monarchy, but in "Governments purely elective, it is a spirit not to be encouraged."[48] The societies bristled at this criticism, especially the "self-created" epithet. What was the hereditary Order of the Cincinnati, queried the Washington County Society?[49] "But self-created as we are supposed," responded Philadelphia's German Republican Society, "hereditary distinction has no place in our code, diplomas, with the insignia of nobility, adorn not our mansions, neither does birth give an exclusive claim to a place among us." The German organization then treated Washington to a powerful dose of Thomas Paine. "All governments are more or less combinations against the people; they are states of violence against individual liberty, . . . and as rulers have no more virtue than the ruled, . . . the power of government can only be kept within its constituted limits by the display of a power equal to itself, the collected sentiment of the people."[50]

Washington's statements and the German society's response reveal an interesting assumption about political controversy throughout the period. Although everyone agreed that only the people were sovereign in the United States, the much older assumption that every advanced society is divided into rulers and the ruled retained tremendous force. Washington was trying to persuade the public that between elections it had one primary political responsibility—obedience to the laws. The societies insisted on their right to criticize and to advocate change, but the claim that "the collected sentiment" of the entire people merely equaled "the power of government" showed how pervasive the older understanding remained in a world still dominated by monarchies. Timothy Dwight, an uncompromising Federalist, continued to talk of "subjects" rather than "citizens" throughout his life.[51] When as late as 1817 radical William Duane proclaimed the "unquestionable truth, that the rulers of a nation have it always in their power to form the habits of a people," he betrayed his own acceptance of the dichotomy between rulers and ruled.[52] The survival of this duality almost guaranteed that fear of aristocracy would thrive after 1790. Rulers, those in power, would almost inevitably try to set themselves apart from the people.

In a word, Democratic-Republicans accepted an enormous challenge when they set out to dismantle the Federalist ascendancy. No Federalist, so far as I am aware, ever proclaimed that he had a right to rule. He had earned high office through some combination of family status, education, and prior service. Federalists insisted they were a true meritocracy. But if they claimed no intrinsic right to govern, they had no doubts that some people—most people—lacked the qualifications to hold major office or even discuss public events intelligently.

In endless repetitions on this theme, Federalists mocked and satirized the pretensions of their opponents. "An Observer" attended a "meeting of Jacobins" in Philadelphia in August 1800. He reported the malapropisms, colloquialisms, confused parliamentary motions, and hiccups of the participants, "the very *refuse* and *filth* of society, . . . a large proportion of [whom] was men of the most infamous and abandoned characters." Some were "notorious for the seduction of *black innocence*," while others had been convicted of perjury, and many had "dared to tear down from the sacred desk, the emblems of mourning in honour of our beloved Washington," who died in 1799. He heaped scorn on the society's black and Jewish members. The conclusion was irresistible. "When persons of such character assume to themselves the order and regulation of a *government,* soon may we expect anarchy, confusion and commotion to ensue."[53] "When men of character accept of small offices," proclaimed a Boston Federalist in 1811, "they raise them to respectability. When men of no character get improtant offices, the office will not bring them up, but they bring the office down."[54] So consistent became this theme among Federalists that Duane still wondered in 1809 why they never learned from their failures. "They have incessantly struggled to regain their honors and dignities," but "they have not grown *one whit* wiser than formerly. They have been employed in one continued endeavor to prove the people *fools*! and their representatives *knaves*!! (as unlikely a way to gain popularity as could be devised!).[55]

V

In the 1790s Democratic-Republicans had not yet had to decide whether some of them were unfit to govern. They were still an opposition party scrambling to win seats in the Pennsylvania legislature when all of Governor Mifflin's patronage could be mobilized against them. They had few college graduates or lawyers in their number, and except for Benjamin Franklin Bache, they had to import their best printers and editors from abroad: William Duane from Ireland and India, John Binns from Ireland and England, Mathew Carey from Ireland.[56] Thus when the Democrats finally won a slim majority in the house in December 1799, they decided not to put Nathaniel B. Boileau—a graduate of the College of New Jersey (Princeton)—up for speaker because "it was concluded that he might be more useful on the floor, the democrats having but few men who were in the habit of public speaking."[57] For that matter, few prominent Democrats other than the printers and the Irish had been born in English-speaking households. Dr. Michael Leib and future governors Simon Snyder and Joseph Hiester were raised in German-speaking families. Boileau came from a Huguenot background. Although he spoke English, Alexander J. Dallas was Scottish and Irish, while future governors Thomas McKean and William Findlay were Scots-Irish. The Federalists knew that they were Pennsylvania's English party, and many of them probably took delight in Thomas Moore's poetic jab at "the piebald polity that reigns/In free confusion o'er Columbia's plains." Moore elaborated:[58]

> Take Christians. Mohawks, democrats, and all
> From the rude wigwam to the congresss-hall,
> From man the savage, whether slav'd or free,
> To man the civiliz'd, less tame than he,—
> 'Tis one dull chaos, one unfertile strife
> Betwixt half-polish'd and half-barbarous life;
> Where every ill the ancient world could brew
> Is mix'd with every grossness of the new.

To Democrats the American Revolution meant not only the achievement of independence, but also the triumph of liberty and equality. What about "fraternity," especially after the French Revolution brought that term to America? It probably never achieved the centrality of the other two, but within the democratic societies and the party, *fraternity* (or some variant of *brethren*) was the word of choice for explaining how good Democratic-Republicans could bridge their conspicuous ethnic differences and reach accord on questions of policy—and, in all probability, patronage. Democrats continued to hold public dinners and civic festivals throughout the Jeffersonian era, and the party clearly used them as ritual occasions for cultivating fraternity and unity. The term could embrace "our magnanimous French brethren" hurling back royalist armies, the victims of legal persecution in Britain, all citizens of the United States willing "to fraternize with us in a common... that the principles of free government may be handed down incorrupt to posterity," and all Democratic and Republican societies in the United States until the glorious day when "the Rights of Man shall become the Supreme Law of every land, and their separate Fraternities be absorbed, in One Great Democratic Society, comprehending the Human Race."[59]

Democrats, in short, were confident that a spirit of fraternity could check any tendency toward factional splintering. Federalists, by contrast, emphasized paternalistic and deferential relationships—the Founding *Fathers* as a group, Washington as the *father* of his country. For Federalists, Washington's birthday even replaced the Fourth of July in the 1790s as their premier national holiday. Quite incongruously, John Adams set himself up as Washington's heir in this respect and expressed acute bitterness as late as 1809 at the failure of the public to respond appropriately. "I always consider the whole nation as my children," he told a pair of visitors, "but they have almost all proved undutiful to me. You two gentlemen are almost the only ones out of my own house, who have for a long time, and I thank you for it, expressed a filial affection for John Adams."[60]

In 1799 Pennsylvania Democrats finally got their chance to exercise power. By a narrow three-seat margin, they took control of the House, but not yet the Senate, and they also elected the new governor, Thomas McKean, a venerable lawyer and patriot who had served as chief justice of the commonwealth for more than twenty years. During his first term, party harmony prevailed, Democrats contributed eight of Pennsylvania's fifteen electoral votes to Thomas Jefferson in 1801, and they began to claim appointive offices. During McKean's second term, the party won full control of the legislature and began pursuing a more radical reform agenda, aimed particularly at simplifying judicial procedures and banning the reading of English common-law decisions in Pennsylvania's courts. McKean resisted strenuously and began to recruit followers among better-educated Republicans, such as Alexander J. Dallas. This group called itself Constitutional Republicans but got dubbed "Quids" or "tertium Quids" (third whats) by their opponents. The legislative majority retaliated by impeaching three justices of the state supreme court (whom the Senate acquitted), by demanding a constitutional convention to enact a series of reforms drafted by Boileau, and then by running a Northumberland County farmer and tanner, Simon Snyder, against McKean in 1805.[61]

By then McKean had arrived at about the same conclusion the Federalists had reached in the 1790s: Most Democrats were unfit to rule. He denounced the Snyderites as the "clodpole" or "clodhopper" faction, began appointing some Federalists to office, and by a narrow margin won a third term through a coalition of Quids and Federalists. He definitely regarded himself as the only bulwark capable of holding back a monstrous Democratic flood, literally the only person fit to be governor of Pennsylvania. (When Duane tried to maneuver him into the vice presidency as Aaron Burr's successor in 1804, McKean spurned the opportunity.) "Who is there to control the wanton passions of men in general respectable, suddenly raised to power and frisking in the pasture of true liberty, yet not sufficiently secured by proper barriers?" he asked. "Who will be my successor, possessing the same advantages from nativity in the State, education, experience, and from long public services in the most influential stations and employments; who can or will take the same liberty in vetoes of legislative acts, . . . as I have done?"[62]

McKean's principal campaign tract, *Address to the Republicans of Pennsylvania* (1805), made these concerns public and explicit. It was written by Alexander J. Dallas, another elite Republican who had arrived from abroad. The son of a Scottish father and an Irish mother, Dallas had grown up in England, studied briefly at the Inns of Court, become a clerk in a mercantile firm, married, moved to Jamaica, and then in 1784, at the age of twenty-four, arrived in Philadelphia. There, while preparing himself for the bar, he strongly encouraged the introduction of the regular theater. Cultural attainments mattered to him and helped define for him who was suitable for office. McKean's opponents were mere "malcontents," he insisted. He looked back fondly on the 1790s, when a spirit of "concert and conciliation gave life and confidence and effect" to the efforts of "the Republican [Snyderites usually said 'Democratic'] party to rescue our civil institutions from danger, and to enforce the right of participation in the service and honors of our country." McKean's administration had brought unprecedented prosperity to Pennsylvania and had ensured that "the stations of power and patronage [were] occupied by *distinguished* republicans." But the state barely had time to enjoy Jefferson's victory in 1801 before "symptoms of ambition and intrigue, of jealousy and discontent, of disunion and disorder, awakened the patriotic mind to a sense of new troubles and new sorrows." Dallas probably never heard the phrase, but like seventeenth-century Puritans his ideal seemed to be a speaking aristocracy presiding over a silent democracy, which every now and then exercised the power or approval or disapproval. "Amidst all our inducements to preserve harmony and peace, the standard of discord has been wantonly unfurled. By specious tales of imaginary wrongs, you have been urged to doubt the reality of the happiness you enjoy." The Jeffersonian revolution had gone as far as it should. More would mean chaos. "And the Republican party of Pennsylvania, outrunning the opprobrious predictions of its enemies, seems eager to become the speedy instrument of its own destruction."[63]

Calling themselves New School Republicans and sometimes even Clodhoppers, the Snyderites pressed their challenge during McKean's third term. Boileau won passage of the resolution that banned from Pennsylvania courts the reading of all decisions and statutes that did not originate in the United States, but McKean killed the measure with a pocket veto. Boileau had a ready reply to the predictable argument that his position was provincial and anti-intellectual and if extended beyond the law would mean the rejection of all scientific and medical discoveries not made in the United States. The resolution, he explained, did not prevent a lawyer from acquiring his knowledge anywhere he chose. It did not even bar him from citing English precedents from memory. It only stopped him from hauling dozens of law books into court and reading interminable cases aloud to perplex and baffle the jury. The analogy with medicine did not hold because physicians had not yet found cause to torment their patients by reading medical treatises at them. He greatly resented the impropriety of the United States proclaiming itself an independent nation while the judiciary in every state but New Jersey slavishly relied on English precedents and statutes. His reform would greatly simplify legal proceedings and permit Americans to acquire "a 'common law' *of our own,* which might from time to time be incorporated into our statutes, and every citizen might then have an opportunity of making himself acquainted with the laws of the land."[64]

Once again, law reform meant a direct clash with McKean. Led by Leib and somewhat reluctantly supported by Boileau, the House in April 1807 narrowly voted to impeach the aging and ailing governor but postponed the trial until after the fall elections. Amidst accusations of monstrous executive corruption and nepotism in Pennsylvania's "royal family," this threat hung over the lame-duck governor until the assembly of 1807–08 voted by a very slim margin not to impeach. By then the Snyderites were already on their way to an overwhelming victory in the 1808 gubernatorial election, which saw Snyder demolish Federalist James Ross with nearly 70 percent of the vote. For the first time in a modern society, "clodhoppers" had taken full control of the government.

VI

Like his two predecessors but none of his successors, Snyder served three consecutive terms, from 1808 to 1817, and had he not died in 1819, he might have been elected again in 1820. His electoral margins were enormous, making him easily the state's most popular governor during the early republic. Just as conspicuously, Snyder's triumph marked a sharp break from the earlier pattern of government by cultivated gentlemen. As Federalist Deborah Logan gleefully recorded in her diary, a judge detained at the governor's country residence by bad weather "sent to his honour to ask the loan of a Book, and received for answer from this semi-barbarian 'that he had none.' "[65] What, then, did Snyder's victory mean to those who enjoyed it?

Pennsylvania Democrats agreed on three central points. First, the history of the United States since the Revolution "is the most pleasing object of historical contemplation in the annals of the world," as William Duane tried to explain in *Politics for American Farmers,* a series of twenty essays published in the *Aurora* in 1807 and reprinted in every

Jeffersonian newspaper in the country.[66] Delaware Democrats agreed that, under Jefferson, Americans "have enjoyed . . . a degree of happiness unexampled, we believe, in the history of any age or nation."[67] Second, the party's Pennsylvania victory in 1799 and its overwhelming confirmation in 1808 had destroyed an incipient ruling class in the commonwealth and—because Pennsylvania was the "keystone" state essential to Democratic-Republican victories at the national level—in the republic at large as well. Democratic spokesmen never tired of making this point because for them it underscored what was truly unique about America, what the Revolution had really been about. "Had it not been for the revolution," declared Duane, "we should have been surrounded by *tithes,* by *privileged colleges,* by a *privileged clergy*—and *nobles of Nova Scotia*! Would not many of our *federal gentlemen* have been among those *privileged barons,* and *knights,* and *nobles,*" he asked, and then, ironically quoting Aaron Burr, added, "—and above the dull pursuits of civil life?"[68] Federalists "care not for the people so that they but rule them," added the *Aurora* two years later.[69] "It shews certainly great blindness in the people to continue so obstinate in *governing themselves,* when the *Doctor* kindly offers with the aid of the federalists to do it for them," agreed the leading Snyderite paper in 1816.[70] The Revolution saw the American "people disavowing any earthly superior, stepping forth in their majesty, and declaring by their representatives that all men were free and equal," affirmed Boileau. "The principles of political and civil organization were gathered out of the chaos of feudal and colonial barbarism, and society was newly created out of her native elements."[71]

The third point of agreement as Snyder took power was that the only serious threat to these achievements arose from British power, British corruption, and the agents and admirers of Britain in America. Pennsylvania Jeffersonians were visceral anglophobes. Some of them admired Napoleon; others did not. Most were inclined to blame Britain rather than Bonaparte for the war that broke out again in 1803 and eventually engulfed the United States. But whatever they thought of Napoleon, they agreed that he could do far less harm to the United States than Britain was already inflicting, even if he did finally conquer all of Europe. As Duane never tired of pointing out, every ally that Britain bought in Europe was then destroyed by France. Americans, he thought, ought to learn the obvious lesson.

This anglophobia no doubt had different sources in different people. Few Pennsylvania Jeffersonians had English roots or any sentimental attachments to the former mother country, but other reasons could be far more personal. The Boileau family farm in Montgomery County, for example, was the site of one of the grisliest atrocities committed by Britain in the northern theater of the Revolutionary War. Just before dawn on 1 May 1778, British raiders out of Philadelphia surprised a detachment of Pennsylvania militia, drove most off, killed many, and then put some of the wounded on buckwheat straw, set it ablaze, and burned them alive.[72] Boileau, a teenager when the event occurred, never forgot the horror and used that field to give a passionate anti-British Fourth of July address to over a thousand people in 1814 at a time when British invaders again menaced the land.[73] Joseph Hiester, successful candidate for governor in 1820, had been held captive on a British prison ship, a truly harrowing experience. The émigré printers, Duane and Binns, had been savagely persecuted by the government of William Pitt the younger. When they contrasted American liberty with British oppression, they spoke from experience.[74]

Federalists certainly made it easy for Democrats to castigate them as "tories" (the favorite radical term for them), British tools, enemies of American independence, and even traitors. Federalist money played a still mysterious role in the Aaron Burr conspiracy of 1806, which Pennsylvania radicals interpreted as nothing less than an attempt to dismember the Union. Around 1804 some Boston Federalists condemned the reading of the Declaration of Independence during Fourth of July festivities as a "pernicious practice" and an "unnecessary insult toward a friendly nation," and this attack soon spread to New York. By 1808 Philadelphia Federalists would not celebrate Independence.[75] The radicals drew obvious conclusions from this pattern. James Ross, Snyder's opponent in the 1808 election, became "a man of high aristocratical habits, and avowed contempt for the people." Even worse, he was a cunning lawyer whose "Machevelian [sic] and Chesterfieldean system is to court, that he may deceive; to flatter, that he may betray.[76]

Yet more than Federalist arrogance sustained this charge. Jeffersonian editors were extremely comfortable with the old paradigm that located the source of political corruption in the executive, and they felt even better when that executive was none other than George III and the British government. As relations deteriorated between Britain and America after

1806, the *Aurora* and the *Democratic Press*—Philadelphia dailies and the party's most important newspapers—found in the British menace a satisfactory explanation for nearly everything amiss in America, particularly the continuing threats of corruption and aristocracy. On the eve of the British crisis, John Binns thought that two words adequately described American parties, "I mean the words *democrats* and *aristocrats*—the friends of the *rights* of the many—and the advocates of a *privileged few*."[77] A single "year's war with England would be cheaply purchased by the *regeneration* of our country," proclaimed a Baltimore paper. "*British* manners—*British* habits—and *British* principles have become so deep implanted in the United States, that nothing but a convulsion will be able to root them out, and restore our soil to its original purity."[78] Eight years later, the war with Britain already concluded, a writer calling himself "Best Blood" still thought that "the late ball at Washington Hall" had done much "to encourage and stimulate the growth of nobility in this country."[79]

The resurgence of Federalism in response to Jefferson's embargo of 1807–09 alarmed the Boston *Democrat*, which called for a national system of schools to counteract an "aristocracy of talents" with a "democracy of education."[80] Nothing appalled Duane more than the hasty repeal of the embargo in early 1809 just before Jefferson left office. "The most humiliating consideration which presents itself on the recent *panic* produced in congress," he explained, "is that it is the absolute and visible effect of British corruption carried on in open day, preceded by murder and insult, accompanied by contumely and contempt." Repeal could not have been favored "by any man possessed of ordinary information, or even of coherent mind," he added. The conclusion was ominous: "From a government which has corrupted, convulsed, and betrayed every government in Europe—and by that corruption overturned them all; a government founded in *virtue* which cannot exist where virtue is extinguished, could not expect either generosity nor [*sic*] justice."[81]

Resistance to the embargo deeply troubled Pennsylvania Democrats, who wrote or reprinted many essays on the decay of virtue in New England, the cradle of the Revolution. Explanations always involved greed and luxury and were always tied to British trade, "British capitalists," and more overt forms of corruption. Many editors, Duane insisted, accepted British pay. New England behavior seemed to illustrate the high importance of republican values even in a liberal world. The pursuit of wealth without regard to the public good not only corrupted individuals. It threatened to destroy independence and the American republic.[82]

VII

The embargo crisis reached its unsatisfying resolution in the early months of 1809, just as the Snyder administration was taking hold in Lancaster. With Duane's permission, the Snyderites had sent John Binns from Northumberland County to establish a second Democratic daily in Philadelphia, a paper that, he boasted inaccurately, was the first in the country to put "Democratic" on its masthead. The two editors probably intended to divide the news roughly along federal and state lines. The embargo certainly diverted Duane's attention from state politics in early 1809 and left that subject open to Binns. Then an unexpected crisis arose. Snyder's clodhoppper government openly challenged the Madison administration on a complex legal issue. Duane was mortified, especially in the context of the embargo struggle. He had been scourging Federalists for condoning violations of the embargo and for denouncing the act as unconstitutional. Now the most democratic government in America took on the United States Supreme Court and President James Madison. Duane's mortification became so acute that, almost without reflection, he found himself asking the forbidden question that had led to the downfall of Federalists and Quids. Were some Democrats simply unqualified to hold office? During the campaign, Duane had defended Snyder against Federalist attempts "to deprecate [his] talents and understanding" and to persuade people "that he was a man of inferior capacity and judgment." The editor also praised the governor's republican simplicity during the inauguration festivities when he declined to be accompanied into Lancaster by a mounted escort. The *Aurora* hailed the result: "An administration of men who consider tilling the soil as no reproach, and when attempted to be made a reproach, only heaping shame on its vulgar author."[83]

Duane's cheerful salutation masked his own reservations. Even while readers of the *Aurora* were heralding Snyder as "the first truly republican governor which Pennsylvania has had since the formation of the present constitution," Duane was beginning to regret that he had helped to create what now seemed a monstrosity of incompetence and corruption.[84]

Gideon Olmstead and others v. *the executrixes of David Rittenhouse* went back to a prize case of 1778. Olmstead, a prisoner aboard the British sloop *Active* en route to New York, persuaded three crewmen to help him lock the others below deck and take the vessel as a prize to a south Jersey port. They were overtaken by a Pennsylvania vessel, *Convention,* which brought the ship to Philadelphia and claimed the prize for itself on the grounds that the crew of the *Active* had not been fully subdued. A Pennsylvania admiralty court, which then used a jury, decided the case for the *Convention.* Under article 9 of the Articles of Confederation, Olmstead appealed to Congress, which reversed the decision. Pennsylvania denied that Congress or any federal agency could overturn facts as established by a jury, and by 1803 insisted that the Eleventh Amendment barred a suit in federal court against a state. Rittenhouse was part of the controversy because as state treasurer he kept the disputed award until somebody would indemnify him for paying it out. He also invested the award in federal certificates in the 1790s and kept the interest. Because of that fact, the United States district court ruled that Rittenhouse had been involved in a private and not a public capacity, that the Eleventh Amendment therefore did not apply, and ordered his executrixes—his daughters Elizabeth Sergeant and Esther Waters—to pay Olmstead.

In February 1809 Snyder ordered General Michael Bright of the state militia to protect "the ladies" from attachment and arrest by the United States marshal. That decision began a confrontation that lasted nearly three months. Many militiamen were reluctant to serve, especially naturalized citizens who had taken an explicit oath to uphold the federal but not the Pennsylvania constitution. The women grew exasperated by their virtual imprisonment at home and threatened to decamp to Lancaster and dump the whole problem at Snyder's door. The federal marshal arrested one of them and then raised a posse large enough to overwhelm the militiamen, who were quickly tried, convicted, fined, and imprisoned. Snyder then agreed to pay the disputed amount (about $14,000), and Madison pardoned the militiamen.[85]

The controversy opened a chasm between the rural Snyderites and the Philadelphia radicals that never closed. Although Duane and Leib had supported Snyder for governor in 1805 and 1808, they were never very happy with the predominance that the Snyderites had obtained within the party. From time to time the *Aurora* called for the use of conventions to replace the legislative caucus as a means of selecting candidates. But in 1809 things would probably have been more satisfactory had Snyder only accepted advice from the "wise men of the east," specifically Leib, whom Duane had hoped Snyder would appoint secretary of the commonwealth. Unfortunately for Duane, both the secretary, Boileau (Montgomery County), and the state treasurer, William Findlay (Franklin County), were from farming communities. Several weeks into the crisis, Duane denounced them as "imbecile and incapable men whom Mr. Snyder has selected for his advisers." The governor "cannot be supposed to possess extensive or critical legal knowledge, and being without a man of integrity or talents in his suite," he had plunged the state into crisis and shame.[86] It never occurred to Duane that on a question as complex as the Olmstead case, intelligent Democrats might reach a principled decision, based on states' rights, and therefore different from his own.

Time and reflection only magnified Duane's rage and disaffection. Since 1798 he had been the most important and most widely read editor in the Union. He was used to having his judgments vindicated eventually, even when things looked truly bleak, as when he opposed John Adams in 1798 or McKean after 1805. Thus, when he began printing a long series of blistering essays by "Conrad Weiser" (an appeal to German farmers?) in January 1810, he almost certainly expected to discredit the Snyder government and overturn it during the 1811 election. The argument regarding incapacity grew more strident. In a number addressed to the governor, the essayist described State Senator Abner Lacock, another Snyder adviser, as "a man deep read in village litigation," yet "something above the mental standard of your excellency." Lacock had also said of Philadelphia, "the first city of the union," that "it would give him no concern to see this city in flames."[87] Because of the Snyder administration, Pennsylvania in the midst of the embargo crisis "was dishonored in the eyes of the world" in a manner "intended to hold up the government to universal derision, and to exhibit the intellectual faculties of the people, through their functionaries, as the most contemptible of the human race."[88] "Those who have known you longest and best," announced one essay, ". . . look round and stare/And wonder how the devil you got there."[89]

But ignorance and incompetence were not even the main problems. In fourteen prolix essays, "Conrad Weiser" set out to expose the "sordid and corrupt intrigue" by which Boileau's support elected Snyder in exchange for his own appointment as secretary, the "sly secret suppleness of intrigue" by which Snyder routinely governed and which "has superceded in a degree everything that sheds lustre on popular government; there is neither the eloquence of genius nor the fervor of patriotism."[90] Boileau in particular became a fiend of malfeasance. After failing to buy one legislator, the *Aurora* proclaimed, "the corrupter retired, not with the dignity of Milton's devils; but with that callous and untouched obduracy of heart, which alone can bear employment in pursuits so derogatory to virtue and probity."[91] Duane's best evidence was his calculation that at least forty-two members of the previous legislature had since accepted patronge positions, presumably as some kind of reward. Quite possibly Snyder and Boileau did have a preelection understanding. They had been good friends since the 1790s. But the *Aurora* also tried to make it an impeachable breach of the separation of powers for Boileau to urge a representative to stand against the incumbent speaker. And the paper raged on for days when a document on the Olmstead case submitted to the legislature was found to be misdated and another was discovered to be missing. Boileau corrected the mistake and supplied the omission, both of which he attributed to clerical errors. Duane, of course, knew better.[92]

In effect, Duane had again revived the old British paradigm of parliamentary corruption and applied it to the most democratic government in America. Snyder clearly did use patronage effectively, and he was not inclined to employ it to reward his enemies. But unlike the Federalists or even the Quids, the governor who dressed in homespun and addressed the legislature in the style of the democratic societies—as "Fellow Citizens," not "Gentlemen"—was hardly aping British manners. He was no aspiring aristocrat in any recognizable sense of that term, although eventually Duane would throw that label at the Snyderites too. But in 1810 the regime had become something else, something even more loathsome, "the most debased and debasing of all governments, an *oligarchy of ignorance and vice*."[93] With telling effect, John Binns regularly defended Snyder in the *Democratic Press* and denounced Duane's Old School Republicans as a pack of disappointed office-seekers. The most important casualty in this process of vilification was, I suspect, the spirit of fraternity. The embargo crisis and Jefferson's retirement had spurred local democratic societies into feverish activity and expressions of solidarity. In the winter of 1810–11, an unknown correspondent described to Leib the torpor that characterized these meetings in Philadelphia. With the explosion of factionalism among genuine radicals, something vital had died.[94]

VIII

During Washington's administration, the Yazoo affair in Georgia became the greatest scandal of the early republic. At the time, Georgia still claimed land west to the Mississippi. In the mid-1790s, a group of speculators bribed most of the men in the Georgia legislature to enable them to buy from the state nearly all of what is now Alabama and Mississippi for $500,000. Congressman James Jackson, whose own group had been turned down even though it offered $800,000 for the same land, resigned his seat in the House and rushed back to Georgia. By then the speculators had sold most of their claims to outsiders, chiefly New Englanders, who later insisted that they had known nothing of the fraud. But Jackson put together what became the Jeffersonian Republican party in Georgia, captured control of the legislature, repealed the law and even burnt the records pertaining to it, and all but obliterated the Federalist party as a force in the state. The aggrieved investors sought redress from Congress under Jefferson and then turned to the courts. They finally won a victory from John Marshall in *Fletcher* v. *Peck* (1810), which declared the original grant a contract that could not be rescinded.[95]

Yazoo was as spectacular a case as anyone could find to illustrate the possibility of society, or business interests, corrupting politics. It had a transforming impact on a youthful visitor, John Randolph of Roanoke, whose loathing of corruption and hatred of speculators took shape while watching the aftermath.[96] To James Jackson, "The corruptions of a Walpole, the squanderings of a Pitt, and the extravagancies of a Marie Antoinette, are all eclipsed by this abominable act." Engrossment of land on such a scale would soon reduce America to lordships. At a moment when France was smashing the feudal system of Europe, he told the voters, "It remains for you fellow citizens to determine if it shall be rebuilt, at the expense of your liberties, within the state of Georgia." The alternative to repeal, he warned, might even be civil war and dissolution of the Union.[97] A correspondent in the *Aurora* was equally alarmed but less hopeful. If Georgians repeal the measure, he predicted, "This will be called a breach of faith in the legislature." If the people violently repudiate "the base deed," their actions "would be insurrection,—rebellion. The people must then bear it; while the rapacious few who will realize vast sums by the infamous scheme insultingly riot on the public spoils." In other words, the only remedy was eternal vigilance, and in this case it came too late. The Georgia indictments, he concluded, "are melancholy proofs of the depravity of human nature."[98]

On a smaller but still alarming scale, the banking question raised similar issues in Pennsylvania. A mania for more banks became noticeable in 1810, acquired momentum in 1811, after the Bank of the United States failed to win renewal of its charter, and grew very powerful in 1813 and 1814. A bill to charter over twenty banks failed in 1813 only because Snyder rejected it—his first veto. In 1814 the investors rounded up still more supporters, passed a bill to incorporate forty-one banks, and just barely managed to carry the measure over a second veto. The veto required courage on the governor's part because the legislative caucus meeting to decide the gubernatorial nomination adjourned to await his decision and did not reconvene until the override had succeeded, when it renominated him for a third term.[99]

Some supporters of the measure defended it on ideological grounds as a dramatic democratization of economic opportunity. "I assure you that there are such Solomons in the legislature," reported one incredulous opponent, "to believe that the bank bill is something like the Agrarian law, that it will make a more equal distribution of wealth."[100] But, anticipating Jacksonian rhetoric by twenty years, enemies of the bill called it "the monster" and expected it to bring apocalyptic evils in its train. One state senator nearly exhausted his ample supply of expletives in describing "this multifarious monster: this kissing serpent which, more deceitful than the one that beguiled our innocent parents, has raised its crest in the chamber of the Senate, and threatens to crawl, emitting its poison and shedding mortality through every corner of the state."[101] On this question Snyder, Boileau, Binns, and Duane all agreed. Among recognized leaders, only State Treasurer William Findlay waffled when the probank forces hinted that if Snyder's veto held, the caucus might give the nomination to Findlay.[102] Yet the banking bill acquired irresistible force, and won a two-thirds majority in both houses. The trend seemed deeply disturbing, to say the least.

Observers noted a pattern of legislative logrolling (as a later generation would describe it) and found it corrupt indeed. The *Aurora's* correspondent in Harrisburg (which the Snyder administration had made the new state capital) scoffed at "the senseless declaration that public opinion is in favor of banks." Instead, "selfishness has got such a mastery in the legislature that unless the purse is to be divided there is to be no purse for any one—hence the compromises and the swapping of votes, and hence there are double the number of banks in the bill than were asked for."[103] "Howard" in the *Democratic Press* similarly attacked the "secret sittings, and meetings, and mutual interests, and accommodations of bank directors" that will "destroy the fame, the honor and more than life, of . . . every man entangled in their toils" who dares to resist them. They "become like a band of brothers, guarding the Golden Fleece, and like a Roman Triumvirate of old, uniting in the destruction of whoever is obnoxious to any one of them."[104] An observer from "west of the Susquehanna" believed he was witnessing the end of republican government. The new banks will become "aristocracies infinitely more dangerous than as many Dukedoms or Earldoms would, or could, be to the liberties of the people," he predicted. In the future all officers of the state government might as well "be appointed by the directors of those banks. This may just as well be done formally as otherwise, for it will be done virtually or *ipso facto*.— Then why bother the people with elections?" If the banks will be worse than titled aristocrats, they will also be more dangerous than rotten boroughs, he added. "They will be fresh and vigorous corporations, possessed of the sinews and marrow of the most powerful influence." If "they are not destroyed," he concluded, "they will destroy the virtue, the patriotism, the public spirit and of course the rights and liberties of the people. We may enjoy the forms of republican government for some time to come, but even that will be as tenants at will."[105]

So alarming was the crisis that the *Aurora's* correspondent, usually a bitter critic of Snyder, generously praised his veto "as the proudest and most independent act of his life. . . . if he deserved the gratitude of the state last year, he has now put in an undisputed claim to contemporary support and posthumous veneration."[106] The bill's opponents, while denying that the measure had broad popular backing, did not suggest still another appeal to the public. Snyder's 1813 veto, a carefully crafted argument, had already tried that strategy without success. The banking interests had organized in response; the "people" had not.[107]

As in the Yazoo crisis, an aroused public responded only after the harm had been done. Two-thirds of the sixty-six representatives who voted to override the veto failed to retain their seats in the fall elections.[108] Perhaps two-thirds or more of the assemblymen were farmers, mechanics, or innkeepers in 1814.[109] Nobody yet drew the further conclusion that Pennsylvania, precisely because of the kind of democracy it had become, was peculiarly vulnerable to corruption of this sort. Many farmers and mechanics probably found bank shares or a seat on a board of directors an irresistible offer. The state legislature still had a distance to go before John D. Rockefeller would be able to do anything he wished with it—except refine it. But it was on that path, and nobody had an answer to the larger question of the Yazoo syndrome.[110]

IX

After the War of 1812, corruption became not just the dominant vocabulary in public life but almost its grammar. Editors had difficulty discussing any issue without putting it in terms of corruption. The Philadelphia Board of Health was an engine of corruption. The post office was corrupt. As Federalism disintegrated and old party labels lost their saliency, John Binns tried to redefine himself as a spokesman for the Anticorruptionist party. While every politician claimed to act "only from the purest of motives," his opponent invariably denounced him as mired in corruption. To an overwhelming degree, the corruption that attracted attention was either the misuse of patronage to undermine the independence of the assembly (classical corruption in republican guise) or the insatiable ambition of disappointed office seekers. Participants had glimpsed Armageddon in the Yazoo syndrome, and they glanced in that direction as little as possible.

The Snyderite heirs might have resisted the trend, but they yielded to it by choosing William Findlay as a successor for the governorship in 1817. In so doing they completed the process of democratizing—and trivializing—the issue of corruption. Despite Duane's denunciation of all caucuses and his demand for a convention of the full party instead of just officeholders, the legislative caucus met as usual in March 1817 to decide between two Snyderites—Boileau, the secretary of the commonwealth, or Findlay, the state treasurer. Boileau's *The Crisis,* distributed free in large quantities, refrained from personal abuse but argued that he, not Findlay, had served in the Revolution, and that his record of Democratic—Republican consistency was much stronger than Findlay's. The pamphlet complained that, because Findlay had courted and won the allegiance of all of the party printers except Binns (Duane had been exorcised), Boileau's supporters had difficulty even making their case to the public. The argument was generally temperate until it thundered to its immodest conclusion: "The annals of this state, or of any state of the union, cannot produce a parallel instance of a man recommended to so high an office, upon pretensions so *bald,* not to say *ineffably* ridiculous." His "*prospect* of success must be in proportion to his *belief* that the democrats are indeed such 'geese,' 'ignoramusses,' and 'clodpoles,' as M'Kean described them to be in 1805."

By deflecting contempt of the people onto Findlay, Boileau—a college graduate—was nonetheless arguing that his opponent was unfit to govern. However, he did not attack his intelligence or even his integrity, just his experience, consistency, and loyalty to Snyder. On Findlay's behalf, *Reply to "The Crisis"* predictably argued that printers throughout the state supported Findlay because they spoke for the people. The tract denounced the "corrupt and prejudiced . . . mind" of the author of *The Crisis* (probably Boileau) and accused him of blackening even Findlay's best achievement "by ascribing it to motives similar to his own."[111]

Findlay won the nomination by a deceptively large margin because at the last minute a bloc of Boileau delegates went over to Findlay to ingratiate themselves with the man expected to become the new governor.[112] A "much depressed" Boileau fled to Lancaster to participate in the Snyder administration's unsuccessful attempt to impeach state judges who had upheld the power of a United States Army court-martial to discipline Pennsylvania militiamen temporarily in national service. He then tried to sit out the campaign.[113] When Duane's Old School Republicans held a convention at Carlisle from which all officeholders and legislators were banned, it nominated Joseph Hiester, a German farmer and Revolutionary War veteran. The Findlay forces then tried to compel Boileau to support their man. Reluctant to reply, Boileau indicated that he preferred to retire to private life in peace but conceded that Hiester's credentials might be better than Findlay's. Findlay's defenders promptly published a circular

that described Boileau's letter as "fraught with falsehood and disappoint-
ment and the most malignant political turpitude imaginable." They
accused him "of traitorously abandoning the democratic party" and of
working to undermine Findlay "to gratify his disappointed ambition and
satiate his revengeful and malignant heart." Men who had worked closely
together for twenty years, and even more intimately in Snyder's cabinet
for nine, savaged each other in full public view.[114]

Boileau, in my estimation, was an interesting and thoroughly decent
man. Born a farmer, he attended the College of New Jersey in his twen-
ties and placed fourth in the talented Class of 1789. Throughout his long
life he loved mechanical pursuits and was never ashamed to work with
his hands. He constructed the paddle wheels for John Fitch's first successful steamboat, and he made most of his own farm implements, including
some plows, carts, and wagons. Grimly anglophobic, he was so galvanized
by the French Revolution that he expected it to spread "and ultimately
emancipate the world from the thraldom of slavery. We fondly fancied
we saw the millenium [sic] approaching, when nations should learn war
no more, and universal peace and good will among men should pervade
the world." Instead "the powers of Hell and the Government of Britain,
equally hostile to the happiness of man, combined to blast our pleasing
anticipations. The era was not yet arrived when Satan was to be bound a
thousand years."[115]

Boileau entered politics in 1797 and became a consistent advocate of
legal reform, internal improvements, and domestic manufactures. He
feared and hated speculators and most banks. He and Snyder differed
from Duane and Leib primarily in their passionate attachment to states'
rights, manifested in the Olmstead case of 1809, the impeachment of
1817, and other issues. The charges of corruption against him can all be
reduced to an accusation that as secretary he helped distribute offices to
reward the governor's supporters rather than his opponents. Although
Duane despised Boileau, two *Aurora* correspondents at the Harrisburg
caucus predicted that he would "be laid aside" because Findlay's "intrigue
and corruption have become more powerful than I had supposed, for
unquestionably, of the two, Boileau has been the most uniform, useful,
and intelligent."[116] Far from being Duane's monster of manipulation,
agreed the other, "*Boileau is but a child in politics,* he is not half enough
acquainted with the underhand work, that marks the bold and discerning

politician."[117] Yet even other Snyderites now denounced him for "the most malignant political turpitude imaginable."[118]

When corruption becomes the grammar of politics, every reputation is at stake. No one escaped, certainly not Findlay after he won a narrow victory over Hiester. Several times the legislature investigated his conduct as state treasurer from 1807 to 1817, though without detecting anything sensationally amiss. He cultivated close relationships with what would soon be called the Family party in Philadelphia, the heavily intermarried Dallas, Sergeant, Ingham, and Bache clans, which included many Quids or their descendants. He tried to destroy Binns and the *Democratic Press* in Philadelphia politics, but Binns responded by engineering an impeachment vote in the House. By now people were so jaded with strident accusations of corruption that even impeachments had become boring. Attendance was low throughout the trial, and Findlay won acquittal. But he had suffered enough damage to turn the governor's office over to Hiester in the 1820 election.[119]

By the 1820s the issue of corruption seemed to have a life and momentum of its own. Despite the public's growing disgust with the tone of political discourse, charges of corruption went on and on.[120] Attacking an opponent became a political necessity in the absence of a visible ruling class, and accusations of corruption had become the most conspicuous way to appeal to "the people." To choose which individuals ought to exercise temporary power over the others, no particular configuration of talents, family, education, or even experience (except heroic military exploits) could combine into an effective argument without raising the fear of aristocracy. It had become easier to discredit an opponent than to make a positive argument for one's own candidate. And the angry factionalism among the Snyderites from 1817 on may suggest another subtle shift. Federalists had routinely denigrated the intelligence of nearly all Republicans, except for a few leaders like Jefferson and Madison, who were denounced instead as wild and irresponsible dreamers. Quids attacked Democrats in the same terms. When the radicals split in 1809, Duane's Old School used the same language in a vain effort to discredit Snyder. But Boileau and Findlay did not question each other's intelligence. The logic of democratic citizenship had left them almost no way to support one man and reject another except by using the rhetoric of corruption. In the nineteenth century, Britain and the United States went in opposite directions with this dichotomy. Members of Parliament often insulted each other's intelligence but always respected an opponent's integrity and honor. Even out-of-doors, charges of corruption faded rapidly after Chartist agitation died out in the 1840s. In American politics, by contrast, it became bad form to demean anyone's intelligence, but the rhetoric of corruption put everyone's integrity at risk.

X

This survey of a seldom-studied theme suggests one general conclusion. For some time, historians have been debating whether, when, how, and/or why republican values yielded to liberalism in the United States. The fullest analysis of this question sees the War of 1812 as the great divide and Jeffersonian Republicans as the main agents of change.[121] An analysis of corruption suggests a rather different formulation. It indicates that, while we surely ought to see republicanism as the recessive and liberalism as the dominant configuration by 1815, we cannot even begin to make sense of the content of public life unless we see the two as a continuing dichotomy. James Madison's dilemma—how to provide a republican government for a liberal society—became America's in Pennsylvania during the age of Jefferson. Without continuing acceptance of republican values, corruption would not have become a serious issue, much less an obsession, in an environment that was rapidly becoming more participatory and democratic. A society completely comfortable with the active pursuit of self-interest would have discovered other ways of discussing political events. But Americans did assume that everyone pursues self-interest and that all officeholders ought to place the public good ahead of private interest. The rhetoric of corruption castigated public men, often for actions that even a Cato would have performed under similar circumstances. By preferring at all phases to blame officials rather than rethink deeper values, this language also trivialized the whole problem and probably made it much easier for serious corruption to take hold later in the century. When everyone is denounced as a Caligula, the real one may be hard to find. But the rhetoric endured—and still endures. It helps define who we are, what we have become. As Jefferson should have said, "We are all republicans; we are all liberals." Republicanism remains the political conscience of a liberal society.[122]

Notes

The author is indebted to the participants at the Lawrence Henry Gipson seminar on corruption in March 1989, when the earliest incarnation of this project was delivered as a lecture. He also wishes to thank the members of Michael Zuckerman's May 1990 colloquium for the Transformation of Philadelphia Project held at the University of Pennsylvania for their many helpful suggestions about a revised version. He is deeply grateful to the project for a fellowship in 1989–90 which made possible most of the original research for this paper. He particularly wishes to thank James Farley, Kim T. Phillips, Daniel T. Rodgers, Thomas P. Slaughter, and Lawrence Stone for their written comments on the 1990 version of this essay. Wayne C. Bodle, Jacob K. Cogan, Richard R. John, Bruce H. Mann, Simon P. Newman, and Scan Wilentz have offered some very helpful suggestions at a later phase. Any remaining errors are the author's responsibility.

1. By far the most thorough discussion of this question for Britain is Philip Harling, "The Rise and Fall of 'Old Corruption': Economical Reform and British Political Culture, 1779–1846" (Ph.D. diss., Princeton University. 1991). See also W. D. Rubinstein, "The End of 'Old Corruption' in Britain 1780–1860." *Past and Present* 101 (1983): 55–86; and Archibald S. Foord, "The Waning of the Influence of the Crown," *English Historical Review* 62 (1947): 484–507. For a helpful survey of the problem in the United States, see *Before Watergate: Problems of Corruption in American Society,* ed. Abraham S. Eisenstadt, Ari Hoogenboom, and Hans L. Trefousse (New York: Brooklyn College Press, 1978).

2. For Britain and France, see Gareth Stedman Jones, *Languages of Class: Studies in English Working Class History, 1832–1982* (Cambridge, Eng.: Cambridge University Press, 1983), esp. 90–178, and William H. Sewell, Jr., *Work and Revolution in France: The Language of Labor from the Old Regime to 1848* (Cambridge, Eng.: Cambridge University Press, 1980), esp. chaps. 11–12.

3. See Muriel St. Clare Byrne, ed., *The Lisle Letters, Selected and Arranged by Bridget Boland* (Chicago: University of Chicago Press, 1983), passim, esp. the foreword by Hugh Trevor-Roper, xiv–xv.

4. See Linda Levy Peck, "Corruption at the Court of James I: The Undermining of Legitimacy," in *After the Reformation: Essays in Honor of J. H. Hexter,* ed. Barbara C. Malament (Philadelphia: University of Pennsylvania Press, 1980), 75–93; J. G. A. Pocock. "Machiavelli. Harrington, and English Political Ideologies in the Eighteenth Century," *William and Mary Quarterly,* 3d ser., 22 (1965): 549–83 (hereafter *WMQ*) and his *The Machiavellian Moment: Florentine Political Thought and the Atlantic Republican Tradition* (Princeton: Princeton University Press. 1975).

5. For a fuller discussion, see John M. Murrin, "The Great Inversion, or Court versus Country: A Comparison of the Revolution Settlements in England (1688–1721) and America (1776–1816)," in *Three British Revolutions: 1641,*

1688, 1776, ed. J. G. A. Pocock (Princeton: Princeton University Press, 1980),
368–453. See also Isaac Kramnick, *Bolingbroke and His Circle: The Politics of
Nostalgia in the Age of Walpole* (Cambridge: Harvard University Press, 1968).
By the mid-eighteenth century, England's courts and judges, unlike the rest
of the government, had won a reputation for unusual integrity. See Wilfrid
Prest, "Judicial Corruption in Early Modern England," *Past and Present* 133
(1991): 67–95.

6. Lower Norfolk County Court Records 1637–46 (Porter transcript), 1: 242–
43 (Virginia Historical Society, Richmond).

7. "Nathaniel Bacon: manifesto concerning the troubles in Virginia
(1676)," in *American Colonial Documents to 1776,* ed. Merrill Jensen, in
English Historical Documents, ed. David C. Douglas. 9 (New York: Oxford
University Press, 1962), 581, 582.

8. Edmund S. Morgan. *American Slavery. American Freedom: The Ordeal of
Colonial Virginia* (New York: W. W. Norton and Co., 1975), chap. 10.

9. For these texts, see *Puritan Political Ideas, 1558–1794,* ed. Edmund S. Morgan
(Indianapolis, Ind.: Bobbs-Merrill Co., 1965), 176–77, 207.

10. See the excerpts from John Winthrop's *Journal* in ibid., 104–08, 114–15,
122–25, and passim.

11. Ibid., 227, 233.

12. The quotation is from "The Declaration of the Gentlemen, Merchants, and
Inhabitants of Boston, and the Country Adjacent," 18 April 1689, in *The
Glorious Revolution in Massachusetts: Selected Documents, 1689–1692,* ed.
Robert E. Moody and Richard C. Simmons (Boston: Colonial Society of
Massachusetts, 1988), 46, 47.

13. See John M. Murrin. "The Menacing Shadow of Louis XIV and the Rage
of Jacob Leisler: The Constitutional Ordeal of Seventeenth-Century
New York," in *New York and the Union: Contributions to the American
Constitutional Experience,* ed. Stephen L. Schechter and Richard
B. Bernstein (Albany: New York State Commission on the Bicentennial of
the United States Constitution, 1990), 29–71.

14. "The Frame of Government and Laws Agreed upon in England," in *The
Papers of William Penn,* ed. Mary Maples Dunn, Richard S. Dunn et al.
(Philadelphia: University of Pennsylvania Press, 1981–86), 2: 213.

15. Jack P. Greene, ed., "The Opposition to Lieutenant Governor Alexander
Spotswood: 1718," *Virginia Magazine of History and Biography* 70 (1962): 41.

16. See generally John M. Murrin, "Political Development," in *Colonial British
America: Essays in the New History of the Early Modern Era,* ed. Jack
P. Greene and J. R. Pole (Baltimore: Johns Hopkins University Press, 1984),
408–56, esp. 435–36. More specifically, see David Alan Williams, *Political
Alignments in Colonial Virginia Politics, 1698–1750* (New York: Garland
Press, 1989); Robert M. Weir, "The Harmony We Were Famous For: An
Interpretation of Pre-Revolutionary South Carolina Politics," *WMQ,* 3d ser.,
26 (1969): 473–501; and W.W. Abbot. *The Royal Governors of Georgia, 1754–
1775* (Chapel Hill: University of North Carolina Press. 1959).

17. James Alexander, *A Brief Narrative of the Case and Trial of John Peter Zenger, Printer of the New York Weekly Journal,* ed. Stanley N. Katz (Cambridge: Harvard University Press, 1963).

18. William Livingston et al., *The Independent Reflector, or, Weekly Essays on Sundry Important Subjects More Particularly Adapted to the Province of New-York,* ed. Milton M. Klein (Cambridge: Harvard University Press, 1963).

19. "The Watchman" essays in the *Pennsylvania Journal.* 1758, quoted in Bernard Bailyn, *The Origins of American Politics* (New York: Alfred A. Knopf, 1969), 140.

20. See specifically Richard L. Bushman, "Corruption and Power in Provincial America," in *The Development of a Revolutionary Mentality,* Library of Congress Symposia on the American Revolution (Washington: Library of Congress, 1972), 62–91: and more generally Bushman. *King and People in Provincial Massachusetts* (Chapel Hill: University of North Carolina Press, 1985); Andrew McFarland Davis, ed., *Colonial Currency Reprints, 1682–1751,* 4 vols. (Boston: Prince Society, 1910–11; reprint, New York: Augustus M. Kelley, 1964); Robert Zemsky, *Merchants, Farmers, and River Gods: An Essay on Eighteenth-Century American Politics* (Boston: Gambit Inc., 1971); John A. Schutz, *William Shirley, King's Governor of Massachusetts* (Chapel Hill: University of North Carolina Press, 1961); Paul Boyer, "Borrowed Rhetoric: The Massachusetts Excise Crisis of 1754."*WMQ,* 3d ser., 21 (1964): 328–51; and Jere R. Daniell. "Politics in New Hampshire under Governor Benning Wentworth, 1741–1767," *WMQ,* 3d ser., 23 (1966): 76–105.

21. Romney Sedgwick, ed., *Letters from George III to Lord Bute, 1756–1766* (London: Macmillan and Co., 1939), 166: 5–6, and passim.

22. Jack P. Greene, "Political Mimesis: A Consideration of the Historical and Cultural Roots of Legislative Behavior in the British Colonies in the Eighteenth Century," with a reply by Bernard Bailyn and a rejoinder by Greene, *American Historical Review* 75 (1969–70): 337–67 (hereafter *AHR).*

23. Submitted as a "trivia" item by Jere R. Daniell to *WMQ,* 3d ser., 20 (1963): 452–53.

24. See especially T. H. Breen, " 'Baubles of Britain': The American and Consumer Revolutions of the Eighteenth Century," *Past and Present* 119 (1988): 73–104; Breen. "An Empire of Goods: The Anglicization of Colonial America. 1690–1776," *Journal of British Studies* 25 (1986): 467–99; and James A. Henretta and Gregory H. Nobles, *Evolution and Revolution: American Society, 1600–1820* (Lexington. Mass.: D. C. Heath and Co., 1987), chap. 3, esp. the charts on 61, 67, 70, 74.

25. Bernard Bailyn and Barbara DeWolfe, *Voyagers to the West: A Passage in the Peopling of America on the Eve of the Revolution* (New York: Alfred A. Knopf, 1986).

26. William H. Kenney III, "George Whitefield, Dissenter Priest of the Great Awakening," *WMQ,* 3d ser., 26 (1969): 75–93; Susan O'Brien, "A Transatlantic Community of Saints: The Great Awakening and the First Evangelical

Network, 1735–1755," *AHR* 91 (1986): 811–32; and Michael J. Crawford, "Origins of the Eighteenth-Century Evangelical Revival: England and New England Compared," *Journal of British Studies* 26 (1987): 361–97.

27. Murrin, "Political Development," esp. 432–45. The one conspicuous exception to this pattern was New York, where the most effective royal governor was undoubtedly Robert Hunter (1710–19).

28. Thomas L. Purvis, "Colonial American Participation in the Seven Years' War, 1755–1763" (Paper presented at the Shelby Cullom Davis Center Colloquium on War and Society in Early America, Princeton University, March 1983). Purvis shows that of all American wars since 1750, this conflict generated the third-highest casualty rate and ranked fourth in percentages mobilized. See also John M. Murrin, "The French and Indian War, the American Revolution, and the Counterfactual Hypothesis: Reflections on Lawrence Henry Gipson and John Shy," *Reviews in American History* 1 (1973–74): 307–18.

29. John M. Murrin, "A Roof without Walls: The Dilemma of American National Identity," in *Beyond Confederation: Origins of the Constitution and American National Identity,* ed. Richard Beeman, Stephen Botein, and Edward C. Carter II (Chapel Hill: University of North Carolina Press, 1987), 333–48; J. M. Bumsted, " 'Things in the Womb of Time': Ideas of American Independence, 1633 to 1763," *WMQ,* 3d ser., 31 (1974): 533–64.

30. Bernard Bailyn, The Ideological Origins of the American Revolution (Cambridge: Harvard University Press, 1967), esp. 144–59; Pauline Maier, *From Resistance to Revolution: Colonial Radicals and the Development of American Opposition to Britain, 1765–1776* (New York: Alfred A. Knopf, 1972); Ira D. Gruber, "The American Revolution as a Conspiracy: The British View," WMQ. 3d ser., 26 (1969): 360–72; Benjamin W. Labaree. "The Idea of American Independence: The British View," Massachusetts Historical Society, Proceedings 82 (1970): 3–20; Gordon S. Wood, "Conspiracy and the Paranoid Style: Causality and Deceit in the Eighteenth Century," WMQ, 3d ser., 39 (1982): 401–41; James H. Hutson, "The Origins of 'The Paranoid Style in American Politics': Public Jealousy from the Age of Walpole to the Age of Jackson," in Saints and Revolutionaries: Essays on Early American History, ed. David Hall. John M. Murrin, and Thad W. Tate (New York: W. W. Norton and Co., 1984), 332–72.

31. Compare Naphtali Daggett's ("Cato's") personal attack on Ingersoll, *Connecticut Courant,* 26 Aug. 1765, with the much broader denunciation of the "infernal, corrupted, detested incendiaries! who hid from the public eye, have invited despotism to cross the ocean, and fix her abode in this once happy land." in *New York Mercury,* 21 Oct. 1765. Both are reprinted in *Prologue to Revolution: Sources and Documents on the Stamp Act Crisis, 1764–1766,* ed. Edmund S. Morgan (Chapel Hill: University of North Carolina Press, 1959), 92–94.

32. Bernard Mason, ed., *The American Colonial Crisis: The Daniel Leonard–John Adams Letters to the Press, 1774–1775* (New York: Harper and Row, 1972):

Jack P. Greene, ed., *Colonies to Nation, 1763–1789: A Documentary History of the American Revolution* (New York: W. W. Norton and Co., 1975), 299.

33. The argument is too complex to pursue here, but the chronology of events in Britain in the final months of 1765 proves that the Rockingham ministry realized that the alternative to repeal was probably civil war and then set about finding a plausible excuse to justify repeal, specifically the argument that the Stamp Act was ruining British trade. The government encouraged merchants to petition for repeal even before receiving news of the colonial nonimportation agreements, which made that contention far more plausible. See Paul Langford, *The First Rockingham Administration, 1765–1766* (New York: Oxford University Press, 1973); P. D. G. Thomas, *British Politics and the Stamp Act Crisis: The First Phase of the American Revolution, 1673–1767* (Oxford: Oxford University Press, 1975).

34. Thomas Paine, *Common Sense* (1776). in *Tracts of the American Revolution, 1763–1776,* ed. Merrill Jensen (Indianapolis, Ind.: Bobbs-Merrill Co., 1967), 419.

35. James Madison, *The Federalist* 14, in *The Federalist,* ed. Jacob E. Cooke (Middletown. Conn.: Wesleyan University Press, 1961), 89.

36. Max Farrand, ed., *The Records of the Federal Convention of 1787,* rev. ed. (New Haven: Yale University Press, 1937), 1: 288.

37. For a fuller discussion, see Gary J. Kornblith and John M. Murrin, "The Making and Unmaking of an American Ruling Class," in *Beyond the American Revolution: Explorations in the History of American Radicalism,* ed. Alfred F. Young (DeKalb, Ill.: Northern Illinois University Press, 1993), 27–79.

38. Farrand, ed., *Records of the Federal Convention, I:* 285.

39. Lance Banning, *The Jeffersonian Persuasion: Evolution of a Party Ideology* (Ithaca: Cornell University Press, 1978), esp. chaps. 5–7.

40. *The Federalist,* ed. Cooke, 56–65, 351.

41. Ibid., 384.

42. Paine, *Common Sense,* in *Tracts,* ed. Jensen, 406.

43. See Donald R. Hickey, "America's Response to the Slave Revolt in Haiti, 1791–1806." *Journal of the Early Republic* 2 (1982): 361–79.

44. See generally Thomas P. Slaughter, *The Whiskey Rebellion, Frontier Epilogue to the American Revolution* (New York; Oxford University Press, 1986); Gerald A. Combs, *The Jay Treaty: Political Battleground of the Founding Fathers* (Berkeley: University of California Press, 1970); and James Morton Smith, *Freedom's Fetters: The Alien and Sedition Laws and American Civil Liberties* (Ithaca: Cornell University Press, 1956).

45. Richard A. Ryerson, *The Revolution Is Now Begun: The Radical Committees of Philadelphia, 1765–1776* (Philadelphia: University of Pennsylvania Press, 1978); Douglas M. Arnold, *A Republican Revolution: Ideology and Politics in Pennsylvania, 1776–1790* (New York: Garland Publishing, 1989); Steven R. Rosswurm, *Arms, Country, and Class: The Philadelphia Militia and the "Lower Sort" during the American Revolution* (New Brunswick, N.J.: Rutgers

University Press, 1987); Owen S. Ireland, "The Crux of Politics: Religion and Party in Pennsylvania," *WMQ,* 3d ser., 42 (1985): 453–75; Ireland, "The Ethnic-Religious Counter-Revolution in Pennsylvania 1784–1786" (Paper presented at the Philadelphia Center for Early American Studies, 22 Jan. 1988). For the text of the 1776 constitution, see *Sources and Documents Illustrating the American Revolution, 1764–1788, and the Formation of the Federal Constitution,* ed. Samuel Eliot Morison, 2d ed. (Oxford: Clarendon Press, 1929), 162–76.

46. Owen S. Ireland, "The People's Triumph: The Federalist Majority in Pennsylvania, 1787–1788," *Pennsylvania History* 56 (1989): 93–113; Joseph S. Foster, "The Politics of Ideology: The Pennsylvania Constitutional Convention of 1789–90," *Pennsylvania History* 59 (1992): 122–43; Harry Marlin Tinkcom, *The Republicans and Federalists in Pennsylvania, 1790–1801: A Study in National Stimulus and Local Response* (Harrisburg: Pennsylvania Historical and Museum Commission, 1950); Kenneth W. Keller, "Rural Politics and the Collapse of Pennsylvania Federalism," American Philosophical Society, *Transactions* 72, Pt. 6 (1982). For the text of the 1790 constitution, see *Pennsylvania Archives,* ed. Samuel Hazard et al. (Harrisburg: State of Pennsylvania, 1852–1949). 4th ser., 4: 113–35 (hereafter. *Pa. Arch.).*

47. Pennsylvania Democratic-Republican Society, resolutions of 10 Apr. 1794; "address to the Patriotic Societies through the United States," 9 Oct. 1794; and "to their fellow Citizens throughout the United States," 18 Dec. 1794, in *The Democratic-Republican Societies, 1790–1800: A Documentary Sourcebook of Constitutions, Declarations, Addresses, Resolutions, and Toasts,* ed. Philip S. Foner (Westport, Conn.: Greenwood Press, 1976), 77, 93, 101.

48. George Washington, 6th Annual Address to Congress, 19 Nov. 1794, and farewell address, 19 Sept. 1796, in *The Writings of George Washington from the Original Manuscript Sources, 1745–1799,* ed. John C. Fitzpatrick (Washington: Government Printing Office, 1931–44), 34: 28–37, quotation at 29; 35: 223–28.

49. To "Fellow Citizens of the United States," 13 Jan. 1795, in *Democratic-Republican Societies,* ed. Foner, 139.

50. To "the free and independent citizens of the United States," Dec. 1794, in *Democratic-Republican Societies,* ed. Foner, 61, 62.

51. John R. Fitzmier, "The Godly Federalism of Timothy Dwight. 1757–1817: Society, Doctrine, and Religion in the Life of New England's 'Moral Legislator'" (Ph.D. diss.: Princeton University, 1986).

52. Philadelphia *Aurora,* 3 Apr. 1817, p. 2, col. 1.

53. Foner, ed., *Democratic-Republican Societies,* 112–16. esp. 112–13.

54. (Boston) *The Scourge,* 28 Aug. 1811. p. 3, col. 1.

55. *Aurora,* 8 Feb. 1809. p. 2, col. 1.

56. See generally Michael Durey, "Thomas Paine's Apostles: Radical Emigrés and the Triumph of Jeffersonian Republicanism," *WMQ,* 3d ser., 44 (1987): 661–88.

57. "A Sketch of the public life of Nathaniel B. Boileau . . . ," Philadelphia *Democratic Press,* 18 Nov. 1816, p. 2, col. 2.

58. Thomas Moore, *Epistles, Odes, and Other Poems* (1806), quoted in Michael Kammen, *People of Paradox: An Inquiry concerning the Origins of American Civilization* (New York: Alfred A. Knopf, 1972), 78.

59. Foner, ed., *Democratic-Republican Societies,* 75, 86, 84, 104.

60. See generally Simon P. Newman, "American Popular Political Culture in the Age of the French Revolution" (Ph.D. diss.: Princeton University, 1991). The Adams quotation is in *Aurora,* 29 March 1809, p. 2, cols. 4–5.

61. See generally Sanford W. Higginbotham, *The Keystone in the Democratic Arch: Pennsylvania Politics, 1800–1816* (Harrisburg: Pennsylvania Historical and Museum Commission, 1952); G. S. Rowe, *Thomas McKean: The Shaping of an American Republicanism* (Boulder: Colorado Associated University Press, 1978); and Richard E. Ellis, *The Jeffersonian Crisis: Courts and Politics in the Young Republic* (New York: Oxford University Press, 1971), chaps. 11–12.

62. Quoted in James Hedley Peeling, "Governor McKean and the Pennsylvania Jacobins (1799–1808)," *Pennsylvania Magazine of History and Biography 54* (1930): 320–54, 333.

63. George Mifflin Dallas, *Life and Writings of Alexander James Dallas* (Philadelphia: J. B. Lippincott and Co., 1871), 9–17, 211–12. Italics added.

64. *Democratic Press,* 13 Apr. 1807, p. 3, cols. 1–2; 22 Apr. 1807, p. 2. cols. 1–3.

65. Deborah Logan Diary, 24 Dec. 1815, 1: 171, Logan Papers, Historical Society of Pennsylvania (Philadelphia). My thanks to Susan Heller for supplying me with this quotation.

66. (William Duane), *Politics for American Farmers: being a Series of Tracts Exhibiting the Blessings of Free Government, as it is Administered in the United States, Compared with the Boasted Stupendous Fabric of British Monarchy* (Washington: R. C. Weightman, 1807), 36. The circulation of this tract may have rivaled that of Paine's *Common Sense* in 1776.

67. *Aurora,* 9 Feb. 1809, p. 2, col. 5.

68. Duane, *Politics for American Farmers,* 30.

69. *Aurora,* 15 Feb. 1809, p. 2, col. 3.

70. *Democratic Press,* 14 Nov. 1816, p. 2, col. 1. The "Doctor" was Michael Leib, who by then was cooperating with Philadelphia Federalists.

71. *Aurora,* 11 Jan. 1805, p. 2, col. 2.

72. For a contemporary description, see Gen. John Lacey to President Thomas Wharton, 4 May 1778, *Pa. Arch.,* 1st ser., 6: 470–71, and the depositions on 500–502. For identification of the Boileau farm as the site, see William J. Buck, "The History of Moorland from Its First Purchase to the Present Time [1853]," Montgomery County Historical Society, *Bulletin 6* (1947–49): 56–58.

73. *An Oration delivered by N. B. Boileau on the Fourth of July, 1814, at the Village of Hatborough, Montgomery County, Pennsylvania* (n.p. 1814). No microtext copy of this oration has been published. I have used the copy in the Bucks County Historical Society, Doylestown, Pa.

74. Kim Tousley Phillips, *William Duane, Radical Journalist in the Age of Jefferson* (New York: Garland Publishing, 1989); John Binns, *Recollections of the Life of John Binns: Twenty-Nine Years in Europe and Fifty-Three in the United States* (Philadelphia: John Binns, 1854); George H. Neff, "John Binns in Northumberland, Pennsylvania—1801–1807," Northumberland County Historical Society, *Proceedings and Addresses 11* (1939): 36–50.

75. *Aurora,* 18 July 1808, p. 2, cols. 2–3; 30 Aug. 1808, p. 2. cols. 2–3.

76. *Aurora,* 24 Sept. 1808, p. 3, col. 3.

77. *Democratic Press,* 15 May 1807, p. 3, col. 3.

78. *Baltimore Evening Post,* n.d., reprinted in *Aurora,* 26 Jan. 1809, p. 2, col. 2.

79. *Aurora,* 3 Mar. 1817, p. 2. cols. 1–2.

80. N.d., reprinted in *Aurora,* 20 Feb. 1809, p. 3, col. 2.

81. *Aurora,* 11 Feb. 1809, p. 2, cols. 1–3.

82. Examples include "British Gold and Gazettes," *Aurora,* 17 Sept. 1808, p. 2. col. 1; "The New Crisis, No. II," *Aurora,* 7 Jan. 1809. p. 2, cols. 1–2; reprint from Washington *Whig* of 6 Jan. 1809, in *Aurora,* 13 Jan. 1809, p. 3. col. 2; *Aurora,* 10 Feb. 1809, p. 2, cols. 1–2; 16 Feb. 1809, p. 2, cols. 1–2: 14 March 1809, p.2, cols. 1–2.

83. *Aurora,* 1 Dec. 1808, p. 2. cols. 1–2.

84. *Aurora,* 14 Feb. 1809, p. 3. col. 1.

85. For Pennsylvania's side in this case, see *Pa. Arch.,* 9th ser., 4: 2651–68, 2771–87. The *Aurora* followed the controversy in great detail and printed the relevant judicial decisions. See the issues of 2, 3, 4, 22, 28, and 30 Mar.; 6, 13, 17, 19, 20, and 27 Apr.; 2, 3, 4 and 6 May 1809.

86. *Aurora,* 6 Apr. 1809, p. 2, col. 1.

87. *Aurora,* 12 Jan. 1810, p. 2, cols. 3–4.

88. *Aurora,* 8 Jan. 1810, p. 2, col. 2.

89. *Aurora,* 12 Jan. 1810, p. 2. col. 3.

90. *Aurora,* 10 Jan. 1810, p. 2, cols. 2–3.

91. *Aurora,* 17 Jan. 1810, p. 2. col. 3.

92. *Aurora,* 9, 16, 22, and 30 Jan. 1810.

93. *Aurora,* 22 Jan. 1810, p. 2, col. 3.

94. Printed in Higginbotham, *Keystone in the Democratic Arch,* 227–28.

95. C. Peter Magrath, *Yazoo: Law and Politics in the New Republic* (Providence: Brown University Press, 1966). See also George R. Lamplugh, "'Oh the Colossus! the Colossus!': James Jackson and the Jeffersonian Republican Party in Georgia, 1796–1806," *Journal of the Early Republic 9* (1989): 315–34.

96. William Partridge, "John Randolph and the Original Great Bugbear Sin of Yazoo" (Senior thesis, Princeton University, 1989), is a careful and penetrating study.

97. [James Jackson], *The Letters of Sicilius to the Citizens of the State of Georgia, on the Constitutionality, the Policy, and the Legality of the Late Sale of Western Lands, in the State of Georgia, considered in a Series of Numbers, by a Citizen of that State* (Augusta, Ga., 1795), esp. 38–39, 9 respectively.

98. *Aurora,* 30 Mar. 1795, p. 2, col. 4.

99. Higginbotham, *Keystone of the Democratic Arch.* 221–22, 224–26, 273–75, 287–88.

100. *Aurora,* 25 Mar. 1814, p. 2, col. 1.

101. *Democratic Press,* 14 Feb. 1814, p. 2. cols. 1–2.

102. So the Boileau people charged in the gubernatorial campaign of 1817. See *The Crisis* (n.p. 1817), 4–5. Findlay's response, *Reply to "The Crisis"* (Harrisburg, Pa.: James Peacock, 1817), savagely attacked Boileau but completely ignored this accusation, an omission that a number of observers detected.

103. *Aurora,* 23 Mar. 1814, p. 2, col. 1.

104. *Democratic Press,* 15 Jan. 1814, p. 2, cols. 3–4.

105. *Democratic Press,* 18 Mar. 1814, p. 2, col. 1.

106. *Aurora,* 23 Mar. 1814, p. 2, col. 1.

107. For Snyder's veto message of 19 Mar. 1813, see *Pa. Arch.,* 4th ser., 4: 836–38.

108. Higginbotham, *Keystone in the Democratic Arch.* 301.

109. In 1823, 1825, and 1829 these occupations accounted for 67 percent, 71 percent, and 67 percent of the membership, respectively. If anything, I would expect the ratios to have been higher under Snyder. See Philip Shriver Klein, *Pennsylvania Politics, 1817–1832: A Game without Rules* (Philadelphia: Historical Society of Pennsylvania, 1940), 27.

110. Whatever their origin, the new banks tried to function cautiously and responsibly but could not overcome the combined pressures of wartime finance in 1814 followed by the Panic of 1819. See Robert M. Blackson, "Pennsylvania Banks and the Panic of 1819: A Reinterpretation," *Journal of the Early Republic* 9 (1989): 335–58.

111. *The Crisis,* esp. 1, 5, 16; *Reply to "The Crisis,"* esp. 4–6, 11.

112. *Aurora,* 7 Mar. 1817, p. 2. col. 1.

113. *Aurora,* 12 Mar. 1817, p. 2. col. 1.

114. *A Private Circular by the Corresponding Committee of Montgomery County, Appointed by the Harrisburg Convention, to Promote the Election of William Findlay for Governor. A Reply by N. B. Boileau, Together with his Correspondence with the Said Committee* (n.p. 1817), esp. 1–2.

115. Boileau, *An Oration* (1814), 7.

116. *Aurora,* 12 Mar. 1817, p. 2, col. 1.

117. *Aurora,* 28 Mar. 1817, p. 2, col. 4.

118. See the brief biography by John M. Murrin and Ruth L. Woodward, in Ruth L. Woodward and Wesley Frank Craven, *Princetonians, 1784–1790: A Biographical Dictionary* (Princeton: Princeton University Press, 1991), 335–49.

119. Philip S. Klein, "John Binns and the Impeachment of Governor William Findlay," Northumberland County Historical Society, *Proceedings and Addresses* 11 (1939): 51–66.

120. See Richard L. McCormick, "Scandal and Reform: A Framework for the Study of Political Corruption in the Nineteenth-Century United

States and a Case Study of the 1820s" (Paper presented at the Philadelphia Center for Early American Studies, 14 May 1982). See also Kim T. Phillips, "Democrats of the Old School in the Era of Good Feelings," *Pennsylvania Magazine of History and Biography* 95 (1971): 363–82; and Phillips, "The Pennsylvania Origins of the Jackson Movement," *Political Science Quarterly* 91 (1976): 489–508.

121. Steven Watts, *The Republic Reborn: War and the Making of Liberal America, 1790–1820* (Baltimore: Johns Hopkins University Press, 1987).

122. See especially Douglas E. Bowers, "From Logrolling to Corruption: The Development of Lobbying in Pennsylvania, 1815–1861," *Journal of the Early Republic* 3 (1983): 439–74; and Mark W. Summers, *The Plundering Generation: Corruption and the Crisis of the Union, 1849–1861* (New York: Oxford University Press, 1987).

10

War, Revolution, and Nation-Making

The American Revolution versus the Civil War

THE WAR FOR American Independence and the War for White Southern Independence were both civil wars. Those who had thought of themselves as one people became two in 1776. The British feared that something of the kind had been developing for 170 years and decided to prevent it from going any further. The colonists denied until the last moment that anything of the sort was happening and then declared their independence anyway.[1] In 1860–61, millions of white Southerners announced that henceforth they would be a separate people. The conservative Confederate position, proclaimed by Jefferson Davis and the South Carolina Secession Convention among others, denied that the South had changed. The North had, until southern coexistence with mad revolutionary Yankees had become morally impossible. "Time and the progress of things have totally altered the relations between the Northern and Southern States, since the Union was established," explained South Carolina. "That identity of feelings, interests and institutions which once existed, is gone. They are now divided, between agricultural and manufacturing, . . . between slaveholding and non-slaveholding states. Their institutions and industrial pursuits have made them totally different peoples." "All fraternity of feeling between the North and the South is lost, or has been converted into hate," South Carolina added, "and we, of the South, are at last driven together by the stern destiny which controls the existence of nations."[2] Other Confederates reached the same conclusion through different arguments. Several Tennessee editors, for instance, insisted that secession was a radical and revolutionary act, a worthy imitation of what

Originally published in Russian in 1997.

the Patriots had done in 1776.[3] Even Northern Republicans, firmly committed to smashing the rebellion, agreed that slavery had made the South into a
distinct people.[4] When Union soldiers invaded Confederate states after 1861,
they shared one sensation in common. All of them believed they were entering a truly foreign country.[5]

Both 1776 and 1861 involved great emotional pain among the seceders,
the rhetoric of unity become disaffection. "But if once we are separated
from our Mother country," warned John Dickinson in near despair in
1768, "what new form of government shall we adopt, or where shall we
find another Britain, to supply our loss? Torn from the body, to which
we are united by religion, liberty, laws, affections, relation, language and
commerce, we must bleed at every vein."[6]

Somewhat more angrily, Thomas Jefferson made a similar point in his
rough draft of the Declaration of Independence when he complained
against the British use of mercenaries. That decision had "given the last
stab to agonizing affection" until "manly spirit bids us to renounce for
ever these unfeeling brethren."[7] The same ambiguity appeared in 1861.
"We repudiate and scorn and spit upon the men and the spirit by whom
and by which the best government the world ever saw has been perverted
into an engine of oppression to one half of its people," raged a Nashville
editor against the Republican Party in May 1861, "because they held
an institution recognized in the fundamental laws, obnoxious to these
Union savers."[8] With no hint of embarrassment or sense of contradiction,
Mississippi could structure its secession ordinance on the Declaration of
Independence and then replace Jefferson's passage on natural rights with
a ringing defense of slavery. "Our position is thoroughly identified with
the institution of slavery—the greatest material interest of the world," the
planters explained, for it was responsible for "by far the largest and most
important portions of the commerce of the earth."[9]

"You have overturned a Government which had become sectional in
policy and sectional in hostility," summarized the satisfied president of
the Georgia Secession Convention after it had completed its task. "It had
lost nationality, and the first requisite of every government—that of protection of person and property. True, you have overthrown the Federal
Union, but you have preserved the Federal Constitution."[10] Presumably
the South had not gained national identity. The United States had lost
it. A North Carolina editor said nearly the same thing when he lamented

that Abraham Lincoln had "completed the sectionalization of the country" and that "the hand of brother [is] uplifted against brother." Despite these underlying affinities, Lincoln had destroyed the Union. "The Union cannot be maintained by force. Men cannot be whipped into freedom."[11] A Tennessee paper could define the crisis in terms of "intersectional troubles which have divided the country for some years" and yet conclude that peace "is altogether out of the question" and union "is gone irretrievably."[12] In both the Revolution and the Civil War, a new nationality found meant an older and larger unity lost. Contemporaries paid a steep emotional price for their novel identities.

I

The parallel between the breakup of the First British Empire and the shipwreck of the American Union has fascinated me since graduate school, when I took a seminar with the late David M. Potter. He gave us, in essence, what soon became a famous essay, "The Historian's Use of Nationalism and Vice Versa."[13] In it through a variety of arguments he discredited the substance of Confederate nationalism. I wondered at the time what would happen if someone applied similar arguments and standards to the aspirations of the United Colonies of 1775–83. I did not know enough in 1959–60 to challenge him, and I probably lacked the nerve. Instead I have waited until he is dead and cannot reply, but I do hope that my challenge is the kind he would have welcomed.

Not only Potter is involved, of course. We get analogous arguments from David Donald, C. Vann Woodward, John McCardell, Paul Escott, Kenneth Stampp and James Oakes.[14] All of them agree that Confederate nationalism was not a legitimate example of the species. It was not nationalism but sectionalism carried to a momentary extreme because the hard interests of South and North had polarized, and northern Republicans had gained control of the presidency. The national identity of the Confederate States of America was superficial, epiphenomenal, and transient. Only because it was indeed ephemeral, Potter explained, could things have turned out as they did. The South did stop fighting in 1865, and it was reabsorbed into the Union with surprising ease after the war. Nobody today doubts that southern whites are Americans.[15]

At first glance, this point has obvious plausibility. At second notice, it is not so obvious. The white South continued to insist into the twentieth century that secession had been morally right and that a magnificent civilization had died at Appomattox. Northerners agreed that Confederate soldiers had fought with extraordinary bravery, but not that the cause had been just. The sections could achieve consensus on the idolization of Robert E. Lee.[16] Likewise, the fighting did stop in 1865, but not southern resistance to northern demands. The KKK, a high percentage of whose membership must have included Confederate veterans or their younger brothers or sons, became one of the world's first paramilitary terrorist organizations and carried on the armed struggle at a lower intensity with a considerable degree of success. The Union was restored and slavery was dead, but the South did not surrender to Yankee values.[17]

To a refugee from the eighteenth century who happens to wander into Civil War historiography, these arguments suggest fascinating parallels. What would happen if we applied to the United Colonies the standards that Potter and others have used to undermine the moral claims of the Confederacy? Of course we must guard against the danger of exploring nothing more than an historical anachronism. Nationalism was a far more potent force in the nineteenth century than it had been in the eighteenth. The Confederates had ways of legitimating their aspirations that had not been as widely available to the colonists, and the very example of 1776 and 1787 made the task much simpler for the people of 1861. With remarkably little debate or tension, the Confederate founders could adopt a formal constitution within a few weeks simply because they had the text of 1787 to draw upon and had to worry only about the few changes that they might wish to make. They also knew about contemporary nationalist movements in Italy and Germany and admired some of the organizers.[18]

It is no huge surprise, in other words, to find a more explicit rhetoric of national identity in the Confederacy than among the United Colonists. And yet the problem will not disappear just because we know that the nineteenth century was different from the eighteenth. National identities did exist in the eighteenth century, and in England (and probably the larger entity of Great Britain as well) this process was already developing into a self-conscious nationalism.

In Gerald Newman's impressive analysis of the phenomenon, English nationalism evolved out of a simpler form of patriotism in the generation after 1740. Powerfully fueled by the mid-century wars with France, this deeper identity emerged as a potentially radical critique of the kingdom's Frenchified aristocracy and the politics of clientage that Sir Robert Walpole left to his successors. The early spokesmen for English national identity loathed French manners and the Englishmen who cultivated them. Most were political outsiders, several steps removed from the levers of power yet deeply troubled by the atmosphere of corruption that pervaded public life. They idealized the constitutional simplicity of Anglo-Saxon England, which was largely their own invention, and castigated the Norman Yoke. In the 1750s only William Pitt the elder met their standard of disinterested patriotism. Most of them sympathized with colonial grievances during the American Revolution, and in the 1780s they would rally behind the younger Pitt and George III against Charles James Fox and Lord North, whom they despised as false patriots and pseudo-reformers. Newman never systematically tries to distinguish between English and British nationalism, although both undoubtedly existed and, in the form of a simple identity, had long histories even before 1740. Scots feared France far less than Englishmen did and worried more about the impact of homegrown English corruption upon themselves, but both shared an urgent need to purify the nation's politics at the center and doubted that the ruling aristocratic elite could ever accomplish the job.[19]

In Newman's estimation English nationalism has been such a completely successful phenomenon that its beneficiaries have scarcely realized that it exists. Until quite recently it had no organized body of scholarship trying to explain it, and most Englishmen seemed content to believe that nationalism was the kind of force that disfigured the past of other countries. It differed elsewhere, he suggests, chiefly in arriving later. Through most of the eighteenth century and beyond in Western and Central Europe, the normal alternative to a sense of national identity was a dynastic loyalty. The two could be combined and could reinforce one another, as with the British monarchy, but few communities could do without one or the other.[20] The American Revolution explicitly rejected dynasticism and any other formal link with Great Britain, and yet the colonists knew that they had to unite or face certain defeat. They had to affirm some degree of national unity. Certainly by 1787–88, the adjective "national" was used routinely by centralizers—and by at least some of their opponents—to describe the government about to emerge under the Constitution. "A nation without a national government," proclaimed Alexander Hamilton in the final paragraph of *The Federalist*, "is, in my view, an awful spectacle."[21] Of course "federal" remained one possible antonym of "national." The Virginia Plan routinely described its proposed government as "national." The New Jersey Plan hoped only to make "the federal Constitution" adequate to the needs of "the Union." As the Virginia Plan evolved into the Constitution, the word "national" disappeared completely from the text, and the centralizers won a major forensic victory in the ratification struggle by appropriating the term "federal" to themselves.[22] The same tension could, no doubt, be traced through the writings of the major Confederate spokesmen of 1861–65, who did believe that they were creating a southern nation and who also insisted that their government would be confederal, not consolidated.

After making proper allowances for all of these qualifications, one point still stands out. By virtually all measurable standards, the Confederate sense of national identity appears to have been deeper, more profound, more passionate (no doubt more of a nationa<u>lism</u>) than the ties that bound the Thirteen Colonies together from 1775 to 1783 and beyond. Yet the colonists won the Revolution and established their independence. The Confederates lost their war and were reabsorbed into the United States. We thus face a big problem in historical explanation, one that simply does not get addressed because of the chronological segments into which American history is routinely divided. The people who write about the Revolution almost never discuss the Civil War in any systematic way, and vice versa.

A full explanation for this contrast would have to go well beyond the dimensions of this paper. It would have to provide a careful analysis of group loyalties in the two situations, asking of each: to what collectivities were people loyal and how did they sort out their priorities? In mid-eighteenth-century America, a person could become quite emotionally attached to his locality (town, county, city), to his province (Massachusetts or Virginia), to the continent of North America, or to the British Empire. A century later, the Empire had disappeared but the others remained and newer regional identities had appeared. Around 1760, any attachment to America was by far the weakest loyalty of the four. It might inspire a Benjamin Franklin to muse about the demographic potential of the continent, or Nathaniel Ames to wax lyrical about coming glories, but it provided no institutional or historical focus.[23] Unlike the Empire, it provided nothing concrete for people to be loyal to. In the most harmonious of all possible worlds, all of these loyalties were mutually reinforcing. Franklin as a loyal Philadelphian tried conscientiously to serve Pennsylvania, even if this meant resisting the Penn family. He did imagine a majestic future for North America, but only within the context of Britain's magnificent empire.

By the mid-1770s, men had been forced to choose among their loyalties. Franklin affirmed province (and therefore continent) over Empire, while Thomas Hutchinson chose Empire over province (and therefore over both continent and city as well, although he was extremely reluctant to recognize these consequences of his imperial loyalties). In the upper Connecticut Valley, most settlers affirmed locality and continent against province and Empire, emerging from the struggle as the nascent state of Vermont, hostile to both New York and Britain. Berkshire County likewise threatened to secede from Massachusetts unless the commonwealth adopted a proper constitution.[24]

Southerners had to make similar choices in 1860–61. Most whites affirmed locality, state, and region over a broader continental union. Appalachia did contain numerous people who preferred to remain part of the old Union, and some of them were compact and coherent enough— and sufficiently close to Union territory—to secede from an existing state and become West Virginia. A complete analysis of this pattern would require more information than I have been able to master even from the secondary literature. David Donald, for example, stresses the localist resistance of North Carolina and Georgia to the manpower and supply demands of the Confederate government. These problems were real and certainly did trouble President Davis, but to me they seem to fall far short of the formidable difficulties amounting to near impotence that beset the American Congress between 1779 and 1781. No doubt unionist sentiment was also a major problem for the Confederacy, but nothing I have read suggests that it approached in scale the problem of the loyalists a century earlier. To consider only one variable, very few white southerners took up arms for the Union. They resisted in other ways, including desertion. By contrast, by 1781 the number of loyalists under arms with the British greatly exceeded the number of Continentals mustered with Washington. The problems were similar in kind in the two situations, but the differences in scale were tremendous.[25]

This paper cannot even try to resolve all of these difficulties. It can hope to demonstrate that the problem—the contrast itself—is real and has serious implications. If so, we may need a fresh perspective to understand both the Revolution and the Civil War.

II

Scattered throughout the South, no doubt, there still survives a breed of unrepentant pro-Confederates who affirm that the South is good, the Confederacy was right, and the Civil War was a terrible tragedy only because the wrong side won. But that is not what historians of the South have been saying for the past quarter of a century.

Only committed Marxists insist that Confederate nationality was real and viable, the unity of a pre-capitalist society against the encroaching "cash nexus" of northern industrialism. Eugene Genovese made this interpretation famous in a series of books culminating with *Roll, Jordan, Roll*.[26] An Italian Marxist, Raimondo Luraghi, gets so enthralled watching the Rebs bash all of those bourgeois Yankees that he barely seems to notice that the Confederacy was a slave society and that southern blacks did not share the same passion.[27]

With few exceptions, non-Marxists have been saying something quite different. Whether conservatives (Potter and Donald) or liberals (Stampp and Oakes), they deny that southern national identity was either pervasive or genuine. Southern sectionalism was real enough, but it was no more extreme or bizarre than, for example, the New England equivalent which led that region to the edge of secession during the War of 1812. For most of his fine study of Jefferson Davis, Paul Escott seems to be arguing, not about real or unreal national identity, but about degrees of intensity. How much pressure could be put upon southern nationalism before it would collapse? But he too finally slips into the categories established by Potter when he concludes that Davis failed completely, in the last analysis, because he was *too much* of a nationalist. He would have served his constituents better by trying to compromise with the Union even at the final moment in order to preserve the institution of slavery. In a word, he should have been a sectionalist, not a nationalist.[28] Among the non-Marxists, only two recent studies think consistently in terms of strong and weak nationalisms, not real and unreal. For Emory Thomas the phenomenon was undoubtedly real, but it lacked the resources and the power to survive against Union hostility.[29] A team of four authors carry this argument to a new extreme in explaining Confederate defeat. At their hands Confederate nationalism becomes a feeble force indeed compared with its Union rival and virtually all successful national movements of the past two centuries.

The Confederacy, they insist, still had sufficient manpower to resist even in 1865 but lacked the national will to continue the struggle. They compare Confederate collapse with the willingness of France to continue to fight and even attack in 1918 after absorbing heavy losses. Other comparisons include the degree of punishment that Nazi Germany absorbed before it surrendered and the truly amazing resistance of Paraguay to the far more powerful alliance of Brazil, Uruguay, and Argentina throughout a longer war that lasted from 1865 until 1871. No one will contest the Paraguayan example, except perhaps to query whether we are dealing with a nationalism or a pan-Indian resistance movement against settler encroachment, a phenomenon with strong parallels elsewhere in the Americas. Nevertheless, at the end of that struggle the country's population had fallen from half a million to 221,000. Among adult survivors women outnumbered men by nearly four to one.

The other comparisons are far less persuasive. To establish their contrast the authors use combat fatalities, not military deaths from all causes. Prior to the twentieth century all armies lost more men to disease than to battle. If we accept the more conventional figure of 260,000 Confederate deaths rather than the 100,000 to 120,000 preferred by the authors, the Confederate toll rises to 4.7 percent of the white population, more than a third again as high as the 3.3 percent lost by France in a war of nearly equal length half a century later, and the Confederacy had no allies to draw upon for a final offensive the way that France could count upon Britain and the United States in 1918. In fact the French army had ceased to be an effective offensive force by the spring of 1917, and its defensive capabilities in the spring of 1918 were not very strong either. The Confederate loss rate even comes close to Nazi Germany's 5 percent and was certainly higher among military personnel, and the losers did not have to face terms of submission nearly as harsh as the unconditional surrender imposed on Germany. "An insufficient [Confederate] nationalism failed to survive the strains imposed by the lengthy hostilities," conclude Richard E. Berringer and his coauthors. This statement is, of course, true. But as an explanation for what happened between 1861 and 1865, it has no more power than any other tautology. Within North America, as we shall see later in this paper, no other nation has ever absorbed remotely comparable punishment.[30]

For Potter—and, I suspect, for Donald as well—the choice of a dichotomy between real and unreal (or nationalist and sectionalist), instead of strong versus weak national loyalties, had profound moral implications. Had Confederate nationalism been genuine, true southerners must conclude that they have been deprived of their right to self-determination. Listening to Potter in 1959, I occasionally wondered whether he had his own peculiar nightmare in which stern duty would compel him to turn terrorist against the United States, sabotaging the government, blowing up railroads, jeopardizing the lives of the innocent. Potter was among the gentlest human beings I have known, and his seminar was an extraordinary intellectual experience for everyone who took it. His sensitivity to nuance and his analytic ability kept all of us in awe. And yet "The Historian's Use of Nationalism and Vice Versa" does seem, upon reflection, to be more an answer to a moral dilemma than a response to a particular historical problem.

Kenneth Stampp, a northerner and a committed neo-abolitionist, has had to face no such tragic choices. Nevertheless his position is equally moralistic at root, with a twist uniquely his own. Southerners, he contends, really wanted to lose the Civil War because the case for Confederate distinctiveness rested upon slavery. "I believe that many of them felt," he writes, "that the fruits of defeat would be less bitter than those of success."[31] Here again one wonders whether what is not said may be more important than what is overtly affirmed. Potter had to find an ethical basis for refusing to resist a government that had conquered his homeland. Stampp, I think, needs a compelling moral reason for permitting the South to rejoin the Union. The brutal fact of northern victory cannot be sufficient for either. Our sympathy for the profoundly human dilemmas that Potter and Stampp have confronted must not, however, blind us to the historical improbability of the argument itself. No army that could execute Pickett's charge could have had serious moral qualms about what it was doing.

John McCardell's reservations about the seriousness of southern nationalism rest upon more practical considerations. The region, he insists, could not agree on what would constitute a viable economy for an independent South. Should it be self-contained and therefore encourage the growth of railroads and local industries? Or should it continue to emphasize the exportation of staple crops for sale on the world market? This debate began long before secession and never reached a satisfactory resolution. But to contend that Confederate national identity could not have been real because it failed to surmount this tension is quite another matter. To put this contention in its eighteenth-century context, it is like arguing that the United States should not have survived the 1790s so long as the new nation tried to contain both Hamilton and Jefferson. Southerners even held eight regional economic conventions between 1849 and 1859, and several before that in scattered years to discuss such problems. One searches in vain for any colonial counterpart to this kind of activity.[32]

III

Most historians of the South now insist that what held the Union together was more important and more permanent in character than what drove the South out of it for a brief four-year period. The ties binding all Americans remained more significant than the differences separating some of them from others, particularly white southerners from northerners. Examples of these affective ties include a common language, a shared religious heritage with roots in the Second Great Awakening and nineteenth-century evangelicalism, a common political culture growing out of similar institutions and allegiance to the same history, and increasingly close economic relations. Trade between the South and New York City or Boston was certainly more important by 1860 than it had been in 1790 or 1820. A genuine continental economy was emerging in the United States, particularly after about 1840.

All of these points are true, and all carry weight. But what happens if we take each and compare it with the colonial situation on the eve of the Revolution? Obviously the British Empire shared a common language. The Revolution meant the affirmation of an identity apart from language, a reality so frightening to Noah Webster that he spent much of his life trying to give the republic its own American English.[33] In linguistic terms, the Confederate rebellion against the United States has to seem less jarring than the first breach in the unity of the English-speaking peoples. If the Civil War was unnatural in these terms, the Revolution was even more so. In between these events the Latin American wars of independence had made revolutions within a linguistic family a political commonplace, indeed the norm for the Americas. What had been without major precedent in 1775 had become typical by 1861.[34]

The argument for a common religious heritage leads to a similar conclusion. What the Second Great Awakening did for the United States, the First did for the Empire. It jolted both the British Isles and North America in an uneven chronological pattern. In the 1730s and 1740s, it sent gigantic shock waves through England, Scotland, New England and the Middle Atlantic region. At this stage it affected the South and the West Indies superficially. Only with the arrival of the Baptists and Methodists in significant numbers during the 1760s and 1770s did the South begin to fall into line. Even then the Awakening in the South never acquired the systematic Calvinist theology that characterized the movement in the northern colonies, Scotland, and among George Whitefield's followers in England. The incipient Wesleyan movement in the South, destined to acquire great power immediately after independence, did, of course, have close affinities to the Methodist movement in England. At no time did simple patterns of religious loyalty forecast the eventual imperial split. At no point did the First Great Awakening establish a sharp cleavage between Britain and the colonies.[35]

Not so in the American South in the nineteenth century. Despite the intensity of the Second Great Awakening, it could not prevent all of the major evangelical churches (Presbyterians, Methodists, and Baptists) from dividing along sectional lines in the 1830s and 1840s. Non-evangelical denominations, such as Episcopalians and Roman Catholics, did not split. If the common wisdom is correct that evangelicals as a group tended to be more deeply committed to their beliefs than non-evangelicals and more likely to wish to transform the world to conform to their values, religious intensity in antebellum America did become a much more accurate barometer of political division and the coming Civil War than such controversies had been a century before. The religious experience of the Empire was far less divisive than that of the republic.[36]

A similar case, though perhaps not quite as strong, can be made about common political cultures. Practically everything that we now affirm about political life in pre-Revolutionary North America rests on the assumption that eighteenth-century British political culture engulfed the American settlements with differential results. If the colonists understood the world as a perpetual struggle between power and liberty and remained nervously alert for every sign of possible corruption, they got these sensibilities from the mother country. Both Britons and colonists revered the Glorious Revolution of 1688 as one of the greatest things that had ever happened in the history of the world and as the event that had sealed the triumph of these values. Much of this rhetoric carried over quite easily to the republic and its idolization of the American Revolution, with one important difference. The War for Independence was a far more violent affair than the Glorious Revolution had been. The events of 1688 were "glorious" mostly because they shed very little blood. But American union had been achieved only through a bloodbath, and nineteenth-century memories of that shared experience were bound to be more visceral than colonial fondness for the men and events of 1688–89.[37]

Even so, one major political contrast stands out starkly. The Deep South seceded first and then went to war to maintain its independence. The colonists, almost to the last moment, insisted that they desired only the traditional rights of Englishmen, that they wished to remain good and loyal subjects of King George III. Resistance to British demands led to war by April 1775, and the imperatives of war produced the Declaration of Independence fifteen months later. But the Deep South first proclaimed its separate nationhood and then started a war to defend it. When Lincoln accepted the challenge with a call to arms, the Upper South (half of the remaining slave states still in the Union) also seceded, joined the Confederacy, and thus gave the Southern Nation most of its industry and roughly half of its white population. The Confederacy in the preamble of its Constitution called itself a "permanent" union, even though it was created by men who loudly affirmed the right to secession. The United States Constitution said nothing of the kind. The Articles of Confederation had, of course, proclaimed a "perpetual" union, but that document had taken more than three years to ratify. As the Revolutionary War ended and the problems of union became more manifest, talk of disunion became quite commonplace from at least 1783 on. Here too, on balance, the Confederates seem to have had a clearer sense than their Revolutionary ancestors of what they were trying to accomplish.[38]

Finally, the closer economic ties that bound North and South together before the Civil War also had their counterpart within the British Empire after about 1740. Commerce became measurably more efficient, and therefore profit margins contracted, to the discomfort of many. The terms of trade were shifting to favor American products against British—that is, the prices of British exports were falling while those of American exports were rising. Per capita imports increased sharply in the generation before independence, and something like a sophisticated land and labor market on an imperial scale was emerging and intensifying rapidly after 1760. North America was acquiring the capacity to depopulate large sections of Scotland and Ireland. Yet none of these integrative trends proved powerful enough to avert the Revolution.[39]

In short, all of the principal arguments used to discredit the substance of Confederate national identity apply with at least equal and sometimes greater force to the United Colonies of 1775. If Potter, Stampp, Donald, and McCardell are right about the South, we ought to conclude that American national identity was superficial, epiphenomenal, and lacked legitimacy. And yet we do know one awkward thing about it. It has not been transient. It has survived. No one since 1783 has favored starting a war to bring back the British crown and Empire. American national identity was indeed weak in the 1770s, but once it achieved independence and acquired secure boundaries within which it could grow, it did just that. It did not, of course, become strong enough to prevent its repudiation by eleven southern states in 1861. May we not ponder the most obvious counterfactual question of relevance here? Had Robert E. Lee smashed George Gordon Meade's army at Gettysburg and marched into Washington to end the war a few weeks later, would we today have the slightest doubt about the intensity and commitment of southern whites to Confederate nationalism?

IV

Are there any weighty and measurable reasons for believing that Confederate national identity was deeper and more passionate than any ties that bound the United Colonies of 1775? There certainly are, and many of them present quite dramatic contrasts between the two sets of rebels.

Who had the stronger sense of common identity, the United Colonies of 1775, or the Confederates of 1861? Only one answer to this question is possible: the Confederates, by a wide margin. Colonial historians have labored mightily to uncover evidence of an emerging American national sense before the Revolution but so far have turned up almost nothing. Prior to about 1772, only two patriots are known to have commented favorably on the idea of an independent American nation within the next century or so. John Adams made a brief remark to this effect during the Seven Years' War, and Charles Carroll of Carrollton expressed a similar thought in a 1763 letter to his father.[40] Far more typical were expressions of Anglo-American loyalty by Franklin, or Nathaniel Ames, or dozens of clergymen in sermons that celebrated colonial and imperial victories from Louisbourg in 1745 to the Treaty of Paris in 1763.[41]

But apparently only the most craven of scholars will permit a mere lack of evidence to deflect him from a favorite hypothesis. Two examples illustrate this point. Richard L. Merritt undertook the immensely tedious assignment of measuring "American" loyalties by counting place names and other words used to identify groups of settlers. For his data base, he uses newspapers from five different colonies in the forty years before Lexington, a highly urban and cosmopolitan (as against localist) source that in all likelihood would exaggerate the extent of common awareness within a continent that was still 95 percent rural. Yet he finds that, in most years, sources with British datelines were more likely to "think American" than sources that originated in North America. And until after 1763, he locates no significant rise in American awareness. It remained at a fairly low level, and it actually declined slightly during each of the last two imperial wars. After 1763, the use of American symbols coincided pretty closely with each of the imperial crises before Lexington. This evidence strongly suggests what Merritt is reluctant to admit. An emerging American identity did not propel the settlers toward resistance and independence. Rather, the severity of the imperial crises drove them to believe, or hope, that they shared enough in common to resist Britain successfully.[42]

Carl Bridenbaugh, an outstanding historian who has done a great deal to enhance our understanding of the colonial period, nevertheless lost most of his sense of discipline when writing *The Spirit of '76: The Growth of American Patriotism before Independence*. He knows what this patriotism means when he finds Samuel Sewall using lyrical language to praise his beloved Plum Island. This attachment to place, this "eloquent burst of pride, affection, and faith of 1697... needs very little added patriotic fervor to turn it into the Spirit of '76." Just because Sewall loved Plum Island does not mean that he had any affection whatever for New Yorkers or Virginians. When Bridenbaugh examines the Virginians, he finds no trace of any comparable local loyalty. He might have carried the point farther, for Ebenezer Cooke's *The Sot-weed Factor* reveals an extraordinary distaste for the Chesapeake environment, just as the earliest chronicles of Virginia history had little but contempt for the colony's past.[43] Yet Bridenbaugh knows how to read the want of sources. "Although no signs of unity or of intercolonial feeling could be discerned in 'these American parts; nevertheless by 1690, much had been accomplished, albeit unconsciously, that laid the foundations so essential for the eventual growth of such a feeling among the colonial people as a whole." After a quick tour of the eighteenth century down to 1763, he concludes that "Americanism was still something the average man felt only deep within himself, something that words could not describe." Think of that! The absence of words, of any significant evidence for what he believes must have happened, somehow gets converted into a positive argument for what is not there.[44]

By contrast, plenty of hard evidence survives to show that people from one colony did not much like those from other parts of America. Viscerally the settlers may have felt more disgust and contempt for one another than hatred for the British, at least until their common fears drove them together in an actual war. New Englanders had never been able to conceal the smug superiority they felt over other colonials from as far back as the days of John Winthrop, who blamed Opechancanough's great massacre of 1644 upon Virginia's expulsion of godly puritan missionaries.[45] In projecting military strategy against New France in the 1750s, Charles Chauncy envisioned an active cooperation between Britain and New England but expected nothing helpful from colonies farther south.[46]

These assumptions remained painfully vigorous as the revolutionary crisis unfolded. When the Massachusetts radical, Josiah Quincy, toured the colonies in 1773 looking for allies in the resistance against Britain, he found almost no one to admire. The political leaders of South Carolina, Virginia, Maryland and Pennsylvania all failed to meet his standards of civility and patriotism. Nor could he even understand why Philadelphia

Quakers distrusted Puritans and considered them bigots and persecu-
tors. He apparently did not know what the Quakers refused to forget,
that Massachusetts had hanged several of them for their beliefs a century before. "Were I to lament anything," he concluded, "it would be
the prevalent and extended ignorance of one colony of the concerns of
another."[47] During the siege of Boston, Abigail Adams revealed a similar
set of assumptions. The British, she told John, were surely wrong in their
denunciation of New Englanders, but after she had watched the behavior of Virginia riflemen, she thought that London might be right about
the barbaric nature of Virginians. "Are not the Genterey Lords and the
common people vassals, are they not like the uncivilized Natives Brittain
represents us to be?" she asked. "I hope their Riffel Men who have shewen
themselves very savage and even Blood thirsty; are not a specimen of the
Generality of the people." John was more charitable. "The Gentry are very
rich, and the common People very poor," he agreed. ". . . But the Spirit of
these Barons, is coming down, and it must submit."[48]

What others said about New Englanders was even less flattering, and
by the 1770s the pattern was already at least a century old. Governor
Sir William Berkeley exulted in the destruction that King Philip's War
brought upon New England in 1675, fitting retribution, he thought, for
a community of regicides.[49] Sixty years later William Byrd II found other
reasons to detest Yankees. The "saints of New England," he warned one of
the organizers of Georgia, would never respect the colony's ban on alco-
hol. "They have a great dexterity at palliating a perjury so well as to leave
no tast of it in the mouth, nor can any people like them slip through a
penal statute."[50] Dr. Andrew Hamilton of Maryland genuinely admired
the civility of Boston, but he too found the cunning and the piety of New
Englanders equally annoying. "It is not by half such a flagrant sin to cheat
and cozen one's neighbour as it is to ride for pleasure on the sabbath day
or to neglect going to church and singing of psalms." Ordinary people,
he found, "are to a degree dissingenuous and dissembling, which appears
even in their common conversation in which their indirect and dubious
answers to the plainest and fairest questions show their suspicion of one
another."[51] The New York merchant Gerard G. Beekman proclaimed in
1754 that "seven Eights of the People I have Credited in New England
has proved to be d--d ungreatfull cheating fellows." Thirteen years later
he was still complaining about Connecticut in particular. "I shall never

trust any more men of that Cuntry. The great Part of them turns Out bad."[52] Sometimes the denunciations of New England appeared quite gratuitously in strange places. Lewis Morris, Jr., could not even keep his disgust out of his will of 1762. He ordered that his heir Gouverneur Morris receive "the best Education that is to be had in Europe or America, but my Express Will and Directions are that he be never sent for that purpose to the Colony of Connecticut least he should imbibe in his youth that low Craft and cunning so Incident to the People of that Country, which is so interwoven in their constitutions that all their art cannot disguise it from the World, tho' many of them under the sanctified Garb of Religion have Endeavored to impose themselves on the World as honest Men."[53]

The revolutionary crisis did not banish these antipathies—not easily, at any rate. One New Yorker in 1774 called New Englanders "Goths and Vandals" and denounced their "Levelling Spirit."[54] Two years later a Marylander described Yankees as "the Huns and Alaricks of the North."[55] "I dread their low Cunning and those levelling Principles which Men without Character and without Fortune in general Possess," agreed Edward Rutledge of South Carolina, "which are so captivating to the lower Class of Mankind, and which will occasion such a fluctuation of Property as to introduce the greatest disorder."[56] When he took command of the Continental Army outside Boston in 1775, George Washington was astonished by what he called "an unaccountable kind of stupidity in the lower class of these people which, believe me, prevails but too generally among the officers of the Massachusetts <u>part</u> of the Army."[57] "No man was ever more disappointed in his expectations respecting New Englanders in general than I have been," agreed Gen. Persifor Frazer of Pennsylvania in a letter to his wife. "They are a set of low, dirty, griping, cowardly, lying rascals."[58] "My crime consists in not being a New England man in principle," reflected New York's Gen. Philip Schuyler when relieved of his northern command in 1777, "and unless they alter theirs I hope I shall never be."[59] Of course men bred to proper gentility found much to despise in the rest of the country as well. "The worst men (was there a degree above the superlative) would be still pejorated by having been fellow-soldiers with that discipline-hating good-living-loving too eternal-fam'd damn'd coxcomatical crew we lately had here from Philadelphia," complained New Jersey's Governor William Livingston of the Pennsylvania Associators in 1776.[60] But no other target quite equalled New Englanders in popularity.

When we do find a colonist extolling American unity, or when we encounter post-Revolutionary patriots rewriting their histories to make the Revolution and American Union explicable outgrowths of earlier events, we should use this evidence with caution.[61] Finding themselves adrift on stormy waters in the Lifeboat Independence in 1776, the occupants began throwing lines at every potentially stable point in their past in the hope that some would take hold. Too many historians have continued the same exercise. It does not work. On the other hand we should treat with the greatest respect the hesitating efforts made by the men of 1776 to understand and respect one another despite the disturbing differences that they encountered. Their unity was always porous, but with generous foreign military, naval, and financial aid, it managed to survive the crisis of a long and often devastating war.

We certainly have far more compelling evidence for an emerging southern identity long before 1860. The first signs of an emerging sectional consciousness appeared during the Revolution.[62] For some people, this attachment became a demand for southern unity and independence as far back as the Nullification Crisis, nearly thirty years before secession.[63] These early nationalists provide an interesting group profile.

Dr. Thomas Cooper, a prominent nullifier, was an Irish immigrant with an earlier career as a radical Jeffersonian in Philadelphia. He then moved south and became president of the University of South Carolina.[64] James Henry Hammond, sometime governor of South Carolina who would be calling for secession by 1836, was the son of a Massachusetts man. Robert Barnwell Rhett, eventually one of the most famous of the fire eaters, was another South Carolinian of Massachusetts ancestry. Similarly, Pierre Soule was an exiled Frenchman, and William Lowndes Yancey of Alabama grew up in the burned-over district of New York, a region that became almost the cradle of American abolitionism. The journalist J.D.B. DeBow was born in South Carolina, the son of a failed New Jersey father.[65]

This pattern did vary somewhat among southern nationalists associated with Virginia. Both Edmund Ruffin and George Fitzhugh had impeccable credentials among the planter gentry. Nathaniel Beverly Tucker, though descended from an immigrant father from Bermuda, fit securely within the same class. He also had a more active fantasy life than most of them. His novel *The Partisan Leader*, published in 1836, predicted a civil war and an eventual southern triumph after wicked Martin Van Buren of New York would attempt to hold the presidency for a fourth term in 1848.[66]

The early nationalists thus seem to have been either Virginians with exceptional state loyalties, or outsiders—marginal men, almost—who took up the cause of southern nationalism long before the locals did. Their counterpart in the Revolutionary generation would be people like Thomas Paine, John Witherspoon, Hugh Mercer, Charles Lee, Alexander Hamilton, or James Wilson, all of whom arrived in America on the eve of independence and became far more nationalistic than most of the older settlers.

Those who deny the substance of Confederate nationalism point to the odd backgrounds of these people and also note that, after rousing everyone to a peak of fury by 1861, they played almost no role in shaping or governing the Confederacy itself. The Montgomery Convention chose Jefferson Davis and Alexander Stephens, both late converts to secession, as provisional President and Vice-President of the Confederacy, thus bypassing Rhett and Yancey, among others. For the most part, this pattern continued to hold for lesser posts as well.[67]

What does it mean? First, the outsider as conspicuous nationalist is by no means a phenomenon peculiar to the Confederacy. England's articulate nationalists after 1750 reflected a similar pattern. Napoleon the Corsican somehow became the embodiment of the French nation. Many of the early German nationalists were men uprooted by Napoleon's reorganization who identified with a greater Germany because they had lost their roots in a special part of it. After playing their role, they had to watch the initiative—and real power—pass to Otto von Bismarck. The careers of Giuseppe Mazzini and Giuseppe Garibaldi in Italy followed a similar pattern, with Count Camillo Benso di Cavour taking charge in this case. Without great difficulty, one could fit Simon Bolivar, Jose de San Martin, and Bernardo O'Higgins into nearly the same mold. To be sure, all exercised more real power in Latin America than, say, Mazzini in Italy. Bolivar, a major figure in the liberation of his native Venezuela, also became an architect of national identity for Peru, Columbia, and Bolivia, where he was an outsider. An Argentinean, San Martin fought for the independence of Chile and Peru. The son of an Irishman in the service of Spain, O'Higgins was educated in England before he became the liberator of Chile.[68]

In the twentieth century, the outsider as supreme nationalist has remained a common phenomenon, but most of them have usually exercised power as well. Mahatma Ghandi, Nicolai Lenin, Josef Stalin, Adolph Hitler, Chou en Lai, Ho Chi Minh, and Syngman Rhee come easily to mind. The explanation for this recurring pattern is not at all obvious, at least to this writer, but it has happened far too often to justify dismissal of the Confederate case because the men who forced the issue of secession were mostly outsiders and never did gain control of the government they helped to create.

One contrast with the Revolution does seem relevant in this context, however. Because the Revolution was primarily a movement that called a nation into being as a means to an end, radical leaders who forced the break with Britain continued to exercise great influence long after independence. The American Revolution was, in Gerald Newman's schematization for England, a patriot movement, not a nationalism. To the extent that radicals shared nationalist values, they were English or British, not distinctively American, but by 1776 colonial patriots discovered that they had to *create* a nation to achieve their political goals. In most states and in Congress, moderates had to wait years to exert an impact comparable to that of the radicals. Meanwhile the actions of the radicals drove something like a sixth of the white population into active loyalism. Even after the adoption of the Constitution, Americans had difficulty agreeing on exactly what sort of people they were, partly because they differed sharply over which Other they most feared. Typical of English nationalists, New Englanders in particular and Federalists generally carried into the early republic the intense English loathing of France. In the middle and southern states, hatred of Britain remained far more powerful than any dread of France. This tension nearly destroyed the republic during the War of 1812.[69]

The Confederacy was very different in this respect. It began as a conservative national movement to protect a slave society. Its nationalism never had the radical reformist potential of England's or the Union's. Secession was, in Arno Mayer's and James M. McPherson's phrase, a "preemptive counterrevolution." From the start, the Confederacy's organizers tried to embrace all or nearly all of white society within its borders. The fire eaters got things going, but it took moderates (ex-unionists) to define and achieve truly national objectives. In a word, the Confederacy was more of a nation than the Thirteen States at any point before 1787—and well beyond. And it took shape after 1848 when nationalism as a social force was also becoming far more conservative in Europe as well.[70]

V

Other compelling reasons indicate that Confederates were more serious about their nation than most settlers about their cause in 1775. Confederates were far more generous in committing their resources to the war, and they fought much harder than the men of 1775.

The Confederate economy of 1861 was closer in structure to America's in 1775 than the Union economy of 1861 was to either. In other words, if one may compare the Union with the Confederacy, one should also be permitted to compare the Confederacy with the United Colonies. The colonies could not have survived even through 1776 without French help (especially gunpowder), and they later received Spanish and Dutch assistance as well. The Confederates took dramatic charge of their largely unintegrated economy, centralized it, and in a remarkably short period of time, made it almost self-sufficient in the production of military material. Ironically, this agricultural cornucopia proved far less successful in providing food and shoes for its armies and civilians. To be sure, printers' type was soon so scarce that 86 percent of Virginia's newspapers and 88 percent of Mississippi's ceased publication by the end of 1862. Confederate artillery fuses were poor, and the society that sent the first ironclad into battle could not even build a good marine engine, but the C.S.A. did invent a usable submarine and also became the first state to sink an enemy warship (the gunboat *Cairo*) through an electronically detonated mine. After every allowance is made for what the Confederates could not do, the amazing thing remains how much they did accomplish. Their performance shames that of 1775, and it has awed Luraghi's Marxist sensibilities. Nothing so close to state socialism had yet appeared anywhere else in the world, he insists. Even a moderate, Emory Thomas, generally agrees. Perhaps because the colonists of 1775 were far more ideological than the Confederates, they never even considered the massive challenge to traditional property rights that some of the Confederate expedients involved. With interesting exceptions, most Confederates were far more serious about their national identity than about states' rights, particularly if 1776 provides the standard. With equally fascinating exceptions, most men of the Revolution had difficulty envisioning liberty except in an intensely localist context.[71]

On a purely military plane, we can learn much by comparing three armies: Washington's, the Union's, and the Confederacy's. The Confederates mustered the highest percentage of their eligible population, compelled them to serve longer terms, and took by far the heaviest proportional losses. Their desertion rate probably fell between Washington's (the highest) and the Union's (the lowest), with most of it coming in the final months of the war.

The Confederacy mustered over 850,000 men out of a potential 1.1 to 1.2 million. This ratio of about 80 percent approaches twentieth-century standards of complete mobilization. That is, it probably included nearly everybody but the halt, the lame and the blind. It did *not* include slaves, of course, and if they are factored into the equation, the percentage of the total population placed under arms drops to about fifty, or about the same as the Union's. We still lack adequate statistics on military service in the Revolutionary War. Participation may well have matched Civil War standards, but far more of it was on a short-term basis with the militia.[72]

About 260,000 Confederates were killed in the Civil War (nearly a third of the men who served), and roughly 240,000 were wounded. Total dead and wounded soldiers would be something less than 500,000 because some men were wounded more than once, and some of the dead had earlier been wounded. Yet it seems likely that over half of those mustered suffered one fate or the other, a rate of carnage comparable to what France experienced in World War I. The social implications of this slaughter remain staggering, but one small fact at least gives us a hint. In Mississippi a third of the white males of military age were killed or maimed during the war. During the year after Appomattox, 20 percent of the state budget went for artificial limbs for crippled veterans.[73]

The Union, by contrast, lost 360,000 killed out of 2.1 million who served, or about one out of six. In the Revolution, 25,000 to 30,000 died out of, at a guess, 250,000, but many of the dead were captured privateers—men who languished in British prisons and ought to be counted against a different population base. Even if we fail to do so, the Revolution's death rate comes in third at somewhere between one out of eight and one out of ten. Nevertheless, this toll exceeds that in any other American war since 1775 except the Civil War.[74]

The Confederates were the first to resort to general conscription and eventually raised 20 percent of their soldiers through this device. The Union quickly followed but used conscription mostly to encourage volunteering. Only about 2.2 percent of the boys in blue were actual conscripts, although another 3.5 percent of those who served were substitutes hired by drafted men. The Revolution never attempted anything of the kind as a uniform policy, although local communities did meet some of their quotas through a draft. Statistics on desertion are even less reliable than for casualties, but something over a quarter of those who served during the Revolution ended up elsewhere without permission. Over 40 percent of the New Jersey Line deserted in 1777, 21 percent in 1778, and then 10 percent in each of the next two years. About two-thirds of all deserters left their units within six months of joining them. In short, only as the Continental Army became a very small body did it achieve stability of personnel. Its defection rate in the early years of the Revolution exceeded the Confederacy's in all but its terminal moments. The Confederate desertion figure was around 13 percent overall and no higher than the Union's until quite late in the war. In North Carolina where the desertion problem became acute, the typical soldier served nearly two years before he finally quit. The Union Army—easily the best fed and supplied force of the three—had the fewest desertions, about 9.6 percent.[75]

As a final military comparison, the Confederates were far more successful than Washington in creating a truly national army and were much more eager to attack than either of the other two armies. Offensive tactics require good morale to succeed, and into 1863 Confederate armies usually did attack their enemies, even though they knew they were on the strategic defensive. Several historians now argue that the Confederacy bled itself to death in a way that the Union or Continental Army never would have. In fact, Bunker Hill so entranced the Revolutionaries that many of them spent the rest of the war looking for hills to defend against stupid British frontal attacks that never again happened, at least not before the Battle of New Orleans in the next war.[76]

Besides economic and military mobilization, popular stereotypes provide another way of contrasting the Revolution with the Civil War. What did the antagonists say about one another in each contest? In the struggle leading to independence, the colonists insisted to the end that they were British who sought only the rights of Englishmen. Britain demanded that they remain British, whatever the precise state of their rights. They differed, obviously, over what it meant to be British.

In America by 1860, *both* northern and southern spokesmen agreed that southerners had become a separate people. They also believed that the two civilizations had evolved into distinctive character types. Planters were brave, reckless, generous, lazy, and sensitive about honor. Yankees were calculating, industrious, morbid, feminized, sickly, and greedy, better at bureaucratic manipulation than at actual command. Could northern patriotism be trusted? Would Yankees die for a cause? Precisely because each side found much truth in these images, they were powerful enough to influence the course of events, including secession and the conduct of the war. "Free Society!" raged one Georgian in the late 1850s. "We sicken at the name. What is it but a conglomeration of greasy mechanics, filthy operatives, small-fisted farmers, and moon-struck theorists . . . hardly fit for association with a southern gentleman's body servant."[77] Contempt so total and widespread could persuade most secessionists that the Confederacy could be established peacefully, that the North would not fight.

Even when the war came and rapidly assumed monstrous dimensions, the stereotype continued to influence behavior. Robert E. Lee humiliated the Army of the Potomac so often on southern soil that the officer corps of the Northeast became thoroughly intimidated for the rest of the conflict. They commanded much larger numbers of healthier and far better supplied troops, but they did not believe that they could defeat the Army of Northern Virginia. Fortunately for the Union, these images carried far less weight among Midwesterners. Under U. S. Grant, the Union Army of the Tennessee began to win battles in early 1862, often without a significant edge in manpower, and it never lost a major engagement throughout the war. The story of Union victory is very much a chronicle of the triumph of this army through 1863 and of the transfer of its leadership to the Atlanta and Virginia theaters in 1864.[78]

In short, the stereotypes did matter. And virtually everyone also agreed on what sustained these differences—slavery. As the Charleston *Mercury* put it in 1858, "on the subject of slavery the North is utterly antagonistic to the South. The South and the North, on this subject, are not only two

Peoples, but they are rival, hostile Peoples."[79] Slavery made planter life and values possible. Its absence committed the North to all of the imperatives of a free-labor society.

VI

In some respects North and South did resemble one another more than the colonies had ever resembled Britain. The question of aristocracy provides such a dividing line. In the eighteenth and nineteenth centuries, Britain remained a society of landed rentiers in a way that no North American community had ever been. On a comparative scale, the South was more aristocratic than the North, even if we accept James Oakes' evidence—which I find persuasive—that in the Jacksonian South, the political center of gravity shifted overwhelmingly toward the small slaveholder instead of the planter. The secession crisis marked a shift in the other direction that had probably started in the 1850s, but Oakes insists that Genovese's concept of planter hegemony simply cannot explain most of what was happening in southern politics after about 1820. Ironically, Union victory in the Civil War may have given the old planter class greater political power within the South by 1900 than it had exercised at any time since the eighteenth century.[80]

In like manner, David Donald has shown a remarkable structural similarity in the way that North and South fought the Civil War. He traces parallel shifts from reliance on volunteers to use of conscripts, and he finds similar patterns in the way that each side financed the war. Nothing remotely comparable happened during the American Revolution. The Continental Army did become more professional over time, and the British learned to place greater reliance upon loyalists. But these changes mark shifts in opposite directions even if the net result was a greater degree of similarity. Congress did not even try to employ orthodox methods of finance until Robert Morris became superintendent of finance in 1781. Despite his efforts, a recognizably British system did not take hold until the triumph of Alexander Hamilton in 1789–91, long after the war.[81]

Clearly the Union and Confederacy did possess broad social and cultural similarities that neither shared with Britain in 1861 or 1775. The Union soldiers who believed without any known exceptions that they were invading a foreign country as they moved south were culturally quite similar to the Confederate enemies they encountered—far more so than American militiamen, or even Continentals, resembled redcoats in the 1770s.[82] Just as clearly, each region shared some features with Britain more than with each other. Southern honor and northern free labor both had major British counterparts.[83] Yet none of these comparisons can resolve the ultimate problem, that of loyalties. Nations are, as Benedict Anderson reminds us, "imagined communities." People who have never met one another readily agree to share a common identity through membership in the same "nation."[84] In measurable social characteristics, Ontario has always resembled the United States more than Britain, but its residents prefer to retain their allegiance to the British crown. Canadians divide on much else, but they have always agreed in rejecting political subordination to or union with the United States. So long as the issue remains one of loyalties, it seems just as clear to this historian that the Confederate South rejected the Union much more decisively than North Americans repudiated the crown in 1776.

I have never had time to research the question, but I doubt that the Confederacy has a literature of mutual execration—Georgians denouncing Alabamians, and that sort of thing—comparable in intensity to what can be found everywhere in late eighteenth-century North America. North Carolina endured a number of humiliations when the Confederate government passed over its officers for promotion above colonel, Virginia newspapers failed to give due credit to North Carolina units after major battles, and contemporaries (and subsequent historians) consistently exaggerated the desertion rate among its soldiers.[85] I also doubt that patriots very often expressed the kind of pure hatred for Britain that Confederates felt for northerners and Abraham Lincoln's Union.

VII

Before drawing a few conclusions, let me stress that, emotionally and intellectually, I am not in any way pro-Confederate. I grew up so far north that my schoolmates and I could not even understand Lee's dilemma of 1861, whether to honor his oath as a soldier or his loyalty to his state. To us, it was no issue. He made the wrong choice.

I got into this question as a colonial historian who started to read about the Civil War, and found mostly enigmas and paradoxes, especially

if anybody would try to apply to 1775 the arguments that seemed persuasive to others about the events of 1861. Why then did the Confederates fail
and the patriots succeed if the Confederate sense of national identity and
will to fight were a great deal stronger than the comparable attributes of
the Revolutionaries? Two differences can explain much. The Confederacy
never won foreign recognition, much less intervention. The United
Colonies did, and without that assistance they would have lost the war.
Similarly, the Union's logistical problems in attacking the Confederacy
were less severe than the difficulties faced by Britain in waging war across
three thousand miles of ocean. The effort to conquer the Confederacy
placed fewer internal strains on northern society than on southern. For
that reason Union nationalism could triumph over its Confederate rival
even though, in objective terms, it was probably a weaker force during the
years of actual warfare. With far more resources to draw upon, it never
had to endure the Confederacy's astronomical losses. Had it faced such a
crisis, it probably would have lost the war.

In a word, conventional military and diplomatic historians have
done fine work in explaining why these two armed conflicts turned
out as they did. The results are not mysteries. They become mysterious
only if we endow the American Revolutionaries with a sense of national
commitment that they had never had time to develop, or if we deprive
the Confederacy of the passion that produced the most brutal war in
the world between Napoleon and the Great War of 1914, apart from the
much smaller Paraguayan conflict.

Conventional histories ought to tell us something more, for if their narratives are correct, the most important variable that explains the different
results of the Revolution and the Civil War is war itself. Who won really
does matter. Had the Confederacy triumphed, the world today would be
much worse off, but we would have no doubts about the depth of white
southern nationalism. War, Clemenceau once remarked, is too serious a
business to be run by generals. Its consequences are also too important
to be ignored by historians. Union victory crushed Confederate nationalism, but then as the Nazis should have taught us, nationalism is by no
means the highest value, even if it is a powerful force that can be either
highly creative or immensely destructive.

The war also destroyed slavery where it was demographically more viable than anywhere else in the world. A Confederate victory would have

meant the survival of slavery into the twentieth century. Perhaps one should inject some nuance here, for the way in which slavery survived would have depended heavily on when the Confederacy won. A victory in 1863, when virtually the whole slave system was still intact, would have been rather different from one in late 1864 (if, for example, the Democrats had won the Union elections), after Union armies had liberated hundreds of thousands of blacks over vast portions of the South. A Confederacy rebuilt on re-enslavement would have had a markedly different tone from one that could simply attempt to perpetuate the Old South. During the Revolution British armies freed something over 10 percent of all slaves in the southern states and almost eliminated the institution in Georgia, but it came back strong anyway.[86] Union armies freed perhaps twice that proportion. Had they reached the point of no return in some parts of the South, even if the Confederacy had somehow won the war? In the absence of a reopened African slave trade, quite possibly, but we cannot be sure. Nevertheless, the main point remains. A Confederate victory would have been a triumph for slavery in most of the South and a disaster for blacks.

Other than Genovese, most southern historians have denied that slavery was an adequate basis for a southern national identity. They prefer to underscore the common racism of all white Americans, North and South.[87] Today no one would deny that they have hit upon a profound truth. And yet it remains incontestable that white southern racists, because many of them also held slaves, proclaimed their independence and fought a terrible war against white northern racists—and eventually 180,000 armed blacks. They almost succeeded. Their remarkable exertions produced the Confederacy's astonishing war effort, but they also antagonized class tensions within the Confederacy, particularly over the draft, and could not hold the loyalty of the slave population when a Union army got close enough to offer a good chance of emancipation. Jefferson Davis's effort to continue the fighting by emancipating and mobilizing slaves in 1865 did nothing to revitalize morale and may even have deflated it further. "Mother I did not volunteer my services to fight for A free negroes country but to fight for A free white mans free country," one North Carolina soldier grumbled, "& I do not think I love my country well enough to fight with black soldiers." A confederate nation without slavery made no ideological sense and attracted few prophets. The armies surrendered instead.[88]

We gain little by taking these truths apart, by trying to use one to bury the other. Rather, we should try to see them as a cumulative whole. The War for Confederate Independence was also a war to perpetuate slavery in the most viable and dynamic slave society in modern history. In the North, the War for the Union became by 1863 a war to destroy slavery, but it was never at any time a war on behalf of black Americans.

We have a tragic dialectic at work here, played out through various stages from 1830 to 1880. The early Jackson years, 1830–33, defined most of the alternatives for the next half-century. John Quincy Adams, Joseph Storey, Daniel Webster, Edward Livingston and Andrew Jackson defined for the first time a coherent concept of a perpetual union.[89] Simultaneously, the idea of a southern nation was born among South Carolina nullifiers.[90] Fused together in the flames of Charles Grandison Finney's revivals, a confident, reforming middle class also took shape in the burned-over district of New York.[91] And an aggressive and outraged abolitionist movement appeared simultaneously in both the district and the Boston area.[92] The interaction of these elements would define American history for the next two generations.

The dialectical process involves liberty and union—"now and forever, one and inseparable," as Webster insisted in his reply to Robert Hayne in 1830.[93] He reaffirmed the formula to sustain the Compromise of 1850, but it did not work. In 1860–61, the Confederates destroyed the Union to save slavery. The North then destroyed slavery and the Confederacy to save the Union. How, then, was reconciliation possible after the intense emotional antagonisms of the war and Reconstruction? Without slavery, the common racism of northern and southern whites could finally assert itself. "Union, white liberty, and racism, now and forever, one and inseparable" became the banner behind which the United States faced the world from the 1890s until after World War II. It was a durable synthesis too, until the Nazis and the deep moral commitment of such American blacks as Martin Luther King, Jr., finally shamed us out of it, North and South.

Notes

1. See J. M. Bumsted, "'Things in the Womb of Time': Ideas of American Independence, 1633 to 1763," *William and Mary Quarterly*, 3rd ser., 31 (1974), 533–64. Bumsted's sources indicate that he is describing a debate about America among Europeans, including British travellers and placemen

in the colonies, with only an occasional contribution from a settler. Colonists did not debate independence until the revolutionary crisis. The British often did.

2. Paul D. Escott, *After Secession: Jefferson Davis and the Failure of Confederate Nationalism* (Baton Rouge, 1978); "The Address of the People of South Carolina, Assembled in Convention, to the People of the Slaveholding States of the United States," in John Amasa May and Joan Reynolds Faunt, eds., *South Carolina Secedes* (Columbia, SC, 1960), 82–92, esp. 88, 91.

3. Dwight Lowell Dumond, ed., *Southern Editorials on Secession* (Washington, 1931), 494, 507, 510.

4. Eric Foner, *Free Soil, Free Labor, Free Men: The Ideology of the Republican Party before the Civil War* (New York, 1970), Chp. 2.

5. Reid Mitchell, *Civil War Soldiers* (New York, 1988), Chp. 4. Professor Mitchell informs me that of the hundreds of soldiers' journals and correspondence that he has read, he has never encountered an exception to this statement.

6. John Dickinson, *Letters from a Farmer in Pennsylvania* (1767–68), in Forrest McDonald, ed., *Empire and Nation* (Englewood Cliffs, NJ, 1962), 18.

7. Julian Boyd *et al.*, eds., *The Papers of Thomas Jefferson* (Princeton, 1950-), I, 427.

8. Dumond, ed., *Southern Editorials on Secession*, 515.

9. Herman V. Ames, ed., *State Documents on Federal Relations: The States and the United States* (Orig. edn., 1900–06; reprint, New York, 1970), 318.

10. Allen D. Candler, ed., *The Confederate Records of the State of Georgia, Compiled and Published under Authority of the Legislature* (Atlanta, 1909–11), I, 616.

11. Dumond, ed., *Southern Editorials on Secession*, 505.

12. *Ibid.*, 509.

13. The essay originally appeared in *American Historical Review*, 67 (1961–62), 924–50. For a fuller version, see David M. Potter, *The South and the Sectional Conflict* (Baton Rouge, 1968), 34–83.

14. David Herbert Donald, *Liberty and Union: The Crisis of Popular Government, 1830–1890* (Boston, 1978); C. Vann Woodward, *The Burden of Southern History* (Baton Rouge, 1960), Chps. 1, 8; John McCardell, *The Idea of a Southern Nation: Southern Nationalists and Southern Nationalism, 1830–1860* (New York, 1979); Escott, *After Secession*; Kenneth M. Stampp, "The Southern Road to Appomattox," in his *The Imperiled Union: Essays on the Background of the Civil War* (New York, 1980), 246–96; James Oakes, *The Ruling Race: A History of American Slaveholders* (New York, 1982).

15. Potter, *The South and the Sectional Conflict*, 76–78. For Potter's detailed narrative of the onset of the Civil War, see his *The Impending Crisis, 1848–1861* (New York, 1976).

16. Thomas L. Connelly, *The Marble Man: Robert L. Lee and His Image in American Society* (Baton Rouge, 1977).

17. James M. McPherson, *Ordeal by Fire: The Civil War and Reconstruction* (New York, 1982), 543–45, 564–67.

18. Emory M. Thomas, *The Confederate Nation, 1861–1865* (New York, 1979), 58, 62–65, 307–22; Drew Gilpin Faust, *The Creation of Confederate Nationalism* (Baton Rouge, 1988), 8–13.

19. Gerald Newman, *The Rise of English Nationalism: A Cultural History, 1740–1830* (New York, 1987). See also, Kathleen Wilson, "Empire, Trade and Popular Politics in Mid-Hanoverian Britain: The Case of Admiral Vernon," *Past and Present*, 121 (November 1988), 74–109; Linda Colley, "The Apotheosis of George III: Loyalty, Royalty and the British Nation 1760–1820," *Past and Present*, 102 (February 1984), 94–129; and Colley, "Whose Nation? Class and National Consciousness in Britain 1750–1830," *Past and Present*, 113 (November 1986), 97–116. For the religious origins of England's earlier sense of itself as a distinct people, see William Haller, *The Elect Nation: The Meaning and Relevance of Foxe's Book of Martyrs* (New York, 1963). For comparable efforts to define a Scottish identity as far back as the sixteenth century but very much within a broader British context, see Arthur H. Williamson, *Scottish National Consciousness in the Age of James VI* (Edinburgh, 1979). I owe to Ned Landsman the suggestion about ways in which Scottish-British nationalism in the age of George III differed from English nationalism as described by Newman.

20. J. H. Hexter, " 'Factors in Modern History,' " in his *Reappraisals in History: New Views on History and Society in Modern History* (Evanston, 1961), 26–44, stresses the dynastic over the national. Sir Lewis Namier, "Nationality and Liberty," in his *Vanished Supremacies: Essays on European History, 1812–1918* (New York, 1963), 31–53, argues that dynasticism and national identity strongly reinforced one another in Britain.

21. Jacob E. Cooke, ed., *The Federalist* (Middletown, CT, 1961), 594.

22. Max Farrand, ed., *The Records of the Federal Convention of 1787*, rev. edn. (New Haven, 1937), I, 20–23, 242–45, and passim.

23. Benjamin Franklin, *Observations concerning the Increase of Mankind* (1755), in Leonard W. Labaree et al., eds., *The Papers of Benjamin Franklin* (New Haven, 1959-), IV, 227–34; Sam Briggs, ed., *The Essays, Humor, and Poems of Nathaniel Ames, Father and Son . . .* (Cleveland, 1891), esp. 284–86, 308–11, 313, 324–25.

24. Benjamin H. Newcomb, *Franklin and Galloway: A Political Partnership* (New Haven, 1972); Bernard Bailyn, *The Ordeal of Thomas Hutchinson* (Cambridge, MA, 1974); Robert J. Taylor, *Western Massachusetts in the Revolution* (Providence, 1954), Chp. 5; Peter S. Onuf, *The Origins of the Federal Republic: Jurisdictional Controversies in the United States, 1775–1787* (Philadelphia, 1983), esp. Chps. 5–6.

25. David H. Donald, "Died of Democracy," in Donald, ed., *Why the North Won the Civil War* (Baton Rouge, 1960), 77–90; Georgia Lee Tatum, *Disloyalty in the Confederacy* (1934; reprint, New York, 1970); H. James Henderson, *Party Politics in the Continental Congress* (New York, 1974),

Chps. 10–12; Jack N. Rakove, *The Beginnings of National Politics: An Interpretive History of the Continental Congress* (New York, 1979), Chps. 11–13; Paul H. Smith, "The American Loyalists: Notes on their Organization and Numerical Strength," *William and Mary Quarterly*, 3rd ser., 25 (1968), 259–77. For the strength of the Continental Line by early 1781, see Charles H. Lesser, ed., *The Sinews of Independence: Monthly Strength Reports of the Continental Army* (Chicago, 1976), xxxi. In the eight months prior to Yorktown, the totals varied from 4,600 to 8,700, not counting perhaps another two or three thousand in the southern department. Although Smith does not give month-by-month accounts of loyalist strength, his data indicate that the total number under arms in 1781 must have been far greater than Continental strength at the same time.

26. Eugene D. Genovese, *The Political Economy of Slavery: Studies in the Economy and Society of the Slave South* (New York, 1965); Genovese, *The World the Slaveholders Made: Two Essays in Interpretation* (New York, 1969); and Genovese, *Roll, Jordan, Roll: The World the Slaves Made* (New York, 1974).

27. Raimondo Luraghi, *The Rise and Fall of the Plantation South* (New York, 1978).

28. Escott, *After Secession*, passim.

29. Thomas, *The Confederate Nation*, passim.

30. Richard E. Beringer, Herman Hattaway, Archer Jones, and William N. Still, Jr., *The Elements of Confederate Defeat: Nationalism, War Aims, and Religion* (Athens, GA, 1988), Chp. 15, esp. pp. 200–05. This book is an abridged version of the same authors' *Why the South Lost the Civil War* (Athens, GA, 1986), but the corresponding section of the longer work, pp. 439–42, does not contain the same explicit comparisons. See also Barrie Pitt, *1918: The Last Act* (London, 1962), for the military situation during the final year of World War I.

31. Stampp, "The Southern Road to Appomattox," in his *The Imperiled Union*, 269.

32. McCardell, *The Idea of a Southern Nation*, esp. Chp. 3.

33. V. P. Bynack, "Noah Webster's Linguistic Thought and the Idea of an American National Culture," *Journal of the History of Ideas*, 45 (1984), 99–114; Noah Webster, *On Being American: Selected Writings, 1783–1828*, ed. Homer D. Babbidge (New York, 1967), passim, esp. pp. 168–74.

34. Benedict Anderson, *Imagined Communities: Reflections on the Origin and Spread of Nationalism* (London, 1983), Chp. 4.

35. For a fuller analysis of the complex literature on this question, see John M. Murrin, "No Awakening, No Revolution? More Counterfactual Speculations," *Reviews in American History*, 11 (1983), 161–71.

36. For the most recent analysis of this question, see C. C. Goen, *Broken Churches, Broken Nation: Denominational Schisms and the Coming of the Civil War* (Macon, GA, 1985), esp. Chp. 4.

37. Bernard Bailyn, *The Ideological Origins of the American Revolution* (Cambridge, MA, 1967); Bailyn, *The Origins of American Politics* (New York, 1968); John M. Murrin, "Political Development," in Jack P. Greene and J. R. Pole, eds., *Colonial British America: Essays in the New History of the Early Modern Era* (Baltimore, 1984), 408–56; Gordon S. Wood, *The Creation of the American Republic, 1776–1787* (Chapel Hill, 1969); Charles Royster, "Founding a Nation in Blood: Military Conflict and American National Identity," in Ronald Hoffman and Peter J. Albert, eds., *Arms and Independence: The Military Character of the American Revolution* (Charlottesville, 1984), 25–49; George B. Forgie, *Patricide in the House Divided: A Psychological Interpretation of Lincoln and His Age* (New York, 1979). Forgie argues that the awesome legacy of the Founding Fathers became almost as heavy a burden to the antebellum generation as it was an asset.

38. For the Articles of Confederation, see Jack P. Greene, ed., *Colonies to Nation, 1763–1789: A Documentary History of the American Revolution* (New York, 1975), 428. For the Confederate Constitution, see Thomas, *The Confederate Nation*, p. 307. On the weakness of American national identity in the 1780s and the widespread fear of disunion, see Eugene R. Sheridan and John M. Murrin, eds., *Letters of Charles Thomson to Hannah Thomson, June to October 1783* (Princeton, 1983), 19, 29–30, 66–67, 73, 83, 86, 91–92; Edmund C. Burnett, ed., *Letters of Members of the Continental Congress* (Washington, D.C., 1921–36), VIII, 247–48, 282, 415–16, 533; Boston's *Independent Chronicle*, Feb. 15, 1787 (the first public call for disunion and separate confederacies); John M. Murrin, "A Roof Without Walls: The Dilemma of American National Identity," in Richard Beeman, Stephen Botein, and Edward C. Carter II, eds., *Beyond Confederation: Origins of the Constitution and American National Identity* (Chapel Hill, 1987), 333–48; and Joseph M. Torsella, "American National Identity, 1750–1790: Samples from the Popular Press," *Pennsylvania Magazine of History and Biography*, 92 (1988), 167–87. For the origins of Confederate national identity, see McCardell, *The Idea of a Southern Nation* and Faust, *Confederate Nationalism*.

39. Among an enormous literature, see especially T. H. Breen, "An Empire of Goods: The Anglicization of Colonial America, 1690–1776," *Journal of British Studies*, 25 (1986), 467–99; James A. Henretta and Gregory H. Nobles, *Evolution and Revolution: American Society, 1600–1820* (Lexington, MA, 1987), Chp. 3; John J. McCusker and Russell R. Menard, *The Economy of British America, 1607–1789* (Chapel Hill, 1985), esp. Chps. 3, 4, and 17; and Bernard Bailyn and Barbara DeWolfe, *Voyagers to the West: A Passage in the Peopling of America on the Eve of the Revolution* (New York, 1986), Chp. 2.

40. The two sources are John Adams to Nathan Webb, Oct. 12, 1755, in Charles Francis Adams, ed., *The Works of John Adams* (Boston, 1850–56), I, 23; and Charles Carroll of Carrollton to Charles Carroll, Sr., Nov. 12, 1763, *Maryland Historical Magazine*, 12 (1917), 21. Carroll wrote as he finished his education in Europe, where the subject of eventual American independence

was a commonplace topic. It was not among the colonists themselves. Even the Adams source is ambiguous. He could mean the transfer of imperial government from England to America in about a century without disrupting Anglo-American union. Cf. Bernhard Knollenberg, *Origin of the American Revolution, 1759–1766* (New York, 1960), 7–8.

41. Benjamin Franklin, *The Interest of Great Britain Considered, with Regard to Her Colonies, and the Acquisition of Canada and Guadeloupe* (1760), in Labaree et al., eds., *Papers of Benjamin Franklin*, IX, esp. 90–91; Briggs, ed., *The Essays, Humour, and Poems of Nathaniel Ames, Father and Son*, passim; Nathan O. Hatch, "The Origins of Civil Millennialism in America: New England Clergymen, War with France, and the Revolution," *William and Mary Quarterly*, 3rd ser., 31 (1974), 407–30. For strong general studies of this theme, see Max Savelle, "Nationalism and Other Loyalties in the American Revolution," *American Historical Review*, 67 (1961–62), 901–23; Paul A. Varg, "The Advent of Nationalism, 1758–1776," *American Quarterly*, 16 (1964), 169–81; and Judith A. Wilson, "'My Country is my Colony': A Study in Anglo-American Patriotism, 1739–1760," *The Historian*, 30 (1967–68), 333–49.

42. Richard L. Merritt, *Symbols of American Community, 1735–1775* (New Haven, 1966), 62, 66, 76, 120, 132, 143, 151, 153.

43. Ebenezer Cook, *The Sot-weed Factor* (London, 1708), in Kenneth Silverman, ed., *Literature in America: The Founding of a Nation* (New York, 1971), 270–83; Timothy H. Breen, "Of Time and Nature: A Study of Persistent Values in Colonial Virginia," in his *Puritans and Adventurers: Change and Persistence in Early America* (New York, 1980), 164–96.

44. Carl Bridenbaugh, *The Spirit of '76: The Growth of American Patriotism before Independence, 1607–1776* (New York, 1975), esp. 33, 37, 117.

45. John Winthrop, *The History of New England from 1630 to 1649*, ed. James Savage, new edn. (Boston, 1853), II, 198–99.

46. Charles Chauncy, *A Letter to a Friend Giving a Concise but Just Account . . . of the Ohio-Defeat* (Boston, 1755), 12; Chauncy, *A Second Letter to a Friend: Giving a More Particular Narrative of the Defeat of the French Army at Lake-George* (Boston, 1755), 15–16.

47. "Journal of Josiah Quincy, Junior, 1773," Massachusetts Historical Society, *Proceedings*, 49 (1915–16), 454–55, 463, 466–68, 470, 477, 481.

48. Abigail to John Adams, Mar. 31, 1776; John to Abigail Adams, Apr. 14, 1776, in Lyman H. Butterfield et al., eds., *Adams Family Correspondence* (Cambridge, MA, 1963–), I, 369, 381.

49. Wilcomb E. Washburn, "Governor Berkeley and King Philip's War," *New England Quarterly*, 30 (1957), 363–77.

50. William Byrd II to John Perceval, Earl of Egmont, July 12, 1736, in Marion Tinling, ed., *The Correspondence of the Three William Byrds of Westover, Virginia, 1684–1776* (Charlottesville, 1977), II, 487.

51. Carl Bridenbaugh, ed., *Gentleman's Progress: The Itinerarium of Dr. Alexander Hamilton, 1744* (Chapel Hill, 1948), 145–46. For his generally

favorable assessment of New Englanders and northerners generally, see
p. 199.

52. Gerard G. Beekman to William Samuel Johnson, Dec. 2, 1754; Beekman to
David and William Ross, Jan. 24, 1768, in Philip L. White, ed., *The Beekman
Mercantile Papers, 1740–1799* (New York, 1956), I, 237, 516.

53. Quoted in Max M. Mintz, *Gouverneur Morris and the American Revolution*
(Norman, OK, 1970), 15.

54. Lyman H. Butterfield et al., eds., *Diary and Autobiography of John Adams*
(Cambridge, MA, 1961), II, 107. Adams reciprocated the distaste: "With
all the Opulence and Splendor of this City [New York], there is very little
good breeding to be found. We have been treated with an assiduous Respect.
But I have not seen one real Gentleman, one well bred Man since I came to
Town." Ibid., 109.

55. James Chalmers, *Plain Truth; Containing Remarks on a Late Pamphlet,
Entitled Common Sense* (1776), in Merrill Jensen, ed., *Tracts of the American
Revolution, 1763–1776* (Indianapolis, 1967), 467.

56. Edward Rutledge to John Jay, June 29, 1776, in Paul H. Smith et al., eds.,
Letters of Delegates to Congress, 1774–1789 (Washington, 1976-), IV, 388.

57. George Washington to Richard Henry Lee, Aug. 29, 1775, in John
C. Fitzpatrick, ed., *The Writings of George Washington* (Washington, D.C.,
1931–44), III, 450–51.

58. "Some Extracts from the Papers of General Persifor Frazer," *Pennsylvania
Magazine of History and Biography*, 31 (1907), 129–44 at 135.

59. Philip Schuyler to Governeur Morris, Sept. 7, 1777, in Henry Steele
Commager and Richard B. Morris, eds., *The Spirit of 'Seventy-Six: The Story of
the American Revolution as Told by Participants* (Indianapolis, 1958), I, 569.

60. William Livingston to William Hooper, Aug. 29, 1776, in Carl E. Prince
et al., eds., *The Papers of William Livingston* (Trenton and New Brunswick,
1979–88), I, 128–29.

61. On the creation of an American past in this period, see Wesley Frank
Craven, *The Legend of the Founding Fathers* (Ithaca, 1956); Arthur
H. Shaffer, *The Politics of History: Writing the History of the American
Revolution, 1783–1815* (Chicago, 1975); and Lester H. Cohen, *The
Revolutionary Histories: Contemporary Narratives of the American Revolution*
(Ithaca, 1980).

62. John R. Alden, *The First South* (Baton Rouge, 1961).

63. McCardell, *Idea of a Southern Nation*, 38–48; William W. Freehling, *Prelude
to Civil War: The Nullification Controversy in South Carolina, 1816–1836*
(New York, 1966), esp. Chps. 9–10.

64. Dumas Malone, *The Public Life of Thomas Cooper, 1783–1839* (New
Haven, 1926).

65. For biographical information, see McCardell, *The Idea of a Southern Nation*,
60–71, 253–54, 280–84, 119–27. Hammond differed from the others in one
major respect. By 1860 he doubted that the South had the unity or resolve
to defeat the North and therefore supported secession only with great

reluctance. See Lawrence T. McDonnell, "Struggle against Suicide: James Henry Hammond and the Secession of South Carolina," *Southern Studies*, 22 (1983), 109–37.

66. Ibid., 107–13, 85–90, and 161–64.

67. Thomas, *The Confederate Nation*, Chp. 3, esp. pp. 60–61.

68. Namier, "Nationality and Liberty," stresses the role of outsiders in establishing the national identity of Italy and Germany. John Lynch, *The Spanish American Revolutions, 1808–1826* (New York, 1973), xi–xxi, contains capsule biographies.

69. Roger H. Brown, *The Republic in Peril: 1812* (New York, 1964); Lawrence S. Kaplan, *Jefferson and France* (New Haven, 1967); Donald R. Hickey, *The War of 1812* (Urbana, 1989).

70. James M. McPherson, *The Battle Cry of Freedom: The Civil War Era* (New York, 1988), Chp. 8, esp. p. 245.

71. Emory M. Thomas, *The Confederacy as a Revolutionary Experience* (Englewood Cliffs, 1971), esp. Chp. 5; Luraghi, *Rise and Fall of the Plantation South*, Chps. 8–11; Faust, *Confederate Nationalism*, 17; McPherson, *Battle Cry of Freedom*, 314–15; Jackson Turner Main, *The Sovereign States, 1775–1783* (New York, 1973); Main, *Political Parties before the Constitution* (Chapel Hill, 1973).

72. McPherson, *Battle Cry of Freedom*, 306–07n; Allan Kulikoff, "The Political Economy of Revolutionary War Service in Virginia," in his *The Agrarian Origins of American Capitalism* (Charlottesville, 1992), 152–80, is the best discussion of cultural constraints upon recruitment during the Revolution. For the significance of the militia in the overall military struggle, see John Shy, *A People Numerous and Armed: Reflections on the Military Struggle for American Independence* (New York, 1976), Chps. 6–9.

73. McPherson, *Battle Cry of Freedom*, 854; Thomas L. Connelly and Barbara L. Bellows, *God and General Longstreet: The Lost Cause and the Southern Mind* (Baton Rouge, 1982), 8.

74. McPherson, *Battle Cry of Freedom*, 854; Howard H. Peckham, ed., *The Toll of Independence: Engagements and Battle Casualties of the American Revolution* (Chicago, 1974), esp. 130–34.

75. James M. McPherson, *Ordeal by Fire: The Civil War and Reconstruction* (New York, 1982), 182–83, 468; McPherson, *Battle Cry of Freedom*, 601 gives a lower total for Union conscription, which I have accepted. See also Richard Reid, "A Test Case of the 'Crying Evil': Desertion among North Carolina Troops during the Civil War," *North Carolina Historical Review*, 58 (1981), 234–62, esp. 246. On desertion during the Revolution, see James Kirby Martin and Mark Edward Lender, *A Respectable Army: The Military Origins of the Republic, 1763–1789* (Arlington Heights, IL, 1982), 130–32. For the dramatic decline in the size of the Continental Army from over 30,000 men in the summers of 1777 and 1778 to 10,000 or fewer in 1780–81, see Charles H. Lessor, ed., *The Sinews of Independence: Monthly Strength Reports of the Continental Army* (Chicago, 1976), xxx.

76. Grady McWhiney and Perry D. Jamieson, *Attack and Die: Civil War Military Tactics and the Southern Heritage* (University, AL, 1982); Thomas J. Fleming, *1776: Year of Illusions* (New York, 1975), nicely develops the theme of what he calls "Bunker Hillism."

77. James M. McPherson, "Antebellum Southern Exceptionalism: A New Look at an Old Question," *Civil War History*, 29 (1983), 230–44. The quotation is on p. 233. The classic study of regional stereotypes is William R. Taylor, *Cavalier and Yankee: The Old South and American National Character* (New York, 1961).

78. Michael C. C. Adams, *Our Masters the Rebels: A Speculation on Union Military Failure in the East, 1861–1865* (Cambridge, MA, 1978).

79. Quoted in McCardell, *The Idea of a Southern Nation*, 270–71.

80. James Oakes, "'We Are Not Free': The Collapse of the Slaveholders' Democracy" (paper delivered at the Shelby Cullom Davis Seminar, Princeton University, May 4, 1984), develops this theme more explicitly than his *The Ruling Race*.

81. Donald, *Liberty and Union*, Chp. 4; E. James Ferguson, *The Power of the Purse: A History of American Public Finance, 1776–1790* (Chapel Hill, 1961).

82. Mitchell, *Civil War Soldiers*, passim. On British soldiers in America during the Revolution, see Sylvia R. Frey, *The British Soldier in America* (Austin, TX, 1981).

83. Bertram Wyatt-Brown, *Southern Honor: Ethics and Behavior in the Old South* (New York, 1982); McPherson, *Battle Cry of Freedom*, Chps. 1, 3.

84. Anderson, *Imagined Communities*, passim.

85. Reid, "A Test Case of the 'Crying Evil,'" esp. 253–55; Richard Bardolph, "Inconstant Rebels: Desertion of North Carolina Troops in the Civil War," *North Carolina Historical Review*, 41 (1964), 163–89, esp. 187–89; and Bardolph, "Confederate Dilemma: North Carolina Troops and the Deserter Problem," *North Carolina Historical Review*, 66 (1989), 61–86, 179–210. Reid's careful calculations have reduced the number of North Carolina deserters from over 24,000 to about 14,000, several thousand of whom eventually rejoined their units.

86. For the best recent scholarship on this question, see Sylvia Frey, "Between Slavery and Freedom: Virginia Blacks in the American Revolution," *Journal of Southern History*, 49 (1983), 375–98.

87. This theme emerged into prominence with Allan Nevins, *The Ordeal of the Union* (New York, 1947), I, Chp. 15. All scholarship now accepts this point, but not everyone draws the same conclusions from it.

88. Faust, *Confederate Nationalism*, emphasizes these internal tensions. Armistead Robinson is completing a full-scale study of this theme. See also Genovese, *Roll, Jordan, Roll*, 97–112. The quotation is from J. Francis Maldes to his mother, Feb. 18, 1865, in Bardolph, "Inconstant Rebels," 177.

89. Kenneth M. Stampp, "The Concept of a Perpetual Union," in his *The Imperiled Union*, 3–36.

90. McCardell, *Idea of a Southern Nation*, 38–48.

91. Paul E. Johnson, *A Shopkeeper's Millennium: Society and Revivals in Rochester, New York, 1815–1837* (New York, 1978).

92. Gilbert Hobbs Barnes, *The Antislavery Impulse, 1830–1844* (Washington, D.C., 1933), was the first major study to see how eastern and western abolitionists differed and how the western wing drew strongly on revivalism.

93. Quoted in Donald, *Liberty and Union*, 33.

CONCLUSION

Self-Immolation

Schools of Historiography and the Coming of the American Revolution

THE COMING OF the American Revolution has almost ceased to interest professional early American historians. A few books covering longer periods have made serious contributions to the subject, especially Jack P. Greene's *Peripheries and Center*, Timothy H. Breen's *The Marketplace of Revolution*, and Brendan McConville's *The King's Three Faces*.[1] But prior to this year only two book-length studies had appeared in the past two decades: J. C. D. Clark's *The Language of Liberty*, which has generated almost no discussion since its publication in 1994, and Woody Holton's *Forced Founders* which contends that underprivileged people drove Virginia's reluctant founding fathers into revolution, an argument that has attracted admiration but not much imitation in the eight years since its appearance.[2] Two excellent books by historians roughly my age pick up the story when revolution was clearly inevitable, David Hackett Fischer's *Paul Revere's Ride* and Pauline Maier's *American Scripture*, which is largely a study of the more local Declarations of Independence that preceded the adoption of Thomas Jefferson's document.[3]

This pattern may finally be changing. Benjamin Carp has just published an outstanding study of the coming of the Revolution in British North America's five largest cities, Brendan McConville has begun a study of what he calls America's revolutions, and Jeremy Stern is completing a Princeton dissertation on the Townshend Crisis in Massachusetts. Nevertheless by 1990 or so I began apologizing to my

Delivered at the Columbia University Seminar on Early American History and Culture on October 9, 2007.

graduate students at the beginning of my seminar on the Revolution and early republic because most of what they would read for the pre-revolutionary era was indeed rather old. Were I to teach it again I'd probably use most of the same titles: *The Stamp Act Crisis* by Edmund S. and Helen M. Morgan, Merrill Jensen's *The Founding of a Nation* which only recently appeared in paperback, Maier's *From Resistance to Revolution*, Richard Brown on Massachusetts committees of correspondence, John Shy on the British army, and David Ammerman on the crisis of 1774–75. I'd have to choose between Gary Nash's *Urban Crucible* and Carp's new book.[4]

Let me intensify the problem. As the Soviet Union collapsed between 1989 and 1991, spokesmen all across the political spectrum began to proclaim that the American Revolution is clearly the most successful and enduring such upheaval in the history of the world. From the left, Sean Wilentz made this claim in several reviews. Closer to the academic center, Joyce Appleby joined in, as did Gordon Wood in the most thoroughly discussed contribution, his *The Radicalism of the American Revolution*. Among evangelicals, Ellis Santoz made a similar claim. Of course, not everyone agrees. Michael Zuckerman published several essays around the 1976 bicentennial that were quite negative about the Revolution, and he has not changed his mind. Yet the pattern remains. Many early American historians regard the Revolution as among the most important events in world history, but they hardly even ask anymore why it happened at all.[5]

This pattern has its positive side. As Maier noted in a thoughtful piece in *Historically Speaking* about two years ago, scholarship on the colonial period (to ca. 1750) is now almost completely divorced from scholarship about the Revolution. She finds the contrast disturbing, but I rejoice that we no longer insist on a teleological component for colonial studies. Most of us can investigate Bacon's Rebellion or the New York slave conspiracy trials of 1741 without digging for a message that will get us to 1776. But the unfortunate side remains dominant. Since around 1980, the origins of the Revolution have almost disappeared from historical scholarship.[6]

Why? I have no answer that satisfies me. Most young historians have found cultural and social history more challenging, and that emphasis has led them away from politics and increasingly into the early republic, not the 1760s. Perhaps, as Jack Rakove suggested in the *Historically*

Speaking forum, the historians from the 1950s through the 1970s did their job so well that we can congratulate them and accept their findings. Much of their scholarship has been superb, but I do not think Maier found that argument sufficient, and nor do I. As many of you know, I have several times claimed that we should conceptualize the onset of the Revolution as a crisis of imperial *integration* that the British imperial state could not handle, rather than a cumulative crisis of imperial disintegration or Jon Butler's gradual emergence of America within the empire over the course of the eighteenth century, a time when most colonists felt more deeply loyal to the British state than almost any of their seventeenth-century ancestors had. But I do not consider my formulation a magical answer to the huge question of the Revolution's origins. I think it can be a constructive beginning that leaves many significant questions for us to pursue.[7]

Instead, let me pursue the historiography of the coming of the Revolution, even though there has not been much of it for almost thirty years. The historiography of what has almost become a non-question may not seem a very promising topic to pursue, but the pattern is truly interesting. The major historiographical schools that addressed these themes from the 1880s into the 1980s did not destroy one another. Most of the time they talked past each other. Instead each school undercut its own foundational insights in a pattern of self-immolation that is, I believe, unique to this particular topic.

I

Let us begin with how the revolutionary generation interpreted its own past. The founders of the republic saw their own epoch in terms that were intensely moralistic and highly contingent. For them the Revolution was preeminently a moral struggle of liberty against tyranny, and equality against bloated privilege. Events were truly contingent rather than inevitable. Leaders of resistance to Britain from 1764 to 1774 always claimed that they had not been struggling for independence. Instead British policy forced that choice upon them. Had Britain listened to their grievances and redressed them, no revolution would have occurred and no new nation would have been created, at least not then or in the way that it happened. And once the fighting started and the British nearly won in the 1776 campaign, contingency again asserted itself. Had George Washington not crossed the Delaware on Christmas night and won victories at both Trenton and Princeton, most contemporaries, including Washington, thought the cause would have been lost.[8]

After the War of 1812, once the republic seemed secure, George Bancroft moved in a new direction. A Yankee and a Harvard graduate who deviated from most of his Brahmin intellectual contemporaries by embracing Jacksonian democracy, Bancroft needed a grander perspective for the American republic. He gave fellow citizens a heady dose of providential nationalism, a theme that took him twelve volumes to develop fully. The United States, he believed, was already God's most favored nation, the one that most fully embraced liberty, equality, Protestantism, and free trade. In other words, he retained the moralism of the founding generation but substituted destiny for contingency. God had foreordained that America would be a great republic, and Britain could not prevent that result, although it tried. He even announced this theme in an early chapter that culminated with the Roanoke colony. He titled it: "England Takes Possession of the United States." His faith survived even the crisis of the Union, although the Civil War forced him to accept a much more vigorous central government than most Jacksonians had ever envisioned.[9]

The next generation of historians came of age during the Civil War. Many received professional training in the nation's first graduate programs, especially at Johns Hopkins University, an advantage that many of them supplemented with extensive study overseas, often exploring medieval topics. For these historians the Civil War had been more than God's obliging effort to relieve the tedium of inevitability. Most of them found Bancroft's nationalism offensive. They revived the founders' sense of contingency but not their moralism. They also accepted a gradualist approach to the origins of American national identity.

Albion W. Small, who later became a famous sociologist at the University of Chicago, launched an early exploration of this problem. The American nation, he believed, was not secure until 1865 or even 1877. It scarcely existed, even in embryo, in 1775 or 1789. For him the early republic displayed a dialectical struggle between Federalist statism and popular (Jeffersonian) anti-statism, until the Civil War finally forged a popular base for a potentially vigorous national government. The United States was not ready for a Hamiltonian constitutional system in the

1790s. Instead Jeffersonians shaped the nineteenth-century republic, at least until the Union came apart.[10]

Henry Adams also quarreled with the nationalist tradition that had emerged in histories written mostly by New Englanders. Although most scholars see Adams himself as part of this tradition, his history dismissed the New England states in the early republic as the most hopelessly Europeanized part of the United States The real America, he insisted, lay south and west of New England and would define the nation's contours after Jefferson's victory in 1800.[11]

Frederick Jackson Turner was both a nationalist and a gradualist. National identity emerged as a social process that had to be realized slowly and without the central government making much of a contribution. What distinguishes the United States from Europe? he asked. The frontier experience, he replied, and he found the 1890 federal census disturbing because, for the first time, there was no visible frontier line. Areas long settled become ever more Europeanized. My own emphasis on Anglicization is, in effect, the flip side of Turner. For this generation of historians the Federalist-Jeffersonian era often seemed more formative than the Revolution itself.[12]

II

Between the 1880s and Word War I, two major new schools of historiography emerged to study the origins of the Revolution. As history became professionalized, that is, increasingly monopolized by Ph.Ds, most of whom had to earn a living by teaching, these new men developed different approaches that grew out of conflicting sets of assumptions. These were the Imperial School and, somewhat later, the Progressives. They, and their Neo-Whig successor after World War II, shared one common pattern. At the outset each school began with a new, liberating assumption. Over time each accumulated inconsistencies severe enough to undercut its starting point. New students in each school ended up affirming some version of what it had begun by repudiating. This pattern is the single most distinctive feature of Revolutionary historiography.

Let us begin with the Imperial School, which began to take shape in the 1880s and 1890s under Herbert Levi Osgood and Charles McLean Andrews. Both detested Bancroft's righteous nationalism, his heady romanticism, and his high rhetorical style. In response, both wrote—deliberately, I suspect—tedious, academic prose. Both also doubted the moral superiority of the United States. They gave the London of Scotland Yard a moral edge over Boss Tweed's New York City. They contrasted the parliamentary reform policies of William E. Gladstone and Bejamin Disraeli at the height of Britain's imperial power with the spoils systems that had taken hold in most large American states. And both were Yankees who had rejected evangelical religion.[13]

Early American history, they contended, had to be written from a British imperial rather than an American nationalist perspective, and the story would have to be reconstructed fact by painful fact, most of them uncovered in unpublished manuscript collections in both Britain and America. Yet neither man ever escaped as far from Bancroft as they thought they had. Both assumed that American nationality, if a misplaced concept for the seventeenth century, certainly did belong in the eighteenth century. Both considered many of the leaders of the American Revolution as dangerous and sometimes unprincipled demagogues who misled themselves by accepting quaint or false social and political ideals. Osgood pointed out with genuine dismay that the Revolution was an illegal overthrow of the existing legal order. (Was he surprised? One wonders.) Andrews was even more pointed. "Men have died for a false creed," he asserted in 1912; "the colonists fought under the banner of a false philosophy." We cannot understand the Revolution, he added during World War I, "if we study, as is usually done, only the radical side and, by calling its supporters 'patriots' and glorifying their every action, disguise the fact that they were agitators and revolutionists—often uncontrolled and lawless men." Did this conviction turn Andrews into a neo-loyalist? No, he made clear in his 1925 presidential address before the American Historical Association. "The American revolutionists had an ideal of living," he explained; "it can hardly be said that in 1776 the Englishmen of the ruling classes were governed in their colonial relations by any ideals that were destined to be of service to the future of the human race."[14]

The underlying assumptions of the imperial school were intensely institutional and legalistic. One should study the formal institutions of government, for there lay legitimacy. They lumped Jamestown and Boston together because both colonies were founded by chartered companies, and they classed New York and Maryland with Barbados

because all began as proprietary colonies. That the economic imperatives of tobacco made Maryland and Virginia quite similar despite
divergent political origins mattered little. In short, neither Osgood nor
Andrews had a coherent social theory.

Their two most important students, George Louis Beer, who studied
with Osgood, and Lawrence Henry Gipson, who worked with Andrews,
went even further. Beer came from a prosperous New York Jewish family,
which probably explains why he never received an academic appointment,
but his wealth enabled him to do enormous amounts of research and to
publish extensively. The Revolution is understandable, he believed, but
it was an unfortunate mistake. As the United States became drawn into
World War I, he went to the Paris Peace Conference hoping to right the
mistakes of the eighteenth century by reuniting the American republic
with the British empire. Instead he soon died.[15]

Gipson was born in Idaho, went to Britain as a Rhodes Scholar during
the Boer War, and apparently fell in love with the British empire. In the
1930s he launched his most important effort, a project that became his
fifteen-volume history of the pre-Revolutionary era. Osgood completed
seven volumes in a sustained series on the colonies, Andrews four, and
Beer four, but none of them got as far as American independence. Gipson
did. His fifteenth volume was delivered to him just days before he died in
1971. In his hands the Imperial School undermined its leading assumption. He made every British policy decision so rational and so beneficial
that, in the end, he had no explanation for the Revolution except his conviction that, under the umbrella of the British empire, the colonists had
evolved into Americans. Unlike Bancroft he found little to celebrate in
this process. American nationalism was narrow and parochial, incapable
of appreciating what Britain had done for the colonies, especially during the French and Indian War, which he renamed the Great War for the
Empire. But Bancroft's nationalism, stripped of its providential qualities,
became his only explanation for why there was a revolution by 1776.[16]

III

The Progressive School, unlike its Imperial predecessor, was dominated
by westerners, several of whom then culminated their careers with prestigious eastern appointments. It first took shape under Frederick Jackson

Turner at the University of Wisconsin, where he earned professional fame with his enormously successful paper "The Significance of the Frontier in American History," delivered in Chicago in 1893. He supervised Orin G. Libby's doctoral dissertation on how states voted in the struggle over ratification of the federal Constitution. The pattern, Libby pointed out, did not conform to existing political boundaries, and in trying to make sense of it he came close to something resembling what Jackson Turner Main would describe—much later, in the 1970s—as a conflict between localists and cosmopolitans. For Turner and Libby, societies exist apart from government, and historians have to be sensitive to the contrast.[17]

Carl Becker, another Turner student, soon became even more influential than Libby. His 1909 study on the development of political parties in pre-Revolutionary New York insisted that these contests were not only about home rule but, even more emphatically, over "who shall rule at home." For Becker, colonial elites were tied to levers of British power. They had grievances, but most of them were cautious about how angry they were likely to get. Ordinary settlers did not share this restraint. Somewhat less eloquently, Charles H. Lincoln had already found a similar pattern in Pennsylvania. For both colonies, the received wisdom became that "the people" took the Revolution away from their superiors and made it a deeper, more democratic event. Finally, Charles A. Beard accomplished much the same purpose with his study of the creation of the Constitution. He desanctified America's most sacred document by explaining its drafting and adoption as the working out of specific economic interests among elite delegates. His dry prose actually increased the power of his less than explicit message, that the people can take control of the government created under the Constitution once they understand how that process had occurred in the first place.[18]

The Imperial and Progressive Schools differed in striking ways. Imperial historians were deeply interested in the founding and early development of the colonies. Progressives were not. Most of what they said about the colonies before 1750 or 1760 was quite perfunctory, but they did have a broader vision of how societies work than anyone in the Imperial School, and they never treated politics as only a matter of institutional development. Nearly all Progressives believed that the most dynamic forces in society operate largely outside government. Society is full of conflict, and a wise historian will always be deeply suspicious of what people, especially elite people, claim they are doing and why. Yet both schools shared a common deficiency. Neither treated slavery, or enslaved people, as questions that demanded serious historical inquiry. As Turner once remarked, "But when American history comes to be rightly viewed it will be seen that the slavery question is an incident," an astonishing perspective for someone who knew that the crisis of the Union had almost destroyed the American republic.[19]

How then did the Progressives run into trouble? They certainly achieved legitimacy. Both Turner and Arthur M. Schlesinger, Sr. (formally an Osgood student but really a disciple of Beard), migrated to Harvard at the peak of their careers. Beard became a power at Columbia until his opposition to American entry into World War I forced him to resign but without doing serious damage to his reputation. His position had far more popular support by the 1930s than it was able to claim in 1917. In the Midwest, the University of Wisconsin remained a bastion of Progressive scholarship for more than half a century after Turner's departure. Progressive interpretations flourished in doctoral dissertations and in mainstream textbooks of American history. Even prominent historians who had seemed even-handed about scholarly disputes adopted a Progressive vocabulary. In *The Growth of the American Republic*, Samuel Eliot Morison and Henry Steele Commager titled the first section of their chapter on the Constitution, "Thermidor: The Annapolis Convention," although they also made it clear that America's Thermidor was less Thermidorian than France's.[20]

But as Progressive monographs piled up, lines of cleavage became blurred. If everybody was a defender of some interest, or collection of interests, did it matter who won? Who were the people? Especially in the 1930s, the people of Revolutionary America seemed to be disappearing as historical actors. "At best," Schlesinger claimed, "an exposition of the political theories of the anti-parliamentary party is an account of their retreat from one strategic position to another"—from basing their rights on their charters, to invoking the rights of Englishmen, and then finally the rights of man. In condemning the Stamp Act, in Becker's version, polemicists attacked internal taxes but said they could accept external ones, or port duties. In the Townshend Crisis (1767–70), they rejected both but still defended Parliament's power to legislate for the colonies. By 1774, in response to Parliament's Coercive (or Intolerable) Acts, resistance spokesmen denied that Parliament had any legitimate legislative power over the colonies, although the First Continental Congress said they were willing to live with the Navigation Acts under which the imperial system had been functioning for more than a century. That left the Crown as Britain's only source of legitimate authority over America, and in July 1776 Congress invoked the rights of man to condemn that too.[21]

In the 1930s both John C. Miller and Philip Davidson explored the role of propaganda in the coming of the Revolution. That theme was potentially explosive in the age of Joseph Paul Goebbels. Becker had pitted the people against contending elite coalitions. Increasingly the result seemed to be that a new, emerging elite was using every available instrument of propaganda to manipulate ordinary people into embracing their cause and, presumably, their quest for power. Ordinary, naive people took the arguments posed by their superiors quite seriously; elite people did not. The emphasis upon economic interests no longer seemed to be liberating anyone by the 1940s. The people were disappearing from Progressive histories, although in this case the *coup de grâce* was delivered after World War II by Forrest McDonald's *We the People*. No Progressive himself, he nonetheless used the cumulative monographic literature of preceding decades to undermine Beard's *Economic Interpretation*. Everyone, he argued, had economic interests, and in any case the cumulative pattern did not support Beard's thesis.[22]

Beard also lost credibility for nonacademic reasons. He opposed the FDR administration on entry into World War II. His resistance to World War I did no permanent damage to his reputation, but the Second World War united the nation as no other military conflict ever had. The overwhelming victory of the United States, Britain, and other allies (with the Cold War looming, the Soviet Union remained problematic for most Americans) convinced many people that maybe our history had generated fewer serious conflicts than our counterparts in Europe and Asia had routinely experienced. Perhaps, they pondered, Beard really was wrong. Maybe the Progressives had exaggerated the persistent tensions over the course of our development. To many younger historians, Americans had been doing some things quite well.[23]

IV

Shortly after World War II a new interpretive paradigm emerged for prerevolutionary America that Jack P. Greene later identified as the

Neo-Whig School.[24] As this shift began, many historians saw it as a clash between "consensus" and "conflict" (or Progressive) perspectives. Edmund S. Morgan led the way in recasting the coming of the Revolution. He has always adamantly rejected the label of "consensus" historian. For early America, Daniel J. Boorstin's *The Americans: The Colonial Experience* certainly qualifies as consensus history, especially in his argument that most of American history has embodied a rejection of European ideologies—and the struggles that they provoked. Many lump Louis Hartz with other consensus historians, but to do so we have to give appropriate weight to a major difference. Hartz's *The Liberal Tradition in America* did argue that America was born Lockean and remains a Lockean society to this day, but unlike Boorstin, he did not celebrate what he saw. For him America's inability to escape its Lockean assumptions had become a trap. Other societies were part of the Marxian dialectic. We are not, and that fact, to our own confusion and discomfort, has disenabled Americans from understanding the rest of the world. Morgan's aspirations were somewhat less grandiose than those of Boorstin and Hartz, but the seriousness with which he has addressed the issue of slavery has fully earned him the right to reject the consensual label.[25]

For the Neo-Whig School the progression to watch is from Morgan to Bernard Bailyn and such early Bailyn students as Gordon S. Wood and Pauline Maier, and then the shift to a post-Bailyn, psychological interpretation.

Morgan's argument took shape between 1948 and 1953. It emerged in two essays in the *William and Mary Quarterly*, and then he pulled together its ramifications in *The Stamp Act Crisis*, co-authored with Helen M. Morgan. Challenging mostly Schlesinger and Becker, he insisted that the revolutionaries took a clear, consistent, and highly principled position in the quarrel with Britain from 1764 to 1774. Hardly any of them distinguished between internal and external taxes. Instead they accepted taxation for the regulation of trade but rejected taxation for revenue. To tax the colonies for revenue within the principles of the British constitution, the home government would have to get the settlers' consent. In the process Morgan rejected a major Progressive assumption, that ideas are mostly devices used by elite people to disguise their real intentions and that the colonial argument had shifted opportunistically from one crisis to the next.[26]

In Morgan's Yale seminar, which I took in 1959–60, we spent one semester on the Puritans and the other on the Revolution. The two topics shared a common denominator. Morgan urged us to start with what people said they were doing and not to challenge a writer's motives unless we had evidence to support our skepticism. Most people mean what they say most of the time. Although he clearly agreed with the revolutionaries, he sympathized more openly with proto-loyalists than anyone yet had while writing from that perspective. He resolved this tension through drama, or narrative. He knew he had a powerful story to tell, and he told it well. For him the loyalists of 1764–66 were honest and decent men trapped on the wrong side of a major historical divide, and all of them paid heavy consequences. Those resisting British policy maintained basically the same arguments during the Townshend Crisis. Only in 1774, when Parliament claimed a power to alter a colonial government without soliciting the settlers' consent, did the mainstream colonial argument shift to no *legislation* without consent. That position quickly became revolutionary.[27]

Like Morgan, Bernard Bailyn took seriously what people said they were doing, but he probed deeply into the underlying assumptions and anxieties that sustained these arguments. Drawing on the wide-ranging scholarship of Caroline Robbins, J. G. A. Pocock, and others, Bailyn emphasized the central antagonism that energized eighteenth-century political ideology in Britain—the continuing struggle between dynamic, aggressive power and beautiful but frail liberty, a contest that power had always won until Britain systematized its mixed and balanced constitution after the Glorious Revolution. Like virginity, liberty, once lost, cannot be recovered, as the ancient Greeks and Romans both learned. If power cannot achieve its objectives directly, it turns to corruption to undermine free institutions. Hence the need for eternal vigilance.

To Bailyn the Revolution became a set of competing conspiracy theses, each of which then emerged as a self-fulfilling prophecy. To alarmed colonists, beginning mostly during the Townshend Crisis, sinister officials in Britain seemed determined to undermine liberty in America. To concerned British officials watching the intensification of the colonial resistance movement, the goal of this agitation had to be independence. Of studies published so far, Pauline Maier's *From Resistance to Revolution* best shows how both sides shifted their anxieties, and eventually their positions, in response to events. By 1776 both sides could shout "I told you so!" The 30,000 redcoats and German mercenaries headed toward New York did not bode well for American liberty. As the vanguard landed on Staten Island on July 2, Congress 90 miles away passed Richard Henry Lee's resolve for independence. Two days later Congress approved the Declaration that justified this step to the world.[28]

V

The powerful psychological dynamic embodied in Bailyn's fear of power and corruption soon proved irresistible. For Morgan, Thomas Hutchinson had been an honest man trapped on the wrong side of a revolutionary divide. For Bailyn, he became, despite a nervous breakdown at one point, almost the only sane man in an increasingly paranoid world. Toward the end of his comprehensive study of Hutchinson, Bailyn directly addressed that question. Was the American resistance movement a manifestation of collective paranoia? After staring briefly over that cliff, he rejected the idea because the Revolution embodied too many generous and positive qualities to be described in these terms.[29]

Many other historians were less cautious. James H. Hutson, a Morgan student and a friend of mine for whom I have the greatest respect, published a bicentennial essay that started with Freud's definition of paranoia and then argued that patriot leaders were *clinically*, not metaphorically, paranoid. Freud traced paranoia in men to fear of homosexual rape in childhood. Nobody, Hutson admitted, could prove that case, but he made the argument for paranoia anyway while also conceding that patriot followers were sane enough.[30]

Philip Greven's study of child-rearing practices and their impact on society and politics contended, by contrast, that ordinary evangelicals who supported the Revolution were *almost* clinically paranoid. Their leaders were troubled, perhaps, and some maybe even neurotic, but if we accepted both studies, there weren't many levelheaded patriots left.[31]

Clearly exasperated by this trend, Gordon Wood responded with a thoughtful essay that located conspiratorial thinking solidly within the emerging pattern of Enlightenment thought. As a providential universe gave way to a thoroughly rational one, negative events could not easily be explained by original sin or even human blunders. Somebody must be planning them, and if no one would take responsibility for them, rational

men looked toward conspiracy which, in Wood's judgment, was a logical response, granting their rationalist assumptions. By then Hutson had
also retreated from his 1976 position. In a paper presented at a conference
honoring Morgan in 1979 but not published until 1984, the paranoid
style became what he called "public jealousy" and characterized much of
Anglo-American politics for more than a century after about 1720.[32]

These conspiratorial studies were offset by a careful and lengthy essay
by Edwin G. Burroughs and Michael Wallace, who explored use of the
parent-child metaphor throughout the imperial debate, with loyalists
urging colonists to obey their lawful superiors, while patriots intensified
their resistance. The authors suggested that patriots were mature adults
who could emancipate themselves from parental authority. Loyalists,
almost by definition, remained immature. Kenneth Lynn, in a short
book, made a similar, more polemical case but without a great deal of evidence. Much as I learned from Burroughs and Wallace, I could not help
wondering what psychological analysis would tell us about the victorious
patriots after the Revolutionary War when they referred quite often to
their "infant republic."[33]

Let me suggest three general points about the Neo-Whig school. To
the extent that intensive psychological analysis became its central thrust
it was utterly repudiating its origins as established by Morgan, Bailyn, and
Maier, all of whom remained close to their original formulations. Various
degrees of paranoia had replaced principled constitutional resistance to
dangerous British policies. Although I am not aware that anyone drew
this conclusion, I thought it obvious that this line of argument could only
end by agreeing with the loyalist contention that patriot resistance had
become a revolution against the best of kings and the freest of nations.
Neo-Whiggery was transforming itself into Neo-Loyalism.

Second, to the degree that a psychological interpretation was emerging as an autonomous school in the 1970s, it started with the kind of
internal contradictions that earlier schools acquired only after one or two
generations. Or we could have thrown in George III's porphyria, Charles
Townshend's epilepsy, William Pitt's severe depression that destroyed
his ministry between 1768 and 1770, and even Lord North's emotional
paralysis that utterly incapacitated him in 1779 when a Franco-Spanish
invasion fleet entered the English Channel. Perhaps the Revolutionary

generation, on both sides, was more than a little mad, but in that case, what would we be explaining?

Third, while the Progressives were deeply skeptical about what people said they were doing, Neo-Whigs derived most of their bite by taking quite seriously what people said during the coming of the Revolution. But during the early republic, when Federalists denounced Democratic-Republicans as potentially murderous Jacobins and Jeffersonians defended themselves against Federalist, whom they denounced as monarchists trying to reimpose corrupt British political practices upon the United States, many historians, reverting to Progressive assumptions, dismissed the rhetoric on both sides as political hyperbole. Richard Hofstadter was one. Lance Banning, strongly encouraged by Pocock, was the first important scholar to take this language seriously. If Banning is right, so was Henry Adams. The new nation was never very secure until after the War of 1812.[34]

VI

While Neo-Whiggery thrived, Merrill Jensen kept a lonely Progressive vigil, more than a little baffled by the attention that Bailyn's formulation was receiving. He continued to supervise outstanding dissertations at Wisconsin, and finally, as the post-war harmonies dissolved into partisan rancor over civil rights, Vietnam, and Watergate, Progressive assumptions began to make sense once again. Like earlier Progressives, his students almost completely ignored race and gender, in part because, unlike Morgan and Bailyn, he did not accept female students. His own *The Founding of a Nation*, now widely recognized as the best one-volume narrative of the coming of the Revolution, appeared in 1968 without attracting much attention. No paperback edition became available until a few years ago, which meant that few teachers used it in the classroom. Yet in the 1970s his students produced some of the best monographs on the Revolutionary era—Ronald Hoffman on Maryland, Stephen Patterson and Van Beck Hall on Massachusetts, and Joseph A. Ernst on monetary issues, to name only four.[35]

Yet despite these successes, much of the initiative was beginning to pass to a disparate group that most of us called either Neo-Progressives or Radicals. They were not a coherent school in the sense that Imperial,

Progressive, and Neo-Whig historians had been. James Henretta and Peter Wood studied at Harvard, Jesse Lemisch at Yale, Staughton Lynd and Eric Foner at Columbia, and Gary Nash at Princeton under mentors who did not claim to be either Neo-Progressives or Radicals. On their own initiatives, the Neo-Progressives became the single most persuasive group when it came to telling us important things about the Revolution that had not yet been systematically addressed. They added race and gender to the earlier Progressive fixation on class. They found severe outbreaks of social conflict in one colony after another. Jackson Turner Main placed beyond doubt Libby's argument in the 1890s that patterns of political cleavage crossed state boundaries.

Soon others, not generally identified as Neo-Progressives, were studying gender and race. Mary Beth Norton, trained under Bailyn, and Linda Kerber, a Richard Morris student at Columbia, produced superb books on women in the Revolutionary Era. At Princeton, Gregory Evans Dowd did the most comprehensive study yet to appear on the responses of Indians of eastern North America to settler expansion, imperial war, and the Revolution between the 1740s and the War of 1812.[36]

VII

So where were we by the 1980s? Each school had suffered a mortal wound but refused to die, until nearly everyone stopped writing about the coming of the Revolution. They seldom talked to one another. For instance, Neo-Progressives, such as Nash, regarded the "republican ideology"[37] (especially before Independence, I, along with Pocock and Banning, have always preferred "country ideology") of Bailyn as an elite language probably not shared by the lower orders, even though when artisans struggled for the right to vote, they claimed that their skills gave them the same kind of personal independence that landowners derived from their property, a staple element of republican ideology. The conspiratorial thinking that first took hold in Hanoverian Britain affected colonial Sons of Liberty before Independence and Democratic-Republican Societies after Independence, as well as elite pamphleteers. For some purposes, this ideology could confer legitimacy well beyond the intimate circles of its original spokesmen. But it was hardly the only available language. New York City's radicals did their best to de-legitimize elite claims that their "independence" enabled them to pursue the common good, while others were tied to self-interest. And in *Common Sense*, Thomas Paine brilliantly trashed the very idea of a balanced constitution of King, Lords, and Commons, often invoking biblical language to do so.[38]

At a 1976 bicentennial session at the annual meeting of the American Historical Association, I helped create a panel in which I argued that historians needed both the Progressive School and Bailyn's Neo-Whigs. The commentators were Richard Buel, a Bailyn student, and Stephen Patterson, a Jensen student. Both did their best to trample me. In response, I remarked that, if you set yourself up as a bridge, others will walk over you. When the essay was published a few years later, it did win a high degree of respect.[39]

Although the three major schools refused to expire, around 1980 they stopped writing about the coming of the Revolution. The last great contribution to this problem for quite some time was Nash's *The Urban Crucible*, which came out in 1979. As we have seen, many historians turned to gender, to the sensibilities of artisans and farmers, to the struggles of black people, both enslaved and free, and to Indians, a subject that generated some of the most imaginative contributions of the past two or three decades. This literature is inherently exciting and makes us question much of what we once took for granted, but through the 1980s I doubted that it would tell us much about why we had a revolution. It was much better on results and consequences than on causes.[40]

VIII

That judgment was premature. If we take North American history from 1750 to 1820 and try to see what was happening from the perspective of ordinary households (settlers, blacks—both enslaved and free—and Indians), we can, I think, detect the lines of force propelling the major changes of the period and begin to merge the social, cultural, and political history that has been written in the past three decades.

To start with gender, or the male-female dichotomy, the most distinctive feature of settler households was the patriarch's goal. He hoped to pass on his status to all of his sons and to marry his daughters to young men of comparable status. They hoped to keep British North America as a paradise for younger sons, as Benjamin Franklin indirectly noted at the beginning of his *Autobiography*. To make this system work properly, women, I believe, had to become more European. As numerous studies have shown, the number of spinning wheels multiplied much faster than the population, and in New England, but not other regions, women did most of the weaving. As the resistance movement took shape, the head of a patriot household told his wife and daughters that they had to make more homespun because the British government was trying to effeminate him and his sons by depriving them of their independence and thus their liberty. I have not yet discovered a document that recounts the content of this conversation, but at least in northern colonies, women responded positively.[41]

If we take a second dichotomy, expansion versus stasis, we learn that to achieve the patriarch's goal in a society that doubled its population every twenty-five years, each successive generation had to take over as much new land as all of their ancestors combined had occupied since the beginning of European settlement. For the first century, that process barely got colonists past the tidewater, but in the eighteenth century, this geographic rate of growth began to engulf everything east of the mountains and was starting to invade the Ohio Valley. Indians, by contrast, fought mostly for stasis, to retain possession of their ancestral lands. By the 1750s this conflict was not compromisable except for short periods of time. American victory in the Revolution meant expulsion from ancestral lands—and cultural desolation—for Indians. Even the few Indians who began to accept patriarchal values could not fend off the result—removal west of the Mississippi by the 1830s.

By contrast, Africans in America and their descendants hoped to share the benefits that white households were demanding, beginning with emancipation. Even those who achieved that intermediate goal soon discovered its limitations. The logic of gradual emancipation trapped them. In most northern states, slaves had to pay for their own freedom by reimbursing their master for the labor he would lose. Most white households could launch their offspring into the economy with the possession of significant resources. But when a black male won emancipation—at age twenty-eight in Pennsylvania, for instance—he had no such advantage. The system allowed him to be free, but never equal.[42]

Clearly the center of gravity for social and political change lay with the autonomous, white, male householder. Especially in the Northeast, women achieved literacy, no doubt because patriarchs thought it advantageous to their families. In that region blacks could win emancipation, but only if they paid for it themselves. White taxpayers would contribute nothing to this project. The biggest losers were Indians. The escalating advance of settlement meant unending retreat for them. Social and political changes occurred only if they were compatible with the needs and desires of white heads of households. But within that group, power was indeed becoming democratized.

A final dichotomy pits Americanization against Anglicization. Both were happening in the colonies, but on the whole, Americanization was an old pattern, established quite early, especially in the systems that allowed all sons equal access, or near-equal access in New England, to land. By the middle of the eighteenth century, many families wondered whether this tradition could be sustained. Another early example of Americanization involved reliance on unfree labor, especially the shift from indentured servitude to slavery. That pattern continued to intensify from Maryland southward. Many settlers could remain free only if Africans remained slaves.

Anglicization, by contrast, marked the effort to bring the benefits of English (and later Scottish) production, thought, culture, and religious institutions to the North American colonists. For the most part, southern colonies imported their ministers, lawyers, master craftsmen, and textiles and other European manufactures. But the New England and Middle Colonies increasingly learned to provide these benefits for themselves. They became the first modernizing societies in the Americas, and after Independence, they were the first to become part of the world metropole. Yet Anglicization was always a race against expansion. By the Revolution, the South in particular could no longer keep pace by importing twice as many ministers, lawyers, and craftsmen from Europe each generation. The results quickly became obvious in religion as Baptists and Methodists drove Anglicans into headlong retreat.

No Anglicization, no Revolution. The very thought structures that sustained the Revolution were rather late imports from Britain. Slowly Anglicization was producing a more stratified society. A father unable to meet the needs of all his children typically favored sons over daughters and, if necessary, the oldest son over his brothers. And gradually some households were becoming structurally more dependent on others. An elite officeholding cadre emerged in the colonies in the eighteenth century, and after adoption of the Constitution, some of them set out to make themselves into a ruling class. Anglicization occurred both before and after Independence, but by 1776 its apostles were almost all seen as would-be aristocrats. It took two revolutions to preserve the achievements of the first Americanization, one in 1776, the other in 1800.[43]

This sketch is not itself a synthesis, but I hope it can lead to one. Any such achievement ought, I believe, to take the form of a braided narrative, showing what was possible in, say, 1750, how that changed over the next generation, what new possibilities emerged with Independence, then with the new Constitution, and finally with the triumph of the Jeffersonians.

But no Americanization, no nineteenth-century American society of autonomous freeholders driving Indians into pathetically small and infertile tracts of land.

Notes

1. Greene, *Peripheries and Center: Constitutional Development in the Extended Polities of the British Empire and the United States, 1607–1778* (New York, 1986); Breen, *The Marketplace of Revolution: How Consumer Politics Shaped American Independence* (New York, 2004); McConville, *The King's Three Faces: The Rise & Fall of Royal America, 1688–1776* (Chapel Hill, 2006).
2. Clark, *The Language of Liberty, 1660–1832: Political Discourse and Social Dynamics in the Anglo-American World* (Cambridge, UK, 1994); Holton, *Forced Founders: Indians, Debtors, Slaves and the Making of the American Revolution in Virginia* (Chapel Hill, 1999). For a sharply critical review of Clark, see Jack P. Greene, "The American Revolution Revisited" (1994), reprinted in his *Interpreting Colonial America: Historiographical Essays* (Charlottesville, 1996), 493–509.
3. Fischer, *Paul Revere's Ride* (New York, 1994); Maier, *American Scripture: Making the Declaration of Independence* (New York, 1997).
4. Carp, *Rising Rebels: Cities and the American Revolution* (New York, 2007); Morgan and Morgan, *The Stamp Act Crisis, Prologue to Revolution* (Chapel Hill, 1953, 1995); Jensen, *The Founding of a Nation: A History of the American Revolution 1763–1776* (New York, 1968); Maier, *From Resistance to Revolution: Colonial Radicals and the Development of American Opposition to Britain, 1765–1776* (New York, 1972); Brown, *Revolutionary Politics in Massachusetts: The Boston Committee of Correspondence and the Towns, 1772–1774* (Cambridge, MA, 1970); Shy, *Toward Lexington: The Role of the British Army in the Coming of the American Revolution* (Princeton, 1965); Ammerman, *In the Common Cause: American Response to the Coercive Acts of*

1774 (Charlottesville, 1974); Nash, *Urban Crucible: Social Change, Political Consciousness, and the Origins of the American Revolution* (Cambridge, MA, 1979).

5. Joyce Appleby, "The Radical Recreation of the American Republic," *William and Mary Quarterly*, Vol. 51, No. 4 (Oct., 1994), pp. 679–83. The best discussion of Wilentz's views of the American Revolution can be found in, Sean Wilentz, *The Rise of American Democracy: Jefferson to Lincoln* (New York: W.W. Norton, 2005). Wood, *The Radicalism of the American Revolution* (New York, 1992); Sandoz, ed., *Political Sermons of the Founding Era, 1730–1805* (Indianapolis, 1991), forward. I have not seen anyone born outside the United States make this claim. Michael Zuckerman, "The Irrelevant Revolution: 1776 and Since" American Quarterly 30 (1978), 224–42.

6. Pauline Maier, Edward G. Gray, Don Higginbotham, Peter S. Onuf, Paul A. Rahe, and Jack Rakove, "The State of Early American History: A Forum," *Historically Speaking*, 6 (2005): 19–32.

7. Murrin, "1776: The Countercyclical Revolution," in Michael A. Morrison and Melinda Zook, eds., *Revolutionary Currents: Nation Building in the Transatlantic World* (New York, 2004), 65–90; Butler, *Becoming America: The Revolution before 1776* (Cambridge, MA, 2000). For a critique of Butler, see the review by Murrin and David Silverman in *Journal of Interdisciplinary History*, 33 (2002–03): 235–46.

8. Arthur H. Shaffer, *The Politics of History: Writing the History of the American Revolution, 1783–1815* (Chicago, 1975); Lester Cohen, *The Revolutionary Histories: Contemporary Narratives of the American Revolution* (Ithaca, NY, 1980).

9. Bancroft, *History of the United States from the Discovery of the American Continent*, 10 vols. (Boston, 1834–74), esp. I, 75. This history terminated with American victory in the Revolutionary War. Bancroft then published *History of the Formation of the Constitution of the United States of America*, 2 vols. (New York, 1893).

10. Small, *The Growth of American Nationality: An Introduction to the Constitutional History of the United States* (Waterville, ME, 1888). This thin volume was printed on cheap paper and must have had a limited circulation, probably for his own teaching purposes at Colby College. I read the copy at Widener Library, Harvard University. Small reworked the first part for publication as *The Beginnings of American Nationality: The Constitutional Relations Between the Continental Congress and the Colonies and States from 1774 to 1789*, Johns Hopkins University Studies in Historical and Political Science, 8th ser., Nos. 1 and 2 (Baltimore, 1890).

11. Adams, *History of the United States during the Administrations of Thomas Jefferson and James Madison*, 9 vols. (New York, 1889–91), esp. I, Chps 1–6; IX, Chps. 7–10.

12. Turner, *The Frontier in American History* (New York, 1920), esp. the lead essay, "The Significance of the Frontier in American History," pp. 1–38.

13. Dixon Ryan Fox, *Herbert Levi Osgood, an American Scholar* (New York, 1924); Abraham S. Eisenstadt, *Charles McLean Andrews, A Study in American Historical Writing* (New York, 1956).

14. The first programmatic statements by the Imperial School appeared in early volumes of the *Political Science Quarterly* in the 1880s and in early volumes of the American Historical Association, *Annual Reports* in the 1890s. See, specifically, Osgood, "England and the Colonies," *Political Science Quarterly*, 2 (1887): 440–69, esp. 441, 463–67; Andrews, *The Colonial Period*, Home University Library (New York, 1916), 252; "The American Revolution: An Interpretation," *American Historical Review*, 31 (1925–26): 219–32, esp. 232.

15. *George Louis Beer: A Tribute to His Life and Work in the Making of History and the Moulding of Public Opinion* (New York, 1924).

16. Gipson, *The British Empire before the American Revolution*, 15 vols. (Caldwell, ID and New York, 1936–91). For an early, concise statement of his position, see *The Coming of the Revolution, 1763–1775*, New American Nation Series (New York, 1954). One can find numerous passages in Osgood and Andrews indicating that, while they rejected any form of American identity in the seventeenth century, they assumed that it was developing in the eighteenth.

17. Turner, "The Significance of the Frontier in American History" (1893), in *The Frontier in American History*, 1–38; Libby, *The Geographical Distribution of the Vote of the Thirteen States on the Federal Constitution, 1787–8* (Madison, 1894).

18. Becker, *The History of Political Parties in the Province of New York, 1760–1776* (Madison, 1909); Lincoln, *The Revolutionary Movement in Pennsylvania, 1760–1776* (Philadelphia, 1901); Beard, *An Economic Interpretation of the Constitution of the United States* (New York, 1913).

19. Turner, *The Frontier in American History*, 24.

20. Morison and Commager, *The Growth of the American Republic*, 4th ed. (New York, 1950), I, 277.

21. Arthus M. Schlesinger, "The American Revolution," in his *New Viewpoints in American History* (New York, 1922), 160–84, quotation on p. 179; Carl L. Becker, *The Declaration of Independence: A Study in the History of Political Ideas* (New York, 1922).

22. Miller, *Sam Adams, Pioneer in Propaganda* (Stanford, 1936); Davidson, *Propaganda and the American Revolution, 1763–1783* (Chapel Hill, 1941); McDonald, *We the People: The Economic Origins of the Constitution* (Chicago, 1958).

23. My understanding of the Progressive School has benefited greatly from Richard Hofstadter, *The Progressive Historians: Turner, Beard, Parrington* (New York, 1968), and from Ray Allen Billington, *Frederick Jackson Turner: Historian, Scholar, Teacher* (New York, 1973).

24. Greene, "The Flight from Determinism: A Review of Recent Literature on the Coming of the American Revolution" (1961), and "The Plunge of

Lemmings: A Consideration of Recent Writings on British Politics and the American Revolution" (1968), both reprinted in his *Interpreting Colonial America: Historiographical Essays*, 311–66. They established Greene as the most comprehensive and thorough historiographer of the coming of the Revolution.

25. Boorstin, *The Americans: The Colonial Experience* (New York, 1958); Hartz, *The Liberal Tradition in America; an Interpretation of American Political Thought since the Revolution* (New York, 1955); Hartz, *The Founding of New Societies: Studies in the History of the United States, Latin America, South Africa, and Australia* (New York, 1964), a book that placed his earlier argument in a global context. Morgan's most comprehensive analysis of early American slavery is his *American Slavery, American Freedom: The Ordeal of Colonial Virginia* (New York, 1975).

26. Morgan, "Colonial Ideas of Parliamentary Power, 1764–1766," *William and Mary Quarterly*, 5 (1948): 311–41 (hereafter, *WMQ*, assumed to be 3d ser.; Morgan, "The Postponement of the Stamp Act," *WMQ*, 7 (1950): 353–92.

27. Morgan and Morgan, *Stamp Act Crisis*.

28. Bailyn, *The Ideological Origins of the American Revolution* (Cambridge, MA, 1967), an earlier version of which appeared as the "General Introduction" to his *Pamphlets of the American Revolution, 1750–1776*, I (Cambridge, MA, 1965), 3–202. Bailyn drew on Caroline Robbins, *The Eighteenth-Century Commonwealthman: Studies in the Transmission, Development and Circumstance of English Liberal Thought from the Restoration of Charles II until the War with the Thirteen Colonies* (Cambridge, MA, 1959), and on J. G. A. Pocock, "Machiavelli, Harrington, and English Political Ideologies in the Eighteenth Century," *WMQ*, 22 (1965): 549–83. See also Maier, *From Resistance to Revolution*. Because Gordon Wood's first book concentrates on the period between independence and adoption of the federal Constitution, it is not discussed in this essay.

29. Bailyn, *The Ordeal of Thomas Hutchinson* (Cambridge, MA, 1974).

30. Hutson, "The American Revolution: The Triumph of a Delusion?" in *New Wine in Old Skins: A Comparative View of Socio-Political Structures Affecting the American Revolution*, ed. Erich Angermann et al. (Stuttgart, 1976), 177–94.

31. Greven, *The Protestant Temperament: Patterns of Child-Rearing, Religious Experience, and the Self in Early America* (New York, 1977), 335–61.

32. Wood, "Conspiracy and the Paranoid Style: Causality and Deceit in the Eighteenth Century," *WMQ*, 39 (1982): 401–41; Hutson, "The Origins of the Paranoid Style in American Politics from the Age of Walpole to the Age of Jackson," in *Saints & Revolutionaries: Essays on Early American History*, ed. David D. Hall, John M. Murrin, and Thad Tate (NY, 1984), 332–72.

33. Burrows and Wallace, "The American Revolution: The Ideology and Psychology of National Liberation," *Perspectives in American History*, 6 (1972), 167–306; Lynn, *A Divided People* (Westport, CT, 1977).

34. Compare Richard Hofstadter, *The Idea of a Party System: The Rise of Legitimate Opposition in the United States, 1780–1840* (Berkeley and Los Angeles, 1969), with Banning, *The Jeffersonian Persuasion: Evolution of a Party Ideology* (Ithaca, NY, 1978).

35. For a list of Jensen's students as of 1976, see *The Human Dimensions of Nation Making: Essays on Colonial and Revolutionary America*, ed. James Kirby Martin (Madison, 1976), 365–67. Of the forty-four who had finished their dissertations and the six who had not, only one was a woman. I do not mean to slight the impressive achievements of Jensen's earlier students, such as Jackson Turner Main, E. James Ferguson, and Roger J. Champagne.

36. Norton, *Liberty's Daughters: The Revolutionary Experience of American Women, 1750–1800* (Boston, 1980); Kerber, *Women of the Republic: Intellect and Ideology in Revolutionary America* (Chapel Hill, 1980); Dowd, *A Spirited Resistance: The North American Indian Struggle for Unity, 1745–1815* (Baltimore, 1992). Although Dowd is my Ph.D student, I can claim little credit for his research or his findings. Most of what I know about Indians in this period I first learned from him.

37. Especially before Independence, I, along with Pocock and Banning, prefer the term "country ideology."

38. Bernard Friedman, "The Shaping of the Radical Consciousness in Provincial New York," *Journal of American History*, 56 (1969–70), 781–801; Edward Countryman, *A People in Revolution: The American Revolution and Political Society in New York, 1760–1790* (Baltimore, 1981); Eric Foner, *Tom Paine and Revolutionary America* (New York, 1976). For two distinct but overlapping efforts to categorize the major political and ethical languages available to Americans by the 1770s and 1780s, see Isaac Kramnick, " 'The Great National Discussion': The Discourse of Politics in 1787," *WMQ*, 45 (1988): 3–32; John M. Murrin, "Fundamental Values, the Founding Fathers, and the Constitution," in *To Form a More Perfect Union: The Critical Ideas of the Constitution*, ed. Herman Belz, Peter J. Albert, and Ronald Hoffman (Charlottesville, 1992), 1–37.

39. Murrin, "The Great Inversion, or, Court versus Country: A Comparison of the Revolution Settlements in England (1688–1721) and America (1776–1816)," in *Three British Revolutions: 1641, 1688, 1776*, ed. J. G. A. Pocock (Princeton, 1980), 368–453.

40. To cite just a few studies of African Americans, see David Brion Davis, *The Problem of Slavery in the Age of Revolution, 1770–1823* (Ithaca, NY, 1975); Gary B. Nash and Jean R. Soderlund, *Freedom by Degrees: Emancipation in Pennsylvania and its Aftermath* New York, 1991); Nash, *Forging Freedom: The Formation of Philadelphia's Black Community, 1720–1840* (Cambridge, MA, 1988); Shane White, *Somewhat More Independent: The End of Slavery in New York City, 1770–1810* (Athens, GA, 1991). The most impressive studies of Indians, in addition to Dowd's, include Richard White, *The Middle Ground: Indians, Empires, and Republics in the Great Lakes Region, 1650–1815* (New York, 1991); and Colin G. Calloway, *The American Revolution in*

Indian Country: Crisis and Diversity in Native American Communities
New York, 1995).

41. Toby L. Ditz, "Ownership and Obligation: Inheritance and Patriarchal
    Households in Connecticut, 1750–1820," *WMQ,* 47 (1990): 235–65; in *The
    Autobiography of Benjamin Franklin*, ed. Leonard W. Labaree et al. (New
    Haven, CT, 1964), p. 46, Franklin noted that he was the youngest son of a
    youngest son for five consecutive generations; Laurel Thatcher Ulrich, *The
    Age of Homespun: Objects and Stories in the Creation of an American Myth*
    (New York, 2001).

42. See especially John Woods Sweet, *Bodies Politic: Negotiating Race in the
    American North, 1730–1830* (Baltimore, 2003).

43. For the colonial pattern, see Jack P. Greene, "Legislative Turnover in British
    America, 1696 to 1775: A Quantitative Analysis," *WMQ,* 38 (1981): 442–
    63. For the immediate aftermath, see Jackson Turner Main, "Government
    by the People: The American Revolution and the Democratization of the
    Legislatures," *WMQ,* 23 (1966): 391–407. For a more detailed exposition
    of some of these themes, see Gary J. Kornblith and John M. Murrin,
    "The Dilemma of Ruling Elites in Revolutionary America," in *Ruling
    America: A History of Wealth and Power in a Democracy*, ed. Steve Fraser and
    Gary Gerstle (Cambridge, MA, 2005), 27–63; and Murrin, "The Jeffersonian
    Triumph and American Exceptionalism," *Journal of the Early Republic*, 20
    (2000), 1–25.